EMOTION
Theory, Research, and Experience

Volume 1

Theories of Emotion

EMOTION
Theory, Research, and Experience

EDITED BY

Robert Plutchik
Albert Einstein College of Medicine
Bronx, New York

Henry Kellerman
Postgraduate Center for Mental Health
New York, New York

Volume 1: Theories of Emotion

In preparation
Volume 2: Emotions in Early Development

EMOTION
Theory, Research, and Experience

Volume 1
Theories of Emotion

EDITED BY

Robert Plutchik
Albert Einstein College of Medicine
Bronx, New York

Henry Kellerman
Postgraduate Center for Mental Health
New York, New York

 1980

ACADEMIC PRESS
A Subsidiary of Harcourt Brace Jovanovich, Publishers
New York   London   Toronto   Sydney   San Francisco

ACADEMIC PRESS, INC.
111 Fifth Avenue, New York, New York 10003

United Kingdom Edition published by
ACADEMIC PRESS, INC. (LONDON) LTD.
24/28 Oval Road, London NW1 7DX

Library of Congress Cataloging in Publication Data
Main entry under title:

Theories of emotion.

(Emotion, theory, research, and experience; v. 1)
Includes bibliographies.
1. Emotions. I. Plutchik, Robert. II. Kellerman,
Henry. III. Series. [DNLM: 1. Emotions. W1 EM668
v. 1 / BF531 K29t]
BF561.E48 vol. 1 152.4'08s [152.4] 79–51685
ISBN 0–12–558701–5

PRINTED IN THE UNITED STATES OF AMERICA

80 81 82 83   9 8 7 6 5 4 3 2 1

CONTENTS

Part I THE EVOLUTIONARY CONTEXT

Chapter 1
A General Psychoevolutionary Theory of Emotion   3

ROBERT PLUTCHIK

Chapter 2
The Function of Emotions in Behavioral Systems:
A Systems Theory Analysis   35

J. P. SCOTT

Chapter 3
Strategies of Social Interaction   57

IRENÄUS EIBL–EIBESFELDT

Chapter 4
An Ethological Assessment of Emotion   81

M. R. A. CHANCE

Chapter 5
Toward a Sociobiological Theory of the Emotions   113

JAMES D. WEINRICH

Part II   THE PSYCHOPHYSIOLOGICAL CONTEXT

Chapter 6
Affect as Amplification: Some Modifications in Theory   141

SILVAN S. TOMKINS

Chapter 7
Aspects of Consciousness and Personality in Terms
of Differential Emotions Theory   165

C. E. IZARD AND S. BUECHLER

Chapter 8
Emotions: A Cognitive–Phenomenological Analysis   189

RICHARD S. LAZARUS, ALLEN D. KANNER,
AND SUSAN FOLKMAN

Chapter 9
The Generation of Emotion: A Psychological Theory   219

GEORGE MANDLER

Chapter 10
The Biology of Emotions and Other Feelings   245

KARL H. PRIBRAM

Chapter 11
The Communication of Emotion: Theory of Sentics   271

MANFRED CLYNES

Part III THE DYNAMIC CONTEXT

Chapter 12
A Constructivist View of Emotion   305

JAMES R. AVERILL

Chapter 13
A Psychoanalytic Theory of Affects   341

CHARLES BRENNER

Chapter 14
A Structural Model of Emotion and Personality: Psychoanalytic and Sociobiological Implications 349

HENRY KELLERMAN

Epilogue 385

ROBERT PLUTCHIK AND HENRY KELLERMAN

LIST OF CONTRIBUTORS

Numbers in parentheses indicate the pages on which the authors' contributions begin.

JAMES R. AVERILL (305), Professor of Psychology and Director of the Graduate Program, Department of Psychology, University of Massachusetts, Amherst, Massachusetts 01002

CHARLES BRENNER (341), Clinical Professor of Psychiatry, State University of New York, Downstate Medical Center, New York, New York 11203; Lecturer, Yale University School of Medicine, New Haven, Connecticut 06510; Training Analyst, New York Psychoanalytic Institute, New York, New York 10029

SANDRA BUECHLER (165), Clinical Supervisor at the Psychological Service Center, University of Delaware, Newark, Delaware 19711

MICHAEL R. A. CHANCE (81), Head, Sub-Department of Ethology, The University of Birmingham, Uffculme Clinic, Birmingham, B13 8QD England

MANFRED CLYNES (271), Research Professor and Head of the Music Research Center, New South Wales Conservatorium of Music, Sidney N.S.W. 2000, Australia

IRENÄUS EIBL-EIBESFELDT (57), Director of the Research Unit on Human Ethology, Max Planck Institute for Behavioural Physiology, 8136 Seewiesen, West Germany

SUSAN FOLKMAN (189), Research Assistant of the Stress and Coping Project, University of California, Berkeley, Berkeley, California 94720

CARROLL E. IZARD (165), Unidel Professor of Psychology, Department of Psychology, University of Delaware, Newark, Delaware 19711

ALLEN D. KANNER (189), Research Associate, Department of Psychology, University of California, Berkeley, Berkeley, California 94720

HENRY KELLERMAN (349, 385), Associate Director of Psychology, and Director of Psychology Internship Training, Postgraduate Center for Mental Health, New York, New York 10016

RICHARD S. LAZARUS (189), Professor of Psychology, Department of Psychology, University of California, Berkeley, Berkeley, California 94720

GEORGE MANDLER (219), Professor of Psychology and Director, Center for Human Information Processing, University of California, San Diego, La Jolla, California 92093

ROBERT PLUTCHIK (3, 385), Professor of Psychiatry (Psychology) and Director of Program Evaluation and Clinical Research, Albert Einstein College of Medicine, Bronx, New York 10461

KARL H. PRIBRAM (245), Professor of Psychology and of Psychiatry and Behavioral Sciences, Neuropsychology Laboratories, Stanford University, Stanford, California 94305

JOHN PAUL SCOTT (35), Director, Center for Research on Social Behavior, Bowling Green State University, Bowling Green, Ohio 43403

SILVAN S. TOMKINS (141), Professor Emeritus of Psychology, Livingston College, Rutgers University, New Brunswick, New Jersey

JAMES D. WEINRICH (113), Junior Fellow, Society of Fellows, Mather House 308, Harvard University, Cambridge, Massachusetts 02138

PREFACE

Emotion, as a psychological concept, is ubiquitous. It appears, in one guise or another, in a large variety of fields, disciplines, and subspecialities. It has been a central idea in general psychology, a fundamental notion in clinical and abnormal psychology, and an organizing concept in ethological and comparative studies of animal behavior. The newly emerging field of sociobiology uses concepts related to emotion, and the medical disciplines of psychiatry and psychosomatic medicine consider emotion as a core concept.

Despite this widespread concern with the topic of emotion, there is, at present, a feeling of disjointedness about the area. Students are still exposed to a century-old theory of emotion (James–Lange) even though it is no longer central to our contemporary understanding. Conceptualizations of the topic provided by recent theorists such as those represented in this volume are not widely known. For example, students are rarely, if ever, exposed to contemporary ethological conceptions related to emotions, and seldom are they made familiar with the psychoanalytic literature on the topic of emotion. In addition, current research on emotions is published in many diverse kinds of sources so that it is very difficult for an individual to keep track of developments in the field.

The present volume, *Theories of Emotion,* is the first of a series on this topic, entitled *Emotion: Theory, Research, and Experience,* and is an attempt to provide some integration to this diverse field. This first volume provides a foundation for the series. It presents broad theoretical perspectives representing all the historical traditions in the study of emotion. This series will serve as a central source of important ideas dealing with emotions. It will draw on the disciplines of psychology, sociobiology, ethology, psychosomatics, psychiatry, linguistics, and neurology. It will provide a central repository for important ideas as they evolve, and will include material dealing with theoretical issues, methodological problems, research findings, and practical and clinical applications. All chapters included in this and forthcoming volumes are and will be written exclusively for the series.

INTRODUCTION

All theories of emotion have developed within a historical context. This can be seen most readily when we consider the major contributors to our thinking about the nature of emotions: Charles Darwin, William James, and Sigmund Freud. From a historical point of view, the first major synthesizer of ideas about the nature of emotion was Charles Darwin. Darwin had come to recognize that the concept of evolution applied not only to the evolution of physical structures, such as skeletons and sensory receptors, but also to the behavior and "mental life" of animals. Not only do intelligence, memory, and reasoning power have an evolutionary history but so too do the emotions expressed by humans and lower animals.

THE EVOLUTIONARY CONTEXT

Darwin's fascinating book, *The Expression of the Emotions in Man and Animals* (published in 1872), contains a large mass of anecdotal and observational evidence concerning the expression of the emotions in lower animals, in infants, in preliterate human groups, and in Western Europeans that led him to certain important conclusions. For example, he concluded that emotions have evolved with definite functions, which are primarily to increase the chances of survival. Basically, emotions communicate information from one animal to another. They provide information about the probability of behavior and they help to prepare an animal for appropriate action. From this Darwinian viewpoint, emotions are basically adaptive and help to organize an animal's behavior in a way that is appropriate to the demands of its environment.

Darwin's work provided the foundation for an entire tradition. Many subsequent investigators, mainly trained within a biological framework, have continued to develop the implications of his ideas. This group of ideas constitutes what we call in this volume *the evolutionary context,* and we have included contributions from a number of authors who may be identified with this tradition.

Part I, The Evolutionary Context, comprises five chapters. In the first chapter, Plutchik presents the latest version of a structural model that he first described almost 20 years ago. The model assumes that there are eight basic emotions which play major adaptive roles in both animals and humans, and that these emotions can be combined in a large number of ways to produce the many derivative states which are actually observed. These include personality traits, behavioral or coping styles, and, in humans, diagnostic syndromes and defenses. Emotions are conceptualized as being a kind of behavioral homeostatic process as well as a fundamental signaling system. Most important, emotions are seen as derivatives of certain nearly universal life problems.

The second chapter, by Scott, presents the thesis that emotions are best understood as parts of general organismic and social systems and that they should be studied at the level of feelings, at the level of expressions, and at the level of physiological changes. He proposes nine classes of social behaviors that can be identified in most species throughout the animal kingdom, and he assumes that emotions are functionally related to these nine systems. Scott proposes connections between these nine functional systems and emotional states, and he supports these ideas with experimental evidence from his research on dogs. Scott also discusses language as a communicator of emotions, and further elaborates on some implications of systems theory.

In Chapter 3, Eibl-Eibesfeldt develops the thesis that expressive patterns of emotion play a major role in controlling human relationships and that certain basic strategies of social interaction are universally observable in human groups. He reports on some of his extensive studies of small, preliterate societies, and points out that many of the universal, facial expressive movements act as unconscious signals of the intentions of the sender and usually trigger appropriate responses in the observer. Also described are some of the important relationships between verbal and nonverbal behavior. Eibl-Eibesfeldt concludes that most social interactions contain elements of both positive and negative emotions. These are balanced in such a way as to maintain existing social positions.

In Chapter 4, Chance contrasts methods of research on emotion used by ethologists with those used by neurophysiologists and experimental psychologists. (Chance accepts the idea that emotions are in some sense derivatives of basic biological functions.) He then defines two modes of mental operation, the "agonic" and the "hedonic," which can be utilized to describe different types of social organizations. He then proceeds to discuss the evidence for these modes and the implications of his formulation.

Chance also accepts the notion that there are certain basic emotions and he provides detailed analyses of a few such as disgust, fear, anger, and mating. However, he devotes special attention to the role of *startle* as a key element in the arousal system. In closing, he also recognizes that personality has an important relationship to emotional states.

In Chapter 5, the concluding chapter in the evolutionary context, Weinrich assumes that every emotion must have an evolutionary history. Because the primary concern of evolution is adaptation, Weinrich's viewpoint implies that all emotions, including those sometimes described as negative, such as aggression, should be considered as adaptive in some sense. Weinrich rejects the idea sometimes made that natural selection works only on physical but not mental structures. According to his concept, displays of emotion as seen in humans must reflect our evolutionary origins, the millions of years that humans spent in a hunter–gatherer existence. An important aspect of Weinrich's chapter is the careful review of sociobiological literature in relationship to emotions.

These five chapters by Plutchik, Scott, Eibl-Eibesfeldt, Chance, and Weinrich provide an in-depth perspective on theories of emotion within the evolutionary context. They define the major concepts in this field with which theorists and researchers will be concerned in years to come.

THE PSYCHOPHYSIOLOGICAL CONTEXT

A second major tradition in the study of emotion may be traced to the writings of William James who was considered the leading U.S. psychologist-philosopher in the nineteenth century. James developed a concept of emotion which emphasizes the relationships between subjective feelings and physiological states of arousal. His theory became the impetus for continued research by many psychologists and physiologists over the ensuing decades.

Among the eminent scientists who were concerned with these issues was Walter Cannon—a colleague of James' at Harvard. Cannon did not question the idea of a relationship between subjective feeling states and physiological and neurological changes; however, he did challenge the assumption that feedback from the autonomic nervous system is the key element in determining emotional feelings. Instead, Cannon proposed that certain brain structures when activated are basically responsible for the feeling of an emotion.

In recent years, many investigators have concerned themselves with one or another aspect of the problem posed by William James and Walter Cannon.

In modern terminology the concepts of *arousal* and *feedback* have been the central elements with which a group of theorists have been concerned. These theorists might be characterized as working within a *psychophysiological context*. Although there are important differences among them, these theorists share a major concern with feedback either from the automatic nervous system, the facial musculature, or brain centers as key determinants of subjective feelings of emotion. Evolutionary factors have either been ignored or given a minor place in their thinking. In addition, most of their concern has been with subjective feelings of emotion as experienced and reported by adult human beings.

Six theorists are included in this volume as representative of the psychophysiological tradition.

In Chapter 6, Tomkins develops his theory that emotions are an amplifier of behavior and act like analogue systems rather than digital systems. He maintains that there are nine basic emotions whose patterns are innately determined and which are associated with particular patterns of neural activity. In earlier statements of his theory, Tomkins emphasized the role of feedback from the muscles of the face as major determinants of the amplification process. Currently, he assumes that the skin of the face is more important than its muscles in providing feedback for emotions. A new element added to his theory is the role of vocalization in connection with the expression or suppression of emotions. Some experimental evidence is provided to show the application of the theory.

In Chapter 7, Izard and Buechler describe their differential emotions theory—that emotions are really a subsystem of a larger model, the personality system. They assume that there are ten basic emotions, each of which has characteristic physiological, expressive, and experiential components, and that each is based on an innate neurophysiological program.

Izard and Buechler emphasize the fundamentally adaptive, organized character of emotions rather than their pathological aspects and point out some important considerations related to the ontogenesis of emotions in infants and children. Izard and Buechler also develop some important ideas about the interaction of emotions with perceptual and cognitive processes.

In Chapter 8, Lazarus, Kanner, and Folkman present an analysis of their cognitive approach to emotions. They argue that cognitive appraisals are fundamental precursors of all emotional states and that all emotions serve both an instrumental and expressive function. Their theory assumes that emotions not only have physiological and expressive components but an action impulse as well. In addition, they devote considerable attention to a relatively neglected problem, namely, the sources and nature of positive emotions. A dominant theme throughout their chapter is the idea that both positive and negative emotions are related to basic coping attempts and strivings and that emotions should be considered as adaptational reactions tied to states of motivation and cognition.

Chapter 9, written by Mandler, also emphasizes a cognitive approach to emotions. However, Mandler devotes a great deal of attention to two additional elements—interruption of ongoing activities and feedback of information from visceral structures. He argues that the inhibition of ongoing organized thought and behavior is followed by activity of the autonomic nervous system. The quality of each emotion is a complex interaction of the arousal feedback and various cognitive evaluations. These cognitive evaluations are called "meaning analyses." Mandler applies his ideas to a number of topics, including the nature of sex and aggression, personality, anxiety, and psychopathology. His theory utilizes the autonomic nervous system as a key element in the explanation of emotional states.

In Chapter 10, Pribram is concerned with the neuroendocrine and brain structures that are involved in the control of emotional states. Pribram describes three control systems involved in the regulation of different aspects of feelings and behavior. He emphasizes the role of novelty or disruptions of stable states as basic elements in the initiation of emotions. He argues that muscle, skin, and visceral inputs are not directly responsible for feelings but are involved only in the registration in memory of changes to which the organism must habituate. He proposes an interesting new distinction between "protocritic" states and "epicritic" states and postulates various cortical centers involved in the regulation of these different feelings states. Although Pribram's work falls within the psychophysiological tradition broadly defined, his major focus is on the role of the brain in the study of emotion.

The final chapter (10) of this section on the psychophysiological context is provided by Clynes. Clynes describes his theory of "sentic states" which is based on his research on the expressive components of different emotions. He also describes his technique for studying the changes that take place in the brain when emotions are expressed. He elaborates some of the clinical implications of this view and discusses in detail the sentic characteristics of specific emotions. The underlying focus of Clyne's theory is on the relationship between subjective prototype patterns of feeling and brain states.

These six chapters by Tomkins, Izard and Buechler, Lazarus, Kanner and Folkman, Mandler, Pribram, and Clynes provide a variety of views on the relationship between emotion as a subjective experience and changes in autonomic, neuroendocrine, or neurological processes.

THE DYNAMIC CONTEXT

A third major tradition in the study of emotion may be identified with the work of Sigmund Freud. Near the end of the nineteenth century, Freud developed a series of revolutionary new ideas concerning the nature of mental functioning. Among them are the concepts of resistance, repression, transference, childhood sexuality, and the unconscious. Fundamentally, Freud developed a theory of mind, a theory of human development, and a theory of psychotherapy. Implicit in his work is the concept that emotions are part of a biological heritage but can undergo a large variety of transformations in the course of one's life history. These transformations included distortion, suppression, repression, and modification in the service of adaptation. These ideas and their later derivatives may be called the *dynamic context*.

Although emotions are frequently mentioned in psychoanalytic writings, there have been very few attempts to develop a systematic view of emotions that could be considered to be derivative of the basic ideas of Freud. In recent years, several contributions have been made which may be viewed within the dynamic context.

In Chapter 12, Averill presents a conception of emotions as transitory social roles. Although he does not deny the contribution of biological factors to emotional expressions, he concludes that the real significance of emotional behavior is to be judged in terms of its role in an interpersonal social context. He describes variables that influence the performance of emotional roles and suggests a typology for classifying emotions within a triadic system. He thus distinguishes between impulsive emotions (e.g., joy and grief), conflictive emotions (e.g., anger and love), and transcendental emotions (e.g., nirvana and enlightment). Within his social-dynamic context, he places considerable emphasis on cognitive factors.

The contribution by Brenner in Chapter 13 sets forth what most closely approximates the classical psychoanalytic position on the nature of affects. In Brenner's view, emotions are fundamentally combinations of certain ideas intimately associated with sensations of pleasure and unpleasure. Emotions are assumed to be present at birth and have a developmental course that is connected to the extent of gratification or its opposite in the life of the individual. Brenner further conceptualizes emotions as an aspect of both ego and superego functioning. Consistent with the general psychoanalytic position, Brenner emphasizes the limited capacity of conscious, subjective feelings to reveal the nature and extent of emotional states. A number of implications for clinical practice and for the understanding of cultural events are described.

Kellerman, in the final chapter of the book, describes a number of psychoanalytic implications of a structural model of emotions. These implications include an analysis of the relationships between emotions and ego defenses, specific intrapsychic forces, dreams and nightmares, and diagnostic dispositions. Kellerman proposes that the entire personality system, which is a derivative of basic emotions, is rooted in certain biological predispositions. Kellerman makes detailed analyses of the clinical implications of each basic emotion and of the defenses and diagnostic dispositions that are entailed by them. Certain broad issues of adaptation are discussed that attempt to provide a bridge between psychoanalytic concepts and sociobiological ones.

This last section of the book, the dynamic tradition, provides a number of exciting new ideas that are helpful in suggesting relationships among all the various traditions. These final chapters taken in conjunction with the chapters in the first two sections of the book provide an overview of the current state of emotion theory.

NEED FOR A SYNTHESIS

The various contributions in this volume appear under three major headings—evolutionary context, psychophysiological context, and dynamic context. However, these categories should not be interpreted as indicating sharp lines of demarcation. In fact, recent theoretical contributions to the study of emotions may be characterized by an increasing tendency to blur distinctions among categories and to use ideas that overlap, not only within a given field, but also among such distinct disciplines as biochemistry, neurophysiology, behavioral medicine, psychopharmacology, psychosomatics, and sociobiology.

Each contribution in this book has attempted to address a series of salient issues which would concern most theories of emotion no matter how disparate they may be. These issues transcend the limits of any particular tradition; for example, definitions of emotion would identify whether they apply to lower animals as well as to humans and whether they focus on subjective experience or behavior. Furthermore, theories of emotion can be concerned with the idea of whether some emotions are more basic than others, how many emotions there are, whether some are "positive" whereas others are "negative," whether each emotion has a developmental history, and whether some emotions are "normal" whereas others are "pathological." Theories of emotion can also address the issue of the extent to which emotional expressions are derived from hereditary sources and the extent to which they are a function of environmental influences. The problem of the effect of learning and stress on the development of emotions and the question of a genetic basis for emotions are other issues that have been addressed in this volume. Finally, some authors have examined the relationships among emotions, motivation, perception, cognition, and personality and have considered the question of the mechanisms involved in the control of emotions.

Although there are still somewhat separate and conflicting viewpoints within the field of emotion, it is reasonable to state that the time may not be distant when there will be no schools of thought, but only a general integrated body of knowledge and theory that helps us to understand the nature of emotions.

EMOTION
Theory, Research, and Experience

Volume 1
Theories of Emotion

Part I

THE EVOLUTIONARY CONTEXT

Chapter 1

A GENERAL PSYCHOEVOLUTIONARY THEORY OF EMOTION

ROBERT PLUTCHIK

ABSTRACT

The general psychoevolutionary theory of emotion that is presented here has a number of important characteristics. First, it provides a broad evolutionary foundation for conceptualizing the domain of emotion as seen in animals and humans. Second, it provides a structural model which describes the interrelations among emotions. Third, it has demonstrated both theoretical and empirical relations among a number of derivative domains including personality traits, diagnoses, and ego defenses. Fourth, it has provided a theoretical rationale for the construction of tests and scales for the measurement of key dimensions within these various domains. Fifth, it has stimulated a good deal of empirical research using these tools and concepts. Finally, the theory provides useful insights into the relationships among emotions, adaptations, and evolution.

Both an explicit and an implicit body of knowledge about emotions exist. The explicit knowledge concerns such things as how well we judge emotions from facial expressions, whether our emotions are revealed by physiological changes, what emotions infants express, and whether aggressive behavior can be produced by brain stimulation. This knowledge, based on formal studies, is often inconsistent and relatively narrow in the sense that only a few key issues have been examined in the laboratory.

Emotion: Theory, Research, and Experience
Volume 1: Theories of Emotion

The implicit knowledge of emotion is probably universal, and most people believe that they already know a great deal about emotions. For example, we believe that emotions are powerful inner forces that affect our behavior and thoughts, even when we would prefer that they did not. We know that some emotions feel good and some bad, and that some people are more emotional than others. Although no school teaches the meaning of emotional expressions of the face, most of us believe we can read emotions on the faces of other people. And almost anyone who has ever had a dog or a cat will insist that these animals show emotions as vividly as do humans.

Despite the existence of these domains of explicit and implicit knowledge of emotions, there are many questions and issues about emotions that are not intuitively known and seldom studied. Examples of these are the following: What functions do emotions serve? How universal are they? Do animals have them? How many are there? Are they inherited, learned, or both?

Such questions have seldom been considered in a systematic way, although it is evident that any adequate theory should have something to say about them. Unfortunately, many of the theories about emotion have dealt with only one or another of these questions, and some are little more than a definition of the term. If a theory is to be general, it should attempt to deal with these and other issues.

EMOTION AS A HYPOTHETICAL CONSTRUCT

A major element in both the implicit and explicit views of emotion is that an emotion is a subjective feeling of a certain kind—the kind for which labels such as angry, disgusted, and afraid are appropriate. However, there is considerable evidence to suggest that this is too narrow a way to define emotion and that the facts available to us imply the need for a broader conceptualization. In contrast, it may be proposed that an emotion is not a subjective experience, per se, but rather a construct or inference based on various classes of evidence. This evidence may include verbal reports about inner feelings, as well as expressive behaviors and peer-group reactions, among others.

The fact that verbal reports alone are inadequate measures of emotion can be illustrated by many examples. Let us consider only three. Davitz (1970) asked a group of students to write brief descriptions of their emotional experiences. Based on these descriptions, he compiled a list of 556 words and phrases describing emotions. To illustrate the complexity of the layman's descriptive language of emotion, consider some of the phrases used in relation to depression:

> I feel empty, tired, sleepy, insignificant, alone, out of touch, not hungry, can't smile, want to withdraw.

These terms present a picture of a complex state having many elements. There are physical symptoms, attitudes toward oneself, impulses to action, and physiological changes. It is evident that any one class of descriptions is therefore only a partial image of the total state called an *emotion*.

A second example of the limitations of subjective reports as measures of emotion is documented in an extensive review of cross-cultural studies of depression (Marsella, 1976). In his review, Marsella cited reports indicating that in some languages there are no terms for depression as such, and that different investigators have reported widely varying prevalence rates for depression depending on their theoretical expectations as well as the specific measures used. It appears that some cultures do not label inner mood states. The more Westernized a culture, the more likely are psychological components to be included in a description of depression. (The fact that a society does not have a word for it does not mean that a particular emotion does not exist.)

The third example of the problematic nature of verbal reports can be found in the Schachter and Singer (1962) study of the role of deception and arousal in reports of emotional states. In this investigation, groups of college students were exposed to conditions designed to arouse feelings of "euphoria" or "anger." To assess the extent to which these emotions were produced, the subjects rated their feelings of "happiness" and "anger" on a scale. The results showed that the subjects reported themselves as more "happy" than "angry" in the "euphoria" condition, as was predicted. However, in the "anger" condition, subjects still reported themselves as more "happy" than "angry." This puzzle was resolved after the experiment was over. It was then learned that the subjects in the anger condition actually felt angry, but many were afraid to say this publicly since the experimenter had promised them two extra points on their final exam for participating: They were afraid that telling the truth might jeopardize their grade. This again emphasizes the point that verbal responses describing emotional states cannot always be taken at face value, particularly when the situation allows various secondary gains (e.g., money, grades, good will, etc.).

Many other examples can be given of the fact that verbal reports of emotions cannot always be taken as a direct index of some presumed inner emotional state. Such examples come from the literature on nonverbal communication (Speer, 1972) and from the psychoanalytic literature (Brenner, 1975; Rado, 1969). In conclusion, it may be stated that the term "emotion" does not necessarily describe subjective feeling states revealed by verbal reports. The evidence against the view of emotion as verbal report may be partly summarized in the following list:

1. Verbal reports of emotions may be deliberate attempts to deceive another person (as in deception experiments).

2. Verbal reports of emotions may be distortions or partial truths for conscious or unconscious reasons.
3. Repression may create false negatives; that is, an observer may erroneously assume that no emotion exists because none has been reported.
4. Reports of emotions depend on an individual's particular conditioning history, as well as his or her facility with words.
5. Reports of inner emotional states usually are retrospective and depend on memory. Remembered events are notoriously subject to distortions such as leveling, sharpening, wishful thinking, and repression.
6. Requests for a report of one's immediate emotional state create the problem that the process of observing can change the thing observed.
7. Emotions are generally believed to occur in infants and in young children. Such young children have not yet acquired the cognitive or motor ability to use language to express their emotions. Therefore, the belief in emotions in infants and young children is based on other classes of evidence.
8. Emotions are generally believed to occur in mentally defective and in mentally deranged humans. In many such cases, the patient is unable to provide any direct verbal reports of his emotional states.
9. The inherent ambiguity of language creates the problem of the "true" meaning of emotion terms. The importance of context in determining meaning implies that the same verbal report of an emotion will have a different referent in another setting.
10. Emotions are rarely if ever experienced in a pure state. More typically, any given situation creates mixed emotions, which are difficult to describe in any simple or unequivocal way.

For these and other reasons to be described in the next section, we must conclude that a verbal report of an inner emotional state is only a rough index of whatever that state is. We conclude that an emotion is not to be considered as synonymous with a presumed inner feeling state. The word *emotion* refers to a complex theoretical term whose characteristics can only be inferred on the basis of a congruence of various classes of evidence. One of these classes of evidence consists of verbal reports of supposed inner states, but such evidence has no greater logical priority than do the other classes of evidence. This approach is exactly analogous to that taken in other parts of psychology or in the physical sciences. Such terms as memory, perceptions, traits, atoms, genes, and DNA molecules are hypothetical constructs whose properties are inferred on the basis of various kinds of evidence.

EMOTIONS IN ANIMALS

Most comparative psychologists and ethologists accept the idea that the concept of emotion applies to lower animals as well as to humans. For example, Hebb (1972) has written: "The dog is definitely capable of jealousy and occasionally, in some dogs, there are signs of sulking. In the chimpanzee, however, we have the full picture of human anger in its three main forms: anger, sulking, and the temper tantrum.'' The validity of such emotion labels resides, in part, in their practical ability to predict an animal's behavior. If an animal is called ''shy,'' caretakers know what to expect of it in the future. If an animal is called ''angry'' or ''hostile,'' the caretakers will be cautious in its presence.

One important way to identify emotional reactions in a given animal is by observing the behavior of other animals toward the identified one. Delgado (1966) gives an example of this method in relation to the effects of electrical stimulation of the brain in monkeys. An electrode was placed in the rhinal fissure at the tip of the temporal lobe in a rhesus monkey. Electrical stimulation of this point produced opening of the mouth, rotation of the head, and scratching of the face, a pattern that, to a human observer, looked like aggression. However, this evoked behavior had no effect on the social behavior of the other members of the monkey colony. In contrast, electrical stimulation of the central gray area of the brain produced behavior that led the other animals to withdraw, grimace, and show submissive behaviors (Delgado, 1964). We can thus reasonably infer that stimulation of the central gray area produced aggressive behavior, whereas stimulation of the rhinal fissure did not, even though there were some superficial similarities in the two patterns of behavior. We may conclude that the behavior of other animals of the same species provides a partial basis for judging the existence and type of emotion present in a given, identified animal.

EMOTIONS AND EVOLUTION

It seems evident that emotions should be considered from a broad evolutionary point of view, since their existence can be inferred in lower animals as well as in humans. Darwin's concept of natural selection implies that almost every feature of each existing species has survival value, and this is as true of an animal's behavior, including its emotional behavior, as it is of its morphology. From an evolutionary point of view, we should therefore try to identify the ways in which emotions function adaptively in the lives of each organism.

In a general way it may be pointed out that all organisms, in order to survive and maintain their populations, must find food, avoid injury, and reproduce their kind. This is as true of lower animals as it is of higher ones. The nature of the environment creates certain functional requirements for all organisms if they are to survive. Any organism must take in nourishment and eliminate waste products. It must distinguish between prey and predator and between a potential mate and a potential enemy. It must explore its environment and orient its sense organs appropriately as it takes in information about the beneficial and harmful aspects of its immediate world. And in organisms that are relatively helpless at birth and for a while thereafter, there must be ways of indicating the need for care and nurturance. The specific behaviors by which these functions are carried out will vary widely throughout the animal kingdom, but the basic prototype functions will remain invariant.

Scott (1958) has listed some basic classes of adaptive behavior recognizable in most species. They include ingestive behavior, shelter-seeking behavior, agonistic (flight or fight) behavior, sexual behavior, care-giving behavior, care-soliciting behavior, eliminative behavior, allelomimetic (imitative) behavior, and investigative behavior. Wilson (1975), the sociobiologist, also suggests the existence of certain general classes of adaptive behavior. For example, in comparing termites and monkeys, Wilson notes the many similarities of function:

> Both [societies] are formed into cooperative groups that occupy territories. The group members communicate hunger, alarm, hostility, caste status or rank and reproductive status among themselves. . . . Individuals are intensely aware of the distinction between groupmates and nonmembers. . . . There is a well-marked division of labor.

In 1962, in my book *The emotions: Facts, theories and a new model,* I also proposed that there are only a few classes of basic adaptive reactions that are identifiable at all phylogenetic levels. From a functional point of view these include such things as *protection* responses (flight, avoidance, hiding, playing dead, etc.), *destruction* responses (clawing, biting, hitting, etc.), and *reproduction* responses (courting, copulating, egg-laying, etc.).

These ideas have been developed to form the bases of a general theory of emotions. The postulates of the theory have been stated explicitly and are listed below (Plutchik, 1980).

Postulates of the Theory

POSTULATE 1. *The concept of emotion is applicable to all evolutionary levels and applies to animals as well as to humans.*

POSTULATE 2. *Emotions have an evolutionary history and have evolved various forms of expression in different species.*

POSTULATE 3. *Emotions serve an adaptive role in helping organisms deal with key survival issues posed by the environment.*

POSTULATE 4. *Despite different forms of expression of emotions in different species, there are certain common elements, or prototype patterns, that can be identified.*

POSTULATE 5. *There is a small number of basic, primary, or prototype emotions.*

POSTULATE 6. *All other emotions are mixed or derivative states; that is, they occur as combinations, mixtures, or compounds of the primary emotions.*

POSTULATE 7. *Primary emotions are hypothetical constructs or idealized states whose properties and characteristics can only be inferred from various kinds of evidence.*

POSTULATE 8. *Primary emotions can be conceptualized in terms of pairs of polar opposites.*

POSTULATE 9. *All emotions vary in their degree of similarity to one another.*

POSTULATE 10. *Each emotion can exist in varying degrees of intensity or levels of arousal.*

The derivatives and implications of these postulates are far-reaching and have been discussed in detail in other publications (Plutchik, 1962, 1970, 1979, 1980; Plutchik, Kellerman, & Conte, 1979). In this chapter, a selection of important ideas will be presented. The theory will be evaluated in terms of its generality, its diversity of application, and its usefulness in integrating old observations and in suggesting new ones. Although one may take issue with any one postulate of the theory, it is important to evaluate the theory as a total conception in terms of its ability to relate psychological, clinical, and biological observations within a common framework.

EMOTIONS AND COGNITIONS

The functional approach to emotions of the present psychoevolutionary theory of emotion (Plutchik, 1980) implies that the recognition by an organism of the beneficial or harmful aspects of its environment means that it must evaluate its environment in some way. This evaluation process represents the cognitive aspect of emotions, and it influences the type of response pattern that is actually observed. So-called "cognitive" approaches to emotion are mainly concerned with the identification of variables that influence the evaluation process in humans, but it should be emphasized that an evaluation is not an emotion. Evaluations are a part of the total process that involves an organism interacting with its environment in biologically adaptive ways.

Cognitions have sometimes been described in a somewhat narrow sense as referring to the interpretations humans and animals make of the events that occur around them. In the present context, cognition will be considered as more or less synonymous with thinking and will include such functions as perceiving, conceptualizing, and remembering. The basic question to be considered concerns the relation between such cognitive or intellectual functions and emotions. This question will be considered from a point of view that recognizes (*a*) that cognitive activities and their material basis, the brain, have a long evolutionary history; (*b*) that cognitive capacities have evolved along with the evolution of the brain; and (*c*) that cognitions are intimately related to emotions.

Before considering these questions, it will be helpful to make explicit the particular postulates concerning cognitions used in the development of the theory (Plutchik, 1977).

Postulates about Cognition–Emotion Relations

POSTULATE 1. *The existence of any emotion presupposes the prior occurrence of a cognition or evaluation. However, although all emotions presuppose evaluations, not all evaluations produce emotions.*

POSTULATE 2. *Cognitions may be based on information obtained from external or internal stimuli.*

POSTULATE 3. *Cognitions are concerned with whether a stimulus is beneficial or harmful, although there are different types of benefits, just as there are different types of harms.*

POSTULATE 4. *Most events are evaluated as both good and bad, beneficial as well as harmful. This is the basis for the wide existence of conflict.*

POSTULATE 5. *In most lower animals, certain cognitions occur without prior learning or experience (e.g., imprinting or courtship rituals).*

POSTULATE 6. *In higher animals, most cognitions depend on learning and can be modified by experience.*

POSTULATE 7. *Cognitions are not always conscious or reportable; they are hypothetical constructs or "maps" whose properties can be inferred on the basis of various kinds of evidence.*

POSTULATE 8. *Cognitions can be in error. It is possible for an individual to evaluate a certain stimulus as beneficial when it is really harmful or, conversely, to evaluate a stimulus as dangerous when it is not (as in most phobias).*

POSTULATE 9. *On the average, most cognitions must be reasonably accurate if an individual is to survive.*

POSTULATE 10. *There are a limited number of cognitions necessary for survival in the face of major life problems.*

Some of the ideas represented by these postulates can be illustrated by means of a diagram showing the sequence of events that occurs in relation to the development of an emotion.

Table 1.1 is meant to show that the occurrence of certain stimulus events,

TABLE 1.1

The Sequence of Events Related to the Development of an Emotion

STIMULUS EVENT		COGNITION		FEELING		BEHAVIOR		EFFECT
Threat by enemy	→	Danger	→	Fear	→	Run	→	Protection
Loss of parent	→	Isolation	→	Sadness	→	Cry for help	→	Assistance

such as a threat by an enemy or the loss of a parent, is followed by a cognition (interpretation) such as "danger" or "isolation." Such cognitions may (or may not) be reflexive and unconscious and will be followed by the introspective feelings such as fear or sadness that we usually think of as emotions. The feeling state is only one step in a chain of reactions and will be followed, with a certain probability, by some kind of appropriate behavior. Such behaviors, if successful, lead to protection of the individual or assistance provided by parent substitutes or other members of the individual's social group. The word emotion refers to this complex chain of reactions, which has adaptive value for the individual in dealing with various kinds of life crises or survival problems.

In describing the complex chain of reactions called an emotion, there are a number of vicissitudes that may befall the emotional sequence. For one thing, the initial cognition may be in error so that the threat is misperceived or misinterpreted. Ego defenses such as denial or projection could certainly play a role here (Postulate 8). If the cognition is accurate, it is still possible for the feeling aspect of the emotional chain to be blocked, modified, or distorted. Ego defenses such as displacement or repression could also operate at this point to transform the feeling state in some way. However, even if the feeling is clearly present, appropriate action may or may not occur. This is simply because environmental or internal restraints may prevent the action. If someone is physically tied up, running away in the face of danger is impossible. Similarly, if one has strong feelings about the importance of bravery, one may not run even if one's life is at stake. Finally, depending on whether appropriate and effective behavior occurred, the goal or purpose of the chain of emotional reactions may or may not be served. It is a lack of attention to these vicissitudes that has largely led to the confusions over whether emotions have purposes and, if so, what they are.

COGNITIONS ARE IN THE SERVICE OF EMOTIONS

Although there have been a number of recent "cognitive" approaches to emotion (Lazarus, 1968; Mandler, 1975; Schachter & Singer, 1962), none has considered cognitions within a broad evolutionary framework. The basic point of view to be presented here is that cognitive capacities have evolved along with the evolution of the brain, and that cognitions have largely evolved in the service of emotions. I have discussed these ideas more fully in a previous publication (Plutchik, 1977) so that only a brief summary will be given here.

The fossil record indicates that the major enlargement of the brain of human-like primate forms took place over a period of less than 1 million years. The stage of *Homo sapiens* is evident in the fossil record beginning about 250,000 years ago; the records indicate a brain volume of approximately 1200 ml. In contrast, the brain of the gorilla is about 500 ml. The brain volume of present-day human adults is about 1400 ml.

Many explanations have been proposed for the large increase in the brain size of humans over a relatively short period of time since only unusual selection pressures could have produced such a rapid change. The following are a few of the explanations that have been proposed.

1. Social grouping evolved as a means of cooperative defense; the stability of relations in social groups required the development of a language for communication, which in turn required a large brain size.
2. The relative scarcity of food on the plains led early man to become a carnivore and hence a predator with a large hunting range. Efficient hunting required a complex signaling system and a relatively large brain (Jerison, 1973).
3. The cold weather associated with glaciation led to the need for artificial climate, as expressed in the use of fire and clothing. Crowding increased the need for social communication with a probable influence on brain size (Campbell, 1966).
4. The appearance of outbreeding (exogamy) in early humans resulted in a large increase in genetic variability, which in turn increased the chances of successful adaptation to changing ecological conditions. Increase in brain size was one such adaptation.

In a broad sense, we may say that the main function of a large brain and a highly developed cognitive system is to ensure survival. We may, however, describe the cognitive process in a more precise way. From the point of view of evolution, *cognition developed in order to predict the future.*

Cognitive activities are a form of map making. Cognition provides a model of the environment and codes information in a time-binding neural code. The development of abstract concepts denoting classes of events meant escape from the present. This increased ability to classify the environment made it possible for humans to develop foresight of future needs. The more precisely the environment could be assessed or mapped, the greater the capacity to make predictions about the likely course of external events and thus to initiate novel patterns of adaptive behavior.

In the most basic sense, any organism must predict on the basis of limited information whether there is food, a mate, or danger in its environment. Depending on the prediction made, the organism makes a decision to run, to attack, to play, or to mate. From this point of view the complex processes of sensory input, evaluation, symbolization, comparison with memory stores, and the like—those processes we call cognitive—are in the service of emotions and biological needs. This idea is not new. Dember (1974) has pointed out that the brain and the body have evolved as an adaptive mechanism and that cognitive processes are instruments, or means to an end—in effect, that the brain is the servant of the stomach and the sex organs. In an article comparing humans with computing machines, Neisser (1963) also discussed the idea of cognitions as being in the service of needs and emotions. He pointed out that human thinking is intimately associated with emotions. In the course of early individual development, information from the environment is evaluated in terms of its need-satisfying and need-frustrating properties. Neisser stated: "One of the most common . . . modes of learning, that of reward and punishment, operates through an open involvement of strong and historically complicated emotions (p. 197)."

There is another important point that should be made in connection with the question of the function of cognition. This concerns the uses to which the cognitive mechanism may be put once it has developed. The original purpose of the evolution of cognition is to enable the organism to map its environment and to predict the future in regard to significant emotional or motivational events. However, once such a complex mechanism has evolved, it can be used for other things. Once developed, the cognitive mechanism can deal with nonemotional events and symbols as well as emotional ones. It can also deal with the symbols of past events as well as future ones, and the symbols, once in the store of memory, can be used for fantasy productions, art, literature, and play.

It is possible to go beyond a general statement of the relation between cognition and emotion and to speculate about various part-functions in the total cognitive process. In contrast to the subjective aspects of emotion, which are usually (but not always) conscious, the processes of thinking are essentially unconscious. Therefore, the structure of cognitive processes can only be inferred from the products of thinking in relation to the inputs to thinking. Another source of insight about cognitive processes is the aberrations that occur when the mechanisms are disrupted by either brain injury, disease, toxicity, or other events.

The following schema represents an attempt to describe the hypothetical part-processes that are involved in all cognitive events. This schema is based on the ideas that have been discussed about cognition as an evolving set of functions based on brain mechanisms, which are designed to make maps, predict the future, and organize appropriate actions. In general, in order for an organism to adapt successfully to a potentially dangerous environment, it must be able to store information about this environment in memory; it must be able to retrieve stored information when necessary; and it must be able to use the retrieved signals as a basis for actions. The details are summarized in Figure 1.1.

The final common pathway of this complex, inferred cognitive process is action, but it is action that is adaptively related to the evaluation of the stimulus event. If the prediction process leads to the implicit conclusion that a predator is attacking, then the appropriate feeling is fear, the appropriate behavior is flight, and the purpose is protection of the individual. If the prediction process leads to the conclusion that another member of one's own

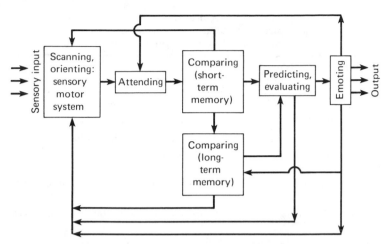

Figure 1.1   Schematic flow diagram of cognitive–emotional functioning. From Plutchik, R. Cognitions in the service of emotions: An evolutionary perspective. In D. K. Candland, J. P. Fell, E. Keen, A. I. Leshner, R. Plutchik, & R. M. Tarpy. *Emotion*. Monterey, Calif.: Brooks/Cole, 1977. Reprinted by permission.

species is threatening, then the appropriate feeling is anger, the appropriate behavior is attack, and the purpose is injury or destruction of the threatener. These complex responses, having multiple components of feeling, behavior, and purpose, are emotions. They are the end results of a complex cognitive process. The appropriateness of the emotional response determines whether the individual lives or dies. The whole cognitive process evolved over millions of years in order to make the evaluations of stimulus events more correct and the predictions more precise so that the emotional behavior that finally resulted would be adaptively related to the stimulus events. It is in this sense that cognitions are in the service of emotions.

THE MULTIPLE LANGUAGES OF EMOTION

Since an emotion is a complex sequence of reactions, one may describe different aspects of the sequence in different terms, or in different languages. Thus, there is a language for describing the stimulus events that produce emotions, a separate language for describing the inferred cognitions that interpret these events, still another language for describing the feeling states, and a language of behavioral reactions. The function of each emotion can be described in yet another way. Table 1.2 gives examples of languages used for each of the eight primary emotions.

The stimuli are all important life-related events that are connected with survival to some degree. The inferred cognitions are probable interpretations made of these events. The feeling states can be weak or strong, as can the associated behaviors. The column marked "Effect" refers to the functions of each emotion-complex.

TABLE 1.2
THE COMPLEX, PROBABILISTIC SEQUENCE OF EVENTS
INVOLVED IN THE DEVELOPMENT OF AN EMOTION

Stimulus event	Inferred cognition	Feeling	Behavior	Effect
Threat	"Danger"	Fear, terror	Running, or flying away	Protection
Obstacle	"Enemy"	Anger, rage	Biting, hitting	Destruction
Potential mate	"Possess"	Joy, ecstasy	Courting, mating	Reproduction
Loss of valued person	"Isolation"	Sadness, grief	Crying for help	Reintegration
Group member	"Friend"	Acceptance, trust	Grooming, sharing	Affiliation
Gruesome object	"Poison"	Disgust, loathing	Vomiting, pushing away	Rejection
New territory	"What's out there?"	Anticipation	Examining, mapping	Exploration
Sudden novel object	"What is it?"	Surprise	Stopping, alerting	Orientation

Another point about Table 1.2 that should be emphasized is the fact that the primary emotion dimensions can be conceptualized in terms of pairs of opposites. Anger and fear are opposites in the sense that one implies attack and the other flight. Joy and sadness are opposites in the sense that one implies possession or gain while the other implies loss. Acceptance and disgust are opposites in the sense that one implies a taking in, and the other implies an ejection, or riddance. Surprise and anticipation are opposites in the sense that one implies the unpredictable and the other implies the predictable.

In addition to the polarities inherent in the structure of emotion, there is another implicit dimension, and that is the relative similarity of the emotions. Thus, anger and disgust are more similar than are anger and surprise.

The combination of these two elements, that is, polarity and similarity, leads to a circle as an analog structure or model since a circle combines the concepts of degree of similarity (nearness) and degree of opposition. I have proposed such a circular model (Plutchik, 1958, 1962) and have also suggested a particular ordering of the primary emotions around the circle.

H. R. Conte and I (Plutchik & Conte, 1978) have largely confirmed the proposed sequence; our method and results will be briefly described. A list of 150 emotion terms was selected as an initial pool of items from various sources (Davitz, 1969; Plutchik, 1962; *Roget's international thesaurus,* 1962; Russell & Mehrabian, 1977). Two independent methods were used to establish the similarity structure of the emotion terms.

The first method was a modified paired-comparison technique. Instead of comparing each term with every other term, which would have required thousands of comparisons, three emotion terms were selected as reference words. All other emotions were compared with these three reference words for degree of similarity on a 7-point scale ranging from "identical" to "completely opposite."

The mean ratings from a group of judges were converted into angular placements on the basis of the convention that an emotion judged to be completely opposite a reference word was placed 180 degrees from it on a circle. An emotion judged to be unrelated to a reference word (i.e., neither similar nor dissimilar) was placed 90 degrees from it on the circle. All other ratings were located at intermediate positions. Since three reference words were used, the actual angular locations were based on the position that was associated with the smallest variability of placement. The results of this method, for a sample of 40 terms, reveal that the emotion terms tend to be distributed around the entire circle. This method for locating the angular placements would not necessarily guarantee such a result, and this finding is not, therefore, an artifact of the method.

Additional support for the reality of this circular structure of similarity relations is the fact that many of the terms that are linguistically opposite (in terms of a simple dictionary definition) fall at opposite parts of the circle. For example, the terms "interested" and "disinterested" are almost 180 degrees apart. This is also true for "affectionate" and "unaffectionate" and for "obedient" and "disobedient."

In addition, emotions that are relatively similar in meaning tend to cluster at neighboring points of the circle. For example, the terms lonely, apathetic, meek, guilty, sad, sorrowful, empty, remorseful, hopeless, and depressed are located in consecutive positions covering a range of 37 degrees on the circle. Finally, it should be noted that the sequence of clusters of emotion terms around the circle is almost identical to the sequence I postulated in 1962 (Plutchik, 1962).

In order to check on the validity of the placements of the emotion terms on the circle, an independent method, based on the semantic differential, was used. A set of 20 semantic differential terms was selected to sample Osgood's three semantic dimensions of evaluation, potency, and activity. A group of judges was asked to rate each of the 40 emotions on each of the 20 semantic differential scales.

The mean ratings on the scales produced a profile of connotative meanings for each of the 40 emotions. Product–moment correlations were then obtained between each pair of profiles to produce a 40 × 40 matrix of correlations. This matrix was then factor-analyzed by means of a principal components analysis and rotated by Varimax rotation. It was found that the first two factors accounted for 88% of the variance. The factor loadings on the first two orthogonal factors were then used to plot the locations of each of the 40 emotions on a two-dimensional space. The ordering of the emotions is shown in Figure 1.2.

It was found that almost all the emotions fell well out on the periphery of a

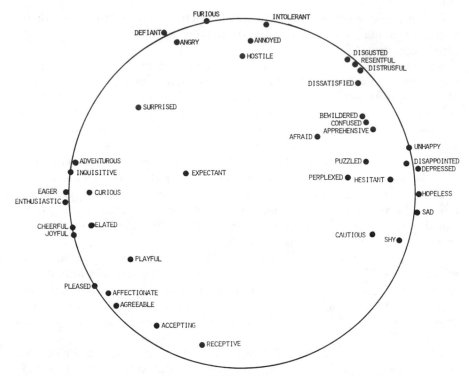

FIGURE 1.2.   Factor analysis of semantic differential profiles for 40 emotion words.

circle. Angular locations for each term were then determined directly from the figure. The angles for the emotions placed by the first direct similarity estimation method were then correlated with the angles for the same emotions placed by means of the semantic differential profile similarity method. The product–moment correlation was found to be .90. This congruence of two independent methods strongly supports the circular similarity structure of emotions.

EMOTIONS AND PERSONALITY

One of the important implications of the theory is the concept of derivatives of emotions. In my 1962 book, I showed that the language of emotions also includes the language of personality traits, if personality is defined as interpersonal relations (and not as abilities, IQ, physical characteristics, or social status). Words like friendly, hostile, gloomy, and impulsive can be used to describe either a brief, emotional state or a long-term personality trait. When judges were asked to imagine what the result would be of the mixing or blending of primary emotions, the names given to the blends can be considered as either emotional states or personality traits. Many writers have stressed the distinction between state measures of anxiety and trait measures. In other words, anxiety can be thought of as describing a temporary mood or an enduring trait. However, the results obtained when considering mixed emotions imply that the state–trait distinction applies not only to anxiety, but to every other emotion as well. Therefore, we can study anger as either a state or a trait, sadness as a state or a trait, etc.

Table 1.3 provides an illustration of the terms used by raters to describe the results of mixing primary emotions. It is important to notice that, although the terms in the first column are usually considered to be personality traits, they can also be descriptions of emotional states if they occur transiently. In other words, even a brave person can be occasionally cautious, just as an optimistic person can have a rare feeling of pessimism.

It is also possible to demonstrate that the circular model proposed for emotions can be used to describe the relations among personality traits. A circular model for personality traits has been proposed by Freedman, Leary, Ossorio, and Coffey (1951), by Stern (1958), by Schaefer (1959), by Becker and Krug (1964), by Lorr and McNair (1965), by Rinn (1965), by Schaefer and Plutchik (1966), and by Bayley (1968), among others. Most of these authors refer to Guttman's concept of a circumplex (1954).

The most extensive documentation of a circular model for personality was presented by Conte (1975). In her investigation, she began by identifying a universe of personality trait terms. This was based on the work of Allport and Odbert (1936), Anderson (1968), Norman (1967), and others. Many words from these various lists were excluded from the final population of terms on the grounds of ambiguity, slanginess, metaphor, etc., or on the grounds that the term did not appear on a majority of the lists. Such terms as kooky, neat, hairy, aghast, larksome, bad, and musical were excluded. The final pool of items contained 223 terms.

Judges were then asked to make direct similarity ratings of each of these

TABLE 1.3
EMOTION COMPONENTS OF A SAMPLE
OF PERSONALITY TRAITS

Personality trait	Emotion components	
	First	Second
Affectionate	Accepting	Joyful
Aggressive	Angry	Expectant
Anxious	Expectant	Afraid
Cautious	Timid	Expectant
Cruel	Rageful	Disgusted
Envious	Angry	Sad
Pessimistic	Sad	Expectant
Resentful	Angry	Dissatisfied

traits against three reference terms, which is, in essence, a modified method of paired comparisons. High positive ratings indicate great similarity of terms, whereas high negative ratings indicate near bipolarity. The average similarity ratings based on all judges were then transformed into an angular placement on a circle, by a method described fully by Conte (1975).

However, since the possibility of bias exists in relation to any given method, Conte replicated the angular placements of a sample of 40 of the terms using an entirely different and independent method: the semantic differential. Each of the 40 trait words was rated for connotative meaning on each of 30 semantic differential scales, such as active, inhibited, powerful, masculine, warm, ugly, and low. The average ratings of a group of judges produced a semantic profile for each trait. These profiles were then correlated in a 40 × 40 matrix. The correlations produce measures of similarity of shape of the different trait profiles in accordance with the descriptions given by Stone and Coles (1970).

The matrix of correlations was then factor-analyzed by the principal components method, and the first two factors were found to account for 91% of the variance; this clearly implied that a two-dimensional surface would be adequate to represent the relations among the traits. The empirical locations of each of the 40 traits were then plotted on the basis of their factor loadings on the first two factors in order to identify a circumplex. This is the method used by Becker and Krug (1964), and by Lorr and McNair (1965), among others, to locate the positions of the elements of a circumplex. Almost all placements were found to fall on the circumference of a circle. These locations were then transformed into angular placements.

In order to check the validity of the placements of the traits on a circle, the angular locations of the 40 traits based on direct similarity estimates were correlated against the angular locations of the same 40 traits using the method of semantic differential profile similarity. The correlation of the placements using the two independent methods was .99, thus strongly supporting the construct validity of the circumplex ordering for personality traits. This circular order is shown in Figure 1.3.

Since the theory of emotion presented in this chapter interprets personality traits as derivatives of emotions, it should be expected that the sequence of traits and emotions around the circle should have some relation to one another. An examination of Figure 1.3 bears this out.

The first cluster of traits (lower right quadrant) relates to the *reproduction* and *incorporation* dimensions of the model. This is followed (going clockwise) by a cluster of terms (e.g., docile, timid) reflecting the *protection* dimension. Following sequentially is the *reintegration* dimension, and it is appropriately described by terms such as depressed and pessimistic. The next dimension, which is *rejection,* is represented by such terms as suspicious, resentful, and critical. This is followed by the *destruction* dimension, and it is expressed by such terms as hot-tempered, quarrelsome, and aggressive. The *exploration* dimension, which follows next, is represented by terms such as adventurous and curious. The *orientation* dimension was not sampled in this

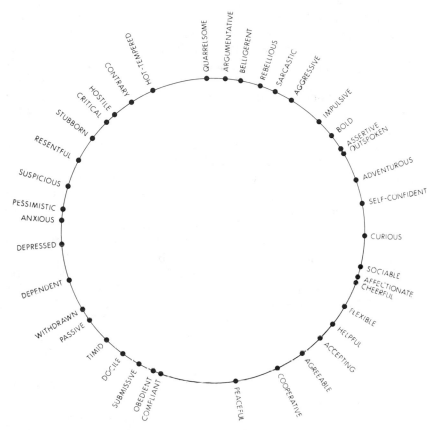

Figure 1.3. Similarity and polarity structure of a sample of 40 personality traits. From Conte, H. R., *A circumplex model for personality traits,* Ph.D. Dissertation, New York University, 1975. Reprinted by permission.

study, but it would be expected that such terms as impulsive and confused would reflect this dimension. There is thus an almost perfect correspondence between the primary emotion dimensions and the clusters of corresponding trait terms. This further supports the concept that personality traits are derivatives of basic emotions.

DIAGNOSTIC CONCEPTS
AS DERIVATIVES OF EMOTIONS

Many of the labels used to describe personality are also labels that are often used to diagnose psychopathology. For example, the traits of distrust and excessive tendencies to be critical are often associated with paranoia. Traits of detachment, inhibition, and passivity are often associated with schizoid personality, etc. It thus seems reasonable to hypothesize a diagnostic circumplex that has certain parallels to the personality circumplex.

Several studies have supported this hypothesis. In one, Schaefer and Plutchik (1966) asked experienced clinicians to make a series of judgments of the extent to which a person who was described by a given diagnostic label (such as paranoid or compulsive) would show each of a number of traits and emotions.

The ratings for all traits were then intercorrelated; this was also done separately for all emotions. These two matrices were then factor-analyzed. Since most of the variance was accounted for by the first two factors, it was evident that a two-dimensional surface would provide a good approximation to the data. The factor loadings of the trait and emotion variables on the first two factors were then plotted. This produced a circular configuration of both traits and emotions similar to the ones shown in Figures 1.2 and 1.3.

However, instead of correlating ratings between pairs of traits, or pairs of emotions, it was possible to correlate ratings between pairs of diagnostic labels. The resulting matrix of correlations was factor-analyzed using the principal components method, and the different diagnostic labels were plotted on the basis of their factor loadings. Here also, two factors accounted for most of the variance. Details of the method are given in Plutchik (1967).

Figure 1.4 shows the approximate circumplex produced by this method of analysis. On an empirical basis, the manic state is opposite the inhibited state, extraverted is opposite intraverted, psychopathic is opposite dependent, and well-adjusted is opposite a grouping consisting of obsessive, compulsive, schizoid, and neurotic labels.

Another method for studying the question of whether diagnostic concepts form a circumplex order was reported by Plutchik and Platman (1977). In this study, 20 psychiatrists were given a list of nonpsychotic personality disorders taken from DSM–II and asked to select personality trait terms that were identified in their minds with each diagnostic label. The personality disorders were compulsive, cyclothymic, hysterical, paranoid, passive–aggressive, schizoid, and sociopathic. To these was added one more term not included in the DSM–II list: well-adjusted.

The psychiatrists were asked to imagine someone who was diagnosed, for example, as paranoid. They were then to select one trait from each pair of trait words on a personality test called the Emotions Profile Index (Kellerman & Plutchik, 1968; Plutchik & Kellerman, 1974). This test consists of 12 personality trait terms selected on the basis of the factor analytic work of Schaefer (1961) and Schaefer and Plutchik (1966). The traits are paired in all possible combinations, yielding 66 pairs. The psychiatrists chose one word from each pair that most closely described the imagined patient. The choices were scored in terms of the eight basic affect dimensions that are considered to be the theoretical components of all traits. This produced a mean judgment for each diagnosis and for each basic affect. In essence, it provided an emotion profile for each diagnosis.

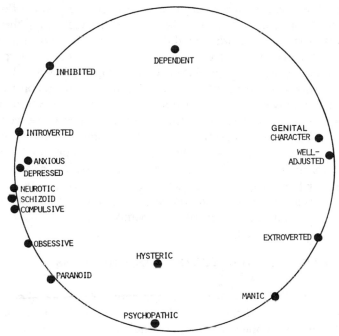

Figure 1.4. A diagnostic circumplex based on relative similarity of emotions implied by each diagnosis. From Plutchik, R. The affective differential: Emotion profiles implied by diagnostic concepts. *Psychological Reports,* 1967, *20,* 19–25. Reprinted by permission.

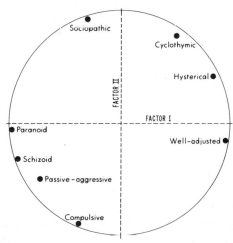

Figure 1.5. Factor analysis based on psychiatrists' definition of diagnostic terms. From Plutchik, R., & Platman, S. R. Personality connotations of psychiatric diagnoses: Implications for a similarity model. *The Journal of Nervous and Mental Disease,* 1977, *165,* 418–422. Reprinted by permission.

These profiles were then intercorrelated for all possible pairs of diagnoses. The matrix of intercorrelations was then factor-analyzed using the principal components method, and it was found that the first two factors accounted for 91% of the variance. The factor loadings for each diagnosis were plotted using the first two axes, which produced the circumplex shown in Figure 1.5.

Figure 1.5 shows that the paranoid, the schizoid, and the passive–aggressive diagnoses are relatively similar and that they are descriptively opposite the well-adjusted diagnosis. The sociopath is midway between the well-adjusted profile and the schizoid, neurotic profile. With some exceptions, the results are fairly similar to those shown in Figure 1.4. It thus appears that a circular model is appropriate for at least a subset of diagnostic labels. This is true simply because these diagnoses represent extremes or exaggerations of certain personality traits, which in turn represent mixtures of basic emotions. It is in this sense that diagnoses are derivatives of emotions.

EGO DEFENSES AS REGULATORS OF EMOTIONS

From a psychoanalytic point of view, ego defenses are mental processes that attempt to resolve conflicts among drives, emotions, and external reality. Despite the original application of the concept to the description of certain aspects of human adult behavior, the concept of ego defenses has gradually achieved a wider generality. Psychoanalysts have written about defenses in relation to both children and infants (Chess, 1964, 1966), and ethologists have demonstrated the operation of certain defense mechanisms, e.g., displacement and regression, in lower animals (Goodall, 1967; Lorenz, 1966). These observations imply the need to place the concept of defense mechanisms in a broad evolutionary framework. This task has been attempted, in a series of studies, by Plutchik *et al.* (1979); therefore, only a brief summary of this research will be presented here.

A review of the literature revealed that there was little agreement among clinicians on just how many defenses there are or even on how they should be defined. However, some conclusions did emerge from this review. First, it became evident that different defenses overlap and vary in their degree of similarity to one another. Second, some defenses were described as polar opposites. Third, some defenses were considered to be more primitive than others.

These descriptions of ego defenses are quite like the descriptions used to characterize emotions. I have shown that emotions vary in their degree of similarity to one another, that they show polarities, and that they vary in degree of intensity (Plutchik, 1962, 1970). These characteristics imply that ego defenses, like emotions, can be topographically represented by a circular model.

In addition to these formal properties of ego defenses, there are important things to say about the nature and function of ego defenses. Clinicians have long recognized the connection between ego defenses and emotions or personality traits. For example, displacement is a defense used to handle anger that cannot be directly expressed. Projection is a defense used to place blame on a person or group in one's environment so as to avoid finding fault with oneself. Denial is used to avoid confronting certain unpleasant facts. These examples imply that defenses are used to deal with emotions.

In the chapter by Plutchik *et al* (1979), a formal model was developed around these observations, and a self-report paper-and-pencil test for measuring ego defenses was described. Empirical data from nine studies were given to show that the hypothesis of a circular structure for ego defenses is a reasonably appropriate analog model. The test is shown to be related to anxiety and self-esteem in predictable ways and is also shown to discriminate between schizophrenic patients and a control group on seven out of eight ego defenses.

Basically, all ego defenses are coping strategies designed to deal with conflicts over particular emotions. If the expression of anger is dangerous, that is, produces threats or invites retaliation, then displacement expresses the anger toward a weaker scapegoat and avoids the danger. When feelings of sadness result from the experience of loss, this is sometimes handled by compensating or sublimating. For example, the bereavement may be handled by increasing one's work for charities. When attempts to "map" or understand the environment begin to fail, or are unsuccessful, then the resulting panic may be handled by arbitrary categorizations—in other words, by intellectualization. The same kind of analysis may be given to show that each basic emotion has an ego defense available to deal with it under conditions of major conflict.

Table 1.4 lists the eight basic emotions and the different languages one can use to describe them and their derivatives. There is a subjective language, a behavioral language, a functional language, and a trait language. In addition, there are diagnostic and ego-defense languages. It is likely that other derivative languages will in time be recognized. One possibility that is currently being considered is a coping style language.

A word should be said about this last point. Ego defenses, by their very nature, imply an unconscious or unaware aspect. We do not choose to repress our fear or displace our anger. The process simply occurs in some individuals under certain conditions. However, many adults are usually aware of their own style of dealing with problems, a style that may, in many cases, be a thoughtful, deliberate result of various life experiences. Thus, some people are perennial optimists and deliberately minimize the apparent seriousness of problems. *Minimization* is thus the conscious derivative of the unconscious process of denial. Similarly, some people handle conflicts by finding fault with other people. This process of fault-finding may represent the conscious derivative of the unconscious defense of projection.

It thus appears that the simple idea of eight basic emotions, when combined with the concept of mixtures and derivatives, leads to a complex world of ideas and reveals systematic connections among diverse concepts. Along the way, many research studies were stimulated by these ideas. The model provides a simple and elegant structure that has many implications, only some of

TABLE 1.4

EMOTIONS AND THEIR DERIVATIVES

Subjective language	Behavioral language	Functional language	Trait language	Diagnostic language	Ego-defense language
Fear	Escape	Protection	Timid	Passive type	Repression
Anger	Attack	Destruction	Aggressive	Aggressive type	Displacement
Joy	Mate	Reproduction	Sociable	Manic state	Reaction formation
Sadness	Cry	Reintegration	Gloomy	Depression	Sublimation
Acceptance	Groom	Incorporation	Agreeable	Hysteric	Denial
Disgust	Vomit	Rejection	Contemptuous	Paranoid state	Projection
Expectation	Map	Exploration	Curious	Obsessive–compulsive	Intellectualization
Surprise	Stop	Orientation	Impulsive	Psychopathic	Regression

which have been explored so far. Chapter 14 examines some important clinical implications of the model.

UNIVERSAL PROBLEMS OF ADAPTATION

This concluding section will consider some broad, but speculative, issues. They concern the possible relations between emotions and certain universal problems of adaptation, which all organisms must deal with or come to terms with. These problems may be labeled as follows: (*a*) the problem of hierarchy; (*b*) the problem of territoriality; (*c*) the problem of identity; and (*d*) the problem of temporality (Plutchik, 1979).

HIERARCHY

The concept of hierarchy refers to the vertical dimension of social life. This is seen almost universally as dominance hierarchies both in lower animals and in humans. In general, the major expressions of high hierarchical positions are first access to food, to shelter, to comforts, and to sex.

The vertical organization of social life is reflected in the age relations among people, in the relations between the sexes, and in the social and economic classes of society and is preeminent in military life. Generally speaking, hierarchical organizations reflect the fact that some people know more than other people, that some people are stronger or more skillful than other people, and that all people vary in affective dispositions. All organisms must face these realities and come to terms with them.

Of great importance is the fact that dominance hierarchies are connected primarily with certain types of basic emotions, namely, anger and fear. They are also connected to the personality derivatives of these emotions, that is, dominance and submission. Organisms high in the hierarchy are typically bossy and irritable, while those at lower levels tend to have anxiety. This has been demonstrated in baboons (Buirski, Kellerman, Plutchik, Weininger, & Buirski, 1973) and in humans (Kellerman, Buirski, & Plutchik, 1974). Depression appears to be related, in part, to perceived downward mobility within a particular hierarchy (Plutchik & Landau, 1973; Price, 1967). Thus, the concept of hierarchy may be reflected in many subtle and indirect ways.

TERRITORIALITY

The second universal adaptation problem for organisms concerns territoriality. In every animal species, each organism must learn what aspects of the environment "belong" to it.

From an evolutionary point of view, territories define an area or space of potential nourishment necessary for survival, or an area that is "safe" from attack or predation. Territories may be explicit or implicit. In the former case, territories may be expressed through scent markings, tree scratches, or boundary lines. In the latter case, they may be defined as the distance one organism allows another to approach before aggression is initiated.

How do boundaries develop? They probably develop through exploration of the environment. When an individual gets to know an environment, he may begin to have some control over it. But the control is possible only within certain limits or boundaries. When boundaries are penetrated by other organisms, this represents a potential threat to survival. It represents a potential loss of control. I propose the hypothesis that the basic emotions related to territoriality are exploration and its opposite, surprise. Or, to use a different but essentially equivalent terminology, the basic affective states centered around the issue of territoriality are control and dyscontrol.

IDENTITY

The third major problem that all organisms encounter, and which is generated by the nature of the social environment, is the problem of identity. In simplest terms, this refers to the basic question of who we are; alternatively, it refers to what group we belong to. This is a fundamental problem for all organisms because isolated individuals in society do not usually survive and certainly they do not propagate. Group membership, therefore, is a fundamental basis for survival.

There are endless examples in nature of specific behavior patterns that have been developed by different groups to increase the chances of survival. These include such things as cooperative hunting, group defense, social signaling, and social communication. However, in order for an individual to benefit by group membership, he has to know what group he belongs to. In lower animals, this knowledge is built in through genetic coding mechanisms. It is obviously too risky for survival to allow a long period of learning to intervene before an animal can determine its own group. Therefore, some genetic coding mechanisms enable an organism to recognize other organisms of the same type. Such recognition is based on a wide variety of cues, which include, for example, size, shape, color, markings, sound patterns, and, particularly in lower animals, chemical or olfactory cues. It is also likely that animals learn not only who their group is but also the nature of other groups with which they have intimate relations either in the form of prey-predator relations or in the form of species occupying the same ecological niche.

What is true for lower animals is also true for human beings. In the evolution of cultures, one may trace the development of different kinds of groups, each of which creates a different problem connected with the handling of the identity relationship. These groups vary from the band, to the tribe, to the chiefdom, to the state. As the complexity of these social organizations increases from band to state, there is, for individuals, a corresponding increase in the problem of knowing the group to which each person belongs.

Another point of major relevance concerns the relation of basic emotions to the identity problem. It is evident that the two basic emotions connected with identity are acceptance and rejection. They both deal with the fundamental issue of who we allow to become part of our group and who we keep out, who is within the circle and who is outside the circle. All animals and humans throughout the course of their lives must struggle with this fundamental question.

TEMPORALITY

The fourth universal problem encountered by all organisms is the problem of temporality. This word refers to the fact of the limited duration of an individual's life. All organisms have a limited life span, part of which is spent in infancy, childhood, and adolescence learning fundamental skills about social living and about getting around in the environment. From an evolutionary point of view, the purpose of the acquisition of skills is to enable the individual to survive as a reproducing adult member of a group.

In lower animals there is probably no individual awareness of age, per se, and death. However, the reality of death creates the inevitability of loss and separation for those who are living, and it creates the need for social solutions to the problems of loss. Individuals without support from other members of their social group do not survive for very long. During the course of evolution, several solutions have evolved for the problem of loss and separation. One solution is the evolution of distress signals on the part of the animal or individual who has experienced the loss. These distress signals are essentially cries for help or social support. This is genetically programmed for all social organisms. The second evolutionary solution to the problem of loss is the evolution of sympathetic or nurturing responses in other members of the social group.

In humans, the problem of the limited span of existence has effected the evolution of a series of social institutions that are designed to deal with this problem. These include mourning rituals; birth, death, and reunion myths; preparation for an afterlife; and possibly certain aspects of religion.

In order to deal with the problem of loss and separation, that is, the problem of temporality, certain emotions have evolved during the course of evolution. The emotion that deals with loss is sadness or distress. The function of this emotion when expressed directly or indirectly as a cry for help is to try to produce reintegration of the individual with the lost person or with a substitute. If the cry functions to produce only a partial or limited reintegration, this may result in a persistent, long-term distress signal that we call depression. If the signal works well and completely, it produces an opposite emotion—joy. Joy is the experience of rejoining or of possession and is thus the opposite of sadness.

IMPLICATIONS

This schema defining four universal problems of adaptation—which I have called problems of hierarchy, territoriality, identity, and temporality—has important implications. First, it provides a general way of looking at life problems at all phylogenetic levels. This is a functional approach to classification that has potential relevance to all animal levels. Second, it provides a set of implicit dimensions that one can use to try to assess the environmental and/or social demands on a given species. For any animal or group of animals, one can ask: How are problems of hierarchy, territoriality, identity, and temporality expressed for that group? What kinds of adaptations has the group made for dealing with each of these problems?

Another important implication of this schema is that it provides another kind of rationale for the existence of certain emotions, since emotions are reflections of the adaptations that animals make to the universal problems. Since these problems are universal, the emotions that are derived from them may be thought of as universal, basic, or primary. Also of great importance is the fact that the primary emotions have a dual or bipolar aspect, with each one entailing an opposite one. Thus, for example, a hierarchy has two poles: the top and the bottom, the dominant and the submissive, the angry and the frightened. Similarly, an identity problem creates the issue of who is in and who is out of the group, who is to be accepted and who rejected.

Finally, the schema presented here of basic life problems suggests the possibility that emotions are functional adaptations for establishing a kind of social equilibrium. This would imply that emotions enter into every social transaction and help to establish a balance of opposing forces. These balances are always temporary and frequently change as we move through life from one conflict to another.

In conclusion, the psychoevolutionary theory outlined in this chapter is broad and comprehensive. It tries to relate certain functional concepts connected with evolution to the origins and nature of emotions. It provides a formal structural model that describes the similarity and polarity relations among emotions. At the same time, the theory is quite explicit in showing that certain areas such as personality and diagnosis are derivative concepts based on emotions. The theory has stimulated research and provided the inspiration for the development of a whole family of new tests: for moods, for personality traits, for ego defenses, and for coping styles. The theory is explicit enough to be empirically tested in order to confirm or disconfirm various elements of the model. The theory is thus an organizer of data, a bridge across disciplines, and a stimulator of research.

REFERENCES

Allport, G. W., & Odbert, H. S. Trait names: A psychological study. *Psychological Monographs,* 1936, *47,* Whole No. 211.

Anderson, N. H. Likeableness ratings of 555 personality trait words. *Journal of Personality and Social Psychology,* 1968, *9,* 272-279.

Bayley, N. Behavioral correlates of mental growth: Birth to thirty-six years. *American Psychologist,* 1968, *23,* 1-17.

Becker, W. C., & Krug, R. S. A circumplex model for social behavior in children. *Child Development,* 1964, *35,* 371-396.

Brenner, C. Affects and psychic conflict. *The Psychoanalytic Quarterly,* 1975, *44,* 5-28.

Buirski, P., Kellerman, H., Plutchik, R., Weininger, R., & Buirski, N. A field study of emotions, dominance, and social behavior in a group of baboons (*Papio anubis*). *Primates,* 1973, *14,* 67-78.

Campbell, B. G. *Human evolution: An introduction to man's adaptations.* Chicago: Aldine, 1966.

Chess, S. *An introduction to child psychiatry.* New York: Grune & Stratton, 1964.

Chess, S. Psychiatry of the first three years of life. In S. Arieti (ed.), *American handbook of psychiatry.* New York: Basic Books, 1966.

Conte, H. R. *A circumplex model for personality traits.* Ph.D. Dissertation, New York University, 1975.

Davitz, J. R. *The language of emotion.* New York: McGraw-Hill, 1969.

Davitz, J. R. A dictionary and grammar of emotion. In M. Arnold (ed.), *Feelings and emotions: The Loyola Symposium.* New York: Academic Press, 1970.

Delgado, J. M. R. Free behavior and brain stimulation. In C. C. Pfeiffer & J. R. Smythies (eds.), *International review of neurobiology,* Vol. VI. New York: Academic Press, 1964.

Delgado, J. M. R. *Emotions.* Dubuque, Iowa: Wm. C. Brown, 1966.

Dember, W. N. Motivation and the cognitive revolution. *American Psychologist,* 1974, *29,* 161-168.

Freedman, M. B., Leary, T. F., Ossorio, A. G., & Coffey, H. S. The interpersonal dimension of personality. *Journal of Personality,* 1951, *20,* 143-161.

Goodall, J. Mother–offspring relationships in the free ranging chimpanzees. In D. Morris (ed.), *Primate ethology.* Chicago: Aldine, 1967.

Guttman, L. A new approach to factor analysis: The radex. In P. F. Lazarsfeld (ed.), *Mathematical thinking in the social sciences.* Glencoe, Ill.: The Free Press, 1954.

Hebb, D. O. *Textbook of psychology.* Philadelphia: Saunders, 1972.

Jerison, H. J. *Evolution of the brain and intelligence.* New York: Academic Press, 1973.

Kellerman, H., Buirski, P. and Plutchik, R. Group behavior in a baboon troop: implications for human group process. In L. Wolberg and M. Aronson (eds.), *Group Therapy 1974,* New York: Stratton, 1974.

Kellerman, H., & Plutchik, R. Emotion–trait interrelations and the measurement of personality. *Psychological Reports,* 1968, *23,* 1107-1114.

Lazarus, R. S. Emotions and adaptation: Conceptual and empirical relations. In W. I. Arnold (ed.), *Nebraska Symposium on motivation.* Lincoln: University of Nebraska Press, 1968.

Lorenz, K. *On aggression.* New York: Harcourt Brace, 1966.

Lorr, M. & McNair, D. M. Expansion of the interpersonal behavior circle. *Journal of Personality and Social Psychology,* 1965, *2,* 823–830.

Mandler, G. *Mind and emotion.* New York: Wiley, 1975.

Marsella, A. J. *Cross-cultural studies of depression: A review of the literature.* Paper presented at the Symposium on Cross-Cultural Aspects of Depression, International Association of Cross-Cultural Psychology, Tilburg, Netherlands, 1976.

Neisser, U. The imitation of man by machine. *Science,* 1963, *139,* 193–197.

Norman, W. T. *2800 personality trait descriptors: Normative operating characteristics for a university population.* Ann Arbor, Michigan: Office of Research Administration, 1967.

Plutchik, R. Outlines of a new theory of emotion. *Transactions of the New York Academy of Sciences,* 1958, *20,* 394–403.

Plutchik, R. *The emotions: Facts, theories and a new model.* New York: Random House, 1962.

Plutchik, R. The affective differential: Emotion profiles implied by diagnostic concepts. *Psychological Reports,* 1967, *20,* 19–25.

Plutchik, R. Emotions, evolution and adaptive processes. In M. Arnold (ed.), *Feelings and emotions: The Loyola Symposium.* New York: Academic Press, 1970.

Plutchik, R. Cognitions in the service of emotions: An evolutionary perspective. In D. K. Candland, J. P. Fell, E. Keen, A. I. Leshner, R. Plutchik, & R. M. Tarpy. *Emotion.* Monterey, Calif.: Brooks/Cole, 1977.

Plutchik, R. Universal problems of adaptation: Hierarchy, territoriality, identity, and temporality. In J. B. Calhoun (ed.), *Perspectives on adaptation, environment and population,* New York: Praeger, 1979.

Plutchik, R. *Emotion: A psychoevolutionary synthesis.* New York: Harper and Row, 1980.

Plutchik, R., & Conte, H. R. *An empirical study of the similarity structure of emotions.* Unpublished manuscript, 1978. (Available from R. Plutchik.)

Plutchik, R., & Kellerman, H. *Manual for the Emotions Profile Index.* Los Angeles: Western Psychological Services, 1974.

Plutchik, R., Kellerman, H., & Conte, H. R. A structural theory of ego defenses. In C. E. Izard (ed.), *Emotions, personality, and psychopathology.* New York: Plenum, 1979.

Plutchik, R., & Landau, H. Perceived dominance and emotional states in small groups. *Psychotherapy: Theory, Research and Practice,* 1973, *10,* 341–342.

Plutchik, R., & Platman, S. R. Personality connotations of psychiatric diagnoses: Implications for a similarity model. *The Journal of Nervous and Mental Disease,* 1977, *165,* 418–422.

Price, J. The dominance hierarchy and the evolution of mental illness. *The Lancet,* 1967, *2,* 243–246.

Rado, S. *Adaptational psychodynamics: Motivation and control.* New York: Science House, 1969.

Rinn, J. L. Structure of phenomenal domains. *Psychological Review,* 1965, *72,* 445–466.

Roget's international thesaurus, 3rd ed. New York: Thomas Y. Crowell, 1962.

Russell, J. A., & Mehrabian, A. Evidence for a three-factor theory of emotions. *Journal of Research in Personality,* 1977, *11,* 273–294.

Schachter, S., & Singer, J. E. Cognitive, social and physiological determinants of emotional state. *Psychological Bulletin,* 1962, *69,* 379–399.

Schaefer, E. S. A circumplex model for maternal behavior. *Journal of Abnormal and Social Psychology,* 1959, *59,* 226–235.

Schaefer, E. S. Conveying conceptual models for maternal behavior and for child behavior. In J. Glidewell (ed.), *Parental attitudes and child behavior.* Springfield, Ill.: C. C. Thomas, 1961.

Schaefer, E. S., & Plutchik, R. Interrelationships of emotions, traits, and diagnostic constructs. *Psychological Reports,* 1966, *18,* 399–410.

Scott, J. P. *Animal behavior.* Chicago: University of Chicago Press, 1958.

Speer, D. C. Nonverbal communication of affective information. *Comparative Group Studies,* 1972, 409–423.

Stern, G. G. *Activities index.* Syracuse: Syracuse University Psychological Research Center, 1958.

Stone, L. A., & Coles, G. J. Correlational similarity: The basis for a new revised method of similarity analysis. *Studia Psychologica,* 1970, *12,* 258–265.

Wilson, E. O. *Sociobiology: The new synthesis.* Cambridge: Harvard University Press, 1975.

Chapter 2

THE FUNCTION OF EMOTIONS
IN BEHAVIORAL SYSTEMS:
A SYSTEMS THEORY ANALYSIS

J. P. SCOTT

ABSTRACT

Emotions are considered as aspects of complex, interactional systems of the organism. There is a relatively small number of emotions whose functions vary according to the level of the system organization in which they appear. Some emotions are primarily concerned with the maintenance of internal stability; others, such as the agonistic and sexual emotions, contribute strongly to the depth of social interactions. Therefore, no one emotion can be taken as a model for all others, rather, each functions within a separate system. A number of studies are described that lead to the conclusion that there is no hard-and-fast line between sensation and emotion, but that these grade into each other and form a continuum. The differences between systems theory, mechanistic theory and reductionism are also examined.

Emotions have usually been studied on three different levels. The first and most important includes the subjective *feelings* or *affect* experienced by humans. Affect has a tremendous effect on behavior, and this fact provides a compelling reason for its study. However, subjective feelings have been the least studied aspect of emotions because of the difficulties of devising techniques for their objective measurement.

Second, there are the *expressions* of emotion: social signals that transmit affect to another individual. This process, which was first studied by Darwin

35

Emotion: Theory, Research, and Experience
Volume 1: Theories of Emotion

(1872), involves both the nature of the signals produced by the transmitter and the responses of the individual who is the receiver. This set of phenomena is amenable to objective study and measurement and has been extensively studied by ethologists in a wide variety of animal species. Two theoretical frameworks have been employed: that of communication theory, and that of instinct theory and fixed action patterns. Neither of these theories directs attention to the underlying emotions involved, although Lorenz has not hesitated to name such feelings in animals like geese.

Third, there are the underlying *physiological changes* that accompany the emotions. These changes can be measured by highly sophisticated and accurate techniques. They have been extensively studied chiefly from the conceptual viewpoint of a mechanistic–reductionistic framework. A reductionistic theory leads to the conclusion that this kind of study should provide the most basic and hence the most important facts concerning the phenomenon of emotions. A great deal of information has been accumulated, and we at least know the parts of the body that are involved in emotional responses and their changes in activity during experimentally produced emotions. The results have nevertheless been disappointing, both in providing a satisfactory theoretical framework and in leading to applied results.

It is the thesis of this chapter that emotions are best understood as parts of general organismic and social systems and that, from this conceptual framework, emotions can be meaningfully studied on all three of the above levels.

SYSTEMS OF SOCIAL BEHAVIOR

THE STUDY OF SYSTEMS

A system is defined as a group of interacting entities. This definition leads to the following scheme of analysis: to study the nature of (*a*) the entities that compose the system and (*b*) the interactions between the entities. At the outset, such studies are largely observational, but the nature of the entities and their interactions will soon suggest theories that can be tested experimentally.

THE NATURE OF SOCIAL ENTITIES

The basic entities in a social system are the organisms that make up a particular species. Since the great majority of animal species reproduce sexually, the most obvious differences between entities are those that involve sex. Thus, we recognize males and females and can further subdivide each of these classes on the basis of age and sexual maturity. The roughest sort of age classification divides individuals into those that are immature and not capable of reproduction and those that are mature and capable of reproduction. We must always recognize that these are gross dichotomies and that both immature and mature individuals change with age. Having applied this classification, an obvious hypothesis that can be tested experimentally and observationally is that males and females, and mature and immature individuals, will vary with respect to the emotions that they feel and express. Since sex is genetically determined, this hypothesis also leads to the study of emotions in the field of behavior genetics. Furthermore, the study of maturational changes in emotions leads to systematic studies of internal physiological changes as well as to developmental studies of emotional behavior.

THE NATURE OF SOCIAL INTERACTIONS

The second major line of study of a system involves the description and analysis of the interactions that take place between its component entities. Social behavior may be defined as behavior that either is stimulated by or has an effect on another member of the same species. Therefore, almost all behavior may be social, though not necessarily so. The social interactions of animals have been widely studied throughout the animal kingdom, and, if we classify these behaviors according to their functions, we arrive at nine general classes (Scott, 1956).

Ingestive behavior is found universally among any animals that show behavior. Its function is the intake of nourishing materials, whether solid, liquid, or gaseous. It therefore includes the behavior that we commonly call eating, drinking, and breathing.

Shelter-seeking or comfort-seeking behavior has the function of moving an organism to a place that is favorable to its survival. In the more complex organisms, this function is partially replaced by shelter-building behavior, usually associated with the care and the protection of the young. Shelter-seeking is almost universal among the members of the animal kingdom that are capable of movement.

Investigatory behavior has the function of discovering and exploring the environment with the aid of various senses. It also appears to be universal, although it is difficult to recognize in animals such as the roundworms of the phylum Nemathelminthes because of the poor sense organs found in these forms.

Sexual behavior has the function of ensuring the union of the sex cells or gametes. It is found in every major animal group except the Sponges, Coelenterates, and the Echinoderms, whose sex cells are simply released into the water.

The preceding four classes of behavior are widely found throughout the animal kingdom, even in the one-celled animals. They therefore may be considered more primitive than the five systems having the following functions.

Epimeletic behavior has the function of providing care and attention to the young of a species, but it may also be extended to other adults or even to the animal itself. With sexual behavior it shares the general function of reproduction. Also associated with it is *et-epimeletic* behavior, which has the function of signaling a need for care and attention. In the higher animals it is usually expressed as crying or some other form of signaling that communicates a need to the parental animals. While the behaviors are often quite simple, it is a hybrid system, in that it may reflect needs for any of the other functions of behavior.

The primary function of *agonistic* behavior is protection against injury, but it may be extended to inflicting injury and so serve a variety of secondary functions, including the regulation of the use of space and thus to territoriality.

Allelomimetic behavior, defined as doing what another individual does, with some degree of mutual imitation, has the primary function of coordinating the behavior of the individuals within the group. Secondarily, it may provide safety for a prey species or more efficient cooperative hunting by predators.

Finally, *eliminative* behavior has the function of disposing of urine and feces. It is found only among terrestrial animals and may acquire a variety of secondary signaling functions.

The last five behavioral classes are prominent only in the three highest phyla of animals. All of them are well developed in vertebrates and in man. Since emotions in subjective experience lead to behavior, we can hypothesize that a different emotion should be associated with each type of social interaction and that emotions should differ from species to species, especially where these species are not closely related. We can, for example, readily recognize the emotional signals of a dog when it is growling and snarling, but the tail-rattling behavior of a mouse is difficult to recognize as being anything that might be related to human behavior.

BEHAVIORAL SYSTEMS

If we study any of the above classes of interactions that take place within social systems, we come to the conclusion that each is also organized on the next lowest level of system organization, that of the individual organism. We can therefore hypothesize that the behavior of an individual organism is organized into subsystems around the major functions of behavior.

The entities that comprise such a behavioral system are patterns of behavior. A *behavior pattern* is defined as a segment of behavior that has a definite function. Thus, the agonistic behavior of the house mouse is composed of the following entities: attack, running away, defense posture, squeaking, hair-fluffing, tail rattling, and passivity. These are expressed in an organized fashion in any situation that involves conflict with another individual.

Some of these patterns are recognizable as emotional signals and some as physiological reactions that may be related to affect (although the latter can only be inferred in a mouse).

Detailed study of the nine classes of behavior in various species leads to the conclusion that each is organized as a system. We can hypothesize that the emotions, whether they appear as affect, expressed emotion, or physiological responses, are functionally related to these systems.

EMOTIONS IN RELATION TO BEHAVIORAL SYSTEMS

This section is based on available evidence from human subjective reports and physiology plus whatever information that either can be inferred from behavior in the higher mammals or is directly derived from the physiological study of these forms. The organization of the material is based on the assumption that behavior patterns are organized into systems around each major life function, and that there is an underlying physiological system corresponding to each behavioral system. As stated above, emotions can appear in the context of these systems as subjective feelings (affect), as behavior patterns (the expression of emotion), and as physiological reactions. I shall also attempt to assess the function of each emotion within the system in which it appears.

THE INGESTIVE SYSTEM

In man and the higher mammals, the functions of this system are divided according to the class of substances being ingested. With respect to food, the predominant emotion is that of hunger. It is expressed in young children and in many young animals as distress vocalization. Babies cry, young puppies whine and yelp, and both are likely to show increased activity. The basic physiology of food intake has been studied for years. Once thought to be relatively simple, it is now known to rest on an extraordinarily complex but highly effective control system involving stomach contractions, the level of blood glucose, hormones such as insulin and the sex hormones, centers in the hypothalamus of the central nervous system, and so on (Silverstone, 1976). More subtle functions affect other nutritive substances such as salt, but these do not involve any major emotions.

The second major function of the ingestive system involves the intake of water. The subjective emotion is thirst, a sensation of dryness in the throat. Like hunger, it can be expressed as distress vocalization. Thirst and drinking behavior are regulated, at least in part, by cells in the hypothalamus that respond to changes in osmotic pressure.

Finally, there is behavior associated with the intake of oxygen. The associated affect is a feeling of breathlessness, which can be relieved by deep breathing. There are no special expressions of emotion, as this is a condition that ordinarily cannot be relieved with the help of others. A control center regulating breathing is located in the medulla of the spinal cord.

In general, the functions of this system are basic to the maintenance of life and range from the provision of oxygen, the lack of which may produce an acute condition within a few minutes, through thirst, where death may ensue within a few days, to the need for food, without which a large animal like man can survive for several weeks. All the emotions are uncomfortable, but their external expression is limited according to whether or not the associated needs can be filled by social interaction. In every case, the emotion stimulates activity that eventually results in behavior that relieves the physiological need, after which the emotion disappears. Thus, the entire system functions as a feedback loop that maintains stability of physiological conditions. The emotions serve to prolong and maintain behavior. Because they are unpleasant, their cessation reinforces the behavior that has brought about relief.

THE SHELTER–SEEKING SYSTEM

The emotions and physiology connected with ingestive behavior are often used as a hypothetical model, especially in instinct theory (Craig, 1918; Tinbergen, 1951) for the organization of other behavioral systems. However, every system appears to be unique, and there are no perfect analogies. In the case of shelter-seeking behavior, the internal sensations are quite different from those of ingestive behavior, in that they are directly related to environmental stimulations. The most common sorts of feelings are those of cold and heat, and these sensations are readily relieved by seeking shelter. Other sorts of unpleasant stimulation are those arising from unpleasant odors, loud sounds, and, in aquatic animals, various sorts of chemicals and alterations of osmotic pressure. The emotional signals are those of distress: crying in man and distress vocalization in dogs. The underlying physiology is relatively simple, e.g., there are sense organs that detect heat or cold and produce sensations of discomfort that, if they are extreme, merge into pain. The general functioning of the system is similar to that of ingestive behavior. The unpleasant sensations lead to activity, which, if appropriate, leads to the cessation of the symptoms, thus forming a feedback loop. As in ingestive behavior, the cessation of the sensations has the effect of reinforcing the preceding behavior.

THE INVESTIGATIVE BEHAVIORAL SYSTEM

The affect connected with this system is a very mild positive emotion usually labeled *curiosity*. The emotion is aroused by novelty and is quite evanescent. No expressive signals are associated with the behavior, although it is quite easy to recognize investigatory behavior in either man or other animals by the nature of the behavior and the obvious use of the sense organs. The neurological basis of investigatory behavior is almost unknown. The emotion has the function of maintaining and reinforcing the external behavior.

THE SEXUAL BEHAVIORAL SYSTEM

There are two kinds of affect associated with this system. One is a vague and almost unrecognizable emotion that leads to an activity that has the function of bringing the individual into contact with one of the opposite sex. In addition, there are the strongly pleasant and specific emotions associated with sexual behavior itself. This kind of affect is different from the preceding in that males and females report different kinds of emotions (Hyde & Rosenberg, 1976).

Emotional expression takes many different forms that vary from species to species. These can be divided into the preliminary patterns of courtship and the expressions of pleasure that accompany sexual activity itself. The physiological changes that accompany this activity are largely hormonal, involving interactions between hormones from the gonads and pituitary gland and associated activity in the hypothalamus of the brain.

The functions of these emotions are to maintain activity that leads to contact and to reinforce strongly the behavior that is involved. The superficial similarity of the functions of these emotions to those in ingestive behavior has often been noted. The difference is that in the sexual system the behavior is primarily social, involving two or more individuals and contributing to attachments between them. In short, this is a behavioral system that leads to a higher order of system organization.

THE EPIMELETIC BEHAVIORAL SYSTEM

The subjective emotions that accompany this behavior are usually labeled tenderness, warmth, and love. In humans the expressed emotions that accompany it may take the form of talking, crooning, or singing. There is often some caressing also. Among other mammals, there is relatively little expression of emotion, although a mother sheep may call a lamb from which she has been separated. Physiological studies of epimeletic behavior have involved the manipulation of three female hormones: estrone, progesterone, and prolactin;

however, the effects of these hormones vary widely from species to species, even in relatively closely related rodents (Zarrow, Gandelman, & Denenberg, 1971). The behavior itself may occur in virgin females and even in males of some species, indicating that the hormones, while they induce changes in the behavior of a parous female, are not necessary for its expression (Rosenblatt, 1975). The principal functions of the emotions in this system are to render associated behavior pleasant and thus to reinforce it and prolong it. Epimeletic behavior is also a response to calls by young animals signaling fright or injury. In humans, the associated internal affect is described as concern and anxiety.

THE ET-EPIMELETIC BEHAVIORAL SYSTEM

This is a hybrid system and a transitory one. In young animals all behavioral systems may be organized so as to produce external emotional expression that functions as a demand for help from some other member of the species, usually a parent. The externally expressed behavior is usually a single simple pattern, such as crying in human infants, but the internal feelings may be those that are associated with any other behavioral system. Consequently, the underlying physiology of the system is also similar to that of other systems. The neurological basis of distress vocalization itself is still largely unknown. The functions of the emotions in the system should be the same as those in the other systems involved.

THE AGONISTIC BEHAVIORAL SYSTEM

This is one of the best known of all the behavioral systems. It is defined as behavior that is adaptive in situations involving conflict between two or more members of the same species. Its behavior patterns include attack, defensive fighting, flight, and freezing. Its social function probably evolved from the defensive response against injury, which is found more widely in the animal kingdom and is adaptive in response to injury by any other animal, whether or not of the same species. The pain of an injury leads to an almost reflexive attempt to bite or otherwise injure the source of the attack. The defensive response to pain is therefore the most primitive type of agonistic behavior. An alternative response to injury is flight, and this is usually associated with fear. The physiologically similar emotion of anger often precedes an attack; thus, the subjective emotions of agonistic behavior are pain, fear, and anger. These may be expressed externally by a wide range of signals. Pain or fear may result in a special kind of distress vocalization, usually expressed as screaming in humans, whereas a puppy may yelp under similar circumstances. In a dog, anger may be expressed by growling, snarling, and threat postures. Angry humans often shout at each other or make motions that indicate an intention to strike.

The underlying physiology is also well known, involving strong reactions of the autonomic nervous system and activity in certain regions of the hypothalamus. Unlike hunger, the emotions do not arise in response to internal physiological changes (Scott, 1971). They primarily serve to maintain behavior over periods of many hours. They also have the function of reinforcing behavior in either a positive or a negative fashion, depending on the emotion involved.

THE ALLELOMIMETIC BEHAVIORAL SYSTEM

The subjective feelings associated with this system are those of unease and loneliness. These are both unpleasant emotions, and their cause cannot always be recognized because they tend to be so persistent. Deprived of companionship, a nonhuman animal will express emotion as distress vocalization over very long periods, with the result that it is difficult to associate the emotion with its actual cause. In addition to the unpleasant emotion associated with separation, there is probably also a milder, positive one of pleasure that is elicited in connection with activities involving companionship and mutual imitation.

The underlying physiology of this emotion is largely unknown except by indirect inference. Some recent studies (e.g., Panksepp, Herman, Conner, Bishop, & Scott, 1978) suggest that it may be connected with the endorphins of the brain.

The general function of the emotion is to ensure contiguity with other members of a group and, along with this, safety and the possibility of cooperative activity. It should also result in social facilitation (Scott, 1968a).

THE ELIMINATIVE BEHAVIORAL SYSTEM

The subjective sensations associated with this behavioral system are those of pressure on the bladder and bowel. In most species there is no emotional expression of the sensations unless they become painful. In some species, however, elimination is used to mark certain locations and thus to communicate the presence of the animal that performed the act to another that may come along later. This behavior may be elaborated into the marking of territories, as it is in rabbits (Mykytowycz, 1965). The internal sensations have no function except to warn the individual that elimination is likely to occur. The expressed behavior has the function of communication, and there is some evidence, especially in rodents, that certain chemical substances (pheromones) associated with urine may communicate the sex and social status of an animal. While this may arouse emotion in the animal that examines the urine, there is no evidence that elimination itself is an expression of internal feelings.

CONCLUSIONS

The preceding material provides us with a list of emotions associated with the basic behavioral functions of the higher animals. As can be seen from Table 2.1, there is a relatively small number of identifiable emotions. Some of these, such as pain and discomfort, are customarily called sensations rather than true emotions. Some emotions appear in more than one system, and we must conclude that evolution has been economical in the creation of emotional responses.

Table 2.1 summarizes this information. In the left-hand column are listed the nine behavioral systems, and in the next column the subjective emotion or affect associated with each is listed. The emotions themselves may have functions on three levels. In the social systems, emotions chiefly have the effect of facilitating or prolonging interaction between individuals. On the organismic system level, the two chief functions are the maintenance and reinforcement of behavior, while on the physiological level the chief function is the maintenance of homeostasis. I have attempted to estimate the relative importance of the function in each case (low, medium, or high) and whether or not its effect is positive ($+$) or negative ($-$). Thus, curiosity has low positive effects on social interaction and the maintenance and reinforcement of behavior in an individual organism, and no function with respect to homeostasis.

There is no one general pattern of emotional function. An emotion may have different functions according to the level of system organization in which it appears. Some emotions are most important at the physiological level, whereas others are more important at the organismic and social levels. Only three sets of emotions are most important on the physiological level: those associated with the ingestive, shelter-seeking, and eliminative behavioral systems. These emotions are directly concerned with the maintenance of internal stability, or homeostasis.

Five of the systems have major functions on the level of social systems, contributing strongly to the depth of social interactions. These are the emotions connected with the sexual, epimeletic, et-epimeletic, agonistic, and allelomimetic behavioral systems.

Finally, all of the emotions have major functions on the level of organismic systems. These functions are the maintenance of behavior over long periods, in order that adaptation may take place, and the reinforcement of behavior in either a positive or a negative fashion, thus contributing to learned responses.

TABLE 2.1

RELATIVE IMPORTANCE OF EMOTIONAL FUNCTIONS AT DIFFERENT SYSTEMS LEVELS[a]

Behavioral system	Associated emotions or sensations	Organismic systems			Physiological systems
		Social systems interaction	Maintenance of behavior	Reinforcement of behavior	Maintenance of homeostasis
Ingestive	Hunger	+	+++	+++	+++
	Thirst	+	+++	+++	+++
	Breathlessness		+++	+	+++
Shelter-seeking	Discomfort (cold, heat, etc.)	+	++	++	+++
Investigative	Curiosity	+	+	+	
Sexual	Unease	+	++	+	−
	Love	+++	+++	+++	−
	Pleasure	+++	+++	+++	−
Epimeletic	Love	+++	+++	+++	−
	Anxiety	+++	+++	+++	−
Et-epimeletic	(Any of the other emotions)	++	++	+	++
Agonistic	Pain	+++	+++	+++	−
	Fear	+++	+++	+++	− −
	Anger	+++	+++	+++	− −
Allelomimetic	Loneliness	+++	+++	+++	−
	Pleasure	+++	+++	+++	
Eliminative	Discomfort (internal)	+	++	++	+++

[a] +, positive function; −, negative function. The number of plus or minus signs indicates estimated importance.

Functions on the social and physiological levels are not necessarily compatible. Sexual, epimeletic, agonistic, and allelomimetic behaviors may actually disturb homeostasis. This means that no one emotion and its associated system can be taken as a model for all others. Rather, each must be considered as a separate system. In classical instinct theory (Craig, 1918; Tinbergen, 1951), the emotion of hunger and its associated physiology has often been taken as a model for other types of behavior. While this was a useful preliminary hypothesis, it is obviously not a correct one.

While these nine systems of behavior exist separately from each other, it does not follow that this is the case in every species. Parts of several systems may be united in cases of such complex activities as hunting by a predator and in many of the complex activities shown by man. Nor are these systems necessarily inclusive of all behaviors and all emotions. The appreciation of beauty, for example, does not fit into any of these systems. What this analysis does is to delineate those systems of behavior and their associated emotions that are general to many species and hence presumably have basic general importance.

EXPERIMENTS ON THE SYSTEMIC NATURE
OF AFFECT IN DOGS

TECHNIQUES

Certain emotions, such as hunger, are very well known and understood. Such is not the case with respect to the emotions connected with allelomimetic behavior and with attachment. We know that dogs express strong emotional reactions to separation from familiar objects and individuals. We do not know whether these emotional responses are separable from other emotional states.

Attacking this problem from the viewpoint of the systems concept, emotions are interactions between entities, not entities themselves. In analyzing a system, a major technique is to remove the constituent entities one at a time. This will verify whether or not the suspected entity is indeed part of the system and may give some clue as to the function of that particular entity in the system. This technique can involve lesions of the nervous system on the physiological level and the removal of individuals from a group on the social level. The technique always has limitations, as it inevitably distorts and may even destroy the functioning of the system as a whole.

A second general technique for the study and analysis of systems is to attempt to modify the nature of the interaction without destroying the system. This has the advantage that it is more likely to reveal the normal functioning of the system. In the case of separation distress in dogs, we have used three techniques: alleviation (the reduction of an emotional response by treatment), the use of psychotropic drugs, and the induction of two emotional reactions at the same time, observing whether or not they produce compatible effects.

The behavior that we have primarily used is the distress vocalization of young puppies in response to separation from familiar objects and individuals. This was first definitively described by Elliot and Scott (1961). From approximately 3 weeks on, puppies separated from their mother and littermates and placed in a strange room will begin to vocalize at high rates, usually more than 100 per minute, and will continue this reaction indefinitely. Vocalization is accompanied by increased activity, which presumably represents an attempt by the puppy to find its way back to the home area, and by increased rates of urination and defecation. The latter responses indicate not only that there is a communicative expression of emotion through behavior but that there are underlying physiological changes. Vocalization reaches a maximum peak at approximately 4 weeks of age and is continued at a high level until 8 weeks, after which it gradually declines. Most of the following experiments were done between 6 and 8 weeks, when the response is relatively constant and the puppies are in a relatively mature state. We also demonstrated that the rate of vocalization in a strange room was approximately twice that of an animal isolated in its home room, indicating that the response is affected by separation both from a familiar area and from individuals. From the viewpoint of the nine major behavioral systems listed in the preceding section, this behavior is one part of the et-epimeletic system, which, as was stated on p. 42, is a hybrid system that reflects emotions from all other systems. In the case of distress vocalization induced by separation, the primary system is that of allelomimetic behavior.

EXPERIMENTS WITH ALLEVIATION

Pettijohn, Wong, Ebert, and Scott (1977) did a systematic experiment on the alleviation of separation distress in young puppies. We already knew that complete alleviation of distress vocalization can be achieved by placing a puppy in its home room with its mother and littermates. These experiments were done in a strange room, and, as a result, complete alleviation was never obtained, but it was possible to rank various social and nonsocial factors in order of effectiveness. Food had little or no effect. If the puppies ate at all, which was seldom, they only stopped vocalizing as long as they were actually eating. Toys, which included various novel objects that could be manipulated by the puppies, were also ineffective, except for soft objects that had a somewhat furry texture, such as towels and a toy woolly lamb. In these cases, contact was the alleviating agent.

In contrast, social interactions produced strong effects. The presence of another dog, including the puppy's own image in a mirror, was moderately effective and might have been more so, except that the other dogs were themselves somewhat upset by the strange situation and did not interact with the experimental pup. In other experiments (Scott & Bronson, 1964), we had found that placing a familiar puppy in the strange room would reduce vocalization 50–75%.

Finally, the behavior of humans could be much better controlled than that of dogs and so was somewhat more effective. A passive human separated from the puppy by a wire fence was moderately effective. Removal of the barrier so that the puppy could make direct contact had a greater effect. Puppies often climbed into the lap of the seated experimenter. The most effective condition was one in which the experimenter not only allowed contact but actively played with the puppy.

We concluded that social interaction was the most effective alleviating agent, followed by social contact, followed in turn by contact with inanimate objects having some properties of a social entity. Agents that modify other emotional responses, such as food alleviating hunger and novel objects stimulating curiosity, had no effect. We concluded that the emotion expressed as separation distress is unique and separable from at least two other emotional states, hunger and curiosity.

EXPERIMENTS WITH PSYCHOTROPIC DRUGS

Certain drugs are known to be effective in controlling undesirable emotions. In particular, tranquilizers are effective in controlling the emotion of anxiety, which may be defined as the fear of anticipated events. If such a drug were to reduce an emotional state such as separation distress in the puppy, we could conclude that the latter emotion is similar to that of anxiety. Actually, we found that neither the major nor the minor tranquilizers had any appreciable effect in reducing distress vocalization (Scott, 1974).

We also did extensive experiments with the effects of amphetamine sulfate. This drug has no effect on distress vocalization in puppies that are isolated in a strange place, but these puppies are already vocalizing at a maximum rate. When puppies are given d-amphetamine sulfate in their home pen, however, the vocalization rate goes up. When adult dogs that have been reared in a kennel to an age of 6 months or more are removed from their usual environment such as a home or strange kennel and consequently develop the separation, or kennel dog, syndrome, those of certain breeds show a striking normalizing effect of amphetamine while they are being given inhibitory training. Without the drug, they are unable to suppress activity, but with the drug they do this quite successfully. One of the major symptoms of the kennel dog syndrome, besides that of increased activity, is a tendency to be fearful toward strange objects and individuals. Amphetamine is a stimulant that has the general effect of increasing wakefulness and activity, but it also is a sympathomimetic drug that inhibits gastric and intestinal mobility. Nausea and diarrhea are symptoms that are associated with fear, and it may be hypothesized that amphetamine is, in this case, reducing fearfulness.

Separation is strongly associated with depression in both man and other animals (Scott & Senay, 1973). For this reason, it seemed logical to assess the effects of antidepressant drugs on distress vocalization in puppies. The drug of choice was imipramine (Scott, 1974). A single dose at the level of 8 mg/kg reduced vocalization to zero in beagles and Australian terrier × beagle hybrids, without side effects. These puppies isolated in a strange situation appeared completely normal. The same dose level administered to Telomians, Telomian × beagle hybrids, and sheltie × Telomian hybrids was only slightly effective. These results support the conclusion that separation distress is uniquely different from other emotional reactions, but also indicate that there are major genetic differences in the response to imipramine in dogs.

The drug morphine has attracted considerable attention because of the discovery of morphine receptor centers in the brain that are normally affected by polypeptide substances called endorphins. Panksepp has observed that morphine addiction in many ways is similar to attachment behavior. He and his colleagues (Panksepp et al., 1978) have done an extensive series of experiments on attachment in a wide variety of animals including dogs. Morphine in low doses that do not produce side effects markedly reduces separation distress in dogs and other animals. The morphine antagonist nalaxone has an enhancing effect upon such distress. These results suggest that the endorphins may form a major element in the physiological system underlying the emotion of separation distress, and thus might explain the very long time periods for which this emotion persists in separated animals.

THE INTERACTION OF SEPARATION DISTRESS WITH OTHER EMOTIONS

A third technique for studying the function of an emotion within a system is to induce experimentally combinations of recognizable emotions. The possible effects of such combinations are as follows: They can be (a) compatible and additive, (b) compatible and multiplicative or mutually enhancing, or (c) compatible but duplicative and nonadditive. They can also be incompatible, in which case (a) one emotion might suppress the other or (b) each might cancel the other out.

There are a limited number of emotional responses that can be readily elicited in young puppies. Hunger will produce distress vocalization at a moderate rate that can be controlled easily by feeding puppies on a regular schedule; just before feeding time the puppies begin to vocalize and continue until they are fed. If a puppy is separated at feeding time, intense distress vocalization is manifested at the same rate as if the puppy were not hungry. Furthermore, puppies, while separated, usually refuse to eat and, if separated for long periods, tend to lose weight. Separation distress is therefore incompatible with hunger and tends to suppress it (Scott & Bronson, 1964).

Another emotion that can be readily aroused in very young puppies is distress vocalization stimulated by discomfort. If a puppy in the neonatal or transition period is placed in a situation that does not provide warmth and contact with soft objects, it will begin to vocalize and keep this up indefinitely. Gurski, Davis, and Scott (1974) found that if such a puppy is placed in a padded enclosure in an incubator maintained at 85° F the vocalization rate is zero, even though the puppy is completely alone. Under these conditions, separation distress does not begin to appear until approximately 2 weeks of age and does not reach a maximum level until 4 weeks. These results indicate that separation distress and discomfort are separable, because they appear at different times in development. We can also conclude that the two emotions are compatible and additive, since an isolated puppy at 3 weeks of age will vocalize at a much higher rate if placed in an uncomfortable situation.

Curiosity, the emotion associated with investigative behavior, is relatively weak. As we have seen in connection with the alleviation experiments, separation overcomes curiosity. Separated animals are active, but this activity is directed solely toward finding a way back to the familiar area and its occupants.

Of the three emotions associated with agonistic behavior, we did not experiment with pain for obvious reasons. We attempted to set up an experiment that would involve eliciting anger and separation distress simultaneously (Davis & Scott, 1978), but were unable to find a successful technique. Anger, as in the case of two dogs competing over a bone, is directed at another familiar animal, and the presence of that animal immediately reduces separation distress.

Fear is an emotion that can be readily elicited in young puppies. In our experiments with genetics and behavior (Scott & Fuller, 1965), we found that fearfulness was not a general characteristic, but rather that certain breeds were fearful in special situations. A dog from one breed might be fearful of strange objects but not of strange dogs, whereas an animal from another breed might react in the opposite way. The expression of fear can be measured independently of separation distress by observing such signals as tail carriage and avoidance of the feared object. Davis, Gurski, and Scott (1977) experimented with the fearful reaction of young puppies to a loud noise under conditions in which the puppy was either isolated or in company with another puppy. They found that the fear reactions and the distress vocalization varied independently, without interactive effects. They concluded that the fear reaction to loud noises is distinct from separation distress.

However, one of the principal characteristics of the separation syndrome seen in adult animals is fear of strange humans, noncanine animals, and strange objects. This particular kind of fear (xenophobia or neophobia) thus appears to be compatible with separation distress and, in fact, may lead to mutually enhancing effects.

In general, all these lines of evidence lead to the conclusion that separation distress is a unique emotion and distinct from all others. It is compatible with discomfort and probably also compatible with one specific kind of fear, the fear of the strange. It is incompatible with hunger and curiosity, and I would predict that it is also incompatible with sexual behavior.

LANGUAGE AND THE EMOTIONS

LANGUAGE AS A SYMBOLIC SYSTEM

One of the major differences between human and nonhuman animals is the human capacity for language, which is immensely more elaborate than any similar form of communication in other species. Language is, of course, a nonliving product of living systems. Nevertheless, it has certain of the characteristics of a system. Words may be considered as entities, and the interaction between them produces meaning. But because symbols are nonliving, they tend to be static, and this is one of the major limitations of language when it comes to symbolically describing and interpreting living systems. Once arranged in a certain order, words do not change and interact with each other as do the entities of a living system. Language can indicate ongoing interactions within a system but never reproduce them.

LANGUAGE AS A COMMUNICATOR OF EMOTIONS

With language, humans can verbally convey their own internal feelings to other individuals, as well as employing the nonverbal signals that other animals use. The verbal symbols themselves ordinarily do not arouse affect in another individual. Producing such affect is a very complex process and a very difficult one, as anyone who has ever attempted to do this with poetry or literature knows. Nevertheless, one person can tell another that he is feeling "angry." Indeed, it is this capacity that is the foundation of the subjective information concerning affect that I have included in this chapter.

The limitations of this information lie in the fact that people find a great deal of difficulty in recognizing and naming their own internal feelings. Even in the case of hunger, young children are usually unable to tell what is the

matter with them, and they only gradually learn to recogniz͏   ͏ernal sensation that is alleviated by food. Eventually most people le͏   ͏cognize a
few of the other strong emotions, such as anger and fear, b͏   n these are
often difficult to recognize without situational cues. The res͏u͏l͏   that people
tend to discriminate emotions, not in terms of the feelings then͏selves but in
terms of the situations that arouse such feelings. For example, one can call the
affect aroused by the sight of Niagra Falls "awe," but the same emotion in
the absence of some external condition would be very difficult to recognize.
There are in the English language some 200 or more names of emotions, but
the vast majority are recognizable only when aroused in particular situations.

AFFECT ASSOCIATED WITH LANGUAGE

Perhaps the most useful way to look at language is as a new behavioral
system. Being a symbolic system, it can overlap with and include any of the
other behavioral systems, but it may still have some independent existence of
its own. Evidence from research on the development of language in human infants indicates that babbling and even words themselves precede any capacity
to use these symbols effectively in communication (Dale, 1976). Babies seem
to enjoy talking, and we can postulate that there is some pleasurable affect
associated with it, although no physiological basis is known. We can also
hypothesize, on less secure grounds, that there is a kind of pleasurable affect
aroused by listening.

DISCUSSION AND CONCLUSIONS

WHAT DOES SYSTEMS THEORY DO?

First, the concept of systems provides a framework for organizing the data
derived from the observation and description of a phenomenon. The result is
a theoretical map denoting explored and unexplored scientific territory. In
this chapter I have performed this task for the phenomenon of emotions. The
systems concept not only shows what has been discovered but also indicates
those areas that have not yet been subjected to scientific analysis.

Second, the systems concept places the focus of research on function,
dynamics, and organizational theory. It deemphasizes mechanistic theory and
the concept of one-way causation and places limitations on the concept of
reductionism. Both mechanistic theory and reductionism can be included
within systems theory, however.

The concept of systems also leads to new directions in experimental research, away from the dissection of systems and toward the interactions between the members of systems. It also leads to the study of interaction between systems themselves (which I have illustrated here) and, even further, to study interactions between systems on different levels. This places reductionism in perspective. Certain aspects of the functions of systems are explainable on the basis of function at lower levels of organization, but it should not be assumed that all such relationships are of this sort.

WHAT CONCLUSIONS CAN WE DRAW?

Following the organization of this chapter, we can summarize the resulting conclusions with respect to current knowledge of affect, signaled or expressed emotions, and the physiology of emotions.

Comparing the sorts of affect seen in the different behavioral systems leads to the conclusion that there is no hard-and-fast line between sensation and emotion, but rather that these grade into each other and form a continuum. The sensation of heat may lead into a general emotion of discomfort, for example. At any point on the scale, the function of emotion is to maintain behavior over long periods, and so to permit adaptation to take place and, from the viewpoint of learning, to reinforce the behavior that is adaptive. Thus, we have reinforcement by internal as well as external factors, a situation that has been largely neglected by the students of learning.

Second, the number of classes of recognizable affect is quite limited (Scott, 1967, 1969). Some behavioral systems have more than one type of affect associated with them, but the total number is certainly not more than 18 or 20, with perhaps half this number being readily recognizable. This suggests that the course of evolution of emotions has been a conservative one, with new emotions being added only where these are of paramount importance.

With respect to the expression of emotional signals, classical instinct theory, based on the assumption of one-way causation, postulated that each emotional signal was a fixed action pattern that aroused a fixed and invariant response in the recipient. While it is true that the function of communication is facilitated by uniformity of expression, and consequently that there is probably considerable selection pressure toward uniformity in such signals, it does not follow that the response is necessarily an automatic, mechanical one. In our experiments with dogs, we have found that the function of a given signal serves primarily to alert the other animal, following which an adaptive response may be made (Scott, 1968b). For example, if we play distress vocalization of puppies to a mother in the absence of her pups, she will attempt to get out of her room and find them. On the other hand, if the same sounds are played to the mother while the pups are with her, she merely takes one look, apparently determines that they are in no actual distress, and pays no further attention. Automatic responses to emotional signals in higher mammals are the result of long training rather than genetically fixed organization.

Furthermore, we have found in humans that there are large individual differences in the expression of emotions. The whole history of the study of the recognition of such signals leads to the conclusion that most people are very poor at it, even after years of contact and experience (Ekman, Friesen, & Ellsworth, 1972; Hall, Rosenthal, Archer, Dimatteo, & Rogers, 1978). Language has the potentiality of increasing the efficiency of such emotional communication, but is still subject to the speaker's difficulty in recognizing his own emotional states.

The study of physiology was the first area in which the concept of systems was fruitfully employed. Cannon's (1929) classical work on the emotions led to the concept of homeostasis. The maintenance of internal stability of a system is one of the basic characteristics of living systems. However, the function of emotions on higher systems levels cannot be reduced to homeostasis, as many emotional states result in disturbing physiological conditions rather than in maintaining them on a constant level. Moyer (1976) has suggested that there is a different neurophysiological basis for each function of agonistic behavior and has collected considerable evidence to support this conclusion. One might expect, therefore, that there would be a different sort of emotion associated with each such subsystem. However, our evidence from studies of fearful behavior (Scott & Fuller, 1965) indicates that, although the neurological bases for specific fears may be different, the emotional bases are probably quite similar. Furthermore, the prevailing theoretical viewpoint in physiology is that in most sorts of behavior there is a nonspecific sort of internal stimulation, which can be called arousal. This again suggests that the evolution of emotions is based on a limited number of physiological systems.

WHAT ARE THE RELATIONSHIPS BETWEEN SYSTEMS THEORY AND MECHANISTIC–REDUCTIONISTIC THEORIES?

The latter theories have been and continue to be extremely useful; they are not false but merely lack universality. The chief concept of mechanistic theory is one-way causation. While this almost never occurs within a system, there are occasional instances where the relationships between systems involve clear-cut, one-way causation. For example, the genetic system of a parent contributes to that of an offspring, but there is no reverse effect. Also, it is often possible to experimentally limit feedback between two entities within a system, thus artificially producing one-way causation and laying a partial (though always incomplete) basis for studying two-way interaction. Thus, in studying agonistic behavior, one can set up a situation in which one animal attacks and the other has no chance to respond (Scott, 1977).

Reductionism is not a totally false doctrine. There are always interrelationships between lower and higher levels of systems organization. The study of these interrelationships is always worthwhile and often produces significant theoretical and practical results. But one must remember that such studies will never produce more than partial explanations. Social behavior will never be completely explained by the study of physiological function, since social behavior represents unique, higher-order phenomena.

Without systems theory, mechanistic theory and reductionism will therefore lead to dead-end research—to insoluble problems that can only be attacked successfully on higher levels within the framework of systems theory.

REFERENCES

Cannon, W. B. *Bodily changes in pain, hunger, fear and rage.* Boston: Branford, 1929, 1953.

Craig, W. Appetites and aversions as constituents of instincts. *Biological Bulletin,* 1918, *34,* 91–107.

Dale, P. S. *Language development* (2nd ed.). New York: Holt, Rinehart & Winston, 1976.

Darwin, C. *The expression of emotions in man and animals.* New York: Philosophical Library, 1955. (Originally published 1872.)

Davis, K. L., Gurski, J. G., & Scott, J. P. Interaction of separation distress with fear in infant dogs. *Developmental Psychobiology,* 1977, *10,* 203–212.

Davis, K. L., & Scott, J. P. Unpublished data, 1978.

Ekman, P., Friesen, W. V., & Ellsworth, P. *Emotion in the human face: Guidelines for research and an integration of findings.* New York: Pergamon, 1972.

Elliot, O., & Scott, J. P. The development of emotional distress reactions to separation in puppies. *Journal of Genetic Psychology,* 1961, *99,* 3–22.

Gurski, J. C., Davis, K. L., & Scott, J. P. *Onset of separation distress in the dog: The delaying effect of comfortable stimuli.* Paper presented at the International Society for Developmental Psychobiology, St. Louis, 1974. (*Developmental Psychobiology,* in press)

Hall, J. A., Rosenthal, R., Archer, D., Dimatteo, M. R., & Rogers, P. L. Decoding wordless messages. *Human Nature,* 1978, *1,* 68–75.

Hyde, J. S., & Rosenberg, B. G. *Half the human experience: The psychology of women.* Lexington, Mass.: D. C. Heath, 1976.

Moyer, K. E. *The psychobiology of aggression.* New York: Harper & Row, 1976.

Mykytowycz, R. Further observations on the territorial function and histology of the submandibular cutaneous (chin) glands in the rabbit, *Oryctolagus cuniculus* (L.). *Animal Behavior,* 1965, *13* (4), 400–412.

Panksepp, J., Herman, B., Conner, R., Bishop, P., & Scott, J. P. The biology of social attachments: Opiates alleviate separation distress. *Biological Psychiatry,* 1978, *13,* 607–618.

Pettijohn, T. F., Wong, T. W., Ebert, P. D., & Scott, J. P. Alleviation of separation distress in 3 breeds of young dogs. *Developmental Psychobiology,* 1977, *10,* 373–381.

Rosenblatt, J. S. Prepartum and post-partum regulation of maternal behaviour in the rat. In *Parent-infant interaction,* Ciba Foundation Symposium No. 33 (New Series), pp. 17–37. Amsterdam: Elsevier, 1975.

Scott, J. P. The analysis of social organization in animals. *Ecology,* 1956, *37,* 213–221.

Scott, J. P. Biology and the emotions. In D. C. Glass (ed.), *Biology and behavior: Neurophysiology and emotion,* pp. 190–200. New York: Russell Sage Foundation and Rockefeller University Press, 1967.

Scott, J. P. Social facilitation and allelomimetic behavior. In E. C. Simmel, R. A. Hoppe, & G. A. Milton (eds.), *Social facilitation and imitative behavior,* pp. 55–72. Boston: Allyn & Bacon, 1968. (a)

Scott, J. P. Observation. In T. A. Sebeok (ed.), *Animal communication: Techniques of study and results of research.* Bloomington, Ind.: Indiana University Press, 1968. (b)

Scott, J. P. The emotional basis of social behavior. *Annals of the New York Academy of Sciences,* 1969, *159,* 777–790.

Scott, J. P. Theoretical issues concerning the origin and causes of fighting. In B. E. Eleftheriou & J. P. Scott (eds.), *The physiology of aggression and defeat,* pp. 11–41. New York: Plenum, 1971.

Scott, J. P. Effects of psychotropic drugs on separation distress in dogs. *Proceedings of the International Congress CINP,* Paris, 1974. Excerpta Medica International Congress Series No. 359, pp. 735–745.

Scott, J. P. Social genetics. *Behavior Genetics,* 1977, *7,* 327–346.

Scott, J. P., & Bronson, F. H. Experimental exploration of the et-epimeletic or care-soliciting behavioral system. In P. H. Leiderman & D. Shapiro (eds.), *Psychobiological approaches to social behavior.* Stanford: Stanford University Press, 1964.

Scott, J. P., & Fuller, J. L. *Genetics and the social behavior of the dog.* Chicago: University of Chicago Press, 1965.

Scott, J. P., & Senay, E. C. (eds.), *Separation and depression: Clinical and research aspects.* Washington, D.C.: American Association for the Advancement of Science, Publication 94, 1973.

Silverstone, T. (ed.) *Appetite and food intake.* Berlin: Dahlem Konferenzen, 1976.

Tinbergen, N. *The study of instinct.* Oxford: Clarendon Press, 1951.

Zarrow, M. X., Gandelman, R., & Denenberg, V. H. Prolactin: Is it an essential hormone for maternal behavior in the mammal? *Hormones and Behavior,* 1971, *2,* 343–353.

Chapter 3

STRATEGIES OF SOCIAL INTERACTION

IRENÄUS EIBL–EIBESFELDT

ABSTRACT

Emotions have an observable and a subjectively experienced dimension. Ethologists deal with observable behavior following a tradition which has been largely established by Charles Darwin's book: The Expression of Emotions in Man and Animals. Evolution, function and physiological causation of the expressive patterns of emotion are their primary concern. The present analysis based on the cross-cultural documentation of unstaged human behavior reveals that phylogenetic adaptations determine man's social interactions in a variety of ways. Many of his expressive movements can be considered as innate motor patterns (fixed action patterns). They trigger certain behaviors and thus act as signals or releasers of innate releasing mechanisms. Systems of friendly approach as well as the agonistic system (ranging in expression from aggression to flight) are activated in human interaction. By antithetic combinations of display and appeasement patterns encounters are managed in such a way as to achieve friendly relations without endangering one's rank position. Expressive patterns control human relations and the cross-cultural comparison reveals the existence of basic strategies of social interactions which occur universally. Whereas children act these strategies out in nonverbal motor patterns, adults verbalize many of these events. However, in doing this, they still obey the same rules which govern the nonverbal strategy. The discovery that a variety of nonverbal and verbal behaviors can substitute for each other as functional equivalents bridges the gap between nonverbal and verbal behavior and opens the way for the study of a grammar of human social behavior covering both verbal and nonverbal behavior.

57

Emotion: Theory, Research, and Experience
Volume 1: Theories of Emotion

Human interactions are structured according to rules that are commonly held to be culturally conditioned. Indeed, if we compare rituals cross-culturally we will encounter a great variability, which is undoubtedly an expression of cultural differences.

Two Nepalese greeting each other fold their hands and bow slightly. The Biami of New Guinea in the same situation grip each other's right hand, similar to the way central Europeans do, but the Biami interlock their pointing finger during this process and part with snapping the fingers in a way of contest. Russians—to give just another example—embrace each other and mutually kiss their cheeks during such an encounter. All these we call "greeting." A great number of greeting rituals can be observed.

Besides this variability, however, we will also discover on closer look a number of features that characterize particular ritualistic events in all cultures alike. Thus, feasts and greeting encounters are characterized by an opening phase, a phase of interaction, and a phase of formalized parting (Eibl-Eibesfeldt, 1977).

Furthermore, cross-cultural comparison reveals that some patterns of behavior occur universally and in the same social context. They are interpreted by the recipient of the signal in all cultures alike. Thus, the eyebrow flash—a rapid raising of the eyebrows—occurs in all cultures as an expression of readiness for contact (Eibl-Eibesfeldt, 1968). Similarly, smiling basically expresses friendly (nonaggressive) intent within a range from slight submission to readiness for contact. The fact that, in addition, cultural variations of smiling occur and that superpositions with other expressive movements can be observed should not prevent us from recognizing the shared cultural invariants in human behavior (Eibl-Eibesfeldt, 1975, 1979b).

But how can these universals be explained? The existence of shared functions may be one answer. If we come to general functions like "appeasing," the following question arises: Why do particular patterns of behavior appease in all cultures? For some patterns we could provide an answer based on learning theory. If a child experiences the particular caretaking behaviors of his mother as comforting, he might conclude that the application of such patterns in contacts with other persons might help to comfort them; thus, this repetition of patterns learned from his mother helps to establish friendly contact. The child may instrumentally apply these behaviors whenever he wants to express friendly intent. Social-imitation learning as well as insightful application could universally lead to similar behaviors. In theory, giving and sharing, and the bonding rituals derived from them, could be traced to such an origin even though suggestive evidence points in another direction. There are cases, however, where learning theory cannot suffice for an explanatory principle. In one of the following paragraphs, we will discuss sulking (pouting and cutoff) as a strategy of agonistic buffering. This strategy can be observed in small children in Europe as well as in the Kalahari Bushmen, the Yanomami Indians, Papuans or Balinese, and in many others. Furthermore, the study of infant behavior reveals that at the age of 3 months babies use the strategy of sulking when neglected by their mother. Murray (1977) asked mothers to stop abruptly for 1 min the flow of friendly interactions with their children. When, after this pause, the mothers tried to continue the friendly interactions, the babies turned their heads away in a clear expression of sulkiness. As sulking is not a very common behavior pattern, it is improbable that the babies learned the pattern from their mother at such an early age.

Coy behavior is another pattern that is universally encountered and appears at an age of 6 to 8 months. It is an expression of ambivalence, of a conflict between intention movements of friendly approach and those of withdrawal (flight). The latter response manifests itself as stranger awareness or fear of strangers regardless of whether the babies experienced anything harmful from strangers. Its occurrence definitely does not depend on bad experience and therefore we have to conclude that at an age of approximately 6 to 8 months babies start to perceive certain features of another individual as arousing fear (Eibl-Eibesfeldt, 1977). Personal acquaintance serves to neutralize this effect. However, if less familiar people approach with friendly intentions, a conflict arises that leads to a superposition of approach and withdrawal responses (Figure 3.1); it persists through adulthood, where it can be observed during flirtatious contacts (Figure 3.2), for example.

PHYLOGENETIC ADAPTATIONS IN ANIMALS

The ethological studies of the last 3 decades have provided us with a wealth of evidence backing the Lorenz–Tinbergen discovery that phylogenetic adaptations determine the behavior of animals in well-defined ways. Animals prove to be outfitted with functional motor patterns at their birth. Porpoises, for example, can swim immediately after birth, newborn gnus can run, and newly hatched chaffinches gape, which releases feeding behavior from their parents. The motor patterns are definitely not learned by imitation or by trial and error. The neuronal network and its specific connection with the effectors and receptors, all responsible for the coordinated motor output, grew in a process of self-differentiation (see Sperry, 1971), according to the programs encoded in the genome. In a way of shorthand description, we call such behavior patterns "inborn" or "innate," well aware that these patterns develop. Not all the behavior patterns constituting the inborn repertoire of a species are manifest from birth. Some mature during ontogeny, as has been proved by deprivation experiments, without the need to imitate a conspecific. Thus, mallards perform the species-specific courtship postures at sexual

(a)   (b)

(c)   (d)

(e)   (f)

FIGURE 3.1. The ambivalence of approach and withdrawal in encounter situations: A Balinese mother waving "hello" to a visitor with her little boy's hand. She indicates her readiness for contact at the same time by an eyebrow flash. Following this, both show gaze avoidance and hiding by cuddling together. The baby finally establishes full face contact again and smiles. [From a 16-mm film by the author.

maturity even if raised in complete social isolation. Similarly, some birds will sing their species-specific songs, even if raised alone in soundproof chambers.

In addition to inborn motor patterns (they are also called fixed action patterns), animals are outfitted with detector devices tuned to the perception of specific stimuli, the perception of which will release certain motor patterns. Experiments have demonstrated that these are unconditioned responses. Thus, a frog immediately after metamorphosis will flick its tongue toward

FIGURE 3.2. Coyness in a Himba girl illustrating successive ambivalence in response to a compliment: After establishing eye contact a smile is signaled, but suppressed; the eye contact is cut off and the head turned away. Following this, eye contact is reestablished from the corners of the eyes (this time with a full smile). Another cutoff follows and the smile is suppressed again. The sequence ends with eye contact and a "coy" smile. [From a 16-mm film by the author.]

small moving objects. The mechanisms that cause this response have been termed "innate releasing mechanisms." Those responsible for the frog's prey-catching behavior have been identified up to the neuronal level by Ewert (1974). Many social responses are triggered via innate releasing mechanisms. In these cases, special signaling devices called "releasers" evolved. Mutual adaptation of receiver and signal-sender took place. Male sticklebacks, for example, developed a red nuptual coloration, which acts as a releaser, triggering the fighting responses in other males and at the same time attracting females. A simple wax model without fins but with a red belly is sufficient to stimulate fighting if presented to males. Females are recognized by their silvery swollen belly. This simple signal, when presented in a wax model, releases courting in males. Since fighting and courting can be released by the adequate stimuli in socially inexperienced males, this discriminative response is not dependent on individual learning (Cullen, 1960; Tinbergen, 1951).

It has been demonstrated that innate releasing mechanisms control animal behavior from invertebrates to primates. Rhesus monkeys reared in social isolation from birth react with fear to conspecifics' expressions of threat (Sackett, 1966).

Another set of phylogenetic adaptations are those that cause an animal's spontaneous behavior. Animals, after all, are not just machines responding to stimuli; they actively seek, through what is called "appetitive behavior," stimulus situations that allow certain behaviors to be performed. Animals are known to be sexually motivated, aggressive, or hungry; depending on the respective "mood," the animal will seek a mate, a rival, or food. In some birds, the motivation to hunt is independent of the motivation to feed. Thus, a well-fed starling deprived of the opportunity to hunt will at intervals fly up from its perch, snap something invisible, return to the perch, and perform the insect-killing movements. Similar findings have been reported by Leyhausen (1965) in small carnivores. In fact, he showed in cats that each of the single acts of prey catching, such as stalking, attacking, grasping, killing, manipulating, and eating, has a motivation of its own. There is a diversity of known mechanisms that motivate an animal to perform in specific ways, including those mediating inner sensory stimuli, hormones, and neuronal mechanisms. The concept of "drives" is not a unitary concept, but a descriptive one pointing to the fact that animals are motivated by inbuilt physiological machineries.

Of great theoretical importance is the concept of neuronal motivation developed by E. v. Holst (1935), who found that completely deafferented spinal eels perform well-coordinated swimming movements. This proved the existence of spontaneously active motor neurons that coordinate their impulses without afferent feedback such that orderly patterned behavior results. This discovery has since been supported by a wealth of further evidence (see, e.g., Fentress, 1976).

Different motivational systems interact either inhibitively or supportively.

Thus, biting (fighting) inhibits courting in the stickleback, but not in other fish. Often an animal has to run through several motivational states before a particular set of behaviors can occur. Sticklebacks must first shoal into shallow water in the spring to stake out territories, after which the males will be responsive to females and nesting materials. The events are structured in a hierarchical order (Tinbergen, 1951).

Learning finally results in adaptive modification of behavior. Since what is adaptive, that is, contributes to fitness, varies, of course, from species to species, phylogenetic adaptations ensure that animals learn the right things at the right time. Chaffinches have to learn their songs, but they know innately what to imitate, because they will pick out—if presented with records of different bird songs—their species song for imitation (Thorpe, 1961). Swamp sparrows will learn an artificially composed song provided it is composed of syllables of their own species' song (Marler & Peters, 1977). Inborn detectors or templates tuned toward these species' characteristics of the song are responsible for the observed learning disposition. In other cases, birds learn during a sensitive period only. Thus, small zebra finches raised for the first 3 months by society finches as foster parents will start to sing like them at sexual maturity. This occurred even when the zebra finches were separated from their foster parents after these 3 months and kept with members of their own species only (Immelmann, 1965).

When nausea is induced in rats by radiation, these animals will associate their ill feeling with what was new in the diet they ate some hours before (Garcia, McGowan, Ervin, & Koelling, 1968). According to classical learning theory, punishing stimuli should serve to stop a behavior associated with it. If a cock is punished electrically whenever he shows display, he will finally stop displaying. However, if he is punished whenever he shows submissive behavior, negative conditioning will not take place; instead, the behavior will be reinforced: The more punishment the animal gets, the more submissive it will become. Under natural conditions—when attacked by a high-ranking individual of the flock—this response is adaptive since it blocks further aggression. The phylogenetically acquired program does not allow the animal to behave in a different way.

By these adaptations the activities of animals are structured in a variety of ways. The hierarchical order of appetites or moods and the inhibiting or fostering influences different drives exert upon each other have been mentioned. In addition, chains of behavioral events are observed when two animals interact, each sending stimuli that in turn release responses that constitute a signal to the partner. The courtship rituals of the stickleback provide an example for such a chain of behaviors. When the female appears, the male starts his courtship dance. The female will then posture, showing her belly to the male. This signal releases his swimming to the nest, which she responds to by following. The male then points with his mouth to the entrance of the nest, which acts as a signal for her to enter. He will then push with his mouth in a rapid "tremolo" against the base of her caudal fin, which causes her to spawn. The appearance of the eggs in turn stimulates the male to fertilize them. The whole orderly sequence is based on a series of stimulus–response relationships. The motor patterns at the level of the fixed action pattern are dependent on external stimuli only as far as their release is concerned. In addition, certain stimuli orient the response in relation to the stimulus source, and coordination is a result of internalized programs.[1]

PHYLOGENETIC ADAPTATIONS IN HUMANS

Lorenz (1943) has suggested that human behavior might be similarly preprogrammed by phylogenetic adaptation. This suggestion has been the target of violent attacks. From the discovery of the conditioned reflex came the hypothesis that all behaviors might be based on conditioned reflexes, which are the building blocks of the more complicated behaviors. This idea paralleled the ideas promoted by Watson (1919). For a long time, it was assumed that humans were born as blank sheets waiting to be written on by educators. Even now, certain scientists (e.g., Montagu, 1976) hold this opinion, but more or less as a doctrinal conviction, because the last decade has provided much evidence in support of Lorenz's hypotheses. Comparative and experimental studies[2] have demonstrated that human behavior is partly preprogrammed by phylogenetic adaptation, in many ways similar to the preprogramming previously discovered in animals. Humans have a repertoire of fixed action patterns. In addition, innate releasing mechanisms bias perception and, during social communication, releasers play an important role. Furthermore, humans are motivated by internal physiological mechanisms, and inborn learning dispositions can be found.

The evidence for these statements comes from the comparative study of primates, from the study of babies and of people born deaf and blind, and from cross-cultural investigations.

Regarding inborn motor patterns, it was mentioned that certain expressive behaviors occur across cultures in the same context. For quite a number of them, such as smiling and laughing, homologies to other primates can be

---

[1] This holds true for stereotyped learned motor patterns.

[2] During the last decade human ethology has become established as a new field. It can be defined as the "biology of human behavior" and is largely congruent with its parent discipline biology. The interests of this field are distributed along corresponding lines, namely, morphology, ecology, genetics, phylogenetics, developmental biology, sociobiology, and physiology. The questions asked and the methods employed in our efforts to answer them are elaborations of the methods employed in these fields, but they are particularly adapted to the study of man. Human ethology is based on the theory of selection; among others, we ask the following question: Which selective pressures have operated to bring the observed structure into being? More about the theoretical background, the methods, and the research program of this new field can be found in Eibl-Eibesfeldt (1975, 1979b).

traced (van Hooff, 1971; Jolly, 1966; van Lawick-Goodall, 1968). In addition, children who are born deaf and blind, and are thus deprived of any perception of how other people act, nonetheless show the basic repertoire of facial expressions (for a detailed discussion, see Eibl-Eibesfeldt [1973].) All of this taken together is clear evidence for the existence of phylogenetic adaptations in the realm of motor behavior.

A number of investigators have discovered corresponding adaptations on the receptor side. Ball and Tronick (1971) projected symmetrically expanding dark blotches in front of 14-day-old babies. The babies responded as if the objects were approaching them on a collision course. They turned their heads away and protectively raised an arm, and their heart beats accelerated. When the blotches expanded asymmetrically, no such response was observed, as if the baby knew that this indicated a bypass course. These experiments were carefully controlled in that babies who did not have aversive experience with colliding objects were chosen to participate. The data presented to the babies must be processed by an innate releasing mechanism. This was confirmed in a number of other experiments, notably that by Bowes (1977), to which the reader should refer for further details.

In the introduction I emphasized that fear of strangers develops in babies without a need for prior aversive experiences. Babies' responsiveness to signals that release flight responses matures. Among others, the eyes are perceived with ambivalence. We need to look at each other to signal readiness for communication, but our looking should not escalate into staring. This is normally prevented by interspersed short gaze shifts serving as cutoffs.

Meltzoff and Moore (1977) discovered that babies are capable of imitating behavior patterns such as tongue protrusion, lip protrusion, and mouth opening at an age of 12–21 days. According to communication with these authors by letter, imitative behavior occurs even in the 1-day-old child. They emphasize that there must be some innate basis for this imitative behavior. Whether the responses are mediated via innate releasing mechanisms is still to be learned. There is no doubt, however, that there exists a given connection between perception of a motor pattern and a motor output, which must be interpreted as a phylogenetic adaptation ensuring that, after perceiving specific behaviors, these can be imitated by the corresponding perceived movements. However, these movements are not necessarily fixed action patterns. For this reason, it might be better not to speak of an innate releasing mechanism at the moment, but to speak in a descriptive way of a matching mechanism or template, this being closer to the original meaning of "angeborenes Schema" used by Konrad Lorenz. If we observe the ability of small children to imitate words heard for the first time, we may expect analogous adaptations matching the "heard" with specific motor outputs of the vocal apparatus. This ability is particularly striking if it is contrasted to the child's apparent inability at this age to imitate the obviously simple task of drawing a circle or other simple geometric figure.

Another receptor bias has been described as categorial perception by Liberman and Pisoni (1977). If individuals are presented with a continuum of
syllables ranging from "ba" to "pa," they will first perceive "ba" and then,
from a certain point in the continuum onward, just "pa" and nothing in between. The point in the continuum where perception shifts from "ba" to
"pa" is the same in all cultures. This holds true for babies who showed
categorial perception at the age of 1 month. Such an adaptation structures the
perception in a way that makes it easier to learn a language. In my opinion, it
is comparable to the adaptation found by Marler and Peters (1977) in swamp
sparrows, who show a receptor bias by being tuned to the syllables of their
own species.

It has been suggested by Lorenz (1943) that our reactions to certain features
of babies that we find cute, as well as certain characteristics of the adult
female or male being perceived as sexually attractive and certain facial expressions being perceived correctly, are a priori understood via innate releasing
mechanisms. Indeed, the features to which we respond can be imitated by very
crude models based upon a few characteristics which then are often grossly exaggerated. Among the features characterizing babyishness are proportional
relations of the baby's body, which is characterized by a large head in relation
to a small body with short extremities. Dolls exaggerate this feature and so do
cartoons. In a similar way, the small face in relation to the large forehead and
the chubby cheeks of the baby are emphasized. Regarding facial expressions:
A friendly or angry expression can be characterized by a few strokes. Ekman
and Friesen (1971) showed videotapes of facial expressions taken from different cultures to people of other cultures. The facial expressions of other people were generally understood.

As far as the physiology of motivation is concerned, there is no indication
that the basic mechanisms are different in different people. They seem to be
alike in all people and to constitute part of a shared heritage. This also applies
to our knowledge of the basic emotions.

All of these adaptations determine human conduct and, in particular,
man's social interactions. Certain types of interactions will be examined in
more detail in the following sections.

SOME BASIC STRATEGIES OF SOCIAL INTERACTIONS

Our extensive cross-cultural documentation program (which we have been
pursuing for 15 years[3]) has revealed that a number of basic strategies of social

[3] One of the main tasks undertaken by the Research Unit for Human Ethology headed by me is
the systematic cross-cultural documentation of rituals and unstaged social interactions in the
natural context. The program has been described (Eibl-Eibesfeldt, 1975). The uncut original is
stored in the Archives for Human Ethology.

interactions exist that are alike in all cultures.[4] They are best observed in the interactions between children because children act out much of their behavior nonverbally. In addition, they are less influenced and inhibited by their culture. In contrast, adults verbalize much of their behavior and cast it in cultural models. Once one has discovered the basic strategies applied by children, one realizes that adults, in principle, follow the same rules, even though they verbalize all action. Upon closer scrutiny, many of the cultural rituals prove to be cultural elaborations of those universally occurring basic strategies.

A few examples will serve to illustrate our thesis. We are restricting ourselves to the strategies we have studied cross-culturally, acknowledging that these are selected examples. We are far from knowing at the moment the complete inventory of interactive strategies available to man, because only recently has this subject started to arouse attention. Besides the human ethologists (Morris, 1977; Eibl-Eibesfeldt, 1975), social anthropologists such as Fox (1977), Goffman (1966), and Marsh, Rosser, and R. Harré (1978) systematically began to study human interactive processes in the natural setting. But we are only beginning to explore the ethogram of man.

AGONISTIC BUFFERING

Competitions leading to aggressive interactions are frequently observed among children, in the Kalahari Bushmen, Yanomami, and Papuan, as well as in Europeans. Several mechanisms of aggression control serve to prevent escalation of the aggressive encounter. According to our investigations, the basic strategies are universal.

One of the behavioral elements seen in aggression control is the smile, a universal facial expression, whose innateness has been confirmed by the study of children born deaf and blind. It occurs as an expression of friendly intent with a submissive connotation that is in accordance with the signal's origin: Homologies can be traced in other primates in which the signal has been described as "fearful grin" with submissive intent (van Hooff, 1971).

A sideways tilt of the head was observed by us to occur as an element of friendly face-to-face interaction. It counteracts the threat effect of eye contact. Coss (1972) showed that the arousal effect of eyespots presented to a subject is greatest when presented horizontally. Any tilt toward the vertical significantly decreases its arousing propensities. Gaze avoidance by looking away is a strategy of switching off aggression-arousing signals, namely, eye contact. This is done in every conversation; however, in this case, eye contact

---

[4] When we speak of "strategies" we refer to the fact that they are a means to achieve certain goals. We do not imply, however, that this is done with insight. As students of animal behavior are well aware, teleonomic behaviors are often a result of natural selection and not of individually adaptive insightful processes.

is reassumed. Here, gaze avoidance is continued, and this is a clear cutoff, signaling that the channels are closed for communication—The bond is symbolically severed. The turning away of the head signals the same. Pouting probably is derived from a pushing-away movement of something offered, by means of the lips, and thus in this derived form signals rejection in a social context.

In certain ways this cutoff constitutes a threat to the opponent because it isolates him as if a bond were severed. As social beings, we live with the security derived from the multitude of bonds that link us with other group members; at a very early age we defend these individual bonds when threatened by rivals. The earliest dramatic manifestation occurs during sibling rivalry (Eibl-Eibesfeldt, 1974). It seems that the cutoff does not only stop further aggression but also gives rise to efforts toward bond repair. I often observed that the previous attacker tried to comfort the insulted, employing a variety of strategies of bond repair, including third parties as mediators. A prerequisite for the cutoff to work is that a bond must exist between the parties involved.

The cutoff can also be verbalized. An insulted person may say "I will not talk to you any more" with the same effect. Verbal behavior in this case acts as the functional equivalent of gaze aversion, head lowering, and pouting. That a variety of behaviors can substitute for each other as functional equivalents is a pecularity of human interactive events, which will be discussed in more detail in a later section.

The fact that humans have two channels available for communication—the verbal and the nonverbal—allows not only substitution of one by the other, but also combinations in a variety of ways. Thus, facial expressions may convey friendly messages, whereas the verbal channel may express aggressive feelings, and vice versa.

Different strategies of agonistic buffering are usually employed between members of different groups. We will discuss them when describing strategies of friendly encounter.

SHARING AND GIVING; REQUESTING AND TAKING

Children share readily at a very early age. I filmed babies in a variety of cultures offering morsels to their siblings and to other members of the group. They apparently enjoyed the resulting dialogues of give and take (Figure 3.3).

As a prerequisite for give and take to occur, the partner must be able to give or to hand back if given something. This may seem to be a trivial statement. However, while observing many mammals, I became aware that, except in very particular situations, it was difficult to teach them to let something go or to give something away. Thus, a dog may invite play by putting his ball in your lap. Turn-taking in play seems to be a related phenomenon. Small babies have difficulty in letting something go which they hold in their hand, but, from a certain age on, they part freely with the object even if apparently not particularly trained to do so. In fact, even in situations where little time would be left for such training the children invite contact by offering their toys as soon as they are able to stand; their efforts to give result in the dropping of their objects to the floor, which often initiates some contact. The habit of throwing their toys from their crib develops from these efforts. In establishing the dialogue, the initiative for contact usually comes from the child.

A girl born deaf and blind was able to return objects given to her for investigation. She did so spontaneously without previous training. When given a small tortoise she would hold it and investigate it by sniffing and touching it with her lips. She would then grasp one leg of the tortoise, hold it out, and wait until it would be taken from her; at just this point she would loosen her grip. She did not simply drop the tortoise, even though she disliked it.

In my opinion, giving and handing back are part of an inherent program. In this context, I would also like to draw particular attention to some observations on the great apes. Fossey (1977), who spent many years observing gorillas in their natural environment, was repeatedly approached by large males which closely watched her and took objects out of her hand out of sheer curiosity. During one such event, which was filmed, one sees a large male approaching her while she is writing in her notebook. He takes her pen gently out of her hand, makes a few steps sideways, sits down, and investigates it thoroughly by sniffing and manipulating it. Having done with it, he walks back to her and passes the pen with his outstretched hand to her. He then takes her notebook, again walks away with it for investigation, and again returns it in an orderly way.

The dialogue characterized by alternation (turn-taking), reciprocity, repetitiveness, and often stereotypes—the latter characterizing more advanced stages of ritualization—is one of the basic patterns of interaction. Dialogues can be performed by a variety of nonverbal and verbal behaviors, and they serve the function of bonding. They are universally encountered and often culturally refined, for example, in the ritualized singing of the Yanomami (Eibl-Eibesfeldt, 1971). The ontogeny of the mother–child dialogue has been studied by Snow (1977), who found that the mother proceeds in a particular fashion first by interpreting every response as an answer and applying strategies of conversation repair if responses fail. As her child gets older, only acoustic utterances and finally only verbal utterances are accepted as responses. Analogously, dialogue-like behavior patterns with a similar bonding function have been described as "duetting" in a great variety of birds. Furthermore, in many mammals, contact calls between mother and child are constantly exchanged in alternation.

The dialogues of give and take are thus just one expression of this bonding strategy, which probably evolved from patterns of mother–child behavior.

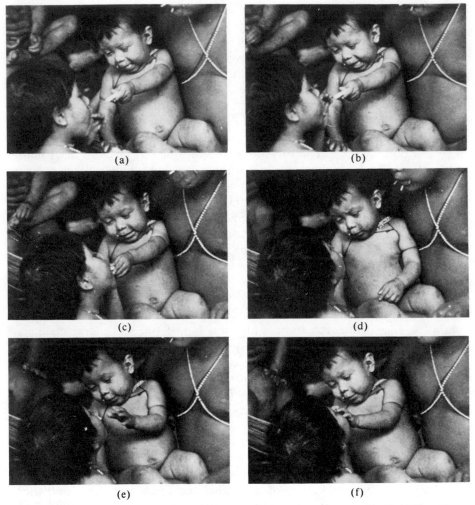

(a)   (b)

(c)   (d)

(e)   (f)

FIGURE 3.3. Dialogues of giving and taking are often initiated by very small children. Here a Yanomami baby offers her sister a morsel. The readiness with which very small children in all

Very small children readily employ this strategy in efforts to establish friendly relations with another child or adult; in particular, in the process of familiarizing with a stranger, they use objects as mediators (Stanjek, 1978). This readiness to share objects, and to use them as a medium for bonding, is in contrast to the primary unwillingness to share social bonds. In fact, children have to learn the hard way that they must share the bond to the mother with the newborn sibling.

In order to be given something, however, a person must acknowledge by his behavior that his partner is the possessor of the wanted object and thus request it appropriately. If he demands by action (grasping) or verbally by using

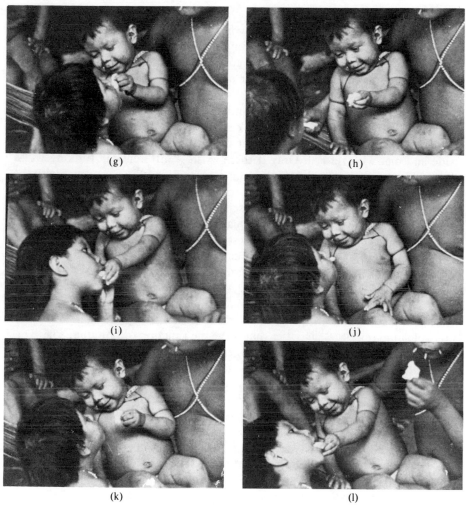

(g)   (h)

(i)   (j)

(k)   (l)

cultures exhibit the pattern suggests a shared disposition. [From a 16-mm film by the author.]

the imperative, his request will normally be refused unless the requesting person has a much higher rank position.

We have as yet no intensive study of the ontogeny of sharing. Imitative learning could play an important role in the ontogeny of this behavior (Rheingold *et al.,* 1976). I am hypothesizing, however, that an inborn disposition to share is prevalent because sharing and giving as a strategy to bond occur promptly and at a very early age and spontaneously in new contexts. I assume that this behavior derives from parental caretaking behavior that became ritualized into an expressive pattern of bonding, as happens very often in vertebrates (Eibl-Eibesfeldt, 1971). Its derivation from feeding intent can be seen ontogenetically. Small children, even babies, like to feed people and to push objects into the mouth. When working with the G/wi Bushmen of the Central Kalahari, little children after having lost their initial fear started to offer berries and other morsels to my co-worker Barbara Hold. They finally pushed little presents of food into her mouth. I had not seen that in another context before.

Again, if the strategies of asking and sharing can be verbalized, the basic grammar of the interaction pattern remains the same. A request must be presented in a form making clear that ownership is respected. Demanding is rude and met with refusal. Only if there exists a difference in ranking will a demand be submissively obeyed, but this is certainly not in agreement with the etiquette. Even the direct asking for something is often done "through the flowers" (German expression!) because this allows an easy refusal without endangering the bond. (Ethnologists speak of *Verblümungssitten*.) I observed the use of this verbal strategy of request in 2-year-old children: A little boy in our neighborhood who liked joining us for breakfast started a friendly conversation upon meeting us at our terrace in front of the house by telling us how much elephants like to eat bread. Afterward, he explained that he indeed liked bread very much too.

Seen in a cross-cultural perspective, sharing and giving play a most important role in many ritual activities that serve the function of bonding. There exists a rich literature on gift exchange and gift chains, which link sparse populations with strings of mutual obligations (Mauss, 1966; Wiessner, 1977). In the Eipo, we studied the patterns of requesting, giving, and taking in everyday interaction on the individual level as well as in the formalized exchange of groups (Heeschen, Schiefenhövel, & Eibl-Eibesfeldt, 1979). Figures in this paper illustrate selected nonverbal patterns of sharing including a long sequence in which five girls were eating and sharing nuts of a pandanus fruit (Heeschen *et al.*, 1979). The reader is referred to these photographs, which illustrate respect of ownership and discriminative sharing according to the closeness of the relationship.

Disrespect of ownership often leads to fairly violent responses, particularly in adults. When a man approximately 25-years old took some bananas from the string bag of his older brother, which was hanging in the men's communal house, his brother inflicted a deep wound on his shoulder with a stone ax. This probably would have led to an exchange of arrows between the brothers if the bystanders had not intervened (see Heeschen *et al.*, 1979).

If an adult verbally comments on someone's possession, this is considered to be a request. Whether this is seen as good or bad behavior depends on the situation. A high-ranking person, for instance, may comment on the possession of someone (and by this very likely receive part of it) without violating the norms. Not familiar with the Eipo's way of life, we often misbehaved by commenting on someone's possessions ("What a nice necklace!" for example). This was taken as a request, but we did not want to obtain the necklace, of course. And there is an interesting parallel. The same etiquette holds true for the Bushmen of the central Kalahari and the Yanomami (Upper

Orinoco area). Here it is nearly compulsory to respond to one's comment by giving.

When the Eipo had returned from hunting, a very particular situation arose. During our first period of contact, Schiefenhövel once commented: "Look how much game and pandanus fruits our villagers brought." He was immediately admonished not to talk. Game and pandanus fruits are very difficult to gather. Therefore, the possessor must not be pressed to share. He must be allowed to unload without being molested. Sharing must be left to his decision. It is a particular situation where the possessor, by a special etiquette, is protected from the demands of others. How commenting functions as a request in a situation corresponding to the etiquette is discussed in Heeschen *et al.* (1979).

A man having much influence, named Babyal and living in the village of Munggona, had come to visit the village Dingerkon in order to perform a curing ritual on a man from Malingdam. This man had been seriously wounded by an enemy's arrows. He belonged to an alliance group headed by Munggona. After the performance, Babyal squatted down on the village ground about 1 m away from Ninke, the most influential man of Dingerkon. In the course of the conversation, Ninke commented on the feathers decorating Babyal's string bag: "*Kwelib Fotong teleb* [Nice feathers of the bird of paradise]." Both had eye contact during this exchange. They continued to converse on other topics while Babyal was untying one of the feathers and passing it on to Ninke, who responded with a long smile—the functional equivalent of "thank you." Babyal was obliged to Ninke, who had agreed to accommodate the wounded man of Babyal's unit in his house.

Refusal of a request can be indicated nonverbally by drawing the requested object away with a rapid movement and by turning the body away in a clear cutoff. The sequence can be initiated by a short threat stare followed by gaze avoidance. Verbal utterances such as *na song* ('I don't want'), *na like* ('I object'), or even *basam kalye* (strong curse referring to the abdominal fat of the pig) or *morone mem* ('Don't beg') accompany the actions.

Such a refusal may release hostile responses such as pushing and hitting the partner just as does verbal abuse. Most of the time it results in a shifting away from each other, often by demonstratively starting a social interaction with another person. If the rejection was less offensive, the questioner can start to repeat his request by arguing—for example, by saying: "You have given to others, but nothing to me!"

Requesting can be combined with an infantile appeal, paralinguistically by speaking in a whimpering, nasalized, and high tone and verbally by establishing a fictive close relationship like *na ka* ('my in-law'), *na ni* ('my father'), or *na nin* ('my mother'). These are appeals that are universally applied. Yanomami men, for example, usually begin a request by addressing another man first as *Shori* ('brother-in-law').

So, too, the infantile appeal is commonly used in a variety of contexts where friendly relationships are sought, as will be exemplified in the following section. Requesting thus can be classified along a scale from the more infantile and submissive begging to a more polite requesting and finally to demanding, which is permissible for a high-ranking individual but otherwise considered rude.

In situations of nonhostile encounter (greeting), the sharing of food and tobacco serves to relieve the tension that always exists when people meet who are less familiar to each other or who meet after a long period of separation. Male visitors are regularly invited into the men's houses and offered tobacco and food. When we established our first contact with the people of the Mairala village in the Fa Valley (who until that time had not had contact with people outside their village), we first were received by a man offering sugar cane to us and shortly afterward by an older woman offering to each of us another piece of sugar cane. The small children obeyed this strategy in a less formalized way. Often we were addressed by children looking at us and holding out their fists with a morsel of steamed vegetable, offering it with an inquiringly friendly *arebnangkin* ('I will give you'). Adults, too (in particular, women), held out their hands with steamed vegetables and sweet potatoes.

Since I could not eat everything that was passed to me, I found a solution that helped to establish very friendly relations. I added some salt to the morsel I received, took just a nibble, and passed the food on to other children, returning a portion of the salted food to the giver.

The Eipo are ready to share among themselves, and the exceptional individual who is not prepared to do so is *mako* ('mean'); they usually emphasize *nuun mako niinye gum* ('We are no mean people'). (Again, in an interesting parallel, the accusation of being stingy is one of the worst judgments for a Bushman or a Yanomami Indian.) Requesting, except for the situation described above, is done either quite directly or more politely by commenting. Direct requests—*arebnilyam* ('Give me')—are frequently uttered, and among intimates these are not considered inappropriate. But such a request may be as openly turned down by *morone mem* ('Don't beg').

On the level of intergroup communication, giving, taking, and requesting are a more formalized matter. Village alliances are strengthened by the exchange of gifts. On the occasion of feasts, visitors bring pigs, stone ax blades, string bags, and other items. According to Schiefenhövel, The Eipo obey the special obligation to give more to their close relatives. Reciprocal gifts are generally not immediately given; sometimes there is a delay of months. This keeps an open obligation in the Kalahari Bushmen, where the exchange takes place more on an individual level; a gift is also usually not immediately paid back on this individual level. This rule seems to be more general. This also holds true for the Kalahari Bushmen (Wiessner, 1977). Sometimes elements of competition enter into the gift exchange. Giving more than the other can be an aggressive act—a fact that was thoroughly studied by Young (1971) in the Goodenough-Islanders. The phenomenon finds its perhaps most dramatic expression in the Potlatch of the Kwakiutl.

Thus, the whole complex of the patterns of sharing, giving, requesting, and demanding is applied as strategy in different functional contexts. Demanding may be employed to assert a dominance relationship and thus be a strategy of dominance achieving. Offering as well as begging and friendly requesting belong to the strategies of friendly bonding.

STRATEGIES OF FRIENDLY ENCOUNTER

The relations between people are characterized by ambivalence. Upon meeting a person the agonistic motivation as well as motivations for seeking friendly contact are activated. The less familiar the persons engaged in the encounter are to each other, the more the agonistic system will be aroused (particularly the flight response and its subjective correlate, fear). A number of strategies serve to overcome these agonistic responses and to establish a friendly relationship. They can be studied particularly well in greeting rituals, which, in spite of great cultural variability of expression, prove to be structured according to universal principles. In order to demonstrate these principles, we will examine the encounter phase of a greeting ritual in a cross-cultural perspective.[5]

Upon the meeting of two individuals of a group, we observe that the interactants engage in a combination of patterns of display on the one hand and patterns of appeasement and bonding on the other. This can be functionally interpreted. An encounter situation is critical when the agonistic system is aroused, and signs of weakness[6] may invite the other to establish a dominance relationship. The display serves as a precaution. Both interactants assert themselves. In order to establish friendly relations, they must also demonstrate their friendly intent. Both goals can be achieved in a variety of ways.

A Yanomami Indian warrior who on the occasion of an invitation to a feast enters the village of his hosts will dance in front of his hosts in a meaningful way, prancing and showing off with his bow and arrow. This aggressive appeal is combined with a friendly appeal demonstrating peaceful intent: A small child dances with the warrior, waving green palm leaves.

If two individuals who know each other well meet in our culture, they will at least acknowledge the other's presence by establishing eye contact at a certain distance. Shortly after this, the head will be lifted with a jerk (head toss) and, simultaneously, the eyebrows will be raised with a rapid movement for about one-sixth of a second. Nodding follows and the persons may smile. During the

[5] The complete ritual, which has been ethologically analyzed by Eibl-Eibesfeldt (1979b), consists of three phases: the encounter phase, the phase of interaction, and the phase of departure, each characterized by specific types of behaviors.

[6] Our social conduct is, in fact, strongly determined by our efforts not to show any signs of weakness. If we do stumble over a stone on the road, we curse it, hit it again, or just comment. We immediately define the situation as an accident, and this demonstrates that we are otherwise in full control of our senses (Goffman, 1979).

approach that follows, gaze aversion occurs. This serves to avoid escalation of eye contact into staring and at the same time to manipulate one's own arousal level.[7] Eye contact will be reestablished on close proximity, except in the case where the interactants just pass and patterns of contact greeting occur (for details, see Eibl-Eibesfeldt [1968], Kendon and Ferber [1973], and Pitcairn and Eibl-Eibesfeldt [1976]). In our culture, a firm handshake combined with a smile, a clap on the shoulder of varying strengths, and verbal utterances may be employed. In the special case of the meeting of people who are well known to each other, the arousal of the agonistic system expresses itself only mildly by gaze aversion and in the displays of the handshake that follows. The firmness of the grip and shake certainly contains an element of display. Between young males, the handshake often slightly escalates in a mutual measure of strength.

It is interesting to note that there exist a variety of ways to display or to appease. A person may appease during greeting encounters by inborn patterns of expression (smiling, eyebrow flash, nodding) or by patterns that are clearly culturally derived, such as lifting the hat. Thrusting a spear into the ground (as the Massai do to express peaceful intentions) and laying down bow and arrow before approaching (as is customary in the !Kung Bushmen) are just other variations of the same strategy. A person may even verbalize the friendly intent in the greeting formula. All of these patterns substitute for each other as functional equivalents. This takes place, however, within the same framework in all cultures. The need to appease and to display in this particular situation derives from our inherited motivational structure, which is the same everywhere.

That certain strategies recur again and again (e.g., the appeal via the child) can be explained by the assumption of innate releasing mechanisms tuned at the appeasing signals of a child. In a similar fashion, we can assume that we understand some of the facial expressions via such mechanisms. Responses such as the sequence head toss–eyebrow flash–nodding–smiling–gaze aversion are universal even though the eyebrow flash can be suppressed in some cultures (e.g., Japanese consider this pattern impermissible among adults). Women, however, may address a small child freely with eyebrow flashes (Eibl-Eibesfeldt, 1973).

SUMMARY AND DISCUSSION

The presentation in this chapter has dealt with selected examples of strategies of social interaction. The examples of different levels of complexity revealed, on cross-cultural comparison, universally shared features that de-

---

[7] Waters, Matas, and Sroufe (1975) registered heartbeat responses of small children as the children were approached by a friendly stranger. The heartbeats rapidly increased upon perception of the approaching stranger. When the children looked away, the heartbeat rate immediately dropped. The children thus were able to manipulate their level of arousal by looking away.

mand explanation. The application of ethological methods and ethological concepts proves to be of explanatory value. Indeed, it can be shown that phylogenetic adaptations determine the events in various ways. Thus, the strategies used to establish friendly encounters are determined extensively by our inborn responses to certain characteristics of our fellow humans, which cause a clear ambivalence of approach and withdrawal responses. Displays, for example, occur as precautions against being dominated, but are combined with patterns that serve bonding and thus resolve the conflict. The patterns by which this is achieved are partly inborn. They can be substituted, however, by cultural patterns, which then serve as functional equivalents. The whole behavior may be verbalized in part or totally. Once having realized this, one may recognize the universal strategies even in their various cultural elaborations.

Unfortunately, we are far from knowing the basic behavioral repertoire of humans. True, many different strategies have been investigated, for example, privacy management, attention seeking, norm control, and the like. However, I would like to emphasize that there is a lack of adequate film documentation, particularly as far as cross-cultural documentation is concerned. Repeatedly I have pointed to the urgent need to document unstaged strategies of social interactions. This is important indeed, because of the rapid cultural amalgamation engulfing, in particular, the few nonliterate cultures that are left. The discovery that verbal and nonverbal behaviors can substitute for each other as functional equivalents bridges the gap between these behaviors. The resulting unifying theory assumes a common grammar of human social interaction, underlying verbal and nonverbal behaviors as well.

The knowledge of our given repertoire for managing our social environment is of the utmost importance. This knowledge could help therapists in their efforts to treat behavioral disturbances in the area of communication and even to prevent their manifestations.

I have mentioned that humans react with ambivalence toward other humans. The less familiar the opponent is, the more the agonistic system[8] becomes aroused, whereas personal acquaintance serves as an efficient buffer. For the greatest part of our history we lived embedded in individualized communities where everyone was familiar with everyone else and agonistic arousal therefore was negligible. Strangers were only met occasionally. This is now just the reverse in our anonymous society. We are constantly exposed to strangers. The individualized group of friends and family members often is scattered to an extent that we meet most of them only occasionally. The constant exposure to strangers has an effect. Complaints about crowding refer to the stranger. The proximity of our friends rarely disturbs us. We cope with the stressor "stranger" by strategies of contact avoidance, as everyone may

[8] The term "agonistic behavior" was introduced by J. P. Scott (1960) to describe the functionally related system that encompasses aggressive behaviors and behaviors of submission and flight.

observe in himself and others when being in an elevator among strangers. Gaze avoidance can be noticed. In the streets people avoid getting involved with other persons to the extent of refusing to help in emergencies. We also tend to mask our expression—a strategy that prevents others from taking advantage of one's particular mood by reading the facial expression. People are on constant alert and this may freeze into a habit, so that finally a person may not be able to communicate even within his family. To prevent such developments everything that diminishes anonymity should be done.

REFERENCES

Ball, W., & Tronick, E. Infant responses to impending collisions: Optical and real. *Science,* 1971, *171,* 818–820.

Bower, T. G. *A primer of infant development.* San Francisco: Freeman, 1977.

Coss, R. G. *Eye-like schemata: Their effect on behavior.* Ph.D. Thesis, Department of Psychology, University of Reading, 1972.

Cullen, E. Experiments on the effects of social isolation of reproductive behavior in the three-spined stickleback. *Animal Behavior,* 1960, *8,* 235.

Eibl-Eibesfeldt, I. Zur ethologie menschlichen grussverhaltens. I. Beobachtungen an Balinesen, Papuas und Samoanern nebst vergleichenden bemerkungen. *Zeitschrift für Tierpsychologie,* 1968, *25,* 727–744.

Eibl-Eibesfeldt, I. Eine ethologische interpretation des Palmfruchtfestes der WaikaIndianer (Yanoama) nebst bemerkungen über die bindende Funktion von Zwiegesprächen. *Anthropos,* 1971, *66,* 767–778.

Eibl-Eibesfeldt, I. The expressive behavior of the deaf and blind born. In M. V. Cranach & I. Vine (eds.), *Social communication and movement.* New York: Academic Press, 1973.

Eibl-Eibesfeldt, I. !Kung-Buschleute (Kungveld, Südwestafrika)—Geschwisterrivalität, mutter-kind interaktionen. Humanethol. Filmarchives Max Planck Society. HF 41, *Homo,* 1974, *24,* 252–260.

Eibl-Eibesfeldt, I. Grundriss der vergleichenden verhaltensforschung. München (Piper) (5th ed.), *Ethology: The biology of behavior* (2nd ed.). New York: Holt, Rinehart and Winston, 1975.

Eibl-Eibesfeldt, I. Krieg und frieden aus der sicht der verhaltensforschung. München (Piper)— *The biology of peace and war.* New York: Viking Press, 1979. (a)

Eibl-Eibesfeldt, I. Rituals and ritualization from a biological perspective. In J. Aschoff *et al.* (eds.), *Human ethology, claims and limits of a new discipline.* Cambridge: University Press, 1979, in press. (b)

Eibl-Eibesfeldt, I. Places in society. In *Cultures.* New York: UNESCO, 1979. Vol. 8. Pp. 105–113. (c)

Eibl-Eibesfeldt, I. Human ethology: Concepts and implications for the sciences of man, 1979, *The Behavioral and Brain Sciences 2,* 1–75. (d)

Ekman, P., & Friesen, W. Constants across cultures in the face and emotions. *Journal of Personality and Social Structure,* 1971, *17,* 124–129.

Ewert, J. P. Neurobiologie und system-theorie eines visuellen muster-erkennungsmechanismus bei Kröten. *Kybernetik,* 1974, *14,* 167–183.

Fentress, J. C. *Simpler networks and behavior.* Sunderland: Sinauer Associates Inc., 1976.

Fossey, D. *The behavior of the free-ranging mountain gorillas of the Virungas.* Film shown at the 15th meeting of the Society of Anthropology and Human Genetic, Hamburg, Sept. 20–Sept. 24, 1977.

Fox, M. W. The inherent rules of fighting. In P. Collet (ed.), *Social rules and social behavior*. Oxford: Blackwell, 1977.

Garcia, J., McGowan, B. K., Ervin, F. R., & Koelling, R. A. Cues: Their relative effectiveness as a function of the reinforcer. *Science,* 1968, *160,* 794–795.

Goffman, E. *Behavior of public places. Notes on the social organization of gatherings.* New York: The Free Press, 1966.

Goffman, E. Response cries. In J. Aschoff *et al.* (eds.), *Human ethology, claims and limits of a new discipline.* Cambridge: University Press, 1979.

Heeschen, V., Schiefenhövel, W., & Eibl-Eibesfeldt, I. Requesting, giving and taking. The relationship between verbal and nonverbal behavior in the speech community of the Eipo, Irian Jaya (West New Guinea). In M. R. Key (ed.), 1979, in press.

Holst, E. v. Über den prozeb der zentralen koordination. *Archiv Gesamelte Physiologie,* 1935, *236,* 149–158.

Immelmann, K. Prägungserscheinungen in der gesangsentwicklung junger zebrafinken. *Naturwissenschaft,* 1965, *52,* 169–170.

Jolly, A. Lemur social behavior and primate intelligence. *Science,* 1966, *153,* 501–506.

Kendon, A., & Ferber, A. A description of some human greetings. In R. P. Michael & J. H. Crook (eds.), *Comparative ecology and behavior of primates.* New York: Academic Press, 1973.

Leyhausen, P. Über die funktion der relativen stimmungshierarchie (dargestellt am beispiel der phylogenetischen und ontogenetischen entwicklung des beutefangs von raubtieren). *Zeitschrift für Tierpsychologie,* 1965, *22,* 412–494.

Liberman, A. M., & Pisoni, D. B. Evidence of a special speech-perceiving subsystem in the human. In T. H. Bullock (ed.), *Recognition of complex acoustic signals,* Life Sciences Research Report, Vol. 5, pp. 59–76. ,1977.

Lorenz, K. Die angeborenen formen möglicher erfahrung. *Zeitschrift für Tierpsychologie,* 1943, *5,* 235–409.

Marler, P., & Peters, S. Selective vocal learning in a sparrow. *Science,* 1977, *198,* 519–521.

Marsh, P., Rosser, E., & Harré, R. *The rules of disorder.* London: Henley, 1978; Boston: Routlege and Kegan Paul, 1978.

Mauss, M. *The gift.* London: Cohen and West, 1966.

Meltzoff, A. N., & Moore, M. K. Imitation of facial and manual gestures by human neonates. *Science,* 1977, *198,* 75–78.

Montagu, M. F. A. *The nature of human aggression.* New York: Oxford University Press, 1976.

Morris, D. *Manwatching. A field guide to human behavior.* New York: H. N. Abrams, 1977.

Murray, L. *Infants' capacities for regulating interactions with their mothers and the function of emotions.* Ph.D. Thesis, University of Edinburgh, 1977.

Pitcairn, T. K., & Eibl-Eibesfeldt, I. Concerning the evolution of nonverbal communication in man. In M. E. Hahn & E. C. Simmel (eds.), *Communicative behavior and evolution.* New York: Academic Press, 1976.

Rheingold, H., Hoy, D. F., & West, M. J. Sharing in the second year of life. *Child Development,* 1976, *47,* 1148–1158.

Sackett, G. P. Monkeys reared in isolation with pictures as visual input. Evidence for an innate releasing mechanism. *Science,* 1966, *154,* 1468–1473.

Scott, J. P. *Aggression.* Chicago: University of Chicago Press, 1960.

Snow, C. E. The development of conversation between mothers and babies. *Journal of Child Language,* 1977, *4,* 1–22.

Sperry, R. W. How a brain gets wired for adaptive function. In E. Tobach, L. R. Aronson, & E. Shaw (eds.), *The biopsychology of development.* New York: Academic Press, 1971.

Stanjek, K. Das überreichen von Gaben: Funktion und entwicklung in den ersen lebensjahren. *Zeitschrift für Entwicklungspsychologie uber Päd. Psychologie,* 1978, *10* (2), 103–113.

Thorpe, W. H. Bird song. The biology of vocal communication and expression in birds. *Cambridge Monograph in Experimental Biology,* 1961, *12.*

Tinbergen, N. *The study of instinct.* London: Oxford University Press, 1951.

van Hooff, J.A.R.A.M. *Aspecten van het sociale gedrag en de communicatie buj humane en hogere niet-humane primaten [Aspects of the social behavior and communication in human and higher non-human primates].* Rotterdam: Bronder-Offset, 1971.

van Lawick-Goodall, J. The behavior of free-living chimpanzees in the Gombe Stream Reserve. *Animal Behavior Monographs,* 1968, *1* (3), 161–311.

Waters, E., Matas, L., & Sroufe, L. A. Infant's reactions to an approaching stranger: Description, validation and functional significance of wariness. *Child Development,* 1975, *46,* 348–356.

Watson, J. B. *Psychology from the standpoint of a behaviorist.* Philadelphia: Lippincott, 1919.

Wiessner, P. *Hxaro: A regional system of reciprocity for reducing risk among the !Kung-San.* Thesis, University of Ann Arbor, 1977.

Young, M. V. *Fighting with food—Leadership, values and social control in Massim society.* Cambridge: Cambridge University Press, 1971.

Chapter 4

AN ETHOLOGICAL ASSESSMENT OF EMOTION

M. R. A. CHANCE

ABSTRACT

This chapter sets out the principles of ethological study and contrasts it with those of neurophysiology and experimental psychology which have provided so much of the framework of thought for the study of emotion. It accepts the scheme proposed by R. Plutchik for defining the fundamental biological functions out of which the emotions arose, and shows how it is necessary to redefine some of these to bring them together with categories of social behavior derived from the essentially social nature of the primates. In particular, it relates emotions to two modes (the agonic and the hedonic) of mental operation uncovered by the study of the social structure of attention.

In addition, it is noted that there is a large measure of agreement between Tomkins, Bull, Ekman and Friesen on the seven basic affects which, being structural features of behavior, are directly comparable with the ethological studies of the infrastructure of behavior in mammals and primates. It is suggested that the prolonged startle reaction is the basis of the agonic mode.

INTRODUCTION: HISTORICAL PRECONCEPTIONS

Research requires exploring (admittedly under the guidance of some ideas that determine the selection of the area of investigation) and then giving up the working hypotheses so as to become aware of the intrinsic pattern of the

81

material, which will require its own *de novo* description. In behavior studies, concepts such as aggression, fear, conflict, and stress have been all too readily used uncritically for relating behavior to other aspects of an organism, for example, its physiology or biochemistry. This is especially true of the concept of emotion. It should be clear now that what we need to start with is a way of describing behavior that is capable of delineating what behavior actually is, before deciding that we know how to divide it up. Ethology is designed to do just this because of its readiness to rely on observation for its awareness of the subject.

Emotion is a widely accepted concept. Is it a satisfactory category? To determine this, we first need to recognize that behavior has a structure which has been revealed by ethologists and then to decide whether emotion forms a recognizable subdivision of that structure or whether what is classified under the rubric of emotion is better divided up and reallocated to other parts of the overall structure of behavior. Moreover, we shall be on firm ground if we can relate "observed" categories in man to knowledge obtained through the observation of animal behavior. However, to appreciate this fully, we need to disabuse ourselves of some old habits of thought.

The late arrival of a separate discipline—ethology, clearly and explicitly based on observation and description, with a view to delineating the underlying structure of behavior—has meant that a great deal of the neurophysiological correlation with behavior has been fragmentary and carried out without the necessary recognition that such a structure exists. We may ask, therefore, the following question: How is it that ethology only became established as a separate discipline in the 1950s, out of the very simple process of observation on which the recognition of acts and postures depends, when, as far back as 1908, Magnus, working in Sherrington's laboratory, had recognized what were regarded as fairly complicated postural reflexes in decerebrate and decorticate mammals?

The reason must lie in the influence that a climate of thought has on our powers of observation, to which the data obtained are referred back as a touchstone of explanation. The major difference between the neurophysiological climate of thought, to which Magnus and Sherrington assented, and the naturalist's, out of which ethology grew, is one that goes far back into the history of European scientific thought.

The essential neurophysiological aspect of Magnus's work was the ascription of the different qualities and components of behavior to the operation of parts of the nervous system. Following him, Liddell (1938), for example, emphasized that the quality of the rigidity in the cat following a cortical extirpation is different from that encountered in the decerebrate state, the former being more plastic in character. Magnus (1908) explains how he defines an act when discussing a problem of the local static reaction:

The reflex transition from a toneless flexible limb to the "stiffness of a rigid pillar" is designated the positive supporting reaction; the relaxation of such a rigid limb, after withdrawal of the stimulus, is called the negative supporting reaction.

These results were spuriously ascribed to the interference procedure of sectioning the CNS.

It is not so much that Magnus's neurophysiological work on the postural reflexes was done in the laboratory and the naturalist's way of observing animals is in the wild, but that Magnus worked on animals whose nervous systems had been interfered with, whereas the naturalist looks at the behavior of the animal itself. Magnus undoubtedly thought that surgical interference was essential to reveal the existence of these postural components. In fact, this is not so, for all of them can be observed in the behavior of animals in appropriate situations—for example, in various acts and postures of rats in social encounters or, as Magnus himself puts it, referring to another reaction, "as when a cat looks under a table."

The lack of contact between different academic disciplines is one of the greatest impediments to progress in the behavioral sciences and in those that impinge on them. Let us take Pavlov's (1927) work. Criticism of his choice of the salivary reflex has come from Lacey, Kagan, Lacey, and Moss (1963) and, although his original description comes from the behavior of his dogs, neither this nor later descriptions of known orientation reactions take into account the zoological status of the organisms he was investigating. Pavlov did not inquire to what extent dogs are social! Even a feeding sheep is showing a partly social response. Denton (1957) showed that sheep constantly salivate but the rate of salivation can be augmented naturally, not at the sight of food, but at the sight of other sheep feeding. When, therefore, food is brought to a solitary sheep in the laboratory, the salivatory reflex is absent and no conditioning by the experimenter is possible, but, if another sheep is brought in and fed in the laboratory, conditioning of the first sheep becomes possible. Here, then, is an innate social response reflected in a change of salivation. This is a clear example of how important is an understanding of the innate organization of behavior to proper experimentation on animals.

Twenty-five years of experimental psychology was pursued on sleepy rats until Chance and Grant (1958) reversed the light cycle of rats to bring their waking life into daylight hours; recent descriptions of human orientating reactions have not taken into account man's anthropoid origin. Hence, the assumptions made about the circumstances under which orienting reactions occur amount to pure speculation and are without an adequate scientific basis. For example, Pavlov (1927) says:

It is this [orienting] reflex which brings about the immediate response in man and animals to the slightest changes in the the world about them, so that they im-

mediately orientate their appropriate receptor organ in accordance with the percep-
tible quality in the agent bringing about the change, making a full investigation of
it. The biological significance of this reflex is obvious. If the animal were not provided with such a reflex, its life would hang at any moment by a thread.

This a priori statement combined with the reductionist tradition turned all
subsequent investigations away from seeking to describe what form the
behavior took and toward seeking under what circumstances the orienting
reaction actually did take place. Such detailed descriptions could provide a
sufficient basis on which to construct a valid hypothesis about its function.
Hence, false assumptions have been the base of the behaviorists' physiological
investigations, as outlined by Lynn (1966):

> Apart from the single turning towards the source of the novel stimulus, it has
> become evident that the orientation reaction involves a large number of
> physiological changes. The purpose of these changes, in general terms, is to make
> the animal more sensitive to incoming stimuli so that it is better equipped to discern
> what is happening and to mobilize the body for whatever action may be necessary;
> for "fight or flight" as Cannon expressed it.

We now know that these fight and flight responses so casually labeled by Cannon take different forms, clearly requiring very different neurophysiological
performances. There are consummated forms of flight and aggression, forms
of both balanced against each other (manifest in equilibration behavior within
a centric social structure involving "cutoff" and displacement acts), and,
finally, forms of blocked escape. In fact, many forms of inhibited aggression
and flight exist, as do many forms of conflict between them, all manifest
within the social structure and not only, as Cannon assumed, between
predator and prey. Even this relationship is much more complex than the
average physiologist has assumed, since escape involves a complex strategy
and not just rapid escape or defensive aggression toward predators (Chance &
Russell, 1959).

Ethology has come into existence by the separation of the processes of
observation from those of investigation requiring interference. In the realm of
scientific inquiry, the procedure of interfering with nature has been converted
into the method of controlled experimentation, whereby the changes in a
system can be ascribed to the process of interference itself: to the neglect,
however, of simple observation. As a result, the method by which simple
observation can reveal information has received relatively little attention.

The philosophy known as *reductionism,* which considers that all explanations in biology can ultimately be expressed in terms of physics and chemistry,
was evident in the desire of Magnus (1908) and his colleagues to interpret a
postural component in terms of simple reflexes, partly because it had been
assumed that the breakdown of behavior into simple components was a prerequisite for neurophysiological localization. But it is equally possible to refer
the postural components to their position in the pattern of the animal's

behavior as a whole. Reductionism tends to regard interference or manipulation in experiment as an essential part of the method of obtaining scientific information, but it is not the whole of scientific investigation. This widespread attitude takes no account, for example, of the fact that astronomy developed, and still is developing, from observing the characteristics and plotting the movement of the stars without (luckily!) interfering with the motions of a single one.

This brings home the point that scientific investigation is essentially the attempt to achieve the maximum correspondence between our ideas of what can be seen to happen and our ideas of what can be made to happen by experimental interference. The contribution of ethology is that it brings back into experimental psychology the technique of observation without interference. So, we may ask, of what does the method of observation consist?

Briefly, it consists of obtaining an overview of the whole behavior of an animal and then examining it in parts by methods strictly designed to enable a part to be isolated for detailed examination (MacKintosh, Chance, & Silverman, 1977). By this process, behavior sequences are obtained and pathways of response are defined, and the presence or absence of social groupings is revealed.

This rather wide-ranging introduction has been necessary to suggest to the reader that far-reaching and fundamental rethinking may be necessary as a result of ethology's contribution to the reassessment of the concept of emotion. In making this assessment, I have been introduced to the view put forward by Robert Plutchik that categories of emotion are derived from fundamental functional categories, and, with modification, I have accepted Plutchik's proposal. In order to facilitate for the reader the integration of these proposals with those now put forward, two points must be made. First, Plutchik's categories (1962) are more fundamental in that they apply to all life forms, whereas ethology deals with the behavior structures that facilitate these processes in specific types of animals. Hence, the first contrast is that Plutchik is speaking of functions, whereas I shall be speaking of structures. Second, while Plutchik is talking of attributes of all animals, I shall be arguing that the specific structures of social life among the primates bring about a re-use of old categories under new circumstances and add new ones in the unique conditions of primate social life.

PRIMATE PECULIARITIES

Geist (1978) describes how one of the features of the ungulate's intraspecific behavior is the attention-attracting displays utilizing the contrast markings on the body. These speciate by the exploitation of different, often exaggerated, anatomical features. Horns, tail, rump, and shoulders, etc., combine in striking ways with the markings. By maximizing visual contrast, symmetrical forms, etc., several eye-catching modes of display are developed: for example, "framing" of the body by the South African oryx antelope; a "picture place balance" by the markhor; and "edge cutting" of Grant's gazelle, whose black and while tail cuts across black and white stripes on the rump as it is switched back and forth. The actual phenotypic outcome is, therefore, the result of the utilization of visual properties that produce modalities, under the selective pressure of functional requirements.

This has produced two types of centric societies in the primates. A centric society is one that coheres about a center, that is, a dominant or prominent individual. Agonic centric societies are those that cohere persistently, in that the members keep within sight of the center and collect about it in response to aggression from without or within. Because individuals respond by submitting to an approaching threat from a dominant, balanced approach and escape motivation is engendered, and attention is bound within the society toward the center. (It must be distinguished from agonistic, which is a term used to describe actual conflictful encounters between two or more individuals.) Hedonic centric societies periodically cohere as a result of mutual (if competitive) display followed by rewards, contact behavior, and food sharing (as in chimpanzee society). There is little if any conflict involved.

The primates and especially humans are unique in three ways that make their intelligence capable of manifesting itself in problem solving: first, the ready availability and flexibility of their manipulative repetoire; second, the social basis of their behavior and mentality; third, their conceptual flexibility, evident in their capacity to use language. What is new in man's nature, apart from the features just mentioned, which he shares with the rest of the higher primates, is expansion of the hedonic mode, in which we shall see the potential emergence of intelligence takes place as a supervisory feature, capable ultimately of discriminating between and controlling the features that man possesses, some of which have been inherited from an agonic phase of his evolution. These are at present held together in a variety of mixes by different cultures and are transmitted by charismatic or religious attention-fixing devices from generation to generation, often within territorial limits. It matters little for the definition of the problem of understanding man's nature (and, specifically, the nature of his emotions) how the individual traits were acquired. What is needed is to understand the structural features of the system; a start in identifying them has been made by Plutchik (1962). The second phase, however, does require a recognition of the specific nature of the primate social cohesiveness system within which it is set, which will alter the expression and role of some of the more primitive vertebrate modalities of mood.

In 1962, when Plutchik published his prescient list of the basic dimensions of emotion, studies of the social behavior of the subhuman primates were only in their infancy. In fact, it was during the following decade that most of the studies of the Old World primates from which man evolved were undertaken and a classification of types of social structures became possible (Chance & Jolly, 1970). As a result, Fox and Bischof were able to put forward schemes for comparing the rules governing human mating with those pertaining in the subhuman primates (Bischof, 1975; Fox, 1975). It is not surprising, therefore, that the significance of persistent social structures incorporating more than one male in some of the higher primates was not recognized as an important distinctive feature separating these species from the rest of the mammalian stock. This means that, with very little seasonal variation, all types of social relations are possible within the group and that the adult individual's social relations assume equal if not greater importance than his direct relationship to the physical environment. We share this dimension with the rest of the primate order. Hence, this dimension must now be brought into the discussion, because the individual's emotional faculties lie in a mental structure formed not only out of characteristics common to all animals (especially mammals), but also out of those behavioral features that have developed in the last 40 million years within the structure required for life in a primate society.

To start with, an obvious but fundamental aspect of the individual's social relations is "being" incorporated into the group. This provides a new and more immediate dimension of protection for the individual that extends to all ages, sexes, and classes of the society. Only when the individual has lost contact with the society does the original prototypic pattern of behavior become relevant and, even then, it does not under all circumstances take the prototypic form. In small mammals, the behavior that emerges when the animal is being chased by a predator is essentially protean in form (Chance & Russell, 1959). *Protean displays* are part of escape and they confuse and disrupt the behavior of a predator. They are unsystematic, and therefore unpredictable, and involve rapid, sudden transitions from one type of behavior to another. Their occurrence in the population is infrequent and thus prevents learning. In the young primate rejected by its mother when she is in social conflict, behavior becomes a subtle blend of protean elements with spatial orientation toward the repudiating mother (Chance & Jones, 1974). Hence, it will almost certainly be found that there are a great variety of protective behaviors based on partial rejection within the group and on desertion by the group when the individual becomes separated from it.

THE TWO MODES

The two modes, the agonic and hedonic, appear in the social behavior of the subhuman primates, notably those termed the higher primates. Response to danger is a type of behavior that contrasts in mood with eating, resting, self-grooming, and sleeping, and this contrast extends through the vertebrates. The higher primates, however, are unique in that, because their social behavior is continuous and their social groups persistently cohesive (through attention to the center), one of the types, the agonically cohesive, has encapsulated within the social group a continuous alertness to danger. Centric attention constitutes a fundamental structure of subhuman primate organization, and in the hedonic mode this cohesion is achieved by display (Chance, 1975, 1976).

THE AGONIC MODE

The way alertness to danger is encapsulated in the agonic societies is a result of the dependence of the individuals in the group on the defensive role of the adult and dominant males, who have evolved large canines and a low threshold of aggression. This means, though, that from time to time these dominant males deal out aggression within the group; this has two consequences for the likely recipients, that is, all the other members of the group. First, it has become built into them to be attracted by low levels of threat, making a number of strategies available to them to ameliorate the intensity of this threat or guard against it. This is the way the members cohere as a group. The strategies that ameliorate the inherent conflict are, for example, spatial equilibration, that is, adjusting the distance between the source of the threat and the recipient and thereby reducing the provocation of proximity; postural or gestural submission; calculated counter threat; and visual "cutoff" (Chance, 1962), which, incidentally, reduces the threat signal implied by looking directly at another monkey. To be effective, these strategies must be readily available and capable of being brought into instant use. Hence, there arises the second consequence of the source of threat arising from the dominant male, namely, that the individuals of an agonic society are constantly alerted to the possibility of having to take instantaneous action to adjust their behavior in the ways described. Indeed, all activities must be undertaken using strategies of movement that are calculated to reduce the likelihood of becoming involved agonistically with the dominant male (Pitcairn, 1976). These are the conditions under which individuals in the agonic society live out most of their active day, though, since they all huddle together in various ways at night, it is likely that the sleeping hours are the only time in the 24 hr day when this state of arousal does not exist. Baboons and macaques exhibit typical agonic societies, though there is a great differentiation between species, and the great apes are the representatives of hedonic societies, especially the society of chimpanzees.

THE HEDONIC MODE

It is important to understand that a pattern of social attention underlies and is the mechanism for social cohesion (Chance & Larsen, 1976). As previously mentioned, Geist (1978) has shown that aspects of social cohesion and the form of communication in ungulates exploit the attention-getting qualities of body markings, combined with posture and movement, and, thereby, certain distinct forms or modalities of contrast are inherent in the geometry of body form. In the same way, social cohesion in the hedonic mode is based on the organization of attention between individuals relying on movement and gesture. The separate existence of the hedonic mode, and thereby its separation from the agonic, is the single most important discovery arising from the recognition that a pattern of social attention exists and can be assessed between members of a primate group. The two modalities are the expression of two essentially separate, though interlocked, brain mechanisms, whose separate existence has so far escaped notice.

This is because ethology was initially built on the study of birds and fishes, whose social relations are phasic and constructed on agonic forms. There has been a carry-over of the principles developed from these studies to later studies on mammals and later still to studies of primates.

From what has just been said, it should be clear that from the start of vertebrate evolution, and for a great part of it, behavior has been constructed within the system of behavior designed for defense against predators. As a result, much differentiation of behavior has occurred within this modality, some of which has been built in. The integrity of the other, hedonic system has been hidden as its components—involving body contact (as in grooming, sitting, or sleeping next to), relaxation, and exploration—appear at different times and not as manifestations of a single alternative system, capable of organizing all aspects of behavior. Only where the elimination of alertness to danger occurs, as within the core of a territory, or when the young are in the presence of the mother and in contact with her, has the hedonic system been seen as a single piece.

The contrast between the two modes as evident in the social relations of primates is given in Table 4.1. The essential properties of the hedonic mode arise from the periodic nature of the social cohesion, which enables attention to be organized in relation to the exploration of objects in the physical environment without the environment itself being regarded as a source of danger. The difference between the agonic and hedonic modes is evident in a simple mammal's reaction to danger, in which the individual employs defensive strategies on its own. As an illustration, the response of a group of hedonic chimpanzees may be cited. They gather together as a group, making body contact, slapping and hugging each other, from which activity each

TABLE 4.1
Characteristics of the Two Social Modes [a]

Feature	Agonic	Hedonic
1. Social cohesion and attention	Continuous	Periodic
2. Attention to a central figure (centric attention)	To modulate threat and avoid being aggressed	In response to display
3. Continuous attention	Confined within the society	Capable of being directed at (non-social) physical environment
4. Arrangement of individuals	Spatially separated	Close contact
5. Social relations	Balanced; successful avoidance of punishment	Rewarded
6. Arousal [b]	Continuous (medium to high)	Fluctuating (low to medium)

[a] 1 to 4 are features of the society; 5 and 6 are features of the individual.

[b] For further information on the consequences of this for behavior, see Wilder (1967).

member gathers confidence to attack the predator on its own. The group is not the source of common defense as in the agonic mode, but a source of mutual confidence from which the individual makes individual assaults, significantly harassing a predator before it is in the mood to attack. Hence, the statement that all activity is rewarded in the hedonic mode applies also to defensive strategies.

Hedonic behavior is therefore a reflection of a brain mechanism that supports flexible attention and hence diverse types of awareness. Hedonic behavior is capable of controlling attention. It also rewards experience, especially in social relations, and maintains through frequent body contact a fluctuating, predominantly low arousal. Such arousal, later in life, is often controlled by facial gestures, by voice modulation, and, in humans, by restricted linguistic codes (Bernstein, 1971).

AROUSAL AND THE TWO MODES

At this point it is worth taking note of perhaps the most distinct advance in neurophysiology, initiated by the work of Morruzzi and Magoun (1949). Since then, the subject has been under active scrutiny by many workers. Albe-Fessard and Kruger (1959) and Bowcher (1961), summarizing much of this evidence (see Figure 4.1), point out that there is now definite anatomical as well as neurophysiological evidence for two distinct afferent pathways by which different aspects of the same stimulus are conveyed initially to different receptive areas of the brain.

Controversy still exists on the degree of separation between these two pathways—the lemniscal system feeding, via the ventroposterior thalamic nucleus, a point to point projection into the postcentral gyrus of the cortex (originally designated the epicritic system by Head [1920]) and the ascending reticular system. This provides a diffuse projection to the whole cortex via the thalamic intralaminar nuclei [Head's [1920] protopathic system].

Nevertheless, these anatomical features just described make clear their distinguishing characteristics. For example, a single shock delivered to a peripheral nerve will evoke a single response in the ventroposterior thalamic nucleus via the lemniscal systems, whereas a bombardment of impulses, spread out over a considerable period of time, will arrive at the intralaminar nuclei. These, in turn, project to the entire cortex by the diffuse thalamocortical circuits and produce desynchronization of the resting EEG pattern, again lasting over a period of time, and which is responsible for arousing or alerting the animal.

Hence, stimulus objects possess an arousal component as well as provide specific information. The conclusion is obvious and inevitable. Changes in the pattern of stimuli, as well as stimuli themselves, cannot be considered only in terms of their influence on orientation, but also must include assessment of their affect on arousal and, therefore, motive structure. The stimulus arriving via the diffuse projection system creates an arousal in the reticular formation of the midbrain, but this takes time to build up. Hence, the full disposition to

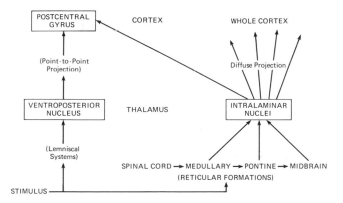

FIGURE 4.1 Brain pathways for two afferent systems (lemniscal and reticular) through thalamus to cortex.

act appropriately is not available. Putting it another way, in order to execute any activity one needs to be warmed up to it and this warming up happens by or is the result of arousal in the reticular formation of the midbrain. This, as we shall see, is the mechanism of arousal in the hedonic mode.

Defensive action, however, requires instantaneous responsiveness to any stimulus. Life in an agonic society requires an anticipatory state of arousal. The reticular system of the midbrain will be in an enhanced state of arousal, which, by instantaneous disinhibition, provides the neurophysiological basis for instantaneous reactivity. The agonic brain, therefore, has an additional element of arousal compared with the hedonic brain, and this enhanced state of arousal is normally prevented from being expressed in behavior by a complimentary cortical inhibition. This state of affairs is in no way different from the relationship of the cortex to the midbrain in the hedonic state because the cortex always keeps the midbrain inhibited. The activity is merely enhanced by the addition of a second inhibited state of arousal. According to the law of initial value (Wilder, 1967), all extraneous stimuli acting on a state of arousal already elevated above the midpoint will enhance the state of inhibition and depress the state of arousal. Although this applies to the agonic mode, the reverse is true of the hedonic mode, where extraneous stimulation leads to directly enhanced arousal.

AUTONOMIC INFRASTRUCTURE
OF BIMODAL AROUSAL

Given the reasoning, I suggest that two modalities of mental operation exist. I propose to show first that this subdivision into two modes of mental function rests on a fundamental division in the neurophysiology of the nervous system and then that recent psychological theory has moved in the same direction, based on the recognition of positive and negative social referent relatedness.

The evidence from neurophysiology concerns the ways in which excitability is organized in the nervous system and is largely the work of Ernst Gellhorn (1966–1967) and the Laceys (1963).

BIMODAL TUNING OF THE NERVOUS SYSTEM

Gellhorn's work is concerned with the reactivity of the autonomic nervous system and, hence, because it is an investigation into an aspect of arousal in the nervous system, links directly, but not simply, to the concepts of agonic and hedonic arousal deduced from the study of social relations. The autonomic nervous system itself has two modes of operation: the energy-expending (ergotrophic) state and the restorative (trophotrophic) state. In the energy-expending state, the excitability of the emotional center (hypothalamus) is enhanced, as assessed by increased heart rate, a rise in the tone of the voluntary muscle, and increased excitability of the neocortex. Conversely, in the restorative state these manifestations are decreased.

Moreover, a shift to the energy-expending state inhibits habituation and so provides a built-in capacity for sustained action, such as we have seen is required by the individual's sustained readiness for action in the agonic mode. Nevertheless, to equate the energy-expending state with the agonic mode would be to misunderstand the state of the nervous system in the agonic mode, and here I need your careful attention. The nervous system is at the same time aroused and inhibited, so that actions characteristic of that state are for most of the time not manifest; the social situation provides the stimulus not only for eliciting the response, but also for inhibiting it. If I may quote again from Gellhorn (1966–1967), you will see that, although physiologists are without any idea of the context in which behavior occurs, they do recognize some of the elements:

> Particularly interesting is the observation that a small cat, which, before brain stimulation by electrodes in the emotional centres, lay close to another cat and purred, fiercely attacked the larger animal on stimulation. In the resting stage the small cat reacted to the large one with increasing cutaneous contact, relaxation and purring (hedonic mode), whereas the large cat became the object of aggression after the energy-expending/restorative balance had been changed to the energy-expending side through stimulation of the brain stem.

This is not equivalent to the agonic mode, which possesses simultaneous inhibition. Fully stimulated into the agonistic mode, the cat would probably arch its back and move away for a short distance. Such behavior may be produced by repeated stimulation. Gellhorn concludes: "There is an increased reactivity to social stimuli in states of increased energy expenditure [as well as] a contrary effect, a lessened energy-expending reactivity in the presence of another animal or person, e.g. in the presence of the mother, the infant is calmed."

Because the neurophysiologists have not inquired into the whole pattern and context of behavior, they are led to conclude that only overt reactivity is a manifestation of a state of arousal, whereas the agonic mode of social existence clearly requires a state of inhibited energy expenditure of the CNS. The simultaneous excitatory and inhibitory influence of a centrally placed or more dominant individual on whom most of the social attention is focused provides just such conflicting stimuli.

TUNING OF THE NERVOUS SYSTEM
AND HUMAN AWARENESS

We are now in a position to appreciate the work of the Laceys (1963) on the neurophysiology of awareness in human subjects. They found that there are very specific patterns of autonomic responses to such stimuli as cold, noise, a flash of light, scent, or mental exercises. Slowing of the heart rate, an indicator of the restorative state, accompanied, and even facilitated, ease of *taking in information from the environment,* whereas cardiac acceleration facilitated rejection of information from the environment. Restorative tuning, therefore, seems necessary for the full development of environmental awareness and, since this autonomic state underlies the hedonic mode, these neurophysiological states provide evidence that, in the mode that liberates attention from confinement to social matters, an enhanced state of environmental awareness comes into being.

Nevertheless, the Laceys readily admit the dangers of oversimplification involved in asserting the existence of a single continuum from "environmental acceptance" to "environmental rejection" and call to mind the common-sense notion that preoccupation with the "mental" solutions of problems is frequently accompanied by inaccessibility and unresponsiveness to external stimuli—for example, closing one's eyes. This facilitates mental retrieval and manipulation of internal information. When studying such conditions, the Laceys found evidence of slight cardiac acceleration, suggesting that a switch had taken place to energy-expending tuning, as they would have predicted when environmental impacts were absent. Clearly, therefore, inventiveness may require an attentional system controlled by environmental awareness and based on restorative tuning, followed by periods during which a switch to slight energy-expending takes place, accompanied by retrieval of internally stored information.

To sum up, we can now say that centric social agonism is a socially induced and sustained imbalance of autonomic arousal in the energy-expending state, to which is added centric fixity of attention. Which comes first, the centric fixity of attention or the readiness for agonistic action, is a meaningless question. They are both part of one pattern set up to meet the requirements of social cohesion under the requirements of survival in a hostile environment; as we have seen that intelligent action requires the relaxation of this state, this results in "environmental acceptance."

PLUTCHIK'S FUNDAMENTAL SCHEME

We now turn to the place of emotion in this scheme. Of all those concerned with emotion, Plutchik has put forward the most advanced biological interpretation, taking as his starting point a scheme put forward by Scott. Plutchik, however, differs from Scott in that he recognizes that emotions are expressed in behavior and therefore must be identified in a behavioral framework. I shall therefore restrict my comments to the scheme outlined by Plutchik. This scheme is directly comparable with the ethological approach because it uses body posture and movement as the basis for recognizing emotion. Plutchik (1962) nevertheless does not fully develop its consequences. For example, he states that "the view to be presented would not restrict the concept of emotion only to the primate level, the mammalian level, or even the vertebrate level; emotion should be conceived of as relevant to the entire evolutionary scale." However, he does not take into account that modes of behavior, the forerunners of moods, which were developed at an early stage in evolution, may be radically altered by a later stage. The starting point of this critique of Plutchik's analysis is based therefore on what a study of the primate's social behavior can teach us about the expression of emotion. The permanent existence of a social structure within which the individual lives and within which it develops behavior patterns, expressing relationships between individuals in the group, is the new dimension. Without more time to study the matter, all that can be done at this stage is to single out particular affects and suggest how they can be related to the bimodal social structure of the higher primates.

Clearly, Arnold and Gasson's (1968) classification of emotions, which classifies them as good and bad, corresponds to those emotions that are punished or rewarded in the agonic or hedonic modes respectively, though they are not in any sense necessarily synonymous with any that can be identified within these modes.

DELINEATION OF EMOTION
BY BULL, EKMAN, AND TOMKINS

Table 4.2 sets out the correspondence between the three sets of authors who have used form and relationships to other parts of behavior as their criteria to identify affects. There is a strong measure of agreement between them. Several of the emotions they describe also occur in the list of prototypic functional categories of emotion listed by Plutchik. We will, therefore, discuss these and commence with startle, which, by definition being a perturbation of behavior, should be classed as an emotion. It is seen by the three tabulated authors as the point of departure of much behavior on which recent information provides a likely link with agonic arousal. First, however, let us be clear about the different ways in which the three authors set about the problem.

We will take them in an order based on the objectivity and concomitant reliability of the information—an order that may surprise some readers. Nina

TABLE 4.2
AFFECTS LISTED BY THREE SETS OF AUTHORS SHOWING EXTENT OF AGREEMENT[a]

Tomkins (1962) [Facial expression]	Bull (1951) [Body posture, gesture, and reported feeling]	Ekman and Friesen (1975) [Facial expression]
Positive		
1. Interest–excitement	Thinking[b]	(Excitement–arousal of interest)
2. Joy–enjoyment	Joy–triumph	Happiness
Resetting		
3. Startle–surprise	(Startle–surprise)	Surprise
Negative		
4. Distress–anguish	Depression	Sadness[b]
5. Fear–terror	Fear	Fear
6. Shame–humiliation	Depression[b]	Shame
7. Contempt–disgust	Disgust	Disgust
8. Anger–rage	Anger	Anger

[a] The brackets indicate modes of expression; The parentheses indicate a doubtful ascription by the author(s).

[b] Possible identity.

Bull (1951), whose work is much less well known than it should be, established "wide areas of correspondence between the behaviour patterns objectively observed in each of six induced affective states and the reports of the subjects as to the feelings they experienced in association with the respective behavior patterns." In order to find out which consistent patterns of body response could be induced and which also corresponded to the familiar affective states known as disgust, fear, anger, depression, triumph, and joy, she hypnotized the subjects into a trance state in which the well-known freedom from self-consciousness and general narrowing of consciousness take place. She then presented each subject on separate occasions with a stimulus word denoting a particular emotion.

This method is the most objective because it takes as its baseline the description of actual behavior. The behavior itself can be related to other aspects of a person's behavior. The method is also repeatable.

Ekman and Friesen's (1975) study is a careful, detailed description of the facial expressions of six emotions: happiness, surprise, sadness, fear, anger, and disgust. After examining the reaction of subjects from different cultures to standard photographs of the six emotions, these investigators found evidence for the belief that the six emotions are transcultural. The cultures from which the subjects were chosen were the United States, Japan, Chile, Argentina, Brazil, and New Guinea. These corroborate the findings of Nina Bull.

The list provided by Tomkins (1962) is confidently asserted on the basis of wide acquaintance with facial expressions, which he regards as the motor equivalents of the emotions he has listed. His work has no systematic basis on which the results of his experience are reported, but his conviction is nonetheless closely and informatively argued. In addition, since he is so conscious of the behavioral context of the affects and/or their anatomical basis, his work will contribute substantially to the next section of this chapter.

One of the values of Table 4.2 is the demonstration of agreement between different authors, suggesting that we have the outline of a universe of discourse about the structure of emotion.

STARTLE AS AN AFFECT

We should take special note of the mention of startle by both Tomkins and Bull. Both refer to the work of Landis and Hunt (1939), who were the first to examine the rapid postural changes following a startling stimulus, that is, flexion followed by extension. Bull refers to startle because "it is a preparatory muscular set—part of the reflexes, which prepare the organism in advance"; startle is, in fact, part of the motor attitude that is the foundation of attention (Ribot, 1911). Bull is critical of Pavlov (1927) because in Pavlov's work the temporal factor is lost sight of and made impossible to investigate by his concentration on the salivary reflex, instead of sticking to the investigation of muscular set and sequence of acts. Nevertheless, having said this, Bull inexplicably leaves out startle as a category. Startle is, however, clearly given a place in the list of affects by recognizing that it intrudes into other ongoing behavior and brings about a resetting, as indicated by Tomkins' (1962) classification in Table 4.2. As he says:

> The startle response . . . clears the central assembly (the transmitting mechanism and those other components of the nervous system functionally assembled to it at the moment) of the immediately preceding information and initiates the tracking reflexes in order to present new information to the central assembly.

Tomkins' great contribution is his recognition of the affect of interest or excitement, now so well understood by Kirkland (1976). Since interest is an activity initially requiring orientation and use of the eyes in a specific way, the face is bound to express the muscular set required for this.

Commenting on Pavlov's position, Tomkins (1962) writes:

> The affect of interest should be distinguished both from the affect of surprise–startle and from what the Russian investigators have called the orientation reactions, which seem to include both the affects of surprise, interest and the orientation reflexes.

Here Tomkins elaborates his concept of resetting because, apart from intruding into ongoing behavior, startle can lead either to surprise and (if the stimulus is threatening) to necessary protective action or, via interest, to investigation and eventually thought. Apart from being a resetting, startle is therefore a potential switch point in behavior.

A defect of Tomkins' position is that, although he makes the point that the face is a focus of emotional expression and can be related to the operation of specific facial muscles, he does not imply (as is the case) that the individual in his lifetime acquires muscular sets or patterns involving his total musculature—into which the facial patterns are integrated and through which constraints on facial expression are imposed.

PROLONGATION OF STARTLE: A LIKELY AROUSAL STATE FOR THE AGONIC MODE

When a mother macaque is in conflict, she glances straight into her infant's face. Since this is a signal of rejection, the infant releases its grasp of her body and drops off, but then dashes wildly about in her vicinity before eventually leaping back onto her to be cradled by her. Close inspection of this behavior on a videotape recording shows that the apparently wild movements consist of a highly coordinated series of erratic twists and turns, with as many as nine separate positions being taken up within a second and the whole active episode lasting perhaps several seconds. At the same time that the infant is dashing wildly about, it is also attending to its mother, ready to take the first opportunity to return to her, which the mother indicates by stretching out her arm, thereby allowing the infant access to her lap or belly. Failing to receive this signal, the infant may bury its head in her thighs if she is sitting or, if for other reasons she is inaccessible, will sit or cling motionlessly on a high perch, occasionally giving out long wails (Chance & Jones, 1974). As elaborated in Chance and Jones' publication, this is nothing less than a protracted startle reaction of the infant, whose attention is rigidly fixed on its mother; the erratic zigzag movements of its behavior express an equilibratory set of movements controlled by a conflict between tendencies to approach and to withdraw. This set of movements provides evidence that the excitement of the initial startle reaction is sustained over at least several seconds and probably throughout the time the infant is separated from its mother, providing it with a defensive escape strategy while it is obliged to be away from her. We have seen that agonic social relations are sustained by a state of ambivalent excitation in every way similar to that of the rejected infant, and these agonic social relations also act as a protective strategy keeping the subordinate members of the society out of conflict with the dominant center of the group. *Hence, I deduce that the agonic mode is sustained by a state of arousal equivalent to that found in protracted startle, which is at the same time inhibited.* Startle is universally regarded as a sudden, instantaneous reaction, but that it can be prolonged in a defensive attitude is shown by the behavior of the young long-tailed macaque. The agonic mode is a sustained defensive attitude and is a feature unique to those primates that display it, for only in the primate order do we have evidence of such a sustained state of arousal, *a form of response to persistent threat together with the threat itself encapsulated within the society.*

STARTLE AND THE TWO MODES

Let us look more closely at the startle reaction since this is the starting point for a number of types of behaviors. Bull makes clear that it leads to orientation toward the stimulus and that subsequently the behavior may take one of two courses: either toward exploration and thinking, essentially a hedonic development, or toward a source of danger, an agonic development. Plutchik makes an additional point, however, that, following the orientation and before the implementation of any particular response, an unequivocal evaluation of the stimulus must take place. Plutchik (1968) writes that, during this initial period, "if direct contact with an unevaluated object occurs a pattern of behavior apparently develops which at the human level is usually called surprise." Startle, surprise, and orientation toward the startling stimulus would, therefore, appear to be essentially outside either mode. But a primate living in one or the other of the two types of social modes, the agonic or hedonic, develops a habit of response to such a stimulus that is predetermined by the fact that he lives in just such a society. In the agonic society, not only does he react as if the stimulus were essentially harmful, but he also does not require the location of the source of the stimulus, since he always orients toward the central individual and derives the information about the startling events from the behavior of the adult male or central social referent. The existence of an agonic social environment determines not only the initial type of reaction, but also the orientation that immediately comes about.

The very opposite occurs for individuals living in a hedonic social environment. Here, a surprise stimulus does not call forth any specific orientation or attention, nor does it predispose an individual (by virtue of the state of that individual) to any particular type of defensive response. Indeed, the animal is left free to investigate the source of the stimulus, which, as often as not, is not necessarily a social one. (This probably accounts for the inability of subordinate chimpanzees to get out of the way of a displaying and charging adult male, which leads the adult male to slap them very hard as he passes [Reynolds & Luscombe, 1976].) Because individual human beings can exist in an agonic or hedonic mental state, one can expect both types of reactions to be found within our species.

SELF-PROTECTION AND PROTECTION
WITHIN THE AGONIC SOCIETY

Humans have come to alter the environment in the process of making things out of it and, in doing so, to destroy much of it. Hence, humans, unlike all other animals, are not adapted to any particular aspect of the environment. This is a crucial distinction. The concept of dominion over nature in practice is largely a process of destruction. This does not apply to animals who are adapted to their particular environments; although they feed on parts of it, rarely do they overexploit it (Wynne Edwards, 1962). The Greek root of agonistic behavior means to struggle, and Plutchik (1968) quotes Scott as defining this in the following way: "All organisms become involved at one time or another in a struggle with other organisms *or with Nature* [my emphasis]." To struggle literally means to struggle with another individual. It is a pure philosophical fiction to suggest that we struggle with nature. The element of struggle or conflict is essentially a description of a dimension of social interaction. The term agonistic behavior, therefore, must be defined in behavioral terms, which is one of Plutchik's basic premises.

The early ethologists, Morris (1970) and Tinbergen (1951) in particular, defined this as the flight-fight continuum, and they only differ from Cannon (1929) in recognizing, through the study of this type of behavior, that it is subdivided in many ways. At one extreme, fighting destroys the opponent, as Plutchik correctly points out, and this creates a situation when the other animal is no longer there. The obverse of aggressive behavior, which itself is graded from mild to severe threat, to chasing, biting, and eventually killing, is flight behavior. Sequence analysis of interactions between two individuals shows that the flight aspect of agonistic behavior divides into two pathways.

Social flight can take the form of one individual simply increasing the distance between it and a more dominant individual who is a potential aggressor, or the subordinate may allow himself to be displaced from his location. Alternatively, he may give a submissive posture, which enables him to remain located where he is when a more dominant individual approaches. The social form that enables individuals to remain in the neighborhood of their social counterparts is submission, which provides a signal to the dominant individual that the other individual, the submissive one, is socially "not there," effectively accepting the aggressive behavior of the more dominant individual (Chance & Jolly, 1970).

The nonsocial pathway is made up of components of escape behavior directed away from a predator. An animal brings about a condition where it is "not there" to the predator in a number of ways, all of which are comprehended by the term *protean behavior* (Chance & Jolly, 1970). Since the elements of these escape strategies are mixed in an erratic sequence, they confuse the observer. The components are erratic flight, inconspicuous immobility, and the achievement of shelter. The essence of this behavior was discovered in a study of what is misconceived as audiogenic seizures in rodents. Protean behavior is a prototypic category and is an escape from dangers in the nonsocial environment—from the physical events such as savannah fires, falling trees, or attack by predators. Its characteristics, therefore, are coordinated by a separate system of behavior. Terror is the emotion expressing the mood of protean behavior and obtrudes into human life only during social and physical disasters or as the basis of some prolonged mental states, as in some forms of mental illness [e.g., schizophrenia (Chance, 1977)].

In one particular study it became clear that the animal considers itself to have achieved shelter when it presses against a solid object as it crouches next to it (Chance, 1954). Strong contact of the body against a solid unyielding object is, therefore, the essential stimulus that turns off the escape behavior and "reassures" an animal. When mammals, particularly the higher primates, developed a social environment, the young obtained this strong body contact through the mother's nursing behavior or through, as Scott (1958) termed it, "care-giving" behavior. Care-seeking behavior, therefore, becomes a form of socialized flight, which in adults is satisfied by "grooming" behavior and "hugging." What I have just outlined is the structure of protective behavior, but agonism certainly incorporates both extreme conditions: destruction and protection, two of Plutchik's prototypic categories. Infants searching for care and adults hugging and grooming relax the underlying arousal and produce the opportunity to convert the relationships from the agonic to the hedonic form. The antagonisms are reduced almost to the point of being eliminated and the growth potential is then realizable. An important distinction must therefore be made between prototypic rejection, that is, vomiting, and allotypic rejection, which involves exclusion from the protection afforded by another member of the group. Care-giving within hedonic-type social relations sustains the hedonic nature of the system by keeping arousal low and affords protection to the young against danger from outside the group.

THE INCLUSION OF PROTOTYPIC REJECTION BEHAVIOR AS A SOCIAL RESPONSE

It is now possible to suggest that Plutchik's prototypic category of rejection behavior is incorporated unchanged into the social repertoire of one species of monkey. For the past 8 years we have studied the behavior of a group of *Macaca fascicularis* built out of two lineages: the progeny of two adult females (Ann and Betty) and an adult male (Percy) (Jones, 1977). Our attention was drawn to a subadult female (Ada) who regularly vomited up her food, and whose weight was and still is half that of her half sister in the other lineage, born at about the same time. Ada, formerly in the dominant lineage, belongs now to the subordinate lineage following a rebellion that reversed the order of the two lineages. Ada was then about 18-months old and her vomiting developed about a year later. Her behavior is, nevertheless, socially competent as she dominates (i.e., location-displaces and occasionally threatens but is not threatened by) her older brothers, who are well over twice her weight. This she does from time to time by soliciting support from other females, all of whom are in the now-dominant lineage; with one of these females, her age peer, she has persistently been a "friend." She now has priority of access to food over three other members of the group, but repeatedly vomits her food shortly after eating it. At other times she has coughing bouts and, from the small amount of phlegm that she brings up, it appears that these bouts are in place of vomiting. This occurs after relatively minor agonistic encounters or when there is agonistic behavior elsewhere in the group.

How are we to interpret this behavior? Observation shows that the vomiting or coughing bouts do not evoke any recognizable response from the other monkeys other than an occasional flicker of attention. So, if it constitutes an adaptive component under the social circumstances of the group, it must do so in a way that can only be understood in the context of the pattern of the group behavior as a whole. This is one of intense agonic balance, between withdrawal and approach, which has depressed the sexual initiative, and hence the experience, of the subordinate mature males, who are, as a result, sexually incompetent. The young mature females of the now-dominant lineage (Betty's) cycle frequently and associate with the adult male (Percy). They possess large swellings at the base of the tail (called sexual swellings, but which are really anti-sexual swellings since they prevent penile access to the vagina).

Ada has a small swelling, cycles regularly, and is occasionally briefly but inexpertly mounted by her elder brothers. Percy inspects but does not mount. Ada's position is similar to but not of higher status than that of the eldest of Betty's line, Bebe, who was displaced from her position of dominance in that lineage. She was the eldest and first to mature. Subsequent to the rebellion, after which she was the supremely dominant female for a year, she possessed a large anti-sexual swelling that collapsed when she was displaced by her younger, now-dominant sisters, who then acquired anti-sexual swellings. So absence of anti-sexual swellings (and possibly lack of vaginal pheromones) goes with low status. Hence, Ada, because she failed to make a status challenge due to her maturing in the subordinate lineage, may have adapted to this position by reducing her status motivation simply by reduced intake of food, but without loss of appetite. The vomiting syndrome can then be seen to bring this about by reducing, at the very source, the input of motivational energy. This stability of status has been achieved without interfering with potential reproductive competence on the one hand or undergoing any marked alteration of her social competence to stay within the group at an intermediate level of social rank on the other, since she is now dominant over Bebe and her brothers, Arlo and Alf. Ada's behavior, therefore, may well represent the inclusion of prototypic rejection into the social repertoire.

ALLOTYPIC REJECTION

The young primate is born into a state of protection and nurture. Nursing provides both. We have seen from the existence of protracted startle that, when temporarily rejected by its mother, the infant pursues a very active equilibrational strategy to maximize the opportunities for return to her. Withdrawal of care from the mother does not, therefore, in itself lead to immobility and lack of resourcefulness, implied by "dejection." This follows only when the infant is abandoned by the whole group. Prior to this, "aunts" and "uncles" and other positive social referents who will at least tolerate the infant's presence are sufficient to fend off allotypic rejection.

After the resetting that follows startle, the alternatives open to the animal are social exploration or escape to another individual. The comparative morphology of agonistic behavior has shown us that, as the capacity for social behavior increases, so the escape tendency is progressively modified into less and less drastic forms of withdrawal from social companions and especially from the central individuals of their groups who are also the sources of internal threat to the individual (Chance & Jolly, 1970). It is true, in fact, that primate social life encapsulates this persistent source of threat, which makes the advent of social life among the primates such a uniquely new feature superimposed on the entire life of the individual. Hence, the initial reactions to new sources of danger are always socially structured reactions. To be rejected by social referents is equivalent to being subjected to aggression from them or *being deprived* by them of access to them in the case of infants and to the space surrounding them in the case of adults. This is the category termed *deprivation* in Plutchik's scheme, but should be called allotypic rejection. Nor can incorporation as used by him be allowed as a term for the opposite of deprivation, which in effect leads to the incorporation of the individual within the group, as the most significant new dimension enters, namely, *not to be deprived,* that is, to be nursed, hugged, or loved. This is not an activity of the individual but something provided by another individual to the subject. By the very fact of its provision, because of the (all) embracing nature of the contact, it provides consummation of the tendency to escape and the consequent lowering of nervous arousal that goes with it. Provided by a mother in sufficient amounts and when demanded, it sets up a built-in stability and calmness in the adult. In adult life, as in the hedonic chimpanzee and many other higher primates, frequent body contact does the same. Cultural factors in "advanced" European societies make this less easy to achieve for human beings, where it is often restricted to mating, but with which it is not necessarily a concomitant.

Prototypic rejection, therefore, is one form, and a second is a specifically social form termed allotypic rejection. However, as we have seen, prototypic rejection may be incorporated into the social dimension as a psychological device for controlling motivation.

In human terms the prototypic category of rejection (illustrated by the emotion of disgust) is, however, different in kind from the others since it is not possible to vomit up another person, but to loathe or to dislike is to attribute a quality to another individual, that is, to project this self-felt state onto the other person. This shows us that a conceptual element can enter into a relationship and yet not describe it, and hence not be reciprocated. The incorporation of an individual within a group means that he may be in receipt of a number of the prototypic categories if these correspond to actual ways in which the individual may relate to others. Thus, he may *be* aggressed (destroyed), *be* left by the group, *be* explored, as well as actively carry out these prototypic actions either primitively in relation to the physical environment or toward another individual. The prototypic reproductive category does not change in the form of copulation. To "be deprived" is the opposite of to "be incorporated" but both are only allotypic phenomena, enhancing or diminishing escape tendencies. The association of prototypic and allotypic responses may be clarified by reference to the work of Nina Bull.

THE ETHOLOGICAL STATUS OF HUMAN EMOTIONS: PROTOTYPIC REJECTION IN THE SOCIAL CONTEXT

THE AGONIC CHARACTER OF DISGUST

Bull's studies (1951) on hypnotized subjects provide important evidence on the relation between the observed behavioral responses and reports by the subjects of their experience, given the stimulus words of the six emotions already referred to.

From these studies a clear and close association was found between "a turning away or averting reflex, which produced an attitude of negative orientation (i.e., 'away from') as if in preparation for bodily escape" and "nausea as if in preparation for vomiting" in response to the stimulus word "disgust." Corroborating the inference that disgust is an emotion associated with escape (which in the primate social context is equivalent to escape from the society, or alienation) was the finding that when traces of anger were present the behavioral aversion was much less.

The specificity of the aversive behavior and congruence between this and the feelings of wanting to get away are remarkable. The aversive behavior most often took three forms:

1. Turning aside of the head and then, less frequently, the body
2. Drawing back and pushing back
3. Drawing up and straightening out, with the head thrown back (typical of the most extreme escape posture in a convulsion, the posture known as opisthotonus)

All three forms of aversion on the one hand and nausea on the other were two kinds of reactions "so closely woven as to be apparently inseparable, but the proportions being quite different in different cases, the total picture varied accordingly" (Bull, 1951). Bull then goes on to make a comment on the adequacy of language that so eloquently bears out the case for creating an appropriate language put forward in the introduction that I quote it here:

> The pattern as a whole could appropriately be called revulsion, there being no other English substantive available to give an adequate picture of its double character. The term revulsion is not usually applied, however, except in cases of rather violent or obvious disgust reactions, and the use of other words (for example, "dislike") for the milder forms of disgust has helped to obscure the actual identity of composition which we believe exists throughout the gamut of intensities.

The gamut of emotion displayed by anger–fear–disgust, in that order, represents suppressed responses built upon positive social aggressive approach, through ambivalence, to negatively incipient escape, and expresses responses typical of behavior in an agonic context. Also, the combination of positive and negative social elements can be seen in this passage, where the "not being socially involved with," that is, treating social relations as not getting involved with rather than retreating from, is also evident as part of the complex of disgust (see the discussion of Ada's behavior on p. 101).

THE AGONIC CHARACTER OF FEAR

We have already discussed Bull's evidence which supports the notion that, ethologically speaking, disgust is equivalent to social withdrawal. Let us now turn to the next most positive state of fear. This statement in itself contradicts the view most widely held that fear is primarily associated with the response to a negative stimulus, which must produce overwhelming withdrawal tendencies. Bull does not characterize it in this way. "The presence of two components," she says, "in the [behavioural] response was not as evident to the observers as in the case of disgust" because, as she later explains, one was the "inability to move." Nevertheless, the dual character was unmistakable, sometimes experienced as conscious conflict in the reports of the subjects as a "desire to get away" opposed by the "inability to move." Bull's (1951) designation of fear is that it is felt in the case of conflict between posture and movement within the same muscular system; that is, the response was predominantly skeletal and not combined, as in disgust, with a separate visceral element (i.e., vomiting):

> The diversity of escape behaviour during *fear* presented a picture quite different from the more channelized avertive pattern that we found so characteristic of disgust. The turning in fear was not all away (from danger) by any means, but some of it was toward (security). There was also turning back—in the direction of the "imaginary" danger to look for it or keep it *under observation*—a very necessary part of the fear orientation with its uncertainty about the stimulus [italics mine].

What could contain a clearer reference to reflected escape and centric attention in "turning toward" the source of fear for security(!) and keeping the center under observation—the true paradigm for a paranoid fear!

THE AGONIC CHARACTER OF ANGER

The impulse to destroy is, as Plutchik points out, the prototypic basis of the emotion of anger. As already described in the allotypic dimension, this is reciprocated by the disappearance of the social partner, or the "not being there" characteristic of the partner's behavior, thereby avoiding destruction. This conservatory character of agonic relations fits Wynne Edwards' (1962) concept of population control by social ranking (see also Chance & Jolly [1970] for a critique of Wynne Edwards). Ranked agonic relations, therefore, by encapsulating aggression, also modify it and modulate it by balancing it against escape, threat, spatial equilibration and social equilibration, submissions, and "cutoff." "Cutoff" postures of various kinds all remove from sight an opponent in an agonistic encounter. Reference to Figure 4.1 will show that afferent impulses have an arousal component as well as provide information. By removing the sight of an opponent, the agonistic motivations of attack and flight are lowered, thereby giving greater flexibility to the behavior. These new categories are, however, significant transformations of a prototypic character into a new form within an allotypic framework.

Bull identifies the allotypic transformation of aggression in facial expression by describing the way it is combined with other actions of a similar form. The aggressive impulse expresses itself as a desire to hit, punch, or throw something and is controlled by clenching of the fists. Bull sees the clenching of the jaw and biting of the lip as a means of checking the primitive vocalizing tendency seen in children's aggressive screams. "Apparently," she says, "the primitive biting reflex is utilized to check the primitive vocalizing tendency, producing a postural closure of the jaws that has no reference to food." It represents a classical displacement of the conflict into a reaction that takes its form through transitional movement. This transition from one type of behavior to a behavior of similar form has been identified by ethologists in many types of animal conflicts.

MATING BEHAVIOR

The earliest studies of social behavior in birds and fishes clearly show mating behavior taking place in an agonistic context and also show that courtship is the process by which the agonistic elements are reduced, enabling mating to occur (Morris, 1970). The final element to this picture is added when we recognize that in the hedonic mode agonism is minimal and that mating occurs without any preliminary courtship, merely by sexual and erotic arousal. Sexual behavior, therefore, takes two forms, or in the structure of the mind is incorporated in two quite different frameworks, the agonic and the hedonic.

Ethology, therefore, has taken Plutchik's initial criteria seriously, especially recognition of psychological features through a study of behavior, and has systematically developed a method by which much of the complexity of the system and its essential structural features have already been revealed.

BIMODAL PSYCHOLOGICAL THEORY

In the early days of psychoanalytic theory, sexuality was regarded as the major source of neurosis, but lately, and even in Freud's time, the cause of neurosis has been seen to reside in unresolved mental conflict. Conflict per se is in essence that mental state supported by the agonic mental infrastructure and, as such, does not itself engender neuroses, but becomes so only insofar as the mental structure does not allow any relaxation of arousal. Sexuality, as we have noted, can exist within either an agonic or a hedonic mental infrastructure. It can now be seen that post-Freudian psychoanalytic theory is concerned with agonic mental structures, from which alone functional psychopathology can arise. The classical psychoanalytic theory is, therefore, restricted in scope, since it does not deal with the hedonic modality. For the first attempt to construct such a comprehensive theoretical basis for mental structure we should turn to the work of Pearce and Newton (1969).

Earlier on, I referred to the discovery of social referents by those investigating the social structure of attention in monkeys and apes (Pitcairn, 1976). Social referents are individuals other than the centrally placed dominant, to whom a high proportion of another individual's social attention is given, and to whom that individual is socially bonded, either negatively in order to avoid involvement or positively as a companion with whom close relationships are possible and sought after.

If we accept the fact that young monkeys become socially independent of their mothers at an early age and that they later set up differential referent relations with other individuals, positive with some, negative with others, then we must realize that this is a statement of the primitive pattern of social relations and the foundation upon which later evolutionary forms have evolved. Agonic social relations develop out of negative referent relationships and hedonic social relations develop out of positive referent relationships. This is the foundation, moreover, on which human sociability, as well as mental structure, is based. We are, therefore, logically bound to ask from this comparative standpoint whether there are any psychological theorists who base their ideas on a fundamental bimodality of this kind.

Pearce and Newton (1969) have found the ontogeny of mental health and illness to be based on just such a duality in the early social bondings of their patients. This is an original theory, important for many reasons. First, it is more comprehensive than any hitherto put forward because it is derived from the experience of human patients viewed from a new angle—one concerned with the definition of mental health as well as illness. It goes back to the psychologists Murray, Kluckholm, and Fromm, writing in the 1940s and 1950s, and later to the work of Harry Stack Sullivan. All see a healthy mentality in our civilization as involving continuous growth of personality in terms of an expanding awareness and ability to meet new problems. They propose an interpersonal psychoanalytic theory based on the quality of social relations. This is nothing new in itself, but its formulation is fundamentally so, for this relationship may be held to have existed in the past, with the individual's attention focused on the memory of it, or to be in the person's present social relations. The young person can at any one time be passing through a phase of social relatedness based primarily on either an integrative or a hostile–denying relationship, essentially similar to the qualities of the hedonic and agonic modes of social cohesion.

The integral aspect of the personality arises from the social relationships being based on validation, tenderness, and cherishing, with respect on a reciprocal basis, and facilitates exploratory and integrative mental faculties (both features of Halstead's [1951] definition of intelligence). The information entering the integral personality does so consciously and through communication with others; this is the hedonic state.

The other component of the personality, which Sullivan calls the security apparatus, is restrictive of exploration and reciprocal communication and arises from denial of love in infancy and from hostile integration in the social relations of later life, which the agonic state helps to define.

SUMMARY

The preceding rather briefly summarized statement of Plutchik's and Bull's positions put within the ethological framework shows that a basically consistent view emerges which suggests that by pursuing this line of investigation we shall achieve an understanding that takes into account the biological origins of human beings. This requires the definition of structure in the mentality at all levels. To complete the human level, we need to expand investigations into the elaborate intersubjective and introspective capacities of the human self as manifest in diverse cultures, much as Ekman and Friesen (1975) have done; to unravel the infrastructure, a much more systematic study of comparative vertebrate and mammalian ethology is required, especially of primate social structures.

There are three unique features of primate society. One is the encapsulation of danger within itself; the second is a reflection of the flight tendency toward the source of the threat; and the third is the consummation of the resulting escape tendency by an act of reciprocation from others within the group. Adults occasionally leave monkey groups and become temporarily, or for a long period, solitary. Allotypic rejection, therefore, occurs only when the individual still seeks consummation of escape within the group.

When, as a result of selection for capabilities, the ability of one individual to provide escape consummation for another through contact behavior was extended from infancy to adult relations, the hedonic capabilities of the species were so enlarged that there could then become an alternative to the agonic as a basis for social cohesion. Hence, there came to the fore the capabilities of growth in the personality and positive social relatedness.

Expansion and growth or diminution are the two directions that the life of a population can take. Both have been developed as adaptive mechanisms under different circumstances, and in a stable population both operate. Corresponding to the balance between these, various physiological states of the individual come about, between debilitation on the one hand and well-being on the other. This has been known from time immemorial—but it had not been so evident until the discovery of the agonic and hedonic mental infrastructures that two distinct modalities of the nervous system exist to facilitate operation under one or the other of these circumstances.

REFERENCES

Albe-Fessard, D., & Kruger, L. Dualité des réponse des cellules du centre médian du thalamus à des stimulations naturelles ou électriques. *Comptes Rendus de l'Academie des Sciences Paris,* 1959, 248–299.

Arnold, M. B. (ed.) *The nature of emotion* (Penguin Modern Psychology). London–Baltimore: Penguin, 1968.

Arnold, M. B., & Gasson, J. A. Feelings and emotions as dynamic factors in personality integration. In M. B. Arnold (ed.), *The nature of emotion* (Penguin Modern Psychology). London–Baltimore: Penguin, 1968.

Bernstein, B. *Class codes and control,* Vols. 1 and 2. London: Routledge, Kegan Paul, 1971.

Bischof, N. Comparative ethology of incest avoidance. In R. Fox (ed.), *Biosocial anthropology.* New York: Malaby Press, 1975.

Bowcher, D. The reticular formation and ascending reticular system: Anatomical considerations. *British Journal of Anaesthiology,* 1961, *33,* 174–181.

Bull, N. The attitude theory of emotion. In *Nervous and mental diseases monographs.* New York: Coolidge Foundation, 1951.

Cannon, W. B. *Bodily changes in pain, hunger, fear and rage.* New York: Appleton, 1929.

Chance, M. R. A. The suppression of audio-genic hyper-excitement by learning in *Peromyscus maniculatis. British Journal of Animal Behaviour,* 1954, *2,* 31–35.

Chance, M. R. A. An interpretation of some agonistic postures: The role of 'cut-off' acts and postures. *Symposia of the Zoological Society of London,* 1962, *8,* 71–89.

Chance, M. R. A. Social cohesion and the structure of attention. In R. Fox (ed.), *Biosocial anthropology.* New York: Malaby Press, 1975.

Chance, M. R. A. Social attention: Society and mentality. In M. R. A. Chance & R. R. Larsen (eds.), *The social structure of attention.* London–New York: Wiley, 1976.

Chance, M. R. A. The infrastructure of mentality. In M. I. McGuire & L. A. Fairbanks (eds.), *Ethological psychiatry: Psychopathology in the context of evolutionary biology.* New York: Grune and Stratton, 1977.

Chance, M. R. A. Biosocial preconditions for the operation of intelligence [Presidential address, Sept. 1977, Univ. of Aston in Birmingham]. *Proceedings of the British Association in the Advancement of Science,* 1979, in press.

Chance, M. R. A., & Grant, E. C. Rank order in caged rats. *Animal Behaviour,* 1958, *1,* 183–194.

Chance, M. R. A., & Jolly, C. *Social groups of monkeys, apes and men.* London: Cape, 1970; New York: Dutton, 1970.

Chance, M. R. A., & Jones, E. A protracted startle response to maternal rejection in infants of *Macaca fasicularis. Folia Primatologica,* 1974, *22,* 218–236.

Chance, M. R. A., & Larsen, R. R. (eds.) *The social structure of attention.* London–New York: Wiley, 1976.

Chance, M. R. A., & Russell, W. M. S. Protean displays: A form of allaesthetic behaviour. *Proceedings of the Zoological Society of London,* 1959, *132,* 65–70.

Denton, D. A. A gregarious factor in natural condition salivary reflexes of sheep. *Nature (London),* 1957, *179,* 341.

Ekman, P., & Friesen, W. *Unmasking the face: A guide to recognizing the emotions from facial clues.* N. J.: Englewood Cliffs: Prentice Hall, 1975.

Fox, R. Primate kin and human kinship. In R. Fox (ed.), *Biosocial anthropology.* New York: Malaby Press, 1975.

Geist, V. On weapons, combat and ecology. In L. Krames, P. Pliner, & T. Alloway (eds.), *Aggression, dominance and individual spacing.* New York: Plenum, 1978.

Gellhorn, E. The tuning of the nervous system: Physiological foundations and implications for behaviour. *Perspectives in Biology and Medicine,* 1966–1967, *10,* 559–591.

Halstead, W. C. Brain and intelligence. In L. A. Jeffries (ed.), *Cerebral mechanisms in behaviour.* New York: Wiley, 1951.

Head, H. *Studies in neurology.* Oxford University Press, 1920.

Jones, E. *The sociobiology of a captive group of long tailed macaques (Macaca fasicularis fasicularis) with particular reference to the mother-infant relationship.* Ph.D. Thesis, University of Birmingham, 1977.

Kirkland, J. Interest: Phoenix in psychology. *Bulletin of the British Psychological Society,* 1976, *29,* 33–41.

Lacey, J. I., Kagan, J., Lacey, B. C., & Moss, H. A. The visceral level: Situational determinants and behavioural correlates of autonomic response patterns. In P. H. Knapp (ed.), *Expression of the emotions in man,* pp. 161–196. New York: International University Press, 1963.

Landis, C., & Hunt, W. A. *The startle pattern.* New York: Farrar and Rinehart, 1939.

Liddell, E. C. T. Differences between experimental rigidities in cats. *Brain,* 1938, *61,* 402–409.

Lynn, R. *Attention, arousal and the orientation reaction.* London: Permagon, 1966.

MacKintosh, J. H., Chance, M. R. A., & Silverman, A. P. Contribution of ethological techniques to the study of drug effects. In L. L. Iversen, S. D. Iversen, & S. H. Snyden (eds.), *Handbook of psychopharmacology,* Vol. 7, pp. 3–31. New York–London: Plenum, 1977.

Magnus, R. Zur Reglung der Bewegungen druch das Zentral-nerven system. *Pflügers Archiv für die Gesamte Physiologie,* 1908, *30,* 219–252.

Morris, D. *Reproductive behaviour.* London: Cape, 1970.

Morruzzi, G., & Magoun, W. H. Brain stem reticular formation and activation of EEG. *Electroencephalography and Clinical Neurophysiology,* 1949, *1,* 455.

Pavlov, I. P. *Conditioned reflexes.* Oxford: Clarendon Press, 1927.

Pearce, J., & Newton, S. *The conditions of human growth.* New York: Citadel, 1969.

Pitcairn, T. K. Attention and social structure in *Macaca fasicularis.* In M. R. A. Chance & R. R. Larsen (eds.), *The structure of social attention.* London–New York: Wiley, 1976.

Plutchik, R. *The emotions: Facts, theories and a new model.* New York: Random House, 1962.

Plutchik, R. The evolutionary basis of emotional behaviour. In M. B. Arnold (ed.), *The nature of emotion* (Penguin Modern Psychology). London–Baltimore: Penguin, 1968.

Reynolds, V., & Luscombe, G. Greeting behaviour; displays and rank order in a group of free-ranging chimpanzees. In M. R. A. Chance & R. R. Larsen (eds.), *The social structure of attention.* London–New York: Wiley, 1976.

Ribot, Th. *The psychology of attention.* Chicago: Open Court Publishing, 1911; London: Kegan Paul, 1911.

Scott, J. P. *Animal behavior.* Chicago: University of Chicago Press, 1958.

Tinbergen, N. *The study of instinct.* London: Oxford University Press, 1951.

Tomkins, S. S. *Affect imagery and consciousness,* Vols. 1 and 2. New York: Springer, 1962.

Wilder, J. *Stimulus and response: The law of initial value.* Bristol: John Wright, 1967.

Wynne Edwards, V. C. *Animal dispersion in relation to social behaviour.* London: Oliver & Boyd, 1962.

Chapter 5

TOWARD A SOCIOBIOLOGICAL
THEORY OF THE EMOTIONS

JAMES D. WEINRICH

ABSTRACT

Sociobiology is the systematic study of the biological basis of social behavior in humans and animals. This chapter begins to build a sociobiological theory of the emotions. The first section discusses some misconceptions about sociobiology, and compares it to its ancestor, classical ethology. The next section summarizes Darwin's work on facial expression, and the portions of the work of other sociobiologists dealing directly with emotion theory. Other relevant work not specifically mentioning emotion is briefly indicated. The third section uses sociobiology to illuminate some central questions in emotion theory. Each emotion should have an adaptive evolutionary history, which implies that emotions can scientifically be termed either "pathological" or "bad" only in extremely restricted circumstances. The author's views on the interaction between cognition and the emotions is discussed, and it is argued on theoretical grounds that the distinction between emotions and drives may be poorly stated. In the last sections, a sociobiological definition of emotion is developed, and genital plethysmography is suggested as an area where future work could produce objective results of interest to both sociobiologists and emotion theorists.

113

Emotion: Theory, Research, and Experience
Volume 1: Theories of Emotion

ANATOMY AND PHYSIOLOGY:
ABOUT SOCIOBIOLOGY

CONCEPTION: INTRODUCTION,
DEFINITIONS, AND HISTORY

This chapter, like mind and body, or nature and nurture, can be divided with some difficulty into two parts. The first half is descriptive: It answers the question, "What have sociobiologists said about emotions as of late 1978?" The second half is speculative—a preliminary attempt to answer some questions about emotion theory that workers in that field have asked, and to answer them in a way that would be agreed upon by most sociobiologists.

Sociobiology is defined as "the systematic study of the biological basis of all social behavior" (Wilson, 1975a, p. 4). It is thus relevant to emotion theory whenever social behavior involves emotion. Although the roots of sociobiology go back a generation, and a few areas can be traced back to Darwin, the field became known to the public only in 1975. Few sociobiologists have mentioned emotions in their works, and none has attempted a general theory.

There are two reasons why this is so. The minor reason is that Wilson defined "social behavior" so as to leave some emotional questions outside of sociobiology's range. He defined it (1975a, pp. 7–8) broadly enough to include any "reciprocal communication of a cooperative nature" yet narrowly enough to exclude "mere sexual behavior" and acts of individuals merely "drawn together by mutually attractive stimuli" (e.g., for territorial competition). For the purposes of this chapter, the term *sociobiology* is broadened to become synonymous with *evolutionary behavioral biology*.

The second, and more important, reason why sociobiologists have tended to overlook emotion is that it seems at first glance to be nonobjective and difficult to study. Sociobiologists attempt to explain behavior and are interested in mechanisms only to the extent that they explain behavior. It is difficult to observe the process of experiencing an emotion. Nevertheless, a few sociobiologists clearly understand that emotions play a pivotal role in motivating the main object of study, the behavior itself, and have phrased their work with this in mind. (Their work will be reviewed in a later section.)

ENEMIES: MISCONCEPTIONS
ABOUT BIOLOGICAL DETERMINISM,
ANIMAL MODELS, AND NATURALNESS

There are three misconceptions about sociobiological models (indeed, about biological models in general) often held by lay people that must be corrected if the following sections of this chapter are to be understood. These misconceptions involve the use of "biological determinism" in models, extrapolation from animals to humans, and using the naturalness of a behavior to justify morally its occurrence in humans.

Biologically deterministic models presume that genetic factors are more important than environmental ones in determining behavior. Sociobiology does embrace a degree of biological determinism when the evidence warrants it; schizophrenia is an example (Kety, Rosenthal, Wender, Schulsinger, & Jacobsen, 1975).

But many other sociobiological models do not exhibit this feature. For example, Figure 5.1 shows a form of genotype–environment interaction called a "behavioral scale" (Wilson, 1975a, pp. 19–21). Here, the proximate cause of an event is environmental. However, genes might have caused the relationship between environment and behavior to be different; for example, there is no automatic reason why humans might not greet strangers in a friendly fashion while directing hostility toward relatives rather than the opposite. That this alternate pattern is uncommon is a fact that can be explained by sociobiology. (Of course, to decide whether this explanation is better than those produced by other disciplines requires further work.)

Likewise, Dawkins (1976, p. 165 and passim) asserted that, when evolutionary arguments predict the evolution of a mixture of several behavioral strategies, it often cannot be predicted from the theory whether some individuals will be genetically predisposed to different behaviors (in the predicted proportions) or whether all individuals will be equally likely to vary their behavior over time (in the predicted proportions), or some mixture of these two extremes.

Indeed, since behavioral responses can occur very quickly after an environmental cause, nondeterministic behavioral–scale models should have wide application. Wilson (1975a, 1979), for example, hypothesized them for such classical emotion topics as aggression and territoriality. These models are discussed in detail in a later section.

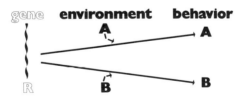

FIGURE 5.1.   Behavioral scaling. Consider a species whose members share a gene (*R*) different from corresponding genes in closely related species, and who live in different environments (*A* and *B*). If the gene affects behavior in a way that changes for the different environments, but adaptively for each, then the situation is described by a model involving a behavioral scale (Wilson, 1975a, pp. 19–21). Several sociobiological behavioral-scale models are discussed in the text. Such models resemble socialization and other environmentalistic models in that the proximate cause of the variation in behavior is environmental. However, the sociobiological model notes that, had the more ultimate cause (the gene) been different, environment *A* could have resulted in behavior *B* (and vice versa). In contrast, a socialization theory would assert that genetic mechanisms are unimportant except as they permit socialization to occur in the first place. [Illustration © 1978 by James D. Weinrich.]

A warning is required here. Sociobiology can produce adaptive explanations for behavior exhibited by hunter–gatherer populations, because it was as hunter–gatherers that humans spent most of their history evolving away from other primates. But behavior in modern societies (and historical, preindustrial societies) can be explained only by working out how a mechanism evolving in hunter–gatherer times would work in the new environment. There has not been much time to evolve new adaptations appropriate to the new environments (although the possibility of genetic change since hunter–gatherer times, some of it substantial, should not be ignored).

A second common misconception about sociobiology concerns supposed "extrapolation" from animals to humans. The lay conception of how models of animal behavior are applied to human beings resembles Figure 5.2. Suppose we want to investigate xenophobia in cross-species perspective. We would begin at the bottom of the evolutionary ladder, looking at slugs, worms, and other slimy things: If we present a group of such animals with a stranger, do they attack it or flee? We would then try our hypothesis out on the next rung, animals with scales. We would work our way up the ladder, crossing our fingers and hoping that results will permit us to ascend to each successive rung. We would eventually proceed to the top of the ladder, humans being the rung from which one is most likely to be toppled. If our hypothesis about the existence of xenophobia holds up through all these evolutionary levels, then we may make an evolutionary generalization: Perhaps xenophobia in humans has a genetic basis and fulfills similar func-

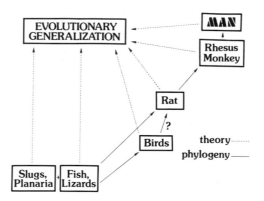

FIGURE 5.2. Extrapolation from animals to man. A common conception of the ladder of nature involves "higher" and "lower" species, with Man in a special position and thus a special typeface. An evolutionary hypothesis is tested first with the lowest species, and successively works its way up the ladder, each step more tentative than the preceding. Lines of phylogeny are followed in order to maximize the likelihood that a truth at a lower level will be confirmed at the next higher level. Finally, an evolutionary generalization emerges from the results at the various levels. This approach, mildly caricatured here (viz., "Man" instead of "Humans"), has been supplanted by the approach in Figure 5.3; for exceptions, see the text. [Illustration © 1978 by James D. Weinrich.]

tions in humans as in animals. Note that the ladder-like nature of the model makes the term "extrapolation" appropriate.

Sociobiologists reason differently—see Figure 5.3. Humans remain an object of special interest, but no longer hold a "higher" status. Instead, the most elevated position is held by evolutionary theory. For xenophobia, a theory might reason that there are both costs and benefits when individuals display hostility, and that the cost should be greater when hostility is directed toward acquaintances. This is because there will be a higher likelihood of encountering an acquaintance in the future and receiving hostility in return, or a higher probability that the acquaintance is genetically related; thus, the hostility hurts that fraction of the actor's genes shared by the recipient. Such a simple model would scarcely suffice in most contexts, of course, but it illustrates how the evolutionary logic can be worked out in some respects regardless of the species to which it will eventually be applied. If the logic is correct, it can be applied to any species that fits the assumptions of the logic, humans included. Note that this process might better be called "interpolating to humans" rather than extrapolating to them. It is analogous to having data points all around the human case, rather than on just one side of it.

Finally, it is sometimes asserted that biology, by producing evidence that a given behavior is "natural," can be used to justify undesired behavior such as racism or sexism. This logic is weak. When people like a biologically-based behavior they sometimes do call it "natural," but when they dislike it they call it "animalistic." It is hard to see how sociobiology per se contributes to either position more than the other.

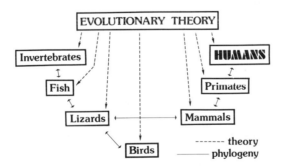

FIGURE 5.3. Interpolation from evolutionary theory. Our own species remains of unusual interest, so humans retain the special typeface. However, the most exalted position is held by evolutionary theory: a logical structure of hypotheses and deductions that is modified by experimental evidence and predicts the distribution of traits across species. If confirmed in enough species, aspects of a theory can tentatively be presumed to apply to others. This process might be called "interpolation," since the theory can be tested in species that are both more and less exemplary of the trait being studied than the species of interest is. There is no evolutionary ladder; all species are presumed to be equally well adapted to the environments they are found in. (Plants are excluded from this diagram because, lacking nervous systems, they are unlikely to have emotions.) [Illustration © 1978 by James D. Weinrich.]

ANCESTORS: A COMPARISON
WITH CLASSICAL ETHOLOGY

Sociobiology grew out of classical ethology less than a generation ago. The two fields still overlap tremendously in their approach. Here I will list two important similarities and one minor difference in the approaches of the two disciplines.

First, sociobiology and classical ethology both emphasize the study of behavior in the wild (while admitting that certain data can only be gathered in a laboratory setting). For example, in zoos, males of certain species kill subordinate males placed in the same enclosure. One cannot interpret this behavior properly before making observations in the wild. There, when the subordinate male is attacked, he escapes death by fleeing—to a distance impossible in a zoo cage. Moreover, zoo and laboratory environments are extremely restricted compared to natural settings; observations in the wild often turn up behavior patterns not seen in captivity because the proper environmental stimuli are never present.

Second, both fields interpret behavior in an evolutionary framework. Both presume that virtually any behavior has some genetic basis, with interspecific (between-species) differences being due to differences in genes in many cases. (In contrast, few assumptions are made about intraspecific genetic variability.) Nor does the genetic contribution need to be very large in order for an evolutionary analysis to be feasible.

Third, there is now a weak tendency for sociobiologists to concentrate on the adaptiveness of the behavior and on the sequence of steps in evolution needed for the behavior to evolve from an ancestral condition. Ethologists, in mild contrast, tend toward investigating the proximate physiological mechanisms producing the behavior and toward using species differences in behavior in the reconstruction of phylogenetic relationships. Although everyone agrees that both approaches are needed to arrive at a relatively complete picture, ethology tends to concentrate on means and sociobiology on ends.

Precisely this difference of emphasis was involved in a controversy about Lorenz's theory of aggression. Lorenz (1966) proposed a "drive" model, in which aggression, like hunger or thirst, could be dammed up until relieved by action resulting from an appropriate stimulus (pp. 55, 279). Another feature was aggression's beneficial effect on the survival of the species: "The best father, the best mother are chosen for the benefit of the progeny" (Lorenz, 1966, p. 47). This conclusion flowed from noting the "ritualized" nature of aggressive interactions, in which injury and killing of conspecifics (members of the same species) were avoided. Bad results of aggression could be explained by an occasional "mishap" or, more commonly, by "unnatural circumstances . . . unforeseen by the 'constructors' of evolution" [e.g., confinement (Lorenz, 1966, p. 47)].

Wilson (1975a) explained why most sociobiologists have come to disagree with this view. First, injury and deliberate killing of conspecifics in the wild are now a commonplace observation (Wilson, 1975a, pp. 246–247). Second, individual-advantage arguments for the ritualization of aggressive interactions have been proposed (Wilson, 1975a, pp. 128–129); Lorenz's reliance on species-advantage (as opposed to individual-advantage) logic would be rejected by most sociobiologists (Wilson, 1975a, Chapter 5). And third, "Aggression evolves not as a continuous biological process as the beat of the heart, but as a contingency plan" (Wilson, 1975a, p. 248). This contingency plan has a genetic basis in the endocrine system (here Lorenz would agree), but it is designed to be used in times of stress and would not become "dammed up" when appropriate stress is not present. I would add that hunger and thirst "dam up" for a comprehensible reason—water and energy are continuously expended by the organism—but there is no comparable rationale for hypothesizing aggression to be similar in this respect.

KINSHIP: OTHER SOCIOBIOLOGICAL TREATMENTS OF THE EMOTIONS

Because ethological writers are represented by two other chapters in this volume (those by Eibl-Eibesfeldt [Chapter 3] and Chance [Chapter 4]), no effort will be made to review purely ethological work on emotion theory. Instead, what follows is a précis of the work of people who have (a) clearly used a sociobiological approach and (b) mentioned emotion theory explicitly in their works.

CHARLES DARWIN

A sociobiological view of the emotions began, and nearly ended, with Darwin. Darwin's book on facial expression (1872/1965) is a good sample of his approach. Today it would be called both sociobiological and ethological, as it discusses the anatomy of the facial musculature and evidence for genetic factors in expression (mechanism), the occurrence across species of different facial and postural expressions (phylogeny), the usefulness of a given expression in the life of the animal (adaptation), and why a given expression would have evolved given the history of selection pressures in a species (evolution).

Darwin's method used natural observations to deduce the adaptive value of an expression; reports from non-Western cultures to show an expression's universality; and cross-species comparisons, anatomical evidence, observations of the insane, and observations of the developmental sequence of expressions in children to establish an expression's genetic basis. This method languished for nearly a century, as biologists pursued other fields. The birth of ethology finally produced new work designed to test Darwin's methods and conclusions, resulting in the fine volume edited by Ekman (1973). Ekman and his collaborators reviewed the evidence accumulated on the similarities and dissimilarities of human facial expression with nonhuman primates, the development of facial expressions in children, and the cross-cultural universality of certain human facial expressions. They concluded that Darwin's work had held up remarkably well, requiring some corrections of detail but few (if any) corrections of overall approach or major conclusions. Darwin's discussion of emotions in *The descent of man* (Darwin, 1871/1905, Chapter 3) was similarly prescient.

ROBERT TRIVERS

Trivers has published one chapter and two papers in which emotions were explicitly or implicitly discussed.

Reciprocal Altruism (Trivers, 1971)

The proverb "You scratch my back and I'll scratch yours" prescribes behavior familiar to all humans. In this paper, Trivers considered the evolutionary conditions under which such reciprocal altruism can be selected for (even when the altruism is not directed toward kin—i.e., is not nepotistic). He concluded that non-nepotistic altruism can become common and persist over evolutionarily significant stretches of time if those predisposed to be altruistic direct their altruism to some degree preferentially toward others similarly predisposed. Over one-third of the paper (pp. 47–54) is devoted to an analysis of the psychological mechanisms in humans that could produce this proaltruist bias, while simultaneously sharpening the abilities of subtle "cheaters" to appear altruistic (thus obtaining some of the benefits of the system without the cost of being altruistic themselves) and improving associated counterstrategies of the altruists. Moralistic aggression, gratitude, sympathy, guilt, trust, and suspicion are all emotional reactions hypothesized by Trivers to have evolved (at least in part) as a result of natural selection for reciprocal altruism.

Parent–Offspring Conflict (Trivers, 1974)

In this paper, Trivers argued that there is inevitably a conflict (in sexually reproducing species) between parents and offspring regarding the situations in which an offspring should be altruistic toward siblings—or toward its parents, if that affects the parents' ability to raise future offspring successfully. In many cases, of course, the parents' and offspring's interests will not conflict regarding whether the offspring should perform a given altruistic act. But Trivers showed that, often, the parents' interests will be maximized by the offspring's altruism, while the offspring's interests will be maximized by its being selfish. In short, "Conflict during socialization need not be viewed solely as conflict between the culture of the parent and the biology of the child; it can also be viewed as conflict between the biology of the parent and the biology of the child" (p. 260). Trivers then extended the analysis into predictions about psychological and emotional predispositions in socialization conflict, about the offspring as a psychological manipulator, and about how the parents might manipulate the offspring's emotional development to produce in adulthood a tendency to optimize parental (rather than offspring) interests regarding choice of mate or becoming a permanent nonreproductive (pp. 257–262).

Parental Investment and Courtship Strategy (Trivers, 1972)

In his chapter in the book *Sexual selection and the descent of man 1871–1971*, Trivers laid out a sociobiological theory of courtship strategy, including the effects that desertion or cuckoldry could have in species in which both parents invest large amounts in offspring (rather than those in which only the female invests beyond the sex cells); for example, "One would expect males of monogamous species to retain some psychological traits consistent with promiscuous habits" (p. 145), if females occasionally do raise young to maturity without help from males. Presumably, these traits and the traits associated with the commoner monogamous pattern would operate through emotional mechanisms, although these mechanisms are not explicitly discussed. Female choice of mate (pp. 165–173) is a similarly emotion-laden topic discussed, although again direct application to emotion theory is lacking. Indeed, many other sociobiological papers on mating systems have subtle, unexplored consequences for the study of emotions like love, lust, and shyness. This literature is large and does not explicitly discuss emotional mechanisms.

These three publications exemplify the qualities of sociobiology asserted in a previous section. The reciprocal altruism paper contains an extended discussion of the model's interface with *social* systems of reciprocity. The parent–offspring conflict paper developed a general evolutionary theory that was then applied to mammals, humans, and other animals—regardless of any supposed "high" or "low" phylogenetic status. The discussion of female choice began rectifying a long-standing bias toward regarding females in all species as passive rewards of male–male competition. These examples could be multiplied at will.

EDWARD WILSON

Wilson has published more material than any other sociobiologist on the connections between evolution, emotion, and behavior. A complete review is impossible, but the outlines will be sketched and sources given.

Sociobiology: The New Synthesis (Wilson, 1975a)

Several animal behavior patterns, said to be emotional in nature, are covered in this book. The chapter on aggression (Chapter 11) exemplifies the sociobiological concept of a behavioral scale: "Aggression evolves not as a continuous biological process as the beat of the heart but as a contingency plan. It is a set of complex responses of the animal's endocrine and nervous system, programmed to be summoned up in times of stress" (p. 248). Moreover, the emotions leading to aggression (hate, disgust, fear, etc.) are multiple and are satisfied by multiple courses of action: "Aggressive behavior serves very diverse functions in different species, and different functional categories evolve independently in more than one control center of the brain" (p. 243).

Another important application of emotion theory in sociobiology concerns altruism. Wilson regarded reproductive altruism as "the central theoretical problem of sociobiology" (p. 3) because fitness-reducing acts are difficult to explain as a result of Darwinian natural selection. But altruism is related to a variety of emotions like love, fear, happiness, and desire. If these emotions are indeed overseen by the "emotional control centers in the hypothalamus and limbic system" (p. 3), then they must be subjected to a sociobiological analysis. Wilson's summary of theories of reproductive altruism is thus highly relevant to emotion theory, although the works he summarized addressed it only indirectly.

On Human Nature (Wilson, 1978)

The question of what to do now about emotions evolving to benefit reproductive success in the past is addressed at length in Wilson's latest book. This discussion merges with a discussion of the "etiology of ethics." Why are certain ethical precepts accepted instead of others? What emotions are those precepts connected to, and by what steps did they evolve?

If we can answer these questions, others present themselves. Should we use our new knowledge to maximize happiness? Reproductive success? Something else? If we choose one of these, what constrains our attempts?

Such constraints can be rigid or flexible. For example, in his chapter on sex

(Chapter 6), Wilson concludes that many sex-role differences can be strikingly reduced with appropriate socialization and reinforcement—without undue emotional strain from those mechanisms that produce a moderate degree of dimorphism in behavior in societies that do not try to affect early sex differences in behavior. In contrast, Wilson suggests that forcing the homosexual members of society into heterosexual patterns of behavior would cause great emotional hardship. The supporting logic amounts to an assertion about the relative lability of two different behaviors closely connected to the emotions: Sex role (performing the tasks associated with rearing children and maintaining a heterosexual pair bond) is apparently more labile than sexual orientation (the sex of the people one falls in love with).

Wilson also views the emotions as a central testing ground for sociobiological theory: "The less rational the decision-making process, the more emotion should be expended in conducting it," and the more amenable it should be to an evolutionary analysis. He thus proposes the study of phobias: They should be easily learned if directed toward natural features like snakes and heights, but not if directed toward evolutionary novelties like guns or electrical outlets.

Wilson's chapter on aggression emphasizes its extraordinarily complex nature in both humans and animals. Hence, the emotions behind it must also be complex, and subject to an evolutionary analysis—since aggression has so often resulted in changes in reproductive success. Extensive evidence is presented that human warlike and territorial impulses are so regularly observed as to require a genetic foundation, but that all this emotional machinery is exquisitely sensitive to environmental and other influences—in an adaptive fashion. Lorenz's theory of aggression is discussed again and rebutted in detail.

Finally, if one defines religion as that aspect of human experience concerned with ritualizing adaptive aspects of culture for which no rational explanation can be given, then sociobiology might sometimes provide the logic showing the adaptiveness of aspects of the ritual. This Wilson attempts to do in his chapter on religion. Clearly, organized religion satisfies deep emotional needs in a majority of humanity, and Wilson suggests that one of its evolutionary functions is to persuade people to subordinate their immediate self-interest to the interests of the group. This process is always opposed by the self-interest of at least some individuals in the group; even if all gain by the self-subordination, some would gain even more by manipulating the subordination machinery itself. Moreover, since no society can predict from moment to moment whether self-subordination or self-aggrandizement is more adaptive, multiple attitudes toward religion are to be expected. Accordingly, Wilson expects an extremely intricate web of emotional mechanisms to guide the religious process and considers how they operate not just in formal religion, but also in various self-fulfillment programs, in Marxism, and in science itself.

OTHERS[1]

I have failed to find any other sociobiologists who specifically addressed emotion theory in their writings (several have confirmed the dearth of such work in personal communications). I hereby apologize to any whose work has been overlooked. Many have, however, written on topics that would clearly be of interest to emotion theorists (viz., aggression, pair bonding, altruism, etc.). For example, two publications by Alexander (1977, pp. 14–15; 1979) contain an intriguing discussion of the emotional aspects of falling in love: specifically, the sense in which one falls, almost literally, "across the chasm from social strangeness to social intimacy." Readers interested in such topics should consult Wilson (1975a) for earlier references. Several new journals report recent work (e.g., *Behavioral Ecology and Sociobiology, Ethology and Sociobiology,* and *Animal Behaviour*).

TERRITORIAL EXPANSION: A SOCIOBIOLOGICAL VIEW OF CENTRAL QUESTIONS IN EMOTION THEORY

Sociobiologists have had relatively little explicitly to say about many aspects of emotion theory. This section, therefore, is exploratory rather than descriptive, personal rather than official, and speculative rather than noncontroversial. I hope any sociobiologist would agree with a majority of what is asserted, although perhaps each would agree with a different majority. I would expect more unanimity regarding the earlier sections in comparison to the later ones.

CHARACTER: WHAT IS AN EMOTION?

It is my impression that a definition of emotion is the conclusion, not the starting point, of many investigations into emotion theory. Perhaps emotion theory is now at a stage analogous to evolutionary theory not too long ago (Figure 5.2): It is a theory that tends to summarize results, rather than predict them. Regardless of the reason, I will follow the custom and present a sociobiologically inspired definition in the next section.

But certain aspects of the definition can be specified here. Most sociobiol-

[1] A prominent ethologist–sociobiologist recently proposed some important and fascinating hypotheses on the sociobiology of emotions. (Happily, he implicitly adopted a definition of "emotion" quite similar to mine.) Consult "emotions" in the index of: Geist, V. *Life strategies, human evolution, environmental design: Toward a biological theory of health.* New York: Springer-Verlag, 1978.

ogists would agree that emotions—like the hormones that are often released with their occurrence—are *mechanisms for motivating or facilitating behavior*. The works of Trivers and Wilson exemplify this view.

Most sociobiologists would, moreover, agree on the following strategy for operationalizing the definition of a given emotion: Find a set of physiological indicators of the emotion, do a validity study showing that human subjects' introspections correlate with these indicators, argue that these indicators reliably reveal the feeling of the emotion, and then enshrine these physiological indicators as the definition of the expression of the emotion in future studies. Precisely this methodology has been used in several studies using a technique called genital plethysmography (the use of devices directly measuring sexual arousal). In a later section this strategy is described in detail, and it is suggested that it may not be possible for all emotions.

Once such a physiological indicator is validated, it can be used in studies of nonhuman animals. Among students of natural history, the assumption that animals have emotions is nearly routine—In fact, some would call it not an assumption, but an observation (Lorenz, 1966, p. 210). Once field workers have observed a species in the wild for a few thousand hours, they "get into the skins" of the animals under study so that small nuances in expression—body stance, facial patterns, actions omitted as well as committed—are no longer overlooked, but become comprehensible indicators of internal states. These field workers assert that it is impossible to understand these aspects of the animals' behavior without making certain assumptions about their internal states. This amounts to an assertion that observations have begun to tap the fundamental mechanisms motivating the behavior.

These workers would readily admit that the actual demonstration of this conclusion to skeptics would be difficult, even though the evidence *against* the notion that animals have internal cognitions or emotions is insubstantial (see Griffin, 1976a, b). This evidence is anti-anthropomorphic, consisting of warnings against projection of human feelings onto "dumb" animals. But this cuts two ways: If it is anthropomorphic to project our own emotions onto animals, it must also be anthropomorphically conceited to assert that emotions are uniquely human. No discipline is more aware of this twin danger than ethology itself. Novices overcome two barriers in becoming experienced field observers: First they learn to overrule their own projections, then they learn to project the way their animals would.

TAXONOMY: THE HISTORY, EVALUATION, NORMALITY, AND NUMBER OF EMOTIONS

Several problems of interest to emotion theorists are readily answered from a sociobiological perspective.

Does Each Emotion Have an Evolutionary History?

By now, the answer is obvious: of course. This should be clear from the preceding discussions, especially the portions discussing the emotional control centers of the hypothalamus and limbic system. The fact that specific sites in mammalian brains respond to pain-killers and euphoria-inducers (like the enkephalins [see, e.g., Frenk, McCarty, & Liebeskind, 1978]) implicates a genetic history behind the receptors at the site.

Are There both "Positive" and "Negative" Emotions?

In one sense, the answer is obviously yes. I have already cited sociobiological considerations concerning aggression (which most people would consider "negative") and altruism and love (presumably considered "positive"). But the separation into "positive" and "negative" categories is based not on theoretical grounds but on cultural ones. Most sociobiologists would agree that the *moral* evaluation of an emotion or its expression in behavior cannot be made on sociobiological grounds.

Incidentally, this cultural division into "positive" and "negative" would not even guarantee that a series of acts motivated by an emotion would all be evaluated in the same category. When one of the male langurs studied by Hrdy (1977a, b) usurps the tenure of another male possessing a harem of females, the emotion he feels is, presumably, joy. But that joy presumably turns to anger or irritation at the unweaned young of females in the harem he takes over, which he proceeds to kill systematically. Nor, of course, does his joy imply anything at all about the emotions felt by the females, their infants, or the displaced male.

Are Some Emotions Pathological?

To a first approximation, sociobiology would equate "pathology" with "maladaptiveness," and, if an emotion has evolved, the explanation of first resort must be that it has been selected for (at the level of the individual, in that environment, over recent stretches of evolutionary time). So if it occurs, a behavior is unlikely to be genuinely pathological.

A closer, second approximation to the optimum definition would permit a behavior to be called pathological under certain exceptional circumstances:

Mutations can create pathology. But even here, qualifiers are needed; after all, evolution itself is a process that regularly turns "abnormalities" into species-wide characters!

Physical damage can result in pathology.

Disease organisms can result in pathology. Natural selection acts to improve the adaptations of both parties to a competition; thus, each might be able to overcome some defenses of the other. Qualification: Many responses to infection, while symptoms of a pathological process, are themselves adaptive (e.g., fever [see Kluger, 1978]).

Some short-term genetic responses to selection can be called borderline pathological. Sickle-cell anemia is the classic example. It apparently evolved when malaria became a problem with the spread of agriculture, an evolutionarily recent event.

Some environmental changes can produce pathology. For humans, this is probably the most important possibility of the five; for example, Konner (1977) argued that the decreasing age at puberty in modern populations (due to better nutrition—an environmental cause) results in an increasing level of adolescent pregnancy, which in turn causes increases in mental illness, birth defects, and child neglect and abuse. "Human beings are not designed by evolution either in body or in spirit for the experience of adolescent pregnancy," Konner noted, whereas in hunter-gatherers the physiological and emotional mechanisms are in balance with nutritional supply.

Note that all the above definitions beg the question of how to decide *precisely* which conditions are pathological; they only outline the cases where sociobiologists would agree that pathology is a defensible term. A behavior can be called maladaptive only after showing that a reasonable alternative would increase one's genetic representation in future generations. But note that deciding this question for a behavior would still not answer most of the questions a society asks.

Enormous variation can occur between individuals of a species regarding any given behavior. Like most students of behavior, sociobiologists have first attempted to model the average (most common, modal) response seen in a population; for example, sociobiologists modeled the emotions behind love leading to reproduction (heterosexuality) before they attempted to model homosexual love. But unlike many social science workers, and even unlike some other biologists, sociobiologists do not first try to model atypical (less common, "deviant") behaviors by fitting them into a scheme of how the modal process can "go wrong." Thus, continuing the previous example, all sociobiological models of homosexuality of which I am aware attempt to uncover the ways in which it might be adaptive (Kirsch & Rodman, 1977; Trivers, 1974, p. 261; Weinrich, 1977a, Pt. 2; Wilson, 1975a, p. 555 and passim, 1975b, pp. 42–43). Contrast this with the pathological models employed by certain psychiatrists (Socarides, 1974), biologists (Swanson, 1974, p. 108), or even emotion theorists (Izard, 1977, p. 179).

Even when two behavior patterns are exhibited by two statistically large groups in a society, there is often a tendency to assume that pathology must be lurking in one or the other. Readers with a college education may consult their own stereotypes (or those of friends) regarding the sexual habits of those men and women who have not had a college education. Then they should compare these stereotypes with the facts (viz., Stycos' introduction to the book by Rainwater [1960]). And before they decide that this behavior pattern is pathological, they should read a recent sociobiological explanation of it (Weinrich, 1977b). A similar course of action is recommended to readers without a college education—especially those who believe that the sexual habits of the well-educated classes are unnatural and perverse (see Kinsey, Pomeroy, & Martin, 1948, Chapter 10).

How Many Emotions Are There?

Sociobiologically, this is not a very interesting question. Just as there are only vague limits to the number of species that can fill the earth, there are only vague limits to the number of emotions that one could conceive of evolving. Two of these limits are the size and the complexity of the nervous system that makes the emotions.

One should not simplistically hypothesize a strong correlation between brain size and emotion number (assuming the latter could be ascertained accurately). But to a very rough approximation, one could hypothesize fewer emotions, and less complex interactions between them, in creatures with simple nervous systems. This is an engineering constraint, however, not a particularly sociobiological one.

More likely to be of (minor) importance is an argument taking into account the evolutionary history of each emotion. New emotional circuits in the brain, like new structural components elsewhere in the body, do not evolve out of thin DNA alone; they evolve from some preceding circuit. This would put some limit on their number and character, although the exact form of this limit would be difficult to specify.

DOMINANCE AND SUBMISSION: SOCIAL CONTROL OF THE EMOTIONS

The control of emotions is not a problem of much theoretical interest to sociobiologists. Again, the reason is that sociobiological theories usually omit mechanisms, and to control an emotion some mechanism must be employed.

However, sociobiology will probably have applications for those who want to control emotions, as does any theory of human nature. Suppose, for example, that sociobiology were to show that, in environment E, it has been adaptive to have aggressive feelings toward strangers, and that this hostility toward strangers has a genetic basis. If the society in question decided that it wanted to reduce such xenophobia (an example of the orthogonality of morality and adaptiveness), what should it do? Such reasoning predicts that simple socialization changes might not suffice.

This is no cause for pessimism. Sociobiology would point out that aggressive reactions to strangers are not inevitably advantageous to hunter–gatherers, so one would expect there to be environments (F and G, say) in which xenophobia was not selected for. The solution would then be to change the environment to resemble *F* or *G,* or those aspects of *F* or *G* that make such xenophobia maladaptive.

Alternatively, one could exploit a preexisting mechanism that evolved to work in a different context. Indeed, some such attempts may already have been made. Foreign exchange student programs forge a bond between members of different countries in a way that has rarely occurred in the course of human evolution. Natural selection has thus not had enough opportunity to select either for or against this practice. Accordingly, mechanisms of within-group bond formation that evolved when genetically related individuals lived in close proximity to each other can be converted to serve the ends of international harmony. This is "perversion" of a sort much to be encouraged.

OUTCROSSING: ONE SOCIOBIOLOGIST'S VIEW OF SCHACHTER, COGNITION, AND DRIVES

Space does not permit examination of the many other theories of emotion that conflict or agree with the sociobiological view. One model, however—that of Schachter and Singer (1962) and Schachter (1971)—has caused a controversy (Plutchik & Ax, 1967) of some size, relevant to some fundamental questions regarding cognition–emotion interactions and drives like hunger and thirst.

Schachter and Singer versus Plutchik and Ax

Schachter and Singer (1962) experimentally manipulated environmental conditions in an attempt to arouse euphoria or anger in their subjects after an injection of epinephrine. They concluded that, in order to obtain euphoric or angry behavior under their conditions, subjects had to be misinformed about the effects of the injected drug. If the subjects were correctly informed about these effects, they acted as if their cognition compensated for the physiological changes they felt. If they had not been correctly informed, they tended to become euphoric or angry; they acted as if their cognition "observed" the physiological changes and inferred that euphoria or anger was actually occurring.

The controversy (as stated by Plutchik & Ax, 1967) is Schachter's conclusion that the "assumption of identity" is not true (1971, pp. 45–46). (The assumption of identity is that there is a one-to-one relationship between a pattern of physiological variables and the feeling of an emotion.) Schachter argued that his results showed that two different emotions can exist with the same set of physiological correlates. Plutchik and Ax objected to this notion "that all emotional states are physiologically identical and are differentiated *only* by cognitive factors" (1967, p. 81; emphasis in original), while readily agreeing with Schachter and Singer's conclusion that cognitive factors interact with emotional ones.

One Sociobiologist's Interpretation of Schachter's Results

Hormones are messengers from one set of cells in the body to another set of cells. In nature, epinephrine is not injected; it travels from center to periphery, which suggests that its function is on the action-producing end of the causal chain, not the emotion-evoking end. The Schachter and Singer finding is thus mildly counterintuitive, since it shows a messenger of a later stage influencing events at an earlier stage.

The paradox disappears when one learns something about how mechanisms directing behavior toward a goal actually work in animals. Even so simple a task as picking up a food item involves an extraordinarily complex interaction between central direction toward the goal, peripheral feedback (from proprioception) regarding progress toward that goal, and observations shutting off the central motivator when the goal is attained. Interference with the proprioceptive feedback, via electrode stimulation or whatever, should not be interpreted as showing that these proprioceptors are part of the *cause* of the central motivation.

Likewise, if there is a complex interaction between the emotion centers for euphoria and anger and the level of epinephrine found in the blood, which helps control the precise level of arousal in responding to whatever motivated the emotion, Schachter and Singer may have incorrectly concluded that euphoria and anger have similar physiological states associated with them. Perhaps the two in a natural state both result in epinephrine being dumped into the bloodstream, yet differ in other physiological respects. (Even the *levels* of epinephrine might differ!) I am struck by the absence of any discussion here of testosterone, progestin, ACTH, or other hormones. What about the studies on fluctuations of hormones during menstruation and pregnancy? Testosterone and fear? A psychohormonal specialist could go on and on.

Cognition and Emotions

All the combatants in the controversy reviewed immediately above agreed that cognitions interact with other factors in the production of emotions. Sociobiologists would agree. But not all emotion theorists have agreed; the James–Lange theory, for example, has sometimes been taken to imply that cognition cannot produce an emotion in the absence of some peripheral event to trigger it (both referring to James, 1890, p. 449; Plutchik, 1977; Schachter, 1971, p. 44).

But at least with beings as cognitive as humans, this is not so. Suppose you collect paintings. When you buy a masterpiece at a good price, you feel happy. When you suddenly deduce that it's a forgery, from information previously known to you but whose significance you hadn't understood, you feel rage. Yet nothing changed in the interim except your deduction of what you had—and this knowledge changed solely through cognition.

Cognition is a complicated mechanism that evolved to handle complicated phenomena. Sociobiologists would assume as a matter of course that it would interact with every other facet of behavior.

Drives

Similarities between drives (or "motivations") and emotions have often been pointed out (Izard, 1977, p. 164; Plutchik, 1962, pp. 167–170; Schachter, 1971, p. 45). Two themes from previous sections are echoed here. First, drives such as hunger and thirst are mechanisms that motivate behavior. Second, many experiments on peripheral and central interactions in hunger and thirst involve an artificial intervention in the causal chain connecting the external stimulus to the eating/drinking response (see, e.g., Schachter, 1971, Pt. 2). These experiments are thus of little theoretical interest to sociobiology. Many of the experiments reporting hyperphagia after lesions of certain areas of the hypothalamus, for example, may amount to interfering with a central circuit that sets the desired weight of the animal—an interesting conclusion, but nature doesn't evolve lesions.

But some of the experiments used intact subjects; these are good candidates for sociobiological analysis. One hypothesis that crossed my mind after reading Schachter's results (1971, Pt. 2) involves different eating strategies in the face of different expectations about the future. If one's food supply is predictable from day to day, one should carry around a low optimal weight and no more. If one's food supply is not reliably available, then when food is plentiful one should gain weight; when it is scarce one is obliged to lose it again. Many environmental variables would correlate, in a hunter–gatherer environment, with predictability of the food supply. High levels of stress (due, say, to fear or anxiety), signaled physiologically by rising ACTH levels, might cause the hypothalamus to raise the set-point of desired body weight. This would cause a higher conversion rate of food into fat, and a more opportunistic strategy directed toward eating as much as one can when one can get it. Unnecessary exercise should also be avoided.

In a modern environment, these environmental indicators of stressful times to come may have become decoupled from actual fluctuations in food supply. If so, some stressed people would follow an opportunistic eating strategy even in the presence of abundant food reliably available over time. The result would be obesity. Obesity should correlate with low socioeconomic status (which is characterized by unpredictability in breadwinners' income streams [see Weinrich, 1977b]), with emotional states such as depression, and with various social–psychological measures of normlessness, helplessness, and uncertainty about the future. The behavior of obese people should exemplify an energy-conserving strategy: moving about less, selecting more energy-rich food when choices are available, and converting a higher proportion of food ingested to fat.

There are also many differences between drives and emotions, or so it is alleged by Plutchik (1962, pp. 168–169) and Izard (1977, pp. 164–166). My own thoughts here are in conflict. On the one hand, these writers and our language make the distinction, so it is reasonable to hypothesize (although obviously insufficient to prove!) that the distinction is theoretically important. On the other hand, the differences listed strike me as post hoc—They do not follow convincingly from a theoretical discussion that shows why they are important. I have tried to come up with a sociobiological argument that would reveal the importance of the distinction, and failed. Perhaps others will be able to succeed—or to show that the distinction is made solely to reflect a linguistic peculiarity.

In particular, I find Izard's main differentiator to be inadequate: that "drives constitute a motivational system of definitely limited functions—the maintenance of the body and the propagation of the species" (1977, p. 164). Not only does this set up a two-tier system—the base feelings are drives, the higher feelings emotions—but it also is anti-sociobiological. First, sociobiology lives and breathes by showing how the propagation of individual genes is itself the cause of both lower and higher feelings. Second, Izard's differentiator forces a distinction between sex toward heterosexual ends and sex toward homosexual ones. Only the former can propagate the species, it would seem, and so Izard was forced to categorize homosexuality as pathological. In fact, he proposed that fear of the opposite sex could produce homosexuality, an assertion against which there is considerable evidence. Sociobiology, in contrast, analyzes both homosexuality and heterosexuality by observing their effects on reproductive success. Both are suspected to result from natural selection, and no invocation of pathology is required.

RECOMBINATION:
TOWARD A SOCIOBIOLOGICAL
DEFINITION OF EMOTION

In an earlier section I noted that definitions of emotion tend to come after, not before, a theoretical discussion of the properties of emotions. This chapter is no exception. With due humility directed toward future emotion theorists within sociobiology, I would define "emotion" as follows:

An emotion is the result of a conscious or unconscious decision-making process; it results from an external event changing what is adaptive for the individual feeling the emotion to do. It is the internal motivator that creates a readiness to change behavior to increase adaptation. An emotion can be discharged by an act that would (if successful) bring the external world more into line with what would be adaptive for the individual having the emotion. Or it can be dissipated by a further change in the environment, or in internal cognition, that reduces the value of adaptive action.

The emotion is defined to begin at the moment when the external event activates the decision-making process leading to further action—as opposed to the moment when, say, it is recorded in memory. The adjective "external" is necessary to exclude drives such as hunger and thirst, which build up over time and can occur without any external stimulus causing a sudden increase in the food or water requirements of the organism. This word was inserted not because I believe it to be sociobiologically important (for the moment), but to make my definition coincide as much as possible with those of others. The last sentence of the definition is required to permit introspection to reduce the need for behavior: Depression after a friend's death, for example, is often "cured" by introspection and the passage of time. The emotion of grief, however, motivated this introspection.

The definition does allow emotions to be unconscious. If it is adaptive to act so as to conceal one's intentions, one could expect the evolution of unconscious mechanisms of emotion. Also note that the definition includes emotions that are latent, becoming conscious only at certain moments. The love of a parent for a child is always there, but it is felt intensely as love only at critical times when this feeling would correctly motivate behavior.

OFFSPRING: GENITAL PLETHYSMOGRAPHY AND ITS RELEVANCE TO EMOTION THEORY

In an earlier section I argued that emotion research can appear to be incompletely rigorous to scientists used to dealing with "harder" data, and that one way to get around this problem defines a specific emotion in terms of a clear-cut physiological response. I then tried to show that we are far from accomplishing this for most emotions. In this section, I suggest that we are not far from attaining this goal for the emotion of sexual attraction, or sexual arousal.

RELEVANCE AND VALIDITY

Genital plethysmography is a technique now used by many sex researchers to study sexual arousal. A *penile plethysmograph* is essentially a volume-measuring device connected to a small chamber placed over a man's penis (see Freund, Sedláček, & Knob [1965] for a description of the device). In this way the degree of erection, and thus of sexual arousal, is measured directly. A *vaginal plethysmograph* is a probe that reflects and measures light off the vaginal wall (see Geer, Morokoff, & Greenwood [1974] and Hoon, Wincze, & Hoon [1976] for a description and validity studies). This indicates vaginal blood volume, which is the most reliable indicator of women's sexual arousal (Masters & Johnson, 1966, Chapter 6).

This technique has several advantages over self-report techniques, besides the obvious one of somewhat less interference from deliberate falsehood and other higher cognitive interactions (Freund, 1961). First, the male measurement is face-valid, and the female measurement is nearly so (once the fundamental physiology is understood). This makes the enshrinement of the physiological response as "the emotion" (rather than the person's communication of that response) a defensible action. Second, the validity studies show that the measure is almost certainly reflecting a single emotion, at least under the experimental conditions tested. In contrast, pupillometry, galvanic skin response, and other correlates of sexual interest also respond to many nonsexual features of the stimuli. Third, the connection of the emotion of sexual arousal to reproduction makes it likely that the results will be interpretable in a sociobiological framework. What, after all, is the adaptive significance of guilt? The number of links in a causal chain between a feeling of guilt and its effect on reproductive success is large, but at least the direction of the effect must be known to begin to make sense of it. This makes sociobiological interpretation not impossible (see Trivers, 1971), but difficult. In contrast, the number of links between a sexual emotion and a reproductive result is often much smaller; therefore, the uncertainties in a sociobiological interpretation are fewer.

PREVIOUS RESULTS

Penile plethysmography was invented before vaginal plethysmography, so there are few results for women. One set reported by Wincze, Hoon, and Hoon (1977), however, would be of relevance to the peripheral-versus-central controversy. These workers found that increases in vaginal blood volume *preceded* by a few seconds their subjects' increases in sexual arousal (as they indicated it by positioning a lever device).

With penile plethysmography, there are many results of interest—more, it turns out, having to do with homosexuality than with heterosexuality. A series of experiments (summarized in Freund, Langevin, Chamberlayne, Deosoran, & Zajac, 1974) showed that homosexual men do not fear women, either as women or as sexual objects; this argues against the position taken by Izard (1977, p. 179) and others. Moreover, if one defines the term "homosexuality" in terms of emotional response as measured by plethysmography (rather than by a purely behavioral criterion taking into account only the sex of one's partners), then plethysmography can be used to measure objectively the degree of change of sexual preference in therapy. There are two behavior therapists who, having formerly presented verbal-report data indicating some degree of "cure" of homosexual men presenting themselves for treatment, now agree that no change in sexual preference occurred when the men were evaluated plethysmographically (Freund, 1977; McConaghy, 1976). Such findings are of extreme importance to the sociobiology of human reproductive strategy. They would also be of importance to emotion theorists, for they describe patterns of human emotions, validating the previously fuzzy concept of "sexual preference." Other minority sexual preferences show up in plethysmographic records (e.g., transsexualism [Barr & Blaszczynski, 1976] and exhibitionism and others [Abel, Levis, & Clancy, 1970]). Finally, the technique has revealed novel and intriguing facets of heterosexual male responsiveness (for example, that young girls and certain adolescent male body parts can be mildly sexually arousing to "nondeviant" adult heterosexual men [Freund, McKnight, Langevin, & Cibiri, 1972]).

SUGGESTIONS FOR FUTURE WORK

In my opinion, genital plethysmography offers an important opportunity to study objectively an emotion of importance to anyone who has ever fallen in love, and of central theoretical importance to sociobiology to boot. Moreover, aspects of other emotions might be studied with the technique; for example, sexual arousal is probably affected by sadness, fear, joy, and other emotions. Subjects could be placed in a situation designed to elicit one of these, and the subsequent effect on sexual arousal could be measured.[2]

Sociobiologists would also be interested in the plethysmographic investigation of sexual responses in animals. Males in many species have erections when they assert dominance over other males; the relationship between this form and "pure" sexual arousal could be clarified. Moreover, the existence or nonexistence of different sexual preferences in animals could be illuminated. As far as I can tell, only technical problems need to be solved: constraint of the animal, validity studies for each species, and so on.

[2] This possibility was suggested to me after hearing of a pilot experiment performed by Gerald Davison.

RECAPITULATION OF ONTOGENY: CONCLUSIONS

Young sciences are always presumptuous, and sociobiology's presumptions regarding the emotions are characteristic of the discipline.

1. Every emotion should have an evolutionary history, which can be rendered sensible by reference to adaptation; maladaptiveness is an explanation of last resort. Thus, explaining the harmful effects of aggression by mishap and unnatural circumstances must be challenged (though such an explanation might have proven true). Maladaptive explanations of the sexual behavior of sufficiently common (but nonmajority) groups are likewise suspect. And adaptation must figure prominently in any definition of emotion.

2. Adaptation should be produced to roughly equal extents in all animals. Hence, hierarchy between species is eschewed, and limits should be placed on assertions of both the uniqueness and the similarity of humans in relation to other animals. Likewise, the tinge of hierarchy implicit in notions of "base" drives and "higher" emotions should be questioned—but not rejected if a sensible, evolutionarily based rationale for discriminating the two can be devised.

3. Mechanisms should be evaluated first by their effects on behavior (and ultimately reproductive success) in evolutionarily realistic environments. Hence, the definition of emotion should stress behavior, explanations of behavioral effects in humans must be keyed to a hunter–gatherer past, and observations of behavior should occur in natural settings.

4. Above all, the mind–body duality of Western thought must be rejected. For too long, the notion that the mind controls the body has caused observers to presume that natural selection—in humans especially—works only on physical, not mental, structures. Emotions are particularly subtle mental processes. If they motivate behavior, then it cannot be presumed—without the most rigorous proof—that their interaction with natural selection is negligible.

ACKNOWLEDGMENTS

Robert Trivers, whose work and life showed me how to fuse emotion and cognition, has contributed greatly to the ideas expressed in this chapter. Michael Denneny helped me think through some important ideas. Edward O. Wilson kindly permitted me access to the manuscript of a forthcoming book.

REFERENCES

Abel, G. G., Levis, D. J., & Clancy, J. Aversion therapy applied to taped sequences of deviant behavior in exhibitionism and other sexual deviations: A preliminary report. *Journal of Behavior Therapy and Experimental Psychiatry,* 1970, *1,* 59–66.

Alexander, R. D. Evolution, human behavior, and determinism. *Proceedings of the Biennial Meeting of the Philosophy of Science Association*, 1977, 2, 3–21.

Alexander, R. D. Natural selection and social exchange. In R. L. Burgess & T. L. Hudson (eds.), *Social exchange and developing relationships*. New York: Academic Press, 1979, in press.

Barr, R. F., & Blaszczynski, A. Autonomic responses of transsexual and homosexual males to erotic film sequences. *Archives of Sexual Behavior*, 1976, 5, 211–222.

Darwin, C. *The descent of man and selection in relation to sex*. New York: P. F. Collier & Son, 1905. (Originally published, 1871.)

Darwin, C. *The expression of the emotions in man and animals* (2nd authorized ed.). Chicago: University of Chicago Press, 1965. (Originally published, 1872.)

Dawkins, R. *The selfish gene*. New York: Oxford University Press, 1976.

Ekman, P. (ed.) *Darwin and facial expression: A century of research in review*. New York: Academic Press, 1973.

Frenk, H., McCarty, B. C., & Liebeskind, J. C. Different brain areas mediate the analgesic and epileptic properties of enkephalin. *Science*, 1978, 200, 335–336.

Freund, K. W. Laboratory differential diagnosis of homo- and heterosexuality—An experiment with faking. *Review of Czechoslovak Medicine*, 1961, 7, 20–31.

Freund, K. W. Should homosexuality arouse therapeutic concern? *Journal of Homosexuality*, 1977, 2, 235–240.

Freund, K. W., Langevin, R., Chamberlayne, R., Deosoran, A., & Zajac, Y. The phobic theory of male homosexuality. *Archives of Internal Medicine*, 1974, 134, 495–499.

Freund, K. W., McKnight, C. K., Langevin, R., & Cibiri, S. The female child as a surrogate object. *Archives of Sexual Behavior*, 1972, 2, 119–133.

Freund, K. W., Sedláček, F., & Knob, K. A simple transducer for mechanical plethysmography of the male genital. *Journal of the Experimental Analysis of Behavior*, 1965, 8, 169–170.

Geer, J. H., Morokoff, P., & Greenwood, P. Sexual arousal in women: The development of a measurement device for vaginal blood volume. *Archives of Sexual Behavior*, 1974, 3, 559–564.

Griffin, D. R. A possible window on the minds of animals. *American Scientist*, 1976, 64, 530–535. (a)

Griffin, D. R. *The question of animal awareness*. New York: Rockefeller University Press, 1976. (b)

Hoon, P. W., Wincze, J. P., & Hoon, E. F. Physiological assessment of sexual arousal in women. *Psychophysiology*, 1976, 13, 196–204.

Hrdy, S. B. Infanticide as a primate reproductive strategy. *American Scientist*, 1977, 65, 40–49. (a)

Hrdy, S. B. *The langurs of Abu: Female and male strategies of reproduction*. Cambridge, Mass.: Harvard University Press, 1977. (b)

Izard, C. E. *Human emotions*. New York: Plenum, 1977.

James, W. *The principles of psychology*. New York: Henry Holt, 1890.

Kety, S. S., Rosenthal, D., Wender, P. H., Schulsinger, F., & Jacobsen, B. Mental illness in the biological and adoptive families of adoptive individuals who have become schizophrenic: A preliminary report based on psychiatric interviews. In R. R. Fieve, D. Rosenthal, & H. Brill (eds.), *Genetic research in psychiatry*. Baltimore, Md.: Johns Hopkins University Press, 1975.

Kinsey, A. C., Pomeroy, W. B., & Martin, C. E. *Sexual behavior in the human male*. Philadelphia: Saunders, 1948.

Kirsch, J. A. W., & Rodman, J. E. The natural history of homosexuality. *Yale Scientific*, 1977, 51(3), 7–13.

Kluger, M. J. The evolution and adaptive value of fever. *American Scientist*, 1978, 66, 38–43.

Konner, M. J. Adolescent pregnancy. *The New York Times*, (Sept. 24, 1977), Vol. 127, 21.

Lorenz, K. *On aggression*. New York: Harcourt, Brace & World, 1966.

Masters, W. H., & Johnson, V. E. *Human sexual response*. Boston: Little, Brown, 1966.

McConaghy, N. Is a homosexual orientation irreversible? *British Journal of Psychiatry,* 1976, *129,* 556–563.

Plutchik, R. *The emotions: Facts, theories, and a new model.* New York: Random House, 1962.

Plutchik, R. Cognitions in the service of emotions: An evolutionary perspective. In D. K. Candland *et al.* (eds.), *Emotion,* pp. 189–212. Belmont, Calif.: Brooks-Cole, 1977.

Plutchik, R., & Ax, A. F. A critique of *Determinants of emotional state* by Schachter and Singer (1962). *Psychophysiology,* 1967, *4,* 79–82.

Rainwater, L. *And the poor get children: Sex, contraception, and family planning in the working class.* Chicago: Quadrangle, 1960.

Schachter, S. *Emotion, obesity, and crime.* New York: Academic Press, 1971.

Schachter, S., & Singer, J. E. Cognitive, social, and physiological determinants of emotional state. *Psychological Review,* 1962, *69,* 379–399.

Socarides, C. W. Homosexuality. In S. Arieti & E. B. Brody (eds.), *Adult clinical psychiatry,* pp. 291–315. New York: Basic Books, 1974.

Swanson, H. D. *Human reproduction: Biology and social change.* New York: Oxford University Press, 1974.

Trivers, R. L. The evolution of reciprocal altruism. *The Quarterly Review of Biology,* 1971, *46*(4), 35–57.

Trivers, R. L. Parental investment and sexual selection. In B. Campbell (ed.), *Sexual selection and the descent of man 1871–1971,* pp. 136–179. Chicago: Aldine, 1972.

Trivers, R. L. Parent–offspring conflict. *American Zoologist,* 1974, *14,* 249–264.

Weinrich, J. D. Human reproductive strategy: The importance of income unpredictability, and the evolution of non-reproduction (Doctoral dissertation, Harvard University, 1976). *Dissertation Abstracts International,* 1977, *37,* 5339–B. (University Microfilms No. 77–8348.) (a)

Weinrich, J. D. Human sociobiology: Pair-bonding and resource predictability (Effects of social class and race). *Behavioral Ecology and Sociobiology,* 1977, *2,* 91–118. (b)

Wilson, E. O. *Sociobiology: The new synthesis.* Cambridge, Mass.: Harvard University Press, 1975. (a)

Wilson, E. O. Human decency is animal. *The New York Times Magazine,* 12 October 1975, pp. 38–50. (b)

Wilson, E. O. *On human nature.* Cambridge, Mass.: Harvard University Press, 1978.

Wincze, J. P., Hoon, P., & Hoon, E. F. Sexual arousal in women: A comparison of cognitive and physiological responses by continuous measurement. *Archives of Sexual Behavior,* 1977, *6,* 121–133.

Part II

THE PSYCHOPHYSIOLOGICAL CONTEXT

Chapter 6

AFFECT AS AMPLIFICATION: SOME MODIFICATIONS IN THEORY[1]

SILVAN S. TOMKINS

ABSTRACT

Four essential modifications in my affect theory are presented. First, an ambiguity in the concept of affect as amplification has been revised so that the affect is now considered to be an analogic amplifier in much the same manner as pain is an analogic amplifier of the injury it amplifies. Second, I now view the skin of the face as more essential than its musculature in providing the feedback which we experience as motivating. It is shown also that the skin in general is a powerful motivational organ in sex, pain, and sleep. Third, I now view innate affect as essentially suppressed and backed up in the adult, exacting a price whose cost is yet to be precisely determined. The mechanism by which this is achieved is through suppression of vocalization of affect. Fourth, I now view the affect as amplifying not only its activation but also the response to the affect, because it coexists with and thereby imprints its form on whatever *response follows it.*

Some empirical studies of this theory in connection with ideology and smoking behavior are described.

---

[1] The modifications in theory presented here are taken from my forthcoming book, *Affect, imagery, consciousness,* Vol. III. New York: Springer, 1979, in press.

Emotion: Theory, Research, and Experience
Volume 1: Theories of Emotion

INTRODUCTION

It is my view that affects are sets of muscular and glandular responses located in the face and also widely distributed throughout the body, which generate sensory feedback that is either inherently "acceptable" or "unacceptable." These organized sets of responses are triggered at subcortical centers where specific "programs" for each distinct affect are stored. These programs are innately endowed and have been genetically inherited. They are capable, when activated, of simultaneously capturing such widely distributed structures as the face, the heart, and the endocrine glands and imposing on them a specific pattern of correlated responses. One does not learn to be afraid or to cry or to startle, any more than one learns to feel pain or to gasp for air.

In short, I propose that affect is primarily facial behavior. Secondarily it is bodily behavior and outer skeletal and inner visceral behavior. When we become aware of these facial and/or visceral responses, we are aware of our affects. We may respond with these affects, however, without becoming aware of the feedback from them. Finally, we learn to generate, from memory, images of these same responses, which we can become aware of with or without repetition of facial, skeletal, or visceral responses.

The affect system provides the primary blueprints for cognition, decision, and action. Humans are responsive to whatever circumstances activate positive and negative affects. Some of these circumstances innately activate the affects. At the same time, the affect system is also capable of being instigated by learned stimuli and responses. The human being is thus urged by nature and by nurture to explore and to attempt to control the circumstances that evoke his positive and negative affective responses. It is the freedom of the affect system that makes it possible for the human being to begin to implement and to progress toward what he regards as an ideal state—one that, however else he may describe it, implicitly or explicitly entails the maximizing of positive affect and the minimizing of negative affect.

BASIC AFFECTS

If the affects are primarily facial responses, what are the major affects? I have distinguished nine innate affects. The positive affects are as follows: first, *interest* or *excitement,* with eyebrows down and stare fixed or tracking an object; second, *enjoyment* or *joy,* the smiling response; third, *surprise* or *startle,* with eyebrows raised and eyes blinking. The negative affects are the following: first, *distress* or *anguish,* the crying response; second, *fear* or *terror,* with eyes frozen open in fixed stare or moving away from the dreaded object to the side, with skin pale, cold, sweating, and trembling, and with hair erect; third, *shame* or *humiliation,* with eyes and head lowered; fourth, *con-*

tempt, with the upper lip raised in a sneer; fifth, *disgust,*[2] with the lower lip lowered and protruded; sixth, *anger* or *rage,* with a frown, clenched jaw, and red face.

If these are innately patterned responses, are there also innate activators of each affect? Consider the nature of the problem. The innate activators must include the drives as innate activators, but *not* be limited to drives as exclusive activators. The neonate, for example, must respond with innate fear to any difficulty in breathing but must also be afraid of other objects. Each affect had to be capable of being activated by a *variety* of unlearned stimuli. The child must be able to cry at hunger or loud sounds as well as at a diaper pin stuck in his flesh. Each affect had, therefore, to be activated by some general characteristic of neural stimulation, common to both internal and external stimuli, and not too stimulus-specific like a releaser. Next, the activator had to be correlated with biologically useful information. The young child must fear what is dangerous and smile at what is safe. The activator had to "know the address" of the subcortical center at which the appropriate affect program is stored—not unlike the problem of how the ear responds correctly to each tone. Next, some of the activators had to be able not to habituate, whereas others had to be capable of habituation; otherwise a painful stimulus might too soon cease to be distressing and an exciting stimulus never be let go—such as a deer caught by a bright light. These are some of the characteristics that had to be built into the affect mechanism's activation sensitivity. The most economical assumption on which to proceed is to look for communalities among these varieties of characteristics of the innate activators of each affect. This I have done, and I believe it is possible to account for the major phenomena with a few relatively simple assumptions about the general characteristics of the stimuli that innately activate affect.

ACTIVATORS OF AFFECTS

I would account for the differences in affect activation by three general variants of a single principle—the density of neural firing or stimulation. By density, I mean the number of neural firings per unit of time. The theory posits three discrete classes of activators of affect, each of which further amplifies the sources that activate them. These are *stimulation increase, stimulation level,* and *stimulation decrease.* Thus, there is a provision for three distinct classes of motives: affects about stimulation that is on the increase, about stimulation that is on the decrease. With respect to density of neural firing or stimulation, then, the human being is equipped for affective arousal for every major contingency. If internal or external sources of neural firing suddenly increase, he will startle or become afraid, or become in-

[2] Data from the Polarity Scale (Tomkins, 1965) revealed that differential magnification of contempt was correlated with normative ideology and that disgust was correlated with humanistic ideology. Originally, contempt and disgust were treated as variants of a unitary response, thus making for eight affects in the original theory, rather than nine.

terested, depending on the suddenness of the increase in stimulation. If internal or external sources of neural firing reach and maintain a high, constant level of stimulation, which deviates in excess of an optimal level of neural firing, he will respond with anger or distress, depending on the level of stimulation. If internal or external sources of neural firing suddenly decrease, he will laugh or smile with enjoyment, depending on the suddenness of the decrease in stimulation.

The general advantage of affective arousal to such a broad spectrum of levels and changes of level of neural firing is to make the individual care about quite different states of affairs in different ways. It should be noted that, according to my views, there are both positive and negative affects (startle, fear, interest) activated by stimulation increase, but only negative affects are activated by a continuing unrelieved level of stimulation (distress, anger), and only positive affects are activated by stimulation decrease (laughter, joy). This latter, in my theory, is the only remnant of the tension reduction theory of reinforcement. Stimulation increase may, in my view, result in punishing or rewarding affect, depending on whether it is a more or less steep gradient and therefore activates fear or interest. A constantly maintained high level of neural stimulation is invariably punishing inasmuch as it activates the cry of distress or anger, depending on how high above optimal levels of stimulation the particular density of neural firing is. A suddenly reduced density of stimulation is invariably rewarding, whether, it should be noted, the stimulation that is reduced is itself positive or negative in quality. Stated another way, such a set of mechanisms guarantees sensitivity to whatever is new, to whatever continues for any extended period of time, and to whatever is ceasing to happen. In Figure 6.1 I have graphically represented this theory.

Thus, any stimulus with a relatively sudden onset and a steep increase in rate of neural firing will innately activate a startle response. As shown also in Figure 6.1, if the rate of neural firing increases less rapidly, fear is activated, and, if the rate increases still less rapidly, interest is innately activated. In contrast, any sustained increase in the level of neural firing, as with a continuing loud noise, would innately activate the cry of distress. If it were sustained and still louder, it would innately activate the anger response. Finally, any sudden decrease in stimulation that reduced the rate of neural firing, as in the sudden

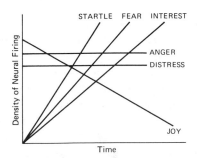

FIGURE 6.1. Graphical representation of a theory of innate activators of affect.

reduction of excessive noise, would innately activate the rewarding smile of enjoyment.

APPRAISAL OF AFFECT

Such a neural theory must be able to account for how the "meaning" in such neural messages operates without the benefit of a homunculus who "appraises" every message before instructing the individual to become interested or afraid. It is clear that any theory of affect activation must be capable of accounting for affect that is triggered in either an unlearned or a learned fashion. Certainly the infant who emits his birth cry upon exit from the birth canal has not "appraised" the new environment as a vale of tears before he cries. Equally certain he will later learn to cry to communications telling of the death of a beloved person and this does depend on meaning and its appraisal. It is my view that theories that postulate such appraisal as a necessary condition for affect activation are more embarrassed by unlearned activation than is a general neural theory embarrassed by learned activators. I would argue that learned information *can* activate affects *only* through the general neural profiles I have postulated. Thus, the novelty of information adequate to trigger interest and the final laughter to a new joke depends on the rate of acceleration of information in the first case and in the rate of deceleration in the second case. If we hear the same information a second time, there is a sense in which it may be appraised as essentially a repetition, but, because we now see it coming, there is neither interest nor enjoyment because the gradients of neural firing are now much flatter, because compressed, than when the information was first received. Similarly with the startle response, a pistol shot is adequate as an unlearned activator, but so is the sudden appearance of a man with two heads. In such a case I would suggest that the rate of neural firing from the conjoint muscular responses of the double-take and the very rapid recruitment of information from memory to check the nature of the apparent message also have the requisite square wave profile of neural firing called for in my model. In short, "meaning" operates through the very general profiles of acceleration, deceleration, or level of neural firing as these are produced by either cognitive, memorial, perceptual, or motor responses. Any such responses singly or in concert can through their correlation between meaning and the profiles of neural firing "innately" fire innate affect programs by stimuli or responses that are themselves learned.

AFFECT AS AMPLIFICATION:
A REFINEMENT

The theory of affect first presented to the XIVth International Congress of Psychology in Montreal in 1954 (Tomkins, 1955), and later expanded in the book, *Affect, imagery, consciousness* (Tomkins, 1962), has since been modified in four essential ways. First, the theory of affect as amplification I now specify as analogic amplification. Second, I believe now that it is the skin of the face, rather than its musculature, that is the major mechanism of analogic amplification. Third, a substantial quantity of the affect we experience as adults is pseudo, backed-up affect. Fourth, affect amplifies not only its own activator, but also the response both to that activator and to itself.

I view affect as the primary innate biological motivating mechanism, more urgent than drive deprivation and pleasure and more urgent even than physical pain. That this is so is not obvious, but it is readily demonstrated. Consider that almost any interference with breathing will immediately arouse the most desperate gasping for breath. Consider the drivenness of the tumescent, erect male. Consider the urgency of desperate hunger. These are the intractable driven states that prompted the answer to the question "What do human beings really want?" [to be] "The human animal is driven to breathe, to sex, to drink, and to eat." And yet this apparent urgency proves to be an illusion. It is *not* an illusion that one must have air, water, and food to maintain oneself and sex to reproduce oneself. What *is* illusory is the biological and psychological source of the apparent urgency of the desperate quality of the hunger, air, and sex drives. Consider these drive states more closely. When someone puts his hand over my mouth and nose, I become terrified. But this panic, this terror, is in no way a part of the drive mechanism. I can be terrified at the possibility of losing my job, or of developing cancer, or at the possibility of the loss of my beloved. Fear or terror is an innate affect that can be triggered by a wide variety of circumstances. Not having enough air to breathe is one of many such circumstances. But if the rate of anoxic deprivation becomes slower, as, for example, in the case of wartime pilots who refused to wear oxygen masks at 30,000 feet, then there develops not a panic, but a euphoric state—some of these men met their deaths with smiles on their lips. The smile is the affect of enjoyment, in no way specific to slow anoxic deprivation.

Consider more closely the tumescent male with an erection. He is sexually excited, we say. He is indeed excited, but no one has ever observed an excited penis. It is a man who is excited and who breathes hard, not in the penis, but in the chest, the face, and the nose and nostrils. But such excitement is in no way peculiarly sexual. The same excitement can be experienced, without the benefit of an erection, to mathematics—beauty bare—to poetry, and to a rise in the stock market. Instead of these representing sublimations of sexuality, it is rather that sexuality, in order to become possible, must borrow its potency from the affect of excitement. The drive must be assisted by affect as an *amplifier* if it is to work at all. Freud knew, better than anyone else, that the blind, pushy, imperious id was the most fragile of impulses readily disrupted by fear, by shame, by rage, by boredom. At the first sign of affect *other* than excitement, there is impotence and frigidity. The penis proves to be a paper tiger in the absence of appropriate affective amplification.

The affect system is therefore the primary motivational system because, without its amplification, nothing else matters and, with its amplification, anything else *can* matter. It thus combines *urgency* and *generality*. It lends its power to memory, to perception, to thought, and to action no less than to the drives.

This theory of affect as amplification was flawed by a serious ambiguity. I had unwittingly assumed a similarity between electronic amplification and affective amplification such that in both there was an increase in gain of the signal. If such were the case, what was amplified would remain essentially the same except that it would become louder. But affects are separate mechanisms, involving bodily responses quite distinct from the other bodily responses they are presumed to amplify.

How can one response of our body amplify another response? It does this by being similar to that response—but also different. It is an analog amplifier. The affect mechanism is like the pain mechanism in this respect. If we cut our hand, saw it bleeding, but had no innate pain receptors, we would know we had done something that needed repair, but there would be no urgency to it. Like our automobile that needs a tune-up, we might well let it go until next week when we had more time. But the pain mechanism, like the affect mechanism, so amplifies our awareness of the injury that activates it that we are forced to be concerned, and concerned immediately. The biological utility of such analogic amplification is self-evident. The injury, as such, in the absence of pain, simply does not hurt. The pain receptors have evolved to make us hurt and care about injury and disease. Pain is an analog of injury in its inherent similarity. Contrast pain with an orgasm, as a possible analog. If, instead of pain, we always had an orgasm to injury, we would be biologically destined to bleed to death. Affect receptors are no less compelling. Our hair stands on end and we sweat in terror. Our face reddens as our blood pressure rises in anger. Our blood vessels dilate and our face becomes pleasantly warm as we smile in enjoyment. These are compelling analogs of what arouses terror, rage, and enjoyment. These experiences constitute one form of affect amplification.

A second form of affect amplification occurs also by virtue of the similarity of their profile, in time, to their activating trigger. Just as a pistol shot is a stimulus that is very sudden in onset, very brief in duration, and equally sudden in decay—so its amplifying affective analog, the startle response, mimics the pistol shot by being equally sudden in onset, brief in duration, and equally sudden in decay. Therefore, affect, by being analogous in the quality of the feelings from its specific receptors, as well as in its profile of activation, maintenance, and decay, amplifies and extends the duration and impact of whatever triggers the affect. Epileptics do not startle (Landis & Hunt, 1939). They experience a pistol shot as sudden but *not* startling. A world experienced without any affect would be a pallid, meaningless world. We would know *that* things happened, but we would not care whether they did or not.

By being immediately activated and thereby co-assembled with its activator, affect either makes good things better or bad things worse by conjointly simulating its activator in its profile of neural firing and by adding a special analogic quality that is intensely rewarding or punishing. In illustrating the simulation of an activating stimulus, for example, a pistol shot by the startle response which was equally sudden in onset, equally brief in duration, and equally sudden in decay, I somewhat exaggerated the goodness of fit between activator and affect to better illustrate the general principle. Having done so, let me now be more precise in the characterization of the degree of similarity in profile of neural firing between activator and affect activated.

Increase, decrease, and level of neural firing are in my model as the sufficient conditions for activating specific affects. Analogic amplification, therefore, is based on *one* of these three distinctive features rather than all of them. It so happens that the startle response simulates the steepness of gradient of onset, the brief plateau of maintenance, and the equally steep gradient of decline of profile of the pistol shot and its internal neural correlate—but this is not the general case. Analogic simulation is based on the similarity to the adequate activator—not on all of its characteristics. Thus, it is only the decay of a stimulus that is simulated in enjoyment. If one places electrodes on the wrist of a subject, permits fear to build, and then removes the electrodes suddenly, invariably a smile of relief will be activated at the moment the electrodes are removed. This amplifies (or makes more so) the declining neural stimulation from the reduction of fear. Therefore, enjoyment amplifies by simulating decreasing gradients of neural stimulation. Interest, fear, and surprise amplify by simulating increasing gradients of neural stimulation. Distress and anger amplify by simulating maintained level of stimulation.

The second modification in my theory concerns the exact loci of the rewarding and punishing amplifying analogs. From the start, I emphasized the face and voice as the major loci of the critical feedback that was experienced as affect. The voice I still regard as a major locus and will discuss its role in the next section. The face now appears to me still the central site of affect responses and their feedback, but I have now come to regard the skin in general, and the skin of the face in particular, as of the greatest importance in producing the feel of affect. My original observations of the intensity of infantile affect, of how an infant was, for example, seized by his own crying, left no doubt in my mind that what the face was doing with its muscles and blood vessels, as well as with its accompanying vocalization, was at the heart of the matter. This seemed to me not an "expression" of anything else but rather the major phenomenon. I then spent a few years in posing professional actors and others to simulate facial affect. McCarter and I (Tomkins & Mc-Carter, 1964) were rewarded by a correlation of .86 between the judgments of untrained judges as to what affects they saw on the faces of these subjects as presented in still photographs and what I had intended these sets of muscular responses to represent. This success was gratifying, after so many years of indifferent and variable findings in this field, but it was also somewhat misleading in overemphasizing the role of innately patterned facial muscular responses in the production of affect. I was further confirmed in these somewhat misleading results by the successes of Paul Ekman and Carroll Izard. Ekman, Sorenson, and Friesen (1969), using some of my photographs, were able to demonstrate a wide cultural consensus, even in very primitive and remote societies. Izard (1969), using different photographs but the same conceptual scheme, further extended these impressive results to many other societies.

The combined weight of all of these investigations was most impressive, but I continued to be troubled by one small fact. The contraction of no other set of muscles in the body had *any* apparent motivational properties. Thus, if I were angry, I might clench my fist and hit someone, but if I simply clenched my fist, this would in no way guarantee I would become angry. Muscles appeared to be specialized for action and not for affect. Why then was the smile so easily and so universally responded to as an affect? Why did someone who was crying seem so distressed and so unhappy? Furthermore, from an evolutionary point of view, we know that different functions are piled indiscriminately on top of structures that may originally have evolved to support quite different functions. The tongue was an organ of eating before it was an organ of speech. The muscles of the face were also probably involved in eating before they were used as vehicles of affect—though we do not know this for a fact. It is, of course, possible that the complex affect displays on the human face evolved primarily as communication mechanisms rather than as sources of motivating feedback. My intuition was, and still is, that the communication of affect is a secondary spin-off function rather than the primary function of facial displays. This would appear to have been the case with a closely related mechanism—that of pain. The cry of pain does communicate, but the feeling of pain does not. It powerfully motivates the person who feels it, in much the same way that affect does. That someone else is informed of this is not, however, mediated by the pain receptors themselves, but by the cry of distress that usually accompanies it. Therefore, I began to look at affect analogs such as pain, sexual sensitivity, and fatigue for clues about the nature of the motivating properties of the affect mechanisms.

THE SKIN: A CENTRAL VARIABLE FOR AFFECT

I soon became aware of a paradox: Three of the most compelling states to which the human being is vulnerable arise on the surface of the skin. Torture via skin stimulation has been used for centuries to shape and compel human beings to act against their own deepest wishes and values. Sexual seduction, again via skin stimulation, particularly of the genitals, has also prompted human beings on occasion to violate their own wishes and values. Finally, fatigue to the point of extreme sleepiness appears to be localized in the skin surrounding the eyes. This area will sometimes be rubbed in an effort to change the ongoing stimulation and ward off sleepiness. But, in the end, it appears to be nothing but an altered responsiveness of skin receptors, especially in the eyelids, which make it impossible for the sleepy person to maintain the state of wakefulness. He cannot keep his eyes open, though he may be powerfully motivated to do so.

I then found further evidence that the skin of diving animals, rather than "expressing" internal events, did lead and command widespread autonomic changes throughout the body in order to conserve oxygen for the vulnerable brain. When the beak of a diving bird is stimulated by the water as it dives for fish, this change produces profound general changes such as vasoconstriction within the body as a whole. Investigators somewhat accidentally discovered that similar changes can occur in a human by putting the human's face in water (without total immersion of the body). I then examined (at the suggestion of Julian Jaynes) the work of Beach and Levinson (1950) on the sexual mechanism in rats. These investigators, examining the structure of the penis under a microscope, found that sensitive hair receptors of the skin of the penis were encased between what resembled the interstices of a cogwheel when the penis was flaccid. When there was a blood flow that engorged the penis, the skin was stretched smooth and the hairs of the receptors were no longer encased but were exposed, and their exquisite sensitivity changed the animal from being in a state of sexual quiescence to one totally sexually aroused. The relevance of such a mechanism for an understanding of the affect mechanism now seemed very clear. It had been known for centuries that, when an individual was angry, the face became red and engorged with blood. It had been known that in terror the hair stood on end and the skin became white and cold with sweat. It had long been known that in enjoyment the blood vessels dilated and the skin felt warm and relaxed. The face as penis would be relatively insensitive in its flaccid condition, its specific receptors hidden, encased within surrounding skin. When, however, there were massive shifts in blood flow and in temperature, changes in the positioning of receptors would be expected, and, pursuing the analogy to its end, the patterned changes in facial muscle responses would serve as self-masturbatory stimulation to the skin and its own sensitized receptors. The feedback of this set of changes would provide the feel of specific affects. Although autonomic changes would be involved, the primary locus would now be seen to be in specific receptors, some as yet to be discovered. Changes in hotness, coldness, and warmth would undoubtedly be involved, but there may well be other, as yet unknown, specific receptors that yield varieties of experience peculiar to the affect mechanism. This suggests that thermography would be one major avenue of investigation for understanding affect. I pursued this possibility in the late 1960s and was disappointed at the relative inertia of the temperature of the skin. However, it may be that advances in the state of the art in recent years may permit a more subtle mapping of the relationships between changes in skin temperature and affect. One implication of such a shift in theory is that the feedback of voluntarily simulated facial muscle responses is not an adequate test of the workings of the innate affect mechanism.

The third modification of the theory concerns the role of breathing and the vocalization of affect. I have not changed my opinion that each affect has as part of its innate program a specific cry or vocalization, subserved by specific patterns of breathing. It is, rather, one of the implications of this theory that took me some years to understand. The major implication that I now understand concerns the universal confusion of the experience of backed-up affect with that of biologically and psychologically authentic innate affect. An analog may help in illustrating what is at issue. Let us suppose that all over the world human beings were forbidden to exhale air but were permitted and even encouraged to inhale air, so that everyone held their breaths to the point of cyanosis and death. Biologists who studied such a phenomenon (who had also been socialized to hold their breath) would have had to conclude that the breathing mechanism represented an evolutionary monstrosity devoid of any utility.

Something similar to this has, in fact, happened to the affect mechanism. Because the free expression of innate affect is extremely contagious and because these are very high-powered phenomena, all societies, in varying degrees, exercise substantial control over the unfettered expression of affect, particularly over the free expression of the cry of affect. No society encourages or permits each individual to cry out in rage, excitement, distress, or terror whenever and wherever he or she wishes. Very early on, strict control over affect expression is instituted and such control is exerted particularly over the voice in general, whether used in speech or in direct affect expression. Although there are large variations between societies, and between different classes within societies, complete unconditional freedom of affect vocalization is quite exceptional. One of the most powerful effects of alcohol is the lifting of such control so that wherever alcohol is taken by large numbers of individuals in public places there is a typical raising of the noise level of the intoxicated, accompanying a general loosening of affect control.

There are significant differences in how much control is exerted over voice and affect from society to society, and Lomax (1968) has shown a significant correlation between the degree of tightness and closure of the vocal box as revealed in song and the degree of hierarchical social control in the society. It appears that more permissive societies also produce voice and song in which the throat is characteristically more relaxed and open. If all societies, in varying degrees, suppress the free vocalization of affect, what is it that is being experienced as affect? It is what I have called pseudo, or backed-up, affect. It can be seen in children who are trying to suppress laughter by swallowing a snicker, or in a stiff upper lip when trying not to cry, or in tightening the jaw when trying not to cry out in anger. In all of these cases, one is truly holding one's breath as part of the technique of suppressing the vocalization of affect. Although this is not severe enough to produce cyanosis, we do not, in fact, know what are the biological and psychological prices of such suppression of the innate affective response. I would suggest that much of what is called "stress" is indeed backed-up affect and that many of the endocrine changes reported by Frankenhaeuser (1979) are the consequence as much of backed-up affect as of affect per se.

It seems at the very least that substantial psychosomatic disease might be one of the prices of such systematic suppression and transformation of the innate affective responses. Furthermore, there could be a permanent elevation of blood pressure as a consequence of suppressed rage, which would have a much longer duration than an innate momentary flash of expressed anger. In 1941, French and his co-workers from the Chicago psychoanalytic group found some evidence for the suppressed cry of distress in psychosomatic asthma. The psychological consequences of such suppression would depend on the severity of the suppression. I have spelled out some of these consequences elsewhere (Tomkins, 1971, 1975). Even the least severe suppression of the vocalization of affect must result in some bleaching of the experience of affect and, therefore, some impoverishment of the quality of life. It must also produce some ambiguity about what affect feels like, since so much of the adult's affective life represents at the very least a transformation of the affective response rather than the simpler, more direct, and briefer innate affect. Such confusion, moreover, occurs even among theorists and investigators of affects, myself included.[3]

The appearances of the backed-up, the simulated, and the innate are by no means the same. While this may be generally recognized, so that typically we know when someone is controlling an affect or showing a pretended affect, with anger the matter is quite confused. Because of the danger represented by this affect and the consequent enormous societal concern about the socialization of anger, what is typically seen, and thought to be the innate, is actually the backed-up anger. Finally, it is on the discontinuity of vocalization of affect that the therapeutic power of primal screaming rests. One can uncover repressed affect by encouraging vocalization of affect, especially when the suppression of vocalization has been severe.

---

[3] By this reasoning, the finding that observers across cultures will agree in identifying affect from facial expression does not tell us whether the faces depicted innate or backed-up affect or whether observers recognized the difference between the two. In these studies, both controlled and innate responses were used as stimuli, but observers were not questioned about the difference between the two. It is my prediction that such an investigation will show a universal confusion, only in regard to anger, in which backed-up anger would be perceived as innate, and innate anger would not be recognized as such.

AFFECT AS AMPLIFIER OF RESPONSE

Although I have maintained for several years that affect has the function of amplifying its activator, I have been equally insistent that it does not influence the response to the activator or to itself. I portrayed the infant who was hungry as also distressed but in no way thereby pushed in one direction or another in behavioral response to its hunger and distress. I was concerned to preserve the independence of the response from its affective precursor. It seemed to me that to postulate a tight causal nexus between the affect and the response that followed would have been to limit severely the apparent degrees of freedom that the human being appears to enjoy and to have come dangerously close to reducing both affect and the human being to the level of tropism or instinct. It seems to me now that my concern was somewhat phobic and thereby resulted in my overlooking a powerful connection between stimulus, affect, and response. I now believe that the affect connects both its own activator and the response that follows by imprinting the latter with the same amplification it exerts on its own activator. Thus, a response prompted by enjoyment will be a slow, relaxed response, in contrast to a response prompted by anger, which will reflect the increased neural firing characteristic of both the activator of anger and the anger response itself. What we therefore inherit in the affect mechanism is not only an amplifier of its activator, but also an amplifier of the response that it evokes. Such a connection is in no way learned, arising as it does simply from the overlap in time of the affect with what precedes and follows it.

It should be noted that by the response to affect I do not intend any restriction to observable motor responses. The response may be in terms of retrieved memories or in constructed thoughts, which might vary in acceleration if amplified by fear or interest or in quantity if amplified by distress or anger, or in deceleration of rate of information processing if amplified by enjoyment. Thus, in some acute schizophrenic panics, the individual is bombarded by a rapidly accelerating rush of ideas that resist ordering and organization. Such individuals will try to write down these ideas as an attempt to order them, saying upon being questioned that if they could separate and clarify all of these too fast, overwhelming ideas they could cure themselves. Responses to the blank card in the Thematic Aperception Test (TAT) by such schizophrenics imagine a hero who is trying to put half of his ideas on one half of the card and the other half on the other side of an imaginary line dividing the card into two.

The great German philosopher Immanuel Kant likened the human mind to a glass that imprinted its shape on whatever liquid was poured into the glass. Thus, space, time, and causality, he thought, were constructions of the human mind imposing the categories of pure reason on the outside thing-in-itself, whose ultimate nature necessarily forever escaped us. I am suggesting that he neglected a major filtering mechanism, the innate affects, which necessarily color our every experience of the world, not only constituting a special categorization of every experience but producing a unique set of categorical imperatives that amplify not only what precedes and activates each affect but also the further *responses* that are prompted by affects.

RESEARCH AND CLINICAL IMPLICATIONS

I have been concerned for some time with a field I have called the psychology of knowledge, an analog of the sociology of knowledge. It is a concern with the varieties of cognitive styles, with the types of evidence that the individual finds persuasive, and most particularly with his ideology. I have defined ideology as any organized set of ideas about which humans are at once most articulate, ideas that produce enduring controversy over long periods of time and that evoke passionate partisanship, and about which humans are least certain because there is insufficient evidence. Ideology therefore abounds at the frontier of any science. But today's ideology may tomorrow be confirmed or disconfirmed and so cease to be ideology. In a review of 2 thousand years of ideological controversy in western civilization, I have detected a sustained recurrent polarity between the humanistic and normative orientations appearing in such diverse domains as the foundations of mathematics, the theory of aesthetics, political theory, epistemology, theory of perception, theory of value, theory of child rearing, theory of psychotherapy, and personality testing.

The issues are simple enough. Is man the measure, an end in himself, an active, creative, thinking, desiring, loving force in nature? Or must man realize himself, attain his full stature, only through struggle toward, participation in, and conformity to a norm, a measure, an ideal essence basically prior to and independent of man? This polarity appeared first in Greek philosophy between Protagoras and Plato. Western thought has been an elaborate series of footnotes to the conflict between the conceptions of man as the measure of reality and value versus man and nature as alike unreal and valueless in comparison to the realm of essence that exists independently of space and time. More simply, this polarity represents an idealization of man—a positive idealization in the humanistic ideology and a negative idealization in the normative ideology. Human beings, in Western civilization, have tended toward self-celebration, positive or negative. In Oriental thought another alternative is represented, that of harmony between man and nature.

I have further assumed that the individual resonates to any organized ideology because of an underlying ideo-affective posture, which is a set of feelings and ideas about feelings that is more *loosely* organized than any highly organized ideology.

Some insight into these ideological concepts held by an individual may be obtained through use of my *Polarity Scale*. The polarity scale assesses the individual's normative or humanistic position on a broad spectrum of ideological issues in mathematics, science, art, education, politics, child rearing, and theory of personality. Following are a few sample items from the scale. The normative position will be A, the humanistic B. The individual is permitted four choices—A, B, A and B, and neither A nor B.

1. A. Numbers were discovered.   B. Numbers were invented.
2. A. Play is childish.   B. Nobody is too old to play.
3. A. The mind is like a mirror.   B. The mind is like a lamp.
4. A. To see an adult cry is   B. To see an adult cry is pathetic.
        disgusting.
5. A. If you have had a bad   B. If you have had a bad experience
        experience with someone,   with someone, the way to
        the way to characterize   characterize this is that it leaves
        this is that it leaves a bad   a bad taste in the mouth.
        smell.

I have assumed that the ideo-affective posture is the result of systematic differences in the socialization of affects. For example, the attitudes toward distress in the items above could be a consequence of the following differences in distress socialization. When the infant or child cries, the parent, following his own ideo-affective posture and more articulate ideology, may elect to convert the distress of the child into a rewarding scene by putting his arms around the child and comforting him. He may, however, amplify the punishment inherent in the distress response by putting himself into opposition to the child and his distress. He will require that the child stop crying, insisting that the child's crying results from some norm violation and threatening to increase his suffering if he does not suppress the response. "If you don't stop crying, I will give you something to really cry about." *If* the child internalizes his parent's ideo-affective posture and his ideology, he has learned a very basic posture toward suffering, which will have important consequences for resonance to ideological beliefs quite remote from the nursery and the home. This is exemplified by the following items from the polarity scale: "The maintenance of law and order is the most important duty of any government" versus "Promotion of the welfare of the people is the most important function of a government."

The significance of the socialization of distress is amplified by differential socialization of all the affects, including surprise, enjoyment, excitement, anger, fear, shame, contempt, and disgust. I have outlined elsewhere a systematic program of differential socialization of each of these affects which together produce an ideo-affective posture that inclines the individual to resonate differentially to ideology (Tomkins, 1979). In the preceding example, excitement and enjoyment are implicated along with distress, anger, shame, fear, contempt, and disgust as it is the relative importance of the reward of positive affects versus the importance of the punishment of negative affects that is involved in law and order versus welfare.

What is less obvious is that similar differences in ideo-affective posture influence such remote ideological options as the following items from the polarity scale: "Numbers were invented." versus "Numbers were discovered."; "The mind is like a lamp which illuminates whatever it shines on." versus "The mind is like a mirror which reflects whatever strikes it."; "Reason is the chief means by which human beings make great discoveries." versus "Reason has to be continually disciplined and corrected by reality and hard facts."; "Human beings are basically good." versus "Human beings are basically evil." The structure of ideology and the relationships between the socialization of affects, the ideo-affective postures, and ideology are more complex than can be discussed here. I wish to present just enough of this theory to enable the reader to understand the relationship of the theory to the face.

IDEO–AFFECTIVE IDEOLOGY AND THE FACE

I have assumed that the humanistic position is one that attempts to maximize positive affect for the individual and for all of his interpersonal relationships. In contrast, the normative position is that norm compliance is the primary value and that positive affect is a *consequence* of norm compliance but not to be directly sought as a goal. Indeed, the suffering of negative affect is assumed to be a frequent experience and an inevitable consequence of the human condition. Therefore, in any interpersonal transaction, the humanist self consciously strives to maximize positive affect insofar as it is possible.

The first hypothesis concerning the face is that humanists will smile more frequently than the normatively oriented, both because they have experienced the smile of enjoyment more frequently during their socialization and because they have internalized the ideo-affective posture that one should attempt to increase positive affect for the other as well as the self. The learned smile does not always mean that the individual *feels* happy. As often as not, it is a consequence of a wish to communicate to the other that one wishes him to feel smiled upon and to evoke the smile from the other. It is often the oil that is spread over troubled human waters to extinguish the fires of distress, hate, and shame. It was known from previous investigations with the stereoscope (Tomkins, 1975) that if one presented humanists and normatives with two pictures of the same face (one of which was smiling and one of which was not) the humanists tended to suppress the nonsmiling face significantly more often than did the normatives. Vasquez (1975) has recently confirmed that humanist subjects actually smile more frequently while talking with an experimenter than do normative subjects. There is, however, no such difference when subjects are alone, displaying affect spontaneously.

The second hypothesis was that humanists would respond more frequently with distress and normatives would respond more frequently with anger. The rationale for this was that when an interpersonal relationship is troubled the humanist will try to absorb as much punishment as possible and so display distress rather than anger—anger is more likely to escalate into conflict being a more blaming extrapunitive response than distress. It was assumed that the normative subject will more frequently respond with anger because he or she is more extrapunitive, more pious and blaming, and less concerned with sparing the feelings of the other, as his or her internalized models did not spare his or her feelings. This hypothesis was *not* confirmed, but neither was it reversed. This failure may have arisen because the differences in polarity scale scores were not as great as I would have wished. In part, this was a consequence of a strong humanistic bias among college students at the time of testing and because of the reluctance of known normatives to volunteer for testing (e.g., very few subjects from the American Legion would cooperate with Vasquez). This is consistent with prior research, including my own, which indicates that volunteers are more sociophilic and friendly.

The third hypothesis was that humanists would more frequently respond with shame and that normatives would respond less frequently with shame but more frequently with disgust and contempt. The rationale was that shame represents an impunitive response to what is interpreted as an interruption to communion (as, e.g., in shyness) and that it will ultimately be replaced by full communication.

In contrast, contempt and disgust are responses to a bad other and the termination of intimacy with such a one is assumed to be permanent unless the other one changes significantly. These hypotheses were confirmed for shame and disgust but not for contempt. Humanistic subjects, while displaying affect spontaneously, did respond more frequently with shame responses than did normative subjects, whereas normative subjects displayed significantly more disgust responses than did humanistic subjects. Biologically, disgust and contempt are drive auxiliary responses that have evolved to protect the human being from coming too close to noxious-smelling objects and to regurgitate these if they have been ingested. Through learning, these responses have come to be emitted to biologically neutral stimuli, including, for example, disgusting and dirty thoughts. Shame, in contrast, is an affect auxiliary to the affect of interest–excitement. Any perceived barrier to positive affect with the other will evoke lowering of the eyelids and loss of tonus in the face and neck muscles, producing the head hung in shame. The child who is burning with excitement to explore the face of the stranger is nonetheless vulnerable to shame just because the other is perceived as strange. Characteristically, however, intimacy with the good and exciting other is eventually consummated. In contrast, the disgusting other is to be kept at a safe distance permanently. In conclusion, it was predicted and confirmed that humanistic subjects respond more frequently with smiling to the good other and with shame if there is any perceived barrier to intimacy. The normative subjects smile less frequently to the other and emit disgust more frequently to the other who is tested and found wanting. The differences represent a correlation between cognition and affect as affect is displayed on the faces of those who differ significantly in what they believe about the world they live in.

I have recently studied more systematically the TAT stories of subjects whose faces were being videotaped as they told their stories. My interest here was the extent to which the structure of the fantasy reflects the sequence of affects on the face. These investigations have only just begun and it is too early to know how successful this attempt will be. It appears that there will be substantial correspondence between the face and *some* of the major themes of the TAT stories. For example, one subject's face was characterized by a disgust response followed by a forced (somewhat reluctant) smile, followed by a biting of her lips. I interpreted this to mean that she found her social environment somewhat repellent, but tried to conform to it reluctantly and then hated herself for her own overconformity. To Card 1 on the TAT she told the following story: "This boy is thinking about playing the violin [the boy's face shows a disgust response]. He doesn't want to do it but as long as he's in this situation, he wants to do well on this lesson. He says, 'Come on violin—let's get together' [at which the subject smiles]. But it doesn't work too well [then the subject bites her lips]." There follow several other stories in which the heroine reluctantly puts up with her uncongenial environment but to the enduring satisfaction of none.

I have also recently been studying the faces of cigarette smokers. I have delineated several types of satisfaction in smoking, ranging from the pure enjoyment of the positive-affect smoker through the varieties of negative-affect smokers who use the cigarette primarily as a sedative to cope with their negative affect, more or less effectively, to the addictive smoker who uses cigarettes primarily to reduce his intolerable craving for a cigarette rather than using the cigarette to cope with negative affect from other sources. Each of these types of dependences is systematically related to ease of cessation on the one hand and to ease of maintenance of cessation on the other.

The purely positive-affect smoker renounces smoking most easily and backslides least of all smokers. He maintains his decision with fewest regrets. The paradox here is that the individual who enjoys smoking the most gives it up permanently most easily. In part, this is because he has numerous alternative sources of positive affect so that the renunciation of smoking evokes some regret, but he is able to renounce it when he becomes aware of its newly discovered hazard to his health.

The negative-affect smoker gives up smoking with more difficulty. He can usually do this if his life goes very well, if he is on vacation, or if enforced illness makes it impossible for him to smoke. His main problem, however, is the maintenance of his decision to cease smoking. He goes back to smoking readily when the burden of negative affect becomes too great. He usually reassures himself that this is no great source of regret since he can and has, again and again, given up smoking whenever he decides he should. His ability to re-nounce smoking is proportional to how much the cigarette really helps him to reduce his negative affect. Paradoxically, the less effective the cigarette is in sedating his negative affect the more difficult it proves to renounce and the more readily he backslides. Similar to the case with the positive-affect smoker, the negative-affect smoker is more in control of the situation the more help he gets from cigarettes in actually reducing his negative affect. This, in turn, ap-pears to depend on the density or quantity of negative affect over time that he normally experiences. As the density of negative affect increases, the fre-quency of smoking increases as it succeeds less and less in sedating his negative affect.

The addictive smoker is, of course, least able to renounce smoking. The cigarette is in fact least helpful to him. His quantity of experienced negative affect is so great that he has taught himself to panic lest he not have cigarettes available. It is not unlike an individual who has learned that aspirin can reduce his headaches and who eventually teaches himself to have a headache just because there is no aspirin available. The addict renounces cigarettes with the greatest difficulty. However, after his period of mourning and trial by fire, he backslides *less* frequently than the negative-affect smoker because he knows that if he takes a cigarette he must again suffer the severe symptoms of psychological withdrawal.

The preferred methods of therapy for these three conditions are systematically different. For the positive-affect smokers, methods based on rationality and persuasion are effective. For negative-affect smokers, support is the method of choice. The buddy system or group therapy works reasonably well. For the addictive smoker, only a heroic method appears effective. These range from cold turkey through conversion experiences following a heart at-tack or the death of a parent from lung cancer. It is my assumption that this provides a general model for psychotherapy. I have proposed that the critical determinant of what is required to produce change in the individual depends on the overall ratio of the relative density of positive to negative affect. Methods ranging from persuasion and rationality, through support, to the most massive heroic interventions depend essentially on the relative quantity of negative affect that must be reduced.

Recently, after several years of systematic research in this field, I have begun to study the relationship of the face to the type of smoking dependency. Ikard and I (1973) established that there is a substantial correlation between the reported quantities of positive and negative affects and the type of dependency of different types of cigarette smokers. We have also established that these reported types of dependencies are *in fact* correlated with the condi-tions under which such individuals smoke. For example, purely negative-affect smokers do *not* smoke when viewing a comedy and do smoke when shown a film about German concentration camps. More recent investigation not yet completed reveals that positive, negative, and addictive smokers display an increasing frequency of negative affect on their faces over time. I interpret this to mean that the relative density of positive to negative affect on the face will correlate more generally with underlying support mechanisms that generate the stable ratios of positive and negative affect which we perceive on the faces of the more or less disturbed smokers and that this ratio is critical in describing the general mental health of individuals. I am suggesting that this ratio is not unlike the optimal temperature of the body and that, when the individual loses his zest for life, it is because support mechanisms fail in their integrative function, thus exposing the individual to a quantity of negative affect that he is no longer capable of neutralizing either by smoking or by any other method.

The preceding discussion summarizes some of our findings in the field of facial affect. Let us now briefly examine some of the difficulties in interpreting these responses.

First, the face is under the joint command of the voluntary and involuntary nervous systems. We rarely see a purely innate involuntary affective response on the face. We often see a purely voluntary response that is used by the individual to serve *any* of several purposes. He may use voluntary simulated affect to deceive the other, to please the other, or in vengeance to hurt the other (e.g., to appear uninterested in the other when the other wants interest and love), or to impress the other, to control the other, to increase intimacy with the other, to praise the other, to plead help from the other, or to appease the other. Facial behavior, because it is *partly* under voluntary control, is as ambiguous in its meanings as any other behavior, and we interpret such behavior at its "face" value at our peril.

Second, voluntary facial behavior is also used as a symbol. The paradox of such use is that the symbolism rests on an assumed and generally true consensus about what an innate facial affective response is. The information in such symbolic use of the face is to be found in the direction and magnitude of the *deviation* of the simulated response from the innate response. Thus, a smile that is either faster or slower and/or more or less wide than an innate smile tells the other that one is really *not* amused. A surprise response that is *slower* than an innate surprise response tells the other that one does not believe what the other is saying, that is, it is *too* surprising. If one then adds to this a simulated contempt response by voluntarily raising the upper lip with the lower lip, one adds to disbelief the *simulated* sneer of contempt. It is simply contemptible as well as unbelievable. If one lowers one's eyelids in a heterosexual encounter, giving the appearance of "bedroom eyes," one is suggesting that one has "shameful" sexual wishes toward the other. In none of these cases is there any confusion between sender and receiver because both know the true characteristics of the true innate response. Startle, smile, and shame responses have known latencies, speeds, durations, and magnitudes. Paradoxically, the symbolic use of simulated affect depends on the sharing of precise deviations of any of these parameters in order to communicate.

Next, the unmodulated, ungraded innate response is in fact relatively rare in acculturated human beings. Normally, what we see on the face of the adult even when an innate affect is triggered is some transformation of the innate response that is superimposed on the innate response. Thus, much innate affect is neither experienced nor communicated as such. It is often suppressed in the form of backed-up affect. Breathing and vocalization are the behaviors that are particularly controlled. Thus, innate anger would normally be expressed as a cry of rage. Instead, the jaws are tightly clenched and the lips tightly pursed, to prevent crying out in rage. So, too, with the cries of distress, enjoyment, and excitement. Sometimes the sexual life is thereby inhibited when the cries of excitement, enjoyment, and sexual pleasure are suppressed.

I have noted one important consequence of the enforced isolation of the innate from the voluntary response. In the case of a child who was overly aggressive, I noted that on those rare occasions when he smiled it was the guileless ungraded smile of the infant that appeared on his face. Because he had smiled so little, the smile had never come under that voluntary control that normally modulates the smile of infancy so that it is differentiated in latency, speed, duration, and width. The same is true of the innate anger response in those for whom inhibition of anger prevents the response from being modulated by the voluntary system. Such isolation characteristically frightens the individual who correctly senses an uncontrollable, dangerous ego-alien force within himself. In order for the affects to be tamed, they must be capable of variable degrees of admixture of involuntary and voluntary innervation. The ratio of involuntary to voluntary controlled affect must itself be variable and must be graded proportionately to the perceived urgency of environmental demand. Murderous rage must never be completely excluded as a response possibility, but graded minor irritation must also not be excluded as a response possibility. Similarly, all of the other affects must not be excluded as response possibilities. Such mixtures radically complicate the use of the face as a diagnostic technique, but also radically enrich its utility for the study of personality.

PERSONALITY IMPLICATIONS
OF FACIAL RESPONSES

We must finally confront yet another problem in the interpretation of facial responses. Thus far, I have described responses that appear not only to be very repetitive and stable but also to be relatively independent of either external or internal stimulation. No matter what happened to the subjects, the face continued to emit the same responses. This is an important phenomenon and it encouraged me to pursue the study of the face further. But it is clearly not the whole story. I have labeled these the *invariant facial responses* simply because they do not vary. Many facial responses are equally lawful and regular but nonetheless are conditional on the occurrence of some external or internal stimulation. I have labeled these the *conditional affective responses*. Thus, one individual smiles whenever he is with others but does not smile when he is alone. In contrast, another individual does not smile when he is with others but does smile when he is alone. By these criteria, the first individual is sociophilic and the second is sociophobic. But a third individual sometimes smiles when he is with people and sometimes does not. He sometimes smiles when he is alone, but sometimes when he is alone he does not smile. It *may* be that it is the size of the group that is critical for his comfort or discomfort, so that he smiles when he is with a few people, but not when he is with a large group. But it may be that being with others or being alone accounts for almost *none* of the variance of his smiling or not smiling. It is my belief that this exposes a fundamental problem in personality theory and in diagnostic testing. This is the question of *what is* a personality variable. It appears to me that what is a personality variable is a function of the particular structure of the individual personality, and we cannot prejudge this matter. In the hypothetical cases we have just considered, orientation toward or against being with others *is* a variable in the first two cases since it produces affective responses that are conditional on the presence or absence of others, but it is *not* or need not be a variable in the third case. The third individual's smile might, for example, be conditional on intellectual stimulation. This might or might not occur in social interaction and might or might not occur when he is alone. He might smile when speaking to someone who interested him intellectually. He might also smile when an interesting thought occurred to him, whether with others or alone. We can, therefore, usefully employ a conditional affective response to determine what are the critical variables in any particular personality. But we must also determine what these variables are if we are to be able to interpret any conditional affective facial response. Unlike the invariant response, a knowledge of *what* is evoking the conditioned facial response is essential for understanding it.

The third type of facial response is one I have labeled a *transient* because it may occur only once or occasionally to a specific stimulus but never recur with sufficient frequency or regularity to become either an invariant or a conditional response. Thus, a startle to a loud noise would be an example of a transient. A distress response to a momentary pain would be a transient. Transients are likely to be innately triggered responses since these are not under voluntary control and the individual is always open to their activation if external or internal stimulation suddenly increases and thus triggers startle, fear, or excitement, or decreases and thus triggers the smile of enjoyment, or reaches a critical level of non-optimal neural firing and thus triggers distress or anger.

Transient responses should not be interpreted in any way as being diagnostic of personality structure since they are in a sense an invariant single response to a stimulus that may or may not recur. Almost everyone except some epileptics will startle to a pistol shot. What can and should be interpreted is the secondary response to such a startle. Does the individual respond to startle with interest in what startled him or does he smile in relief, become ashamed that he was surprised, or become angry or frightened? The variability of response to an innately triggered transient can be indicative of the individual's posture toward sudden uncontrolled change. Such a secondary response to a transient startle response may itself be a conditional response that is regular and predictable whenever the individual is startled. Thus, one could employ a series of standardized stimuli known to be capable of eliciting innate affective responses as a test in which one discarded the innate response and studied only the secondary response to each innately activated affect for its illumination of a profile of affective responses to the entire spectrum of the primary affects.

In conclusion, it is important to distinguish between facial affects that are emitted independently of inner or outer stimulation, that is, the *invariant* responses, facial affects that are emitted lawfully but that are dependent on specific differences in stimulation, that is, the *conditional* responses, and facial affects that are emitted as a consequence of single or rarely repeated stimulation (most often innately and involuntarily), that is, the *transient* responses. The interpretation of invariants is not always obvious, but they represent the most stable structures in the personality. The interpretation of conditional responses is usually simpler because these responses depend so critically on specific differences in the stimulating circumstances. Since these differences are also stable, they too represent stable structures in the personality but are more situation dependent than are the invariant responses. Transients, in contrast to invariants and conditionals, are generally devoid of specific diagnostic significance.

These are a sample of some of the problems inherent in decoding the information on the face. The human face is sometimes opaque, sometimes ambiguous, but often enough deeply illuminating to provide the next frontier for the study of personality.

REFERENCES

Beach, F. A., & Levinson, G. Effects of androgen on the glans penis and mating behavior of castrated male rats. *Journal of Experimental Zoology,* 1950, *114,* 159–171.
Ekman, P., Sorenson, E. R., & Friesen, W. V. Pan-cultural elements in facial displays of emotions. *Science,* 1969, *164* (3875), 86–88.
Frankenhaeuser, M. Psychoendocrine approaches to the study of emotion. In *Nebraska Symposium.* Lincoln: University of Nebraska Press, 1979, in press.
French, T. M., Alexander, F., *et al.* Psychogenic factors in bronchial asthma. *Psychosomatic Medicine,* 1941, Monograph No. 2.

Ikard, F., & Tomkins, S. The experience of affect as a determinant of smoking behavior: A series of validity studies. *Journal of Abnormal Psychology,* 1973, *81,* 172–181.

Izard, C. The emotions and emotion constructs in personality and culture research. In R. B. Catell (ed.), *Handbook of modern personality theory.* Chicago: Aldine, 1969.

Landis, C., & Hunt, W. A. *The Startle Pattern.* New York: Farrar and Rinehart, 1939.

Lomax A. *Folk song style and culture.* Washington, D.C.: American Association for the Advancement of Science, 1968.

Tomkins, S. S. Consciousness and the unconscious in a model of the human being. In *Proceedings of the XIV International Congress of Psychology.* Montreal: I.C.P., 1955.

Tomkins, S. S. *Affect, imagery, consciousness,* Vol. I. New York: Springer, 1962.

Tomkins, S. S. *Affect, imagery, consciousness,* Vol. II. New York: Springer, 1963.

Tomkins, S. S. Affect and psychology of knowledge. In S. Tomkins & C. Izard (eds.), *Affect, cognition and personality.* New York: Springer, 1965.

Tomkins, S. S. A theory of memory. In J. Antrobus (ed.), *Cognition and affect.* Boston: Little, Brown, 1971.

Tomkins, S. S. The phantasy behind the face. *Journal of Personality and Assessment,* 1975, *39,* 551–562.

Tomkins, S. S. *Affect, imagery, consciousness,* Vol. III. New York: Springer, 1979, in press.

Tomkins, S. S., & Messick, S. (eds.) *The computer simulation of personality.* New York: Wiley, 1963.

Tomkins, S. S., & McCarter, R. What and where are the primary affects? Some evidence for a theory. *Perceptual and Motor Skills,* 1964, *18* (1), 119–158.

Vasquez, J. *The face and ideology.* Ph.D. Thesis, Rutgers University, 1975.

Chapter 7

ASPECTS OF CONSCIOUSNESS AND PERSONALITY IN TERMS OF DIFFERENTIAL EMOTIONS THEORY

C. E. IZARD AND S. BUECHLER

ABSTRACT

Differential emotions theory is presented as a framework for the study of the emotions as a personality subsystem. A major focus of the theory is the process by which emotions interact with other subsystem functions. This emphasis necessitates the integration of the theory's theoretical conceptions with formulations (and empirical findings) from diverse disciplines in the social and biological sciences.

Basic to the theory is its conception of a fundamental emotion as a complex motivational phenomenon with characteristic neurophysiological, expressive, and experiential components. Ten discrete emotions are described, each with its innately programmed neurophysiological substrate, universally recognized facial expression, and motivational subjective experience. These emotions are seen as activators and organizers of behavior, rather than as inherently pathological forces.

One of the most persistent problems in the human sciences is the independent creation of theories of personality, theories of behavior, and theories of emotion. While personality and behavior theorists often make use of concepts of motivation, they have, for the most part, neglected the impact of the discrete emotions in the experience of their subjects. Emotion theorists, on the other hand, have frequently concentrated on a circumscribed aspect of the

165

emotion process (such as its neurophysiology, its expression, or self-reports of its experiential qualities) while failing to relate their research to the wider domain of personality growth.

Differential emotions theory (Izard, 1971, 1972, 1977) represents a framework for investigating the interrelationship between the emotion processes and other subsystems of human personality. The theory draws from a wide array of classical works (including the writings of Darwin, Spencer, James, Dewey, Freud, and Woodworth) and was influenced by the more contemporary writings of Sinnott, Harlow, Bowlby, Holt, Tomkins, and Singer. While the central focus of differential emotions theory is the role of the discrete emotions in personality development and functioning, it attempts to relate these emotion concepts to findings from disciplines as diverse as the cognitive theories of Kagan (1966, 1970, 1972, 1974) and the neurophysiological research of investigators such as Gellhorn (1964) and Simonov (1972).

Since the framework of differential emotions theory has been presented in detail elsewhere (Izard, 1959, 1971, 1972, 1977, 1979a,b; Izard & Tomkins, 1966; Tomkins, 1962, 1963), this chapter will present a brief synopsis of its central tenets, followed by an attempt to focus specifically on its current formulations in the fields of emotion patterning, emotions and early development, emotions and personality growth, and the self-regulation of emotion.

BASIC PREMISES OF DIFFERENTIAL EMOTIONS THEORY

The key premises and definitions of differential emotions theory address the role of the discrete emotions in the functioning of the personality as a whole. Taken together, these central tenets provide a view of the subsystems of personality, the functions of the fundamental emotions, and the process of emotion activation. This section outlines several of the basic premises of differential emotions theory. It omits some concepts that are more readily discussed as introductory material to subsequent topics.

THE SUBSYSTEMS OF PERSONALITY

The theory conceptualizes human personality as a complex organization of six subsystems: the homeostatic, drive, emotion, perceptual, cognitive, and motor subsystems. Each subsystem functions relatively autonomously but influences and interacts with the others. The homeostatic subsystem, which includes the endocrine and cardiovascular systems, is auxiliary to the emotion system, functioning to regulate and sustain emotions once they have been activated. The drives (such as hunger, thirst, and sex) are motivational states brought about by changes or deficits in tissues other than that of nerve cells. Although they have some of the characteristics of emotions, they are more limited in the timing of their occurrence, the range of their objects, and the freedom of alternatives for their satisfaction. Their importance in interaction with the fundamental emotions will be examined further below.

FUNDAMENTAL EMOTIONS AS MOTIVATIONAL STATES

Differential emotions theory proposes that the six personality subsystems produce four types of motivations: drives, emotions, affect–perception and affect–cognition interactions, and affective–cognitive structures and orientations. After basic survival and comfort needs are met, drives generally only assume psychological importance in their interactions with the emotions. Affects (which include both emotions and drives) frequently direct perceptual and cognitive processes. The resulting affect–perception and affect–cognition interactions contribute to the complexity and variety of human motivation. When a particular affect (or pattern of affects) interacts frequently with an image or cognition, the pattern assumes the stability of an affective–cognitive structure. A complex configuration of such structures constitutes an affective–cognitive orientation or personality trait, such as passivity, skepticism, or egotism.

The emotions constitute the principal motivational system in the human being. There are ten fundamental emotions, each with its unique motivational properties. The fundamental emotions are innate, transcultural phenomena. Although each culture has its own "display rules" (Ekman, 1972) and attitudes toward emotion experience (Izard, 1971), these emotion processes are recognized and identified as part of the human experience by individuals from widely varying cultural backgrounds.

A fundamental emotion is defined as a complex motivational phenomenon, with characteristic neurophysiological, expressive, and experiential components. No single component of the three suffices as a description of an emotion; all three are essential to the concept. At the neurophysiological level, a fundamental emotion is defined as a particular, innately programmed pattern of electrochemical activity in the nervous system. The expressive component consists mainly of a characteristic pattern of facial activity, but may also include bodily responses (postural–gestural, visceral–glandular) and vocal expressions. At the experiential level, each fundamental emotion is a unique quality of consciousness.

The theory holds that consciousness is organized by the fundamental emotions, which provide direction and focus to the processes of sensation, perception, and cognition. Differential emotions theory stresses the concept that it is the emotions that determine the range of input in consciousness, by controlling the processes of awareness. The relationship between emotion development and consciousness will be treated more fully in a subsequent section (pp. 175–179).

The ten fundamental emotions are experienced as interest, joy, surprise, sadness, anger, disgust, contempt, fear, shame/shyness, and guilt. None of these experiences can be categorized as inherently "positive" or "negative," since its effect depends on intraindividual and person–environment interactions. However, for convenience, the fundamental emotions are frequently divided into positive and negative classes based on their most likely consequences for the individual. The most frequently experienced positive emotion is interest. Interest motivates learning, the development of skills, and, more generally, much of our involvement in the environment. Joy is conceived as a positive emotion characterized by a sense of confidence and contentment, which may occur during reverie, daydreaming, or even sleep, as well as active, alert states. Surprise is a transient state, typically brought about by a sudden, unexpected event that serves the purpose of clearing away ongoing emotion, thus readying the individual to respond to change. That is, surprise momentarily dominates consciousness. Thus, it interrupts ongoing emotion or emotion–cognition processes and, in effect, clears the "channels" of the nervous system for processing the information relevant to the eliciting event. Sadness, the most common negative emotion, may include feelings of loneliness, discouragement, rejection, and dissatisfaction with oneself. Sadness in the infant, and throughout life, communicates a need for change and may elicit empathic responses. Anger, which is frequently stimulated by the feeling of being physically or psychologically restrained, mobilizes energy, providing a feeling of power and confidence. Disgust can be a response to something either physically or psychologically deteriorated or spoiled. Contempt is a feeling of superiority that can foster the kind of aggressive behavior that can be directed toward a depersonalized target. Fear is a particularly toxic negative emotion, experienced as apprehension, uncertainty, and the feeling of threat or danger. Shame/shyness is a feeling of overexposure of a vulnerable aspect of the self, a heightened self-awareness. Guilt is a sense of being accountable for violating internal standards.

The fundamental emotions are motivators and organizers of behavior, not merely responses to an appraisal process. The perceptual–cognitive process of appraisal is itself motivated and directed by emotion. And interest in the object dictates a quite different appraisal than anger or fear. Of course, the information derived from appraisal influences the emotion process. Contrary to theories that view emotions as functions of prior cognitive assessments of a stimulus situation, differential emotions theory emphasizes the two-way interactions between emotion and cognition (further discussion of these interactions is presented on pp. 180–182).

Both the subjective, motivational component and the expressive component of the fundamental emotions serve adaptive functions in the life of the individual. From infancy onward, the felt experience of the emotions gives impetus and directedness to behavior. Contrary to theories that view emotions as disrupting, disorganizing phenomena, differential emotions theory emphasizes their functional role. In addition, the expressions of the emotions are seen as integral to the development of human attachments, communication, and self-regulation.

THE PROCESS OF EMOTION ACTIVATION

Emotion activation is mediated by the somatic nervous system, although once an emotion is activated it may arouse autonomic–visceral–glandular activity. This view of emotion activation has important implications for the self-regulation of the emotions, since the somatic system is under voluntary control. For example, if the hypothesis is correct, a person who needed to suppress anger in order to avoid a potentially serious consequence of its expression should be able to attenuate the emotion either by inhibiting the expressive movements of the face and body or by relaxing the muscles involved.

Since the theory postulates the continual presence of emotion in consciousness, the description of emotion activation pertains to the activation of a new emotion. As a first step, an internal or external event changes the level or pattern of electrochemical activity in the nervous system, resulting in new sensory data or "information." The theory proposes that the event may be either an intraindividual process (a memory, image, thought, proprioceptive impulse, or other activity affecting neural mechanisms) or a person–environment interaction. The change in level or pattern of neural activity directs which of the innately determined facial expressions is effected. Sensory feedback from the face then generates the subjective experience of a particular fundamental emotion. Once an emotion is activated, the glandular–hormonal, cardiovascular, respiratory, and other life systems are involved in its amplification or regulation.

Facial expressions may be partially or fully inhibited. Voluntary suppression of the emotion expression does not entirely preclude the experience of the emotion (since rapid "micromomentary expressions" or alternative pathways for the usual feedback pattern may still be triggered), but under certain circumstances voluntary expression control can play a role in the regulation of emotion experience.

These, then, are some of the basic premises of differential emotions theory. The following section presents a discussion of patterns of emotion.

PATTERNS OF EMOTIONS

Human motivation owes its complexity, in part, to the patterns of fundamental emotions that are formed as a result of the individual's genetic makeup and experience. The differential emotions theory of patterns of emotion has implications for the development of emotion traits and for an understanding of the experience of anxiety, depression, and hostility. A discussion of these issues will also suggest some implications of differential emotions theory for the fields of psychodiagnostics and psychotherapy.

Izard (1972, 1977) has defined a pattern of emotions as two or more fundamental emotions experienced simultaneously or in rapid sequence. The facial expression of a pattern of emotions may show a blend of the emotions involved.

In a pattern of emotions, all of the discrete emotions have some motivational impact on the individual. As expressed by Izard (1972, p. 24), "Discrete emotions retain their essential genotypical characteristics when they occur in patterns."

Two or more fundamental emotions often combine in a pattern, and, when they do, they may produce a relatively stable emotion trait that is likely to be elicited by a particular set of conditions.

As opposed to theorists who view anxiety as a unidimensional experience, differential emotions theory defines anxiety as a pattern of emotions including fear and two or more of the emotions of sadness, anger, shame/shyness, guilt, and interest (Izard, 1972, 1977). While fear is an essential component of the anxiety pattern, the other fundamental emotions are variable elements. Individuals differ in terms of the emotions they experience as part of their anxiety pattern (except for the fact that fear is always included). This suggests that scientific efforts to study "anxiety" should take into account the lack of precision of the term. It may prove more fruitful to study the various forms of anxiety that result from combinations of fear with other discrete emotions. Empirical investigation (Bartlett & Izard, 1972) of the emotions experienced during real and imagined anxiety conditions lends support to the premise that fear is central to the experience of anxiety, but interest, guilt, anger, and shame/shyness are frequent components.

The differential emotions theory views depression as a complex pattern of emotions, with sadness as its key component. Anger, disgust, contempt, fear, guilt, and shyness may be included in the pattern. The theory suggests that the pattern of depression may differ from individual to individual and may also vary from time to time within the same individual. Izard (1977) suggests that these differences may have important psychodiagnostic and psychotherapeutic implications. The experience of the individual whose depressive pattern is dominated by acute sadness and extreme fear is quite different from the experience of another person (or the same person at a different time) whose depression results from sadness and a less toxic accompanying emotion, such as anger. Izard (1977) reports empirical data and clinical observations in support of this premise.

Hostility is viewed as a complex pattern of emotions, drives, and affective–cognitive orientations, with anger, disgust, and contempt as its most prominent emotions. In the differential emotions framework, hostility differs from aggression in that it does not include verbal or physical activity to harm the object, but refers to the motivational state, facial expression, and accompanying cognitive processes that may instigate subsequent aggressive behavior. While the hostile affect expression is viewed as affecting the threshold for aggressive behavior, the direction of this change may vary depending on the relative social status of the potential adversaries and on other situational factors.

Savitsky, Izard, Kotsch, and Christy (1974) studied the effect of a confederate victim's facial expression on subjects' aggressive responses (delivery of shock). The results supported the premise that perceiving an anger expression influences subsequent aggressive behavior. Subjects whose "victims" showed anger administered less shock, whereas smiling "victims" were given increased levels of shock. Aside from suggesting the importance of facial expressions in determining aggressive interchanges, these data imply that studies of aggression should include the face-to-face encounter to make their results generalizable to real situations. The differential emotions theory viewpoint also suggests the importance of studying the experiential and behavioral differences between hostility patterns greatly dominated by anger and those with disgust or contempt as a prominent component. The composition of the hostility pattern might be hypothesized to affect the facial expression of the potential aggressor, the message received by the potential victim, and the subjective experience and behavioral consequences for both.

More generally, the position of differential emotions theory suggests that studying patterns of emotion such as anxiety, depression, and hostility as though they were unidimensional constructs is overly simplistic. The clinical significance of patterns such as these suggests the importance of research into the individual and situational factors that determine the composition of a pattern of emotions and its experiential and behavioral consequences.

THE DEVELOPMENT OF THE EMOTION SYSTEM

Before proceeding to discuss emotion system development, several additional premises of differential emotions theory should be presented. While not unrelated to the propositions outlined in the first section, these additional components of the theory extend its implications to the issues of the onset of emotion expressions and experiences, their hereditary and environmental basis, their effect on social development, and their relationship to the development of consciousness.

The emotions emerge as they become adaptive in the total life experience of the infant. Development, particularly in the sphere of infant–caregiver communications, is facilitated by the innately determined ontogenesis of the emotion expressions. For example, the distress cry is present from birth, serving survival needs by maintaining the proximity of the caregiver. On the other hand, the potentially toxic emotion of fear, which could add little to adaptiveness in the early months of infancy, emerges in the second half-year and contributes to the motivation for the newly mobile infant's efforts at self-protection, self-cognition, and self-control.

As each emotion emerges, it increases the individual's conscious awareness of a broad set of contingencies, setting the stage for a particular type of learning and development. The emergence of anger, for example, makes salient the attributes of frustrating restraints and motivates efforts to deal personally with barriers, instead of relying solely on the cry of distress to elicit the attention of the caregiver. This increases the infant's experience of itself as a causal agent, a separate, capable individual.

Each emotion adds to the complexity of consciousness through its relationships to sensory, perceptual, and cognitive processes. This and related premises are elaborated further in a subsequent portion of this section which deals specifically with the relationship between emotion development and consciousness.

A given stimulus may elicit different emotions, depending on the infant's level of perceptual, cognitive, emotional, and motor development. Maturation in these interacting subsystems may be expected to affect the expressive responses of the growing infant to any standardized stimulus condition.

The facial expressions of emotion, which have an evolutionary and biological basis, play a significant role in the establishment of the infant–caregiver bond. The development of emotion communication, synchrony or mutual responsiveness between infant and caregiver, and attachment depends, in large measure, on the genetically programmed messages conveyed through facial expressions.

THE ONTOGENESIS OF THE EMOTION EXPRESSIONS

From the viewpoint of differential emotions theory, the ontogenesis of fundamental emotion expressions and experiences is primarily a function of maturational processes and secondarily a function of learning and experience. While the neural mechanisms for the expressions of all the fundamental emotions are innate, only five can be elicited at birth (Izard, 1971, 1978). The onset of the other fundamental emotion expressions awaits age-related maturational processes.

This viewpoint on the ontogenesis of the fundamental emotions differs substantially from the alternative formulation of the process conceptualized as the differentiation hypothesis. As first enunciated by Bridges (1932), the differentiation hypothesis holds that by a process of differentiation the separate emotions derive from a single emotion or arousal state. Thus, there are no emotions in the first weeks of life, unless one considers "excitement" or generalized distress as an emotion.

The research supporting the differentiation hypothesis has been previously reviewed and its methodological weaknesses were noted (Ekman, Friesen, & Ellsworth, 1972; Izard, 1971; Izard & Buechler, 1979). Contemporary proponents of the differentiation hypothesis of emotion ontogenesis, such as Sroufe (1976), have attempted to address some of the problems in Bridges' formulation, especially the lack of theoretical explication or empirical evidence for the development of each emotion from its derivatives. Sroufe suggests, for example, that "early obligatory attention" differentiates into wariness and finally into fear, while early distress gives rise to rage and then anger, angry mood, and defiance.

The work of Darwin (1872, 1877), the early research of Goodenough (1931, 1932–1933), the theoretical writings of Tomkins (1962, 1963) and Spitz (1959, 1965), and the empirical findings of Emde, Gaensbauer, and Harmon (1976) contributed to the differential emotions conceptualization of the ontogenesis of the emotions (Izard, 1971, 1972, 1977, 1978, 1980). The major implications of this viewpoint, as contrasted with the differentiation hypothesis perspective, may be briefly summarized as follows:

1. There are separate, innately programmed neural mechanisms for each of the fundamental emotions.
2. The fundamental emotions are qualitatively different experiences from their earliest inception. The phenomenal experience (and facial expression) of each emotion is distinctive from its onset throughout life, lending continuity to conscious experience.
3. The emotion process is a function of the somatic nervous system. Autonomic arousal is seen as an auxiliary process that may sustain emotion after its neural activation by sensory feedback from the face. This differs substantially from the differentiation hypothesis, which focuses on generalized arousal as the basis for the emotions.
4. Emotions emerge according to an innate maturational pattern. In contrast, Bridges considers anger, disgust, and joy to emerge as a result of continuous learning processes (the formation of bonds of association between provoking situations and combinations of emotion reactions).

Further elaboration of the differential emotions viewpoint on the ontogenesis of the emotions is presented in a subsequent portion of this section which discusses the age of onset and adaptive value of each of the fundamental emotions as they direct the development of conscious experience. A more extensive presentation of this subject has been provided elsewhere (Izard, 1979b).

EMOTION SYSTEM DEVELOPMENT AND SOCIAL INTERACTION

The implications of differential emotions theory for clarifying the complex interplay between emotion system development and infant–caregiver interaction have been treated at length (Izard, 1977, 1978, 1980). Considerations of brevity limit the present discussion to an examination of only three areas within this broad field: the emotion communication theory of attachment, the concept of emotion "contagion" or induction, and the socialization of emotion expressions.

Emotion Communication Theory of Attachment

Differential emotions theory proposes that the first human attachment, the infant–caregiver bond, evolves, in part, from emotion communication experiences via the visual, aural, and somesthetic senses. In early infancy the facial–visual system is particularly salient, although vocal expressions and the sense of touch also play significant roles. The theory holds that the infant's communication system is largely based on facial expressions whose morphology is biologically determined. The infant's expression of meaningful emotion signals elicits caregiver responses that are the basis of the earliest experience of mutual responsiveness.

A number of recent studies have explored the importance of synchrony in these early infant–caregiver interchanges. Klaus, Trause, and Kennell (1975, p. 77) defined synchrony as a repertory of "specific interlocking behavior patterns that develop so early between mother and infant and which serve to unite them." Research findings suggest that the absence of this interlocking communication pattern may result in failure to thrive (Sander, 1969; Brazelton, Tronick, Adamson, Als, & Weise, 1975; Thoman, 1975). While the importance of establishing a mutually responsive signal system has considerable support, the study of infant–caregiver cues (and, more specifically, the role of infant–caregiver facial expression interchanges) has received little empirical attention. (Notable exceptions include work on the social signal value of infant facial expressions by Emde, Katz, and Thorpe [1979] and Emde, Kligman, Reich, and Wade [1978].)

Emotion Induction

The concept of emotion "contagion" or emotion-induced emotion suggests that some emotion expressions serve as innate releasers (or environmentally stable activators) of a similar emotion experience and expression in an interactant (Simner, 1971; Sagi & Hoffman, 1976). This premise seems important to the development of synchrony, as outlined in the preceding section. The infant's smile elicits a smile of joy from the caregiver, providing a basis for the infant's experience of affecting others. Izard (1977, p. 106) has suggested that there are probably a number of other instances of emotion-induced emotion, but their understanding awaits further research.

The Socialization of Emotion Expressions

Although the emotion expressions are innate, and their onset is largely a function of maturation, the infant's human encounters play an important role in determining the impact of emotions in its life experience. Differential emotions theory suggests that each fundamental emotion has a "history" as a quality of consciousness and motivator of sensory, perceptual, cognitive, and motor acts. The theory is that the life experience of the individual determines the affective–cognitive interactions and affective–cognitive structures that are formed. The events that are associated with the expressions of a fundamental emotion are important factors in the development of these structures or orientations, which, in turn, mediate much of the individual's later experience.

Like so many other areas in emotion development, elaboration of the process of socialization of each of the fundamental emotions awaits future empirical investigation. As an example of differential emotions theory's viewpoint on the socialization of emotions, Izard (1977, p. 369) outlines Tomkins' (1965) analysis of the socialization of fear. It is suggested that parental patterns of socialization of fear greatly influence the child's development of humanistic or other affective–cognitive orientations. When the parents minimize the child's exposure to fear experiences, reassure the child after unavoidable fearful events, and help the child become increasingly able to tolerate and counteract fear, the child is hypothesized to develop a humanistic orientation. The way each emotion is socialized may be expected to influence the development of major aspects of personality.

In summary, the ontogenesis and morphology of the facial expressions of the fundamental emotions are largely functions of maturation and innate, biological "givens." They play a significant part in the infant's earliest human interaction, forming the basis for the development of the attachment bond. Throughout development, experience determines the individual's unique "history" of emotion expressions, affect interactions, and affective–cognitive structures. These enduring orientations result, in part, from the ways in which the growing individual's emotion expressions have been "socialized" by the caregivers and other significant adults in the child's human environment.

EMOTIONS AND THE DEVELOPMENT OF CONSCIOUSNESS

In considering the relationship between the emerging emotions and the development of consciousness in the first 2 years of life, differential emotions theory proposes several interrelated premises (Izard, 1980).

1. Phenomenologically, that is, in terms of subjective experience, the fundamental emotions are invariant from the time of their emergence. This provides an essential continuity to conscious experience.

2. The cognitive accompaniments of an emotion vary with age, experience, and context. This provides flexibility and freedom in the operations of consciousness.

3. Each emotion that emerges adds to the complexity of consciousness, increasing the capacity for processing and responding to a wider range of inputs.

4. Emerging emotions facilitate changes in the level of conscious experience through their relationships to sensory, perceptual, and cognitive processes. The infant's conscious experience is initially dominated by sensory–affective processes. With maturation, a greater range of emotion experiences shifts the dominant conscious experience to affective–perceptual processes. Further maturation and emotion emergence result in a third level, in which consciousness is dominated by affective–cognitive structures. Each of these three "levels" of consciousness builds on the experiences at the previous level and still includes examples of the prior types of processes.

5. Consciousness changes in three basic ways as a result of emerging emotions. Awareness widens, so that an increasing proportion of time is spent in conscious activity. The predominant mode of experience shifts, from sensory–affective to affective–perceptual and then to affective–cognitive. Finally, the contents of consciousness include an ever-increasing array of inputs. Emerging emotions motivate and sustain each of these three basic changes in conscious experience.

The first premise proposes that from their onset throughout life the fundamental emotions retain their experiential distinctiveness and specific motivational properties. This proposition follows from the view that emotion expressions are innately programmed, universal, and associated with phenomenologically distinct experiences. These enduring emotion processes lend continuity to conscious experience, which contributes stability to the sense of self and self–environment interactions.

The second premise suggests that there is change in the quality and complexity of conscious experience throughout life as affects become linked with cognition. Conscious experience, which is initially dominated by relatively simple, global sensory–affective events, increases in focus, allowing for greater complexity and facilitating the development of emotion control. These broad, qualitative changes in conscious experiencing result from the emergence and elaboration of affective–cognitive structures that increasingly focus attention and enhance the capacity for orderly thought.

The remaining premises provide the basis for the conception of three levels of consciousness in infancy. In the first level, consciousness is dominated by rather simple, sensory–affective experiences. In the first weeks of life, the infant is primarily an affective being, responding to inner sensory events, but it is not insensitive to its surround. Awareness is limited, for the most part, to how changes in stimulation make the infant feel, with little or no cognitive accompaniment. The first interactions with persons and objects are based largely on their effects on the infant's interoceptive processes, rather than on the infant's perception of the object's stimulus properties. At this level, emotion expressions are essential for communication of the infant's inner needs to the primary caregiver and for establishment of the rudiments of the mother–infant bond.

In the initial weeks of life, interest motivates the attentive state. Although the infant is as yet unable to form a stable concept, it shows preferences among visual stimuli based on the arousal of different qualities or intensities of affective experience. This interest-motivated attention pattern forms the basis upon which selective attention to perceptual properties of the environment will later develop. The movement from simple immediate awareness of single events without benefit of memory or anticipation to perception attuned to distinguishable properties of persons and objects and the capacity for storage and retrieval is largely a function of the power of interest to focus, direct, motivate, and sustain attention.

In early infancy, sadness is the most frequently experienced "negative" emotion. Tissue deficits or discomfort result in sensory data that impinge on awareness, and the resulting physiological pain recruits sadness. This Pain–Sadness interaction completely dominates consciousness. The pain cry alerts the caregiver to the infant's needs. Not only is this affect signal obviously crucial for physical survival for the helpless infant, but it also forms the basis for the first experience of a relationship between a behavioral event and its consequence. The cry eventually is followed by relief from pain. This experience is the first of many interactions that will contribute to the growing discrimination between self and other. The expression of sadness may also foster the caregiver's empathic bond to the infant.

The second level of consciousness builds on the patterns established in the first, but it is variegated by the emergence of other emotions. While the infant has already established a pattern of preferential responding, beginning in the second quarter of the first year of life interest directs attention to separate, distinguishable perceptual aspects of persons and objects. With the advent of affective–perceptual processes, consciousness changes from minimally discriminating to more focused and selective experiencing, and from domination by sensory–affective processes to greatly increased awareness of the surround.

This interest-motivated change takes on new meaning with the advent of the social smile, beginning in the third month of life. At this time the infant will smile in response to any facial configuration moving toward it. The social smile differentiates a particular positive experience, the joyful interchange with the human interactant, from other positive events. Positive experience is no longer merely a function of gradations of interest. The rudiments of the distinctions between interacting with the object world and interacting with humans are facilitated by this differential response to faces. The rhythmic give-and-take of mutual responsiveness, the earliest experience of initiating joy in others, and awareness of self as causal agent are furthered by the social smile.

Two additional emotions that emerge into consciousness during this period, surprise and anger, further the infant's perceptual awareness. Surprise, which functions to clear the information-processing channels of the nervous system, readies the infant for affective–cognitive processes appropriate to the situation that follows the unexpected event. Surprise alerts attention to change, an essential component of perceptual processes. The emergence of anger motivates attempts to deal directly with restraints and barriers, resulting in a new form of the experience of self as agent. In the anger experience the infant can become conscious of its own capability for direct action. The infant experiences its own distinctness from the frustrating object, in part, through the latter's opposition.

The third level of consciousness is characterized by the development of affective–cognitive processes. Awareness is freed from reliance on perceptions of presently impinging stimuli. Affective responses to an image, symbol, or concept of an object or person can now continue despite their absence. With increased capacity for memory of the past and anticipation of the future, the realm of awareness is infinitely broadened. Distinctions between classes of objects and the development of particular attachments allow for awareness of ownership. The limits and capabilities of the self as causal agent take on increasing meaning. The child is becoming capable of considering itself as an object, with all the evaluations, trepidations, and opportunities for growth that this entails.

These changes, which begin in the last quarter of the first year of life, once again build on already established patterns, but are a function of the emergence of new emotion experiences into consciousness. Shame/shyness and fear both increase awareness of the self and its vulnerabilities. Once the stranger can be discriminated from familiar others, the possibility for the experience of shame exists. Shame is a heightened awareness of the self, occasioned by the awkwardness of attempting interaction with strangers who do not respond in the familiar way to the infant's patterns of interaction. Such experiences eventually foster the development of competencies and skills to increase self-esteem and decrease shame experiences.

Beginning around the seventh to ninth month of life, the infant responds with fear and avoidance to certain situations that previously elicited other emotions. The stranger, and later the separation experience, may elicit fearful expressions and flight to the caregiver. With this experience, awareness of the vulnerability of the self and awareness of the particular attributes of attachment figures acquire consciousness.

Fear and shame and the anticipation of these experiences make certain aspects of the self and the surround particularly salient. To counter the vulnerability of the self, the infant must classify events as presently or subsequently dangerous (relying on memory and anticipation, as well as affective–cognitive processes and, eventually, affective–cognitive structures or stable orientations toward aspects of the self and environment). The infant scans the surround, not merely to perceive its properties, but to recognize the meaning of the situation. By this point in development the conscious awareness of the infant, alerted to change and familiarity in the self and surround, is a highly complex, directed flow of affectively motivated experience.

EMOTIONS AS INTERACTANTS WITH OTHER SUBSYSTEMS OF PERSONALITY

Differential emotions theory focuses on the importance of harmonious interaction between the subsystems of personality for effective behavior. Maladjustment is viewed as resulting from difficulties in interaction of subsystems rather than from any inherently disrupting or disorganizing influence of the fundamental emotions themselves.

Although the personality subsystems (homeostatic, drive, emotion, perceptual, cognitive, and motor systems) can function relatively autonomously, they are complexly interrelated. As has already been suggested (see p. 167), the homeostatic and drive systems generally achieve psychological importance through their interactions with emotions. Interactions of the other four systems form the basis for most of the higher-order functioning in the human being. This section focuses attention on the implications of differential emotions theory for effective subsystem interaction. After brief elaboration of the interaction between emotions and other motivators, attention will center on the interplay between the emotions and perceptual–cognitive processes since this area has been the subject of much theoretical discussion.

EMOTIONS AS INTERACTANTS WITH OTHER MOTIVATORS

As has been suggested (see p. 167), differential emotions theory postulates four major types of motivation: the drives, emotions, affect–cognition interactions, and affective–cognitive structures. This premise implies a great diversity in human motivation since motivating conditions include single fundamental emotions, dyads and triads of emotions, drives acting alone or in interaction with emotions, and the interplay between cognitions or cognitive structures and affects. Emotion–emotion interactions give rise to significant patterns such as anxiety, depression, and hostility (as elaborated under "Patterns of Emotions''). The interaction of emotions (such as fear) with drives (such as sex) has behavioral implications that are the focus of much clinical and experiential attention (see Izard [1977, pp. 161–188] for an extensive discussion of the relationships between emotions and drives).

EMOTIONS AND THE
PERCEPTUAL-COGNITIVE PROCESSES

While theorists generally agree that the emotion and perceptual-cognitive systems frequently interact, cognitive theorists consider the appraisal process (cognition) as the initiator of emotion experiences, while differential emotions theory maintains that affective experience can occur without cognitive appraisal. Differential emotions theory also suggests that, through its control of consciousness, affect paves the way for perceptual and cognitive processes. The issue involves more than a discussion of which step is the first in the causal chains that result in emotion and perceptual-cognitive experiences. The viewpoint of differential emotions theory on this issue reflects its conception of the operations of the conscious mind.

Differential emotions theory maintains that the emotion and perceptual-cognitive systems are relatively autonomous but frequently interacting processes. As was described in the first section (p. 169), differential emotions theory suggests that conscious emotion experiences result from the cortical integration of facial feedback, which can occur without the mediation of cognition. Thus, although cognitions can affect the experience of an emotion (for example, through voluntary regulation of facial expressions, as will be outlined in a subsequent section), an initial appraisal process (which is indeed a frequent antecedent of a change in the intensity or quality of emotion experience) is not essential for an emotion experience to be activated. Furthermore, one may respond to an emotion experience without cognizing, or labeling it. The entire experience of an emotion, from its neural activation through its behavioral expression, can occur without cognitive mediation.

Differential emotions theory agrees in some important respects with the cognitive and social theories of emotion, such as those of Lazarus (Chapter 8), Mandler (Chapter 9), Plutchik (1977 and Chapter 1), and Averill (Chapter 12). All of these theories recognize the role of cognition in emotion activation and all recognize the importance of cognition-emotion interactions. Both Lazarus and Plutchik have made significant contributions to our understanding of cognition-emotion relationships, and Averill has emphasized the importance of the social context. The point of difference here is the assumption of differential emotions theory that emotion is always present in consciousness, thus affecting ongoing cognitive processes (including appraisal), which in turn can change the intensity or quality of emotion.

The theory suggests that, through its control of the limits of conscious awareness, affect precedes and shapes perceptual and cognitive events. This premise of differential emotions theory provides a framework for understanding the experimental findings that show the influence of affect on perception and cognition (for example, the results of work by Bruner and Goodman [1947], Levine, Chein, and Murphy [1942], and Sanford [1936, 1937]).

Affect also influences cognition by motivating behavior that results in the availability of learning experiences. This premise of differential emotions theory parallels Elkind's (1972) concept that "intrinsic growth forces" motivate seeking behavior in the child and Piaget and Inhelder's (1969) suggestion that all intellectual behavior patterns "involve affective factors as motives." Some empirical evidence for this view is provided by the finding that an index of pleasure in the tasks on the Cattell Infant Intelligence Scale at 18 months was significantly correlated with Binet I.Q. at 3 years (Birns & Golden, 1972).

One implication of differential emotions theory concerns current research efforts to relate cognitive attainments to emotion development. Theorists have hypothesized that particular cognitive advances must precede certain emotion responses. Thus, for example, Schaffer (1966, p. 103) suggested that "the establishment of the object concept is therefore a precondition to the onset of fear of strangers." However, several experimental studies have failed to support this assertion (Scarr & Salapatek, 1970; Emde, Gaensbauer, & Harmon, 1976). The differential emotions theory, while acknowledging the importance of affect–cognition interactions, suggests that milestones in affective development (such as the emergence of fear) proceed according to an innately programmed maturational timetable (see the section "The Development of the Emotion System" and see Izard [1978, 1980]). In this framework, the ontogenesis of emotion expressions does not result from the cognitive ability to complete an appraisal process but rather has a separate, independent progression. Some empirical support for this assertion is suggested in the finding that Down's syndrome infants equated in intelligence with younger normals showed different affective responses to looming objects (Cicchetti & Sroufe, 1978). The differential emotions viewpoint stresses the importance of studying the ontogenesis of emotion expressions for an understanding of the factors affecting emotion development.

Differential emotions theory provides a framework for investigating intuitive processes and altered states of consciousness, as well as the factors affecting analytical thought. Izard (1977) suggests that intuitive knowing may result from sensory cues "filtered" by the state of consciousness that is created when interest blends with joy. This receptive mode or tacit awareness differs from the more logical, critical, analytical knowing that results from interest in interaction with other emotions, such as sadness.

By interfering in the usual pattern of consciousness (in which focused interest initiates rapid conversion of sensory cues to perceived and cognized information) it may be possible to sense more directly. This is, however, extremely difficult, since in the adult the operations of ordinary consciousness are firmly entrenched. In the adult mind affective–cognitive orientations are so well learned that they seem to operate automatically. The strength of these affect–cognition bonds (which is determined by the quality and intensity of the affective component) makes the pure sensing that occurs in infancy almost impossible for the adult to achieve.

THE REGULATION OF EMOTIONS

Several of the implications of differential emotions theory regarding the regulation of emotion expression are implicit in the basic premises of the theory. In the following brief discussion of these implications, attention will center on the processes by which emotions can be amplified or attenuated.

Differential emotions theory views the emotion process as primarily a function of the somatic system. The fact that this system is under voluntary control is the basis for the theory's conception of the individual's capacity for self-regulation of the emotions.

More specifically, the theory views each emotion as based on interaction between its neural, expressive, and experiential components. Cortically integrated sensory feedback from the face generates the subjective experience of a particular fundamental emotion. Since the facial muscles involved in producing expressions are under voluntary control, this component of the feedback system may be used to regulate emotion experience when, for example, the individual willfully controls facial movements. Several recent research efforts support this conclusion. Studies by Kleck, Vaughan, Colby, Cartwright-Smith, Vaughan, and Lanzetta (1976) and Lanzetta, Cartwright-Smith, and Kleck (1976) suggest that intensification or suppression of facial expressions in pain can amplify or attenuate both the physiological response and the self-report of the affective experience.

The premise that the emotion process can operate independently of the cognitive system (although the two interact frequently) suggests that, while at times emotion regulation is mediated by cognition, this is not always the case. That is, since conscious experience of an emotion follows cortical integration of the facial expression, modification of the expression and consequent emotion experience can be initiated by any of the subsystems. Emotions can be amplified or attenuated by drives, the motor system, cognitions, and other emotions.

Voluntary suppression of strong anticipated or initiated emotions (exertion of control over the facial expression, thereby attenuating the emotion experience) when used chronically may lead to psychological problems, since it involves repetitive blockage of the normal emotion process. The resulting unexpended energy that has not been channeled into the normal emotion feedback process may amplify undifferentiated arousal. Since, in contrast to the motivating experience of a specific fundamental emotion, the message one obtains from nonspecific arousal is vague, one's actions may become ineffective or maladaptive.

Cognitive processes (such as imagery) can, however, be constructively used to help alleviate negative emotion experience. Izard (1971) and Singer (1974) have described techniques of imagery that have proved useful in psychotherapy and behavior modification. Perhaps part of the explanation of the effectiveness of these techniques is that they rely not merely on the exertion of cognitive control over emotion expression, but on imagery-induced positive emotions. When cognitive processes recruit energy from within the emotion system itself, successful emotion regulation seems more likely than when the individual merely attempts to actualize a message to "control himself."

The early learning of voluntary emotion expressions and the suppression of emotion expression through imaginative play, imitation, and role assumption are a significant area for research. Understanding normal development in this area will have important psychotherapeutic implications, since self-regulation of the emotions can play a part in the larger domain of the attainment of self-control.

RESEARCH AND CLINICAL IMPLICATIONS

The differential emotions theory conception of the nature of emotions and emotion patterns, and their interactions with other personality subsystems, suggests directions for future research and clinical practice. Most generally, it implies that our understanding of human motivation requires study of the neural, expressive, and subjective components of the emotions as they affect development and adult experience. In this section several more specific implications of the theory are noted.

Experimental investigations should use criteria of the presence of an emotion that are specific to that emotion expression. Studies using "arousal" as a measure of fear or crying as a measure of an infant's distress lack precision since these may be indications of any of several fundamental emotions and emotion patterns. Research efforts should include several measures that are capable of differentiating among the emotions, such as objective analyses of facial expressions and self-reports of subjective experience.

The premise that conscious awareness is directed by emotion states suggests the study of perceptual and cognitive processes during experiences of each of the fundamental emotions and emotion patterns. Design of these investigations might include the use of simulated and imaged emotion experiences, particularly when data have been reported that indicate an essential similarity in the emotion profiles reported by subjects under real and imaged emotion conditions (as, for example, was reported by Bartlett and Izard [1972] in studying anxiety profiles of subjects imagining anxious situations versus subjects undergoing real anxiety-provoking circumstances).

Viewing emotions as adaptive, organizing forces during development and throughout life suggests the use of psychotherapeutic techniques based on emotion theory. In particular, a better understanding of the dynamic interplay between component emotions in patterns such as depression might suggest fruitful therapeutic interventions. Therapists might employ measurement devices such as the Differential Emotions Scale (or its modified form used in a study of hospitalized depressives reported by Marshall and Izard [1972]) to understand the pattern of emotions currently experienced by a particular depressed client. This could result in better understanding of the client's emotion states as well as insights into recurrent emotion patterns or emotion traits in the life of the client. For the depressed client in whom sadness is nearly matched by fear, the optimal therapeutic intervention might begin with techniques to cope with the fear since this toxic emotion constricts thought and narrows the perception of alternatives. Following reduction in the fear experience of the client, effective intervention for the relief of the sadness might be more easily accomplished.

The study of the development of individual differences in emotion experience could involve several lines of longitudinal research. Differential emotions theory suggests the possibility that individuals may differ from birth in their thresholds for experiencing each of the fundamental emotions. Using standardized emotion-eliciting situations and objective measures of emotion responses, such issues as the degree of individual variation in the pattern and intensity of infant emotion responses, the extent to which emotion responses to a standardized situation are related to age, level of cognitive development, sex, and social class, and the stability of these differences over time could be investigated.

The differential emotions theory of emotion communication has research as well as clinical implications. The concept of emotion "contagion," and the suggestion that it facilitates human bonding (and infant–caregiver attachment in particular), invites observation and analysis of this process in laboratory experiments, therapeutic settings, and naturalistic home situations. Some work on empathic distress (Hoffman, 1978) suggests that distress in one infant elicits distress in others. Whether other emotions are similarly induced between infant and caregiver, therapist and client, and actor and television viewer, for example, might be examined.

Differential emotions theory conceptions suggest the study of the relationship between emotion states and creativity. The theory implies that the receptive, intuitive mode of thinking is facilitated when consciousness is shaped by a blend of interest and joy. This invites the measurement of expressive behavior and self-reports of emotions during simulated and real creative experiences, such as listening to music, attempting to compose music, viewing or creating a painting, and perhaps attempting to follow intuitive leads in understanding a therapeutic client.

Differential emotions theory is a framework for integrating the study of the fundamental emotions and emotion patterns with investigations of normal personality growth and pathological processes.

REFERENCES

Bartlett, E. S., & Izard, C. E. A dimensional and discrete emotions investigation of the subjective experience of emotion. In C. E. Izard (ed.), *Patterns of emotions: A new analysis of anxiety and depression.* New York: Academic Press, 1972.

Birns, B., & Golden, M. Prediction of intellectual performance at three years from infant test and personality measures. *Merrill-Palmer Quarterly,* 1972, *18,* 53-58.

Brazelton, T. B., Tronick, E., Adamson, L., Als, H., & Weise, S. Early mother-infant reciprocity. In *Parent-infant interaction.* Amsterdam: CIBA Foundation, Associated Scientific Publishers, 1975.

Bridges, K. M. B. Emotional development in early infancy. *Child Development,* 1932, *3,* 324-341.

Bruner, J. S., & Goodman, C. C. Value and needs as organizing factors in perception. *Journal of Abnormal and Social Psychology,* 1947, *42,* 33-44.

Cicchetti, D., & Sroufe, L. A. An organizational view of affect: Illustration from the study of Down's syndrome infants. In M. Lewis & L. A. Rosenblum (eds.), *The development of affect.* New York: Plenum, 1978.

Darwin, C. R. *The expression of emotions in man and animals.* London: John Murray, 1872.

Darwin, C. R. A biographical sketch of an infant. *Mind,* 1877, *2,* 286-294.

Ekman, P. Universal and cultural differences in facial expression of emotion. In J. K. Cole (ed.), *Nebraska Symposium on Motivation, 1971.* Lincoln: University of Nebraska Press, 1972.

Ekman, P., Friesen, W. V., & Ellsworth, P. C. *Emotion in the human face.* New York: Pergamon Press, 1972.

Elkind, D. Cognitive growth cycles in mental development. In J. K. Cole (ed.), *Nebraska Symposium on Motivation, 1971.* Lincoln: University of Nebraska Press, 1972.

Emde, R. N., Gaensbauer, T., & Harmon, R. J. *Emotional expression in infancy: A biobehavioral study.* New York: International Universities Press, 1976.

Emde, R. N., Katz, E. L., & Thorpe, J. K. Emotional expression in infancy. II. Early deviations in Down's syndrome. *Journal of Psychiatry,* 1979, in press.

Emde, R. N., Kligman, D. H., Reich, J. H., & Wade, T. D. Emotional expression in infancy. I. Initial studies of social signaling and an emergent model. In M. Lewis & L. A. Rosenblum (eds.), *The development of affect.* New York: Plenum, 1978.

Gellhorn, E. Motion and emotion: The role of proprioception in the physiology and pathology of the emotions. *Psychological Review,* 1964, *71* (6), 457-472.

Goodenough, F. L. The expression of the emotions in infancy. *Child Development,* 1931, *2,* 96-101.

Goodenough, F. L. Expression of emotions in a blind-deaf child. *Journal of Abnormal and Social Psychology,* 1932-1933, *27,* 328-333.

Hoffman, M. L. The arousal and development of empathy. In M. Lewis & L. A. Rosenblum (eds.), *The development of affect.* New York: Plenum, 1978.

Izard, C. E. *Positive affect and behavioral effectiveness.* Unpublished manuscript, Vanderbilt University, 1959.

Izard, C. E. *The face of emotion.* New York: Appleton-Century-Crofts, 1971.

Izard, C. E. *Patterns of emotions: A new analysis of anxiety and depression.* New York: Academic Press, 1972.

Izard, C. E. *Human emotions.* New York: Plenum, 1977.

Izard, C. E. On the development of emotions and emotion-cognition relationships in infancy. In M. Lewis & L. A. Rosenblum (eds.), *The development of affect.* New York: Plenum, 1978.

Izard, C. E. Facial expression, emotion, and motivation. In A. Wolfgang (ed.), *Nonverbal behavior.* New York: Academic Press, 1979. (a)

Izard, C. E. Emotions as motivations: An evolutionary-developmental perspective. In R. A. Dienstbier (ed.), *Nebraska Symposium on Motivation.* Lincoln: University of Nebraska Press, 1979. (b)

Izard, C. E. The emergence of emotions and the development of consciousness in infancy. In J. M. Davidson & R. J. Davidson (eds.), *The psychobiology of consciousness.* New York: Plenum, 1980.

Izard, C. E., & Buechler, S. Emotion expressions and personality integration in infancy. In C. E. Izard (ed.), *Emotions in personality and psychopathology.* New York: Plenum, 1979.

Izard, C. E., & Tomkins, S. S. Affect and behavior: Anxiety as a negative affect. In C. E. Spielberger (ed.), *Anxiety and behavior.* New York: Academic Press, 1966.

Kagan, J. Reflection-impulsivity: The generality and dynamics of conceptual tempo. *Journal of Abnormal Psychology,* 1966, *71,* 17-24.

Kagan, J. The determinants of attention in the infant. *American Scientist,* 1970, *58,* 298-306.

Kagan, J. Motives and development. *Journal of Personality and Social Psychology,* 1972, *22,* 51-66.

Kagan, J. Discrepancy, temperament and infant distress. In M. Lewis & L. A. Rosenblum (eds.), *The origins of fear.* New York: Wiley, 1974.

Klaus, M. H., Trause, M. A., & Kennell, J. H. Does human maternal behavior after delivery show a characteristic pattern? In *Parent-infant interaction.* Amsterdam: CIBA Foundation, Associated Scientific Publishers, 1975.

Kleck, R. E., Vaughan, R., Colby, C., Cartwright-Smith, J. E., Vaughan, K., & Lanzetta, J. T. Effects of being observed on expressive, subjective, and physiological responses to painful stimuli. *Journal of Personality and Social Psychology,* 1976, *34* (6), 1211-1218.

Lanzetta, J. T., Cartwright-Smith, J. E., & Kleck, R. E. Effects of nonverbal dissimulation on emotional experience and autonomic arousal. *Journal of Personality and Social Psychology,* 1976, *33,* 354-370.

Levine, R., Chein, I., & Murphy, G. The relation of the intensity of the need to the amount of perceptual distortion: Preliminary report. *Journal of Psychology,* 1942, *13,* 283-293.

Marshall, A. G., & Izard, C. E. Depression as a pattern of emotions and feelings: Factor-analytic investigations. In C. E. Izard *Patterns of emotions: A new analysis of anxiety and depression.* New York: Academic Press, 1972.

Piaget, J., & Inhelder, B. *The psychology of the child.* New York: Basic Books, 1969.

Plutchik, R. Cognitions in the service of emotions: A evolutionary perspective. In D. K. Candland, J. P. Fell, E. Keen, A. I. Leshner, R. Plutchik, & R. M. Tarpy (eds.), *Emotion.* Monterey, Calif.: Brooks/Cole, 1977.

Sagi, A., & Hoffman, M. Empathic distress in the newborn. *Developmental Psychology,* 1976, *12,* 175-176.

Sander, L. Regulation and organization in the early infant-caretaker system. In R. J. Robinson (ed.), *Brain and early behavior.* New York: Academic Press, 1969.

Sanford, N. The effects of abstinence from food upon imaginal processes: A preliminary experiment. *Journal of Psychology,* 1936, *2,* 129-136.

Sanford, N. The effects of abstinence from food upon imaginal processes: A further experiment. *Journal of Psychology,* 1937, *3,* 145-159.

Savitsky, J. C., Izard, C. E., Kotsch, W. E., & Christy, L. Aggressor's response to the victim's facial expression of emotion. *Journal of Research in Personality,* 1974, *7,* 346-357.

Scarr, S., & Salapatek, P. Patterns of fear development during infancy. *Merrill–Palmer Quarterly,* 1970, *16,* 53–90.

Schaffer, H. R. The onset of fear of strangers and the incongruity hypothesis. *Journal of Child Psychology and Psychiatry,* 1966, *7,* 95–106.

Simner, M. Newborns' responses to the cry of another infant. *Developmental Psychology,* 1971, *5* (1), 136–150.

Simonov, P. V. On the role of the hippocampus in the integrative activity of the brain. *Acta Neurobiologica Experimentalis,* 1972, *34,* 33–41.

Singer, J. L. *Imagery and daydream methods in psychotherapy and behavior modification.* New York: Academic Press, 1974.

Spitz, R. A. *A genetic field theory of ego formation: Its implications for pathology.* New York: International Universities Press, 1959.

Spitz, R. A. *The first year of life.* New York: International Universities Press, 1965.

Sroufe, L. A. *Emotional expression in infancy.* Unpublished manuscript, 1976.

Thoman, E. B. How a rejecting baby affects mother–infant synchrony. In *Parent–infant interaction.* Amsterdam: CIBA Foundation, Associated Scientific Publishers, 1975.

Tomkins, S. S. *Affect, imagery, consciousness,* Vol. 1: *The positive affects.* New York: Springer, 1962.

Tomkins, S. S. *Affect, imagery, consciousness,* Vol. 2: *The negative affects.* New York: Springer, 1963.

Tomkins, S. S. Affect and the psychology of knowledge. In S. S. Tomkins & C. E. Izard (eds.), *Affect, cognition and personality.* New York: Springer, 1965.

Chapter 8

EMOTIONS: A COGNITIVE-PHENOMENOLOGICAL ANALYSIS

RICHARD S. LAZARUS, ALLEN D. KANNER, AND SUSAN FOLKMAN

ABSTRACT

We have attempted four main tasks in this chapter. First, a systematic overview is given of the cognitive–phenomenological theory of emotions put forth by Lazarus and his colleagues. The concepts of cognitive appraisal, coping, and several key principles in the theory, including transaction and flux, are reviewed. Second, we offer a working definition of emotion which also serves to summarize the main tenets of the theoretical point of view. Third, we draw upon this point of view to deal with a number of phylogenetic issues concerning the nature of emotion in humans and infra-humans. Finally, we attempt to redress the traditional imbalance of thought in which positively toned emotions have been neglected in favor of the negative. We systematically examine some of the conceptual issues that have made it difficult to integrate positively toned emotions into emotion theory. In this discussion, emphasis is placed on the functions of physiological changes in positively toned emotions and on the ways that positively toned emotions affect coping. Throughout, our view has been that the neglect of positively toned emotions in emotion theory has obscured their importance in human adaptation and in psychological growth and change.

Emotions are central to our understanding of human behavior and experience on every level of scientific analysis—sociological, psychological, and

189

Emotion: Theory, Research, and Experience
Volume 1: Theories of Emotion

physiological (Lazarus, 1978; Lazarus & Cohen, 1977; Lazarus, Cohen, Folkman, Kanner, & Schaefer, 1980; Lazarus & Launier, 1978). Since few meaningful encounters, actions, and thoughts occur without emotion, or at least the potential for it, the presence of an emotion provides an important clue to the significance of a person's ongoing adaptational encounter with the environment. It is surprising, therefore, to find that in psychological studies dating approximately from the turn of the century emotions as such have received less attention than other significant psychological processes such as motivation and cognition. And in the light of the powerful role played in life by positively toned emotions such as love, joy, contentment, and exhilaration, it is equally surprising that, when emotions are considered in psychology, it is almost exclusively in terms of negatively toned emotions such as fear, anxiety, anger, guilt, and sadness–depression.[1]

The purpose of this chapter is twofold: First, to review Lazarus's *cognitive-phenomenological* theory of emotions (Lazarus, Averill, & Opton, 1970) and to consider some general issues about emotion from this theoretical perspective. Second, we shall use this theoretical perspective (see Lazarus, 1966, 1979; Lazarus, *et al.,* 1970; Lazarus & Launier, 1978) to examine some dilemmas concerning positively toned emotions.

BACKGROUND

For a long time the predominant approach to emotions in psychology has been drive-oriented rather than cognitive (Lazarus, 1968), despite the fact that cognitive approaches dominated psychological thought for most of its history (Bolles, 1974). However, there has been a marked resurgence of interest in cognitive approaches in recent years (Arnold, 1970; Dember, 1974; Mandler, 1975; Weiner, 1974), which can be traced in part to a previously existing and even growing concern with the regulating functions of cognition on emotion and motivation (e.g., Averill, 1973; Horowitz, 1976; Klein, 1970; Schachter, 1966; Zimbardo, 1969). This renewed emphasis on cognitive factors also brings current conceptualizations of emotions more in tune with the older ideas of William James, Lewin, Tolman, Heider, George Kelly, and H. A. Murray and perhaps also recent social learning theory as represented by Rotter, Bandura, Mischel, and others.

To emphasize the causal influence of cognitive processes on emotion—as we do—does not mean that emotion, in turn, does not causally affect cogni-

---

[1] Interestingly, it appears that the formula by which emotions have been labeled positive or negative is a combination of the experienced pleasantness or unpleasantness of a particular emotion and our attitudes toward that emotion. Smugness, for example, which *feels* good but is looked upon with disapproval, is therefore difficult to label as either positive or negative. In light of this, it seems best to us to use the cautious phraseology of positively toned and negatively toned emotions in order to avoid implications that we think are false.

tion. The latter effect has been amply discussed and documented by Lazarus, Deese, and Osler (1952), Young (1959), Korchin (1964), Easterbrook (1959), Sarason (1972), and others—in fact, by all those who have contributed to the Yerkes–Dodson law.[2] The relations between cognition and emotion are, no doubt, exceedingly complex two-way streets, with emotion often redirecting or interfering with cognitive activity, as well as vice versa. In an article on emotion in the *Encyclopedia Britannica,* Endre Grastyán (1975) discusses the *fusion* of cognitive and emotional activity as well as their interdependence (see also Folkman, Schaefer, & Lazarus, 1979).

This position is consistent with Altman (1976), who has criticized the traditional way of thinking of cause and effect in the linear terms of environmental stimulus (S) to person response (R), or even the neobehavioristic modification of this that adds organismic mediation, as in an S–O–R formulation. Since the theoretical route from cognitive activity to emotion has been underemphasized for a long time (Lazarus, 1968), we attempt to redress the imbalance by emphasizing how cognitive processes shape the quality and intensity of a given emotional response, rather than the other way around. Ultimately any comprehensive model will have to focus on the ongoing interplay of emotions and cognitions (Folkman *et al.,* 1979), a point to which we will return later.

The growth of cognitively oriented theories of emotion seems to have produced two parallel lines of thought about emotion and coping that are only now beginning to converge (Roskies & Lazarus, 1980). One arises from academic psychology and laboratory research and is illustrated by our own position. For example, during the period between 1962 and 1972, the role of cognitive mediation was extensively investigated by Lazarus and his colleagues in the laboratory (for reviews, see Lazarus, 1966, 1968; Lazarus *et al.,* 1970; Lazarus & Launier, 1978). A second line arises from the therapeutic work and thought of cognitive behavior therapists such as Ellis (1962), Beck (1971), Goldfried (1979), Meichenbaum (1977), and Mahoney (1977). Although their primary concerns are with treatment interventions, they have adopted an approach to emotion that explicitly argues that the beliefs or assumptions a person holds about himself or herself in the world determine the emotional response to daily events. When such beliefs are irrational, as in "the idea that it is a dire necessity for an adult human being to be loved or approved by virtually every significant other person in his community" (Ellis, 1962, p. 61), then the likelihood of misconstruing a situation and responding with a negatively toned emotion is greatly increased. There is a parallel between the key tenets of our cognitive approach to emotions and the premises underlying cognitive behavior therapists. The clinical implications are that if one changes what the person thinks and believes one can also change the pattern of emotional reactions to ordinary social transactions.

---

[2] The Yerkes–Dodson law (Yerkes & Dodson, 1908) states, in effect, that, as drive tension or arousal increases, performance first improves to an optimal level and then declines. This is the classic inverted U-shaped curve.

EMOTIONS FROM A COGNITIVE-
PHENOMENOLOGICAL PERSPECTIVE

A cognitive theory of emotion, at its bottom line, assumes that emotion arises from how a person construes the outcome, actual or anticipated, of a transaction or bit of commerce with the environment. This perspective suggests that adult humans may well be the most emotional creatures on earth, since our ability to use complex, symbolic cognitive processes permits subtle distinctions to be made and later recalled among many types of information.

COGNITIVE APPRAISAL

The concept used to denote the evaluative processes that are central to the cognitive theory of emotions is *cognitive appraisal* (Folkman, *et al.*, 1979; Lazarus, 1966; Lazarus *et al.*, 1970; Lazarus & Launier, 1978). Whether it is couched in terms of information processing (Folkman *et al.*, 1979), tacit knowing (Polanyi, 1958), personal constructs (Kelly, 1955), self-efficacy (Bandura, 1977), or whatever, such a concept is essential to understand and deal with the great individual differences in emotional intensity, quality, and fluctuation observed in comparable environmental settings. Were it not for such individual differences, found even within the same cultural settings, we would not need to speak of cognitive mediation. However, in the face of such variation among and within persons, theories of emotion *must* take into account the way what is happening is construed by the person.

In its fullest expression, a cognitively oriented theory states that each emotion quality and intensity—anxiety, guilt, jealousy, love, joy, or whatever—is generated and guided by its own particular pattern of appraisal (see Beck, 1971; Ellis, 1962; Lazarus & Launier, 1978). Learning, memory, perception, and thought—in short, cognitive activity—are always key causal aspects of the emotional response pattern.

The renewed emphasis on cognition brings with it a shift in the central variables of psychological analysis. Instead of needs and transient drives, we must speak of motivational constructs such as commitments (e.g., Klinger, 1975, 1977), goals, and values. These variables affect the personal stakes with respect to which well-being is defined. We say, for example, that a person will not be threatened or challenged if the endangered goal is minor in importance (Mahl, 1952; Vogel, Raymond, & Lazarus, 1959). Moreover, these motivational constructs cannot be defined without including cognitive variables (Klein, 1970).

In addition to motivational constructs (such as commitments), beliefs about oneself and the world are also important antecedent variables in emotion. Along with motivational constructs, such beliefs serve in the theory as determinants of the appraisal process. Motivational and cognitive antecedents of appraisal are also fused with emotional possibilities in actual life contexts and should not be regarded as separate and distinct except for convenience of discussion. For example, if we ask the question, "What makes a commitment powerful, a goal salient, or a value strong?" we must answer that it is the intensity of the emotions that accompany each of these "cognitive" phenomena that gives them their full meaning. With strong commitments come high hopes, intense fears, and the emotionally laden possibilities of exhilarating successes and depressing failures. Likewise, goals and values about which we feel blasé are simply not important enough to evoke either powerful emotionalized attractions or feelings of repulsion. The point is that, although cognitive variables are crucial in adaptation, beliefs and ideas become emotionally charged only when they are held so strongly that they are bound up in the person's sense of well-being or ill-being. Emotions, cognitions, and commitments are inextricably intertwined and are best understood in that way.

In the theoretical analysis presented by Lazarus and his colleagues, cognitive appraisal comes in three forms: primary, secondary, and reappraisal. The process of *primary appraisal* is the evaluation of every transaction or encounter for its significance for well-being. Three fundamental evaluations are possible: An *irrelevant* encounter is one that has no personal significance and hence can be ignored; a *benign-positive* encounter signifies a state of affairs that is considered beneficial or desirable; and a *stressful* encounter can take three forms, namely, harm–loss, threat, and challenge. Harm–loss refers to injuries that have already occurred, threat to ones that are anticipated, and challenge to the potential for positive gain, mastery, or growth rather than the harms or dangers that such a confrontation might entail.

Secondary appraisal is the process of evaluating coping resources and options that might be available in a stressful encounter. Although it need not follow primary appraisal in time, since we can know something about such resources even when not in a stressful encounter, stress potentiates such appraisal because coping efforts are required to overcome, tolerate, or accept the actual or potential harmful outcome or, if the appraisal is one of challenge, to bring about the gain. In recent years we have increasingly come to believe that secondary appraisal is of even greater importance in adaptation than originally assumed (Lazarus & Launier, 1978). Indeed, it may be even more important than the occurrence of the stressful event itself, for the person's evaluation of the adequacy of his or her resources will in large part determine whether, for example, he or she feels threatened, challenged, or hopeful.

Reappraisal points to the feedback process wherein changes in primary and secondary appraisals can be brought about by changes in the adaptational encounter; as the person reacts and the environment counterreacts, these reactions are, in turn, perceived and appraised by the person, perhaps leading to altered appraisals of the person–environment relationship and an altered emotional response. The processes of appraisal are continuous. That is, the person never stops making evaluative judgments about what is happening. Nor is the appraisal process necessarily conscious, although it commonly is.

We shall see that reappraisal takes two forms: one in which the person takes in information about his or her changing relationship with the environment and evaluates its significance and the other in which the evaluative judgment represents an intrapsychic effort of coping with stress. (See Folkman *et al.* [1979] for a discussion of the limitations of information-processing models for explaining the mental processes involved in cognitive appraisal.) Thus, denial of danger and avoiding thinking about it are ways of regulating the emotion. Since they are not totally dependent on actual information from the environment, but are generated from within, as it were, Lazarus (1966) has previously referred to this as "defensive reappraisal." The more recent tendency is to speak of this as intrapsychic coping as distinguished from direct actions. Such a process uses a form of reappraisal to reduce emotional distress rather than to accurately assess the troubled relationship with a view to changing it (see Lazarus, 1978; Lazarus & Launier, 1978). In any case, this type of reappraisal gets us directly into a second key mediating process in emotion theory, namely, coping.

COPING

Like cognitive appraisal, coping also functions as a mediator between an environmental event and an emotional response (see Lazarus and Launier [1978] for a fuller exposition). And, as we noted above, some types of coping are in themselves forms of thought, as when a person in a potentially harmful transaction searches for information on which to predicate adaptive action, or when she or he attempts to regulate an emotional response to the transaction, say, by avoidance, denial, or intellectualized detachment. We call these *intrapsychic modes*. Another mode of coping is *direct action* designed to change a troubled person–environment relationship, by either planned interventions, altering one's own behavior, or altering the environment itself. The experience of emotions is either prolonged, attenuated, ended, or changed by the ways in which we cope with a particular event, whether the event is actual, imagined, or anticipated (Kemper, 1978). This is why, in our view, there cannot be a complete theory of emotion without taking into account the coping processes mediating between an adaptational transaction and the emotional reaction. Coping is not just a consequence of emotion as in the standard wisdom of the past. It has causal significance; that is, it shapes the emotional outcome by changing the appraisal of the past, present, or future person–environment relationship, either through cognitive appraisal processes or through direct action. The concept of coping, to which we will return later, also shifts attention away from the more simplistic idea of environmental "stressors" and stress responses and toward a more complex, ongoing, and inclusive view of person–environment transactions.

OTHER CORE PRINCIPLES

Before coming to a definitional statement about emotions, two other principles on which our thinking and research are predicated need to be outlined. One concerns the relational aspects of emotions, which is discussed below in the concept of transaction. A second principle concerns our emphasis on flux as much as stability, the latter having been the long-standing emphasis of psychology. A corollary of both transaction and flux is an emphasis on process rather than structure in thinking about and describing the adaptational encounters from which emotion springs.

TRANSACTION

Emotions arise out of ongoing relationships or *transactions* (Lazarus & Launier, 1978) in which the person influences and is influenced by the environment, especially the social environment. Such a view forces us to examine what is happening at a given moment as well as over time. To understand any given encounter in which there is an emotional episode, attention must be given to the changing *relationship* between the person and environment as the encounter proceeds. Transactions refer to and describe this relationship rather than the traditionally separated variables of person and environment (see Lazarus, 1978).

Potentially, any person–environment transaction may have emotional significance. However, it is only during those transactions that the person judges as having implications for her or his *well-being* that emotions actually occur. Such transactions are exceedingly common, perhaps the rule of life for many persons, although we do not really know much about this since there is little naturalistic study of daily emotional activity in normally functioning persons at various periods of life. Thus, when a transaction is seen as threatening or harmful, negatively toned emotions will arise. Similarly, a transaction that is viewed as potentially or actually benign or beneficial will evoke positively toned emotions.

A transaction is harmful when it hinders, delays, or makes impossible (or signals any of these) the gratification of needs, the attainment of goals or commitments, or the realization of positive values. The strength of the need, commitment, or value influences the appraised severity of the harm or threat. Most people share some needs and commitments and hence are harmed or threatened in more or less similar degrees by certain transactions. Thus, danger to life, a mortal illness, incapacitation, severe and prolonged bodily pain, loss of loved ones or of cherished possessions, and many more related transactions are calamities for most people to which they respond with strong negatively toned emotions. Similarly, receiving praise and recognition, acquiring new skills or desired possessions, being loved, and sharing with loved ones are nearly universal positive experiences.

However, sociocultural factors, individual history, and stage of life, which determine patterns of commitment, values, and belief systems, also vary greatly so that the kind and strength of emotional response even to common human experience can range quite dramatically. For example, one person may respond to the prospect of an extended period alone with relief or even enthusiasm while another reacts with apprehension or even terror. A woman who announces her love may generate highly positive feelings of joy or affection in one man, but another man may react with fear or annoyance. Since the definition of well-being is to some extent sculptured by socioeconomic forces, individual history, and personality, any complete theory of emotions must account for these forces and characteristics. The influence of social forces in emotion has been elaborated convincingly by Kemper (1978), a sociologist who, like ourselves, views emotions as the result of the outcomes of ongoing interpersonal relationships. For Kemper, the important relationship variables underlying emotions are power and status, and he views the social system as a template that shapes the patterns of such relationships and the personal values underlying them.

FLUX AND STABILITY

It is our view that emotions are experienced in fleeting episodes, as distinguished from the more stable sentiments and longer lasting moods. Such episodes are set in motion by some particular transactional event usually involving both intrapsychic and environmental activity. Emotion episodes have a beginning and an end and do not usually last long because the transaction inevitably changes as it unfolds, although it may repeat itself often. Each strong emotional episode is, in a sense, a little world of its own, a little drama with a particular background of beliefs, sentiments, and goals, thoughts infused with feelings, behavioral impulses and acts, and physiological reactions. Tied to these internal processes are environmental events and continuing changes in the person–environment relationship. Here, too, we follow a classic distinction and view moods as longer lasting, less intense, and more diffuse than an emotion episode, and sentiments as relatively stable disposi-tional judgments of social and physical objects and events, judgments that often underlie an emotion episode when triggered by a relevant cue (see also Ketal, 1975). In addition to being short-lived, each emotion in a complex en-counter expresses a different facet of the person's relationship with the en-vironment, or occurs at a different stage of the changing relationship.

Emotional life, therefore, is best understood as characterized by flux and change. As we shall see, several emotions can occur simultaneously, although some will be transformed into yet other emotions while others intensify or weaken over the course of a transaction or series of transactions. Such flux is anchored to cognitive appraisals and reappraisals of unfolding events that have changing relevance to one's well-being.

Stability of emotional patterning can come about in two ways: First, a per-son may re-enter essentially the same environment repeatedly and therefore be exposed to recurrent environmental conditions. Thus, an argument may ensue between husband and wife in the morning at home, and, as they separate to pursue their daily tasks with new adaptational requirements, the anger dissipates or is replaced with new thoughts, feelings, and actions. There may be some residual disturbance for a time, due either to the hormonal substances that have been sent coursing through the blood and tissues or to continuing rumination and intrusive thoughts (Horowitz, 1976). Usually, however, the anger gives way to other reactions that are tied to the immediate events of the working day. However, on returning home, the unresolved issue recurs perhaps in an anticipatory thought, or in a word or action by the partner, and another anger episode—with a structure similar to the last—ensues. In effect, stability in the environment may create a stable pattern of recurring emotions, each with similar dynamics.

Second, personality factors make some emotional reactions and patterns more likely than others. Stable patterns of commitment, values, and belief systems about oneself in relation to the environment, and unresolved childhood conflicts, such as difficulties accepting male or female authority, strong needs to be approved or to dominate or control, and so one, illustrate developmentally based determinants of stability in emotional pattern. Such factors create important agendas for the emotional episodes of the day. They serve as the background, as it were, against which the precipitating figure is a specific interpersonal transaction. The emotional response of the person to the figural event often cannot be understood without a knowledge of the background factors, that is, the motivational and cognitive agendas that help define for any given individual what is appraised as harmful, benign, or beneficial. Stability or flux in emotion is an empirical question that can be assessed by examining the pattern of emotion in the same person across en-vironmental settings and over time. We would expect the degree of flux or stability to vary greatly from person to person as a function of person and environment characteristics.

DEFINING EMOTION

Using the preceding discussion as a backdrop, we can now generate a summary definition of emotion: Emotions are complex, organized states (analogous to, not the same as, syndromes [see Lazarus *et al.,* 1970]) consisting of cognitive appraisals, action impulses, and patterned somatic reactions. Each emotion quality (e.g., anger, anxiety, joy) is distinguished by a different pattern of components, which is what urges the analogy to a syndrome. Moreover, the three components of emotion are subjectively experienced as a whole, that is, as a single phenomenon as opposed to separate and distinct responses. When one component is missing from the perception the experience is not a proper emotion although it may contain some of the appropriate elements.

Having indicated the three key components of the emotion itself and the perception or experience of it, we need to say a few things about each component as part of the total syndrome. We have already dealt at some length with *cognitive appraisal* processes. By including appraisals in the definition we are saying that not only do emotions arise as the result of evaluation of the transaction or encounter, but the ongoing appraisals are themselves an integral and intrinsic component of the emotion. Anger, for example, includes the attribution of blame for a particular kind of injury or threat, and guilt also involves such attribution of blame to oneself, with the further implication that one has not only done harm but has acted badly in accordance with personal standards of behavior. These attributions are forms of cognitive appraisal that are more than initial evaluations; they become an ongoing and critical dynamic in the experience of anger and guilt. Emotions not only involve an action impulse and somatic disturbances, but include as part of the emotional process and experience the cognitive appraisal on which they are based. Emotions and cognitions are thus inseparable, since appraisal comprises a part of the emotional reaction.

In referring to an *action impulse* rather than an action per se, we are expressing the thought that an action that is set in motion internally (psychophysiologically) need not be carried out or visible; it can be suppressed, denied, or transformed. We are inclined to treat even inaction as an action impulse when doing nothing involves suppression, a usage that recognizes that "freezing" in mammals is one kind of built-in emergency response. On the other hand, it is not clear to us what should be done with inaction when it is associated with depression, disappointment, or being relieved or content. We shall have something to say about this later in connection with somatic response in the context of positively toned emotions. In any event, the action impulse is an integral part of an emotion process and of its subjective experience or perception.

Action impulse also encompasses the expressive aspects of emotion, since facial expression, postural patterns, verbal styles, and body gestures are an aspect of an emotion-linked action, and they are capable of expressing or communicating what the person is feeling. All acts serve both an instrumental and an expressive function, these often being difficult to distinguish one from the other. For example, striking when angry can be a form of expression and instrumentality, knowingly or not, as is embracing when feeling love. Screaming in fear and whooping for joy are also examples that have expressive–instrumental value, as are voice modulation and intonation during speech. Along with other mammals, we use expressive cues in interpreting our own and others' feelings.

The instrumental aspects of emotion-linked actions also make it difficult to distinguish these acts or action impulses from what we have earlier called coping. For example, the dominant action impulse in anger is usually to injure or destroy the object of the anger; in fear it is to escape or avoid the harm or danger. The actions of anger and fear, which are among the clearest instances of instrumentality, also serve coping functions in that they can be seen as evolution-linked efforts, successful or not, to overcome the harm or master the danger by eliminating or weakening it. Thus, negatively toned emotions are ordinarily viewed as having survival value because of their close ties with adaptive actions. They are also useful because of the physiological mobilization they engender, the better through which to cope with emergencies. On the other hand, this very mobilization for action is also the basis of the stress disorders discussed by Cannon (1935) and Selye (1956).

Finally, in speaking of a *patterned somatic reaction,* we are taking the controversial position that each emotion is associated with a particular physiological response *profile.* This is in sharp contrast to the widespread current belief that physiological arousal is the same in any emotion regardless of quality (Holmes & Masuda, 1974; Schachter & Singer, 1962; Selye, 1976). Although the evidence is weak, overall, we note that Lacey (1967) has demonstrated the *specificity* of autonomic end-organ reactions to different types of person–environment transactions, and Mason (1975; Mason, Maher, Hartley, Mougey, Perlow, & Jones, 1976) has found a different profile of hormonal response for each of a number of physical stressors. These and other researchers, in our view, have effectively demonstrated the inadequacy of general arousal theory. However, this is not the place to argue such a controversial position since it is not central to our cognitive–phenomenological treatment of emotions or to our definition. In addition, elsewhere (Lazarus *et al.,* 1980) we have suggested reasons why today the dominant position in psychosomatic medicine, social psychology, and social epidemiology is that there is little or no specificity in the somatic patterning connected with emotional states. In any case, and whatever the nature of the somatic response, this response is an intrinsic feature of emotion.

PHYLOGENETIC ISSUES

The topic of emotions is usually seen in phylogenetic perspective because humans share the emotion function with other, simpler mammalian species. This raises a number of interesting and important issues that need to be addressed. For example, although emotion occurs in all mammalian life, this does not imply that the same process is occurring from one species to another, although it probably does imply that some of the elements overlap, at least physiologically, and possibly even socially and psychologically.

For us the key differences between human and infra-human emotions are best summarized by two very general principles, namely, that as one goes up the phylogenetic scale variability increases, and that such variability results from the growing dependence in higher mammals on learning and symbolic thought and the lessening dependence on wired-in stimulus–response linkages. From a cognitive theory perspective, human emotions depend on subtle social shadings and meanings that are absent or minimal in infra-human animal life. This, in turn, means that sociocultural forces have a far more powerful influence on human than infra-human emotions, in both the contemporaneous and the long-term developmental sense.

Is there a finite number of emotions in human life? Diverse writers, including Plutchik (1962), who is well known for his phylogenetically oriented theory and a "circumplex" arrangement of eight primary emotions, have proposed between five and fifteen basic emotions. Kemper (1978) makes the interesting point that, to the sociologist, the number of emotions is irrelevant, but the number of different social conditions from which emotions can flow, whether serving as cues, socialization parameters, or interactional and relational outcomes, is a key concern.

A cognitive theorist might make a parallel argument, namely, that what is most important are the major categories of appraisal from which action impulses and different mobilization patterns might arise. That is, every emotion has its own cognitive theme. Negatively toned emotions, in general, arise whenever a transaction is appraised as harmful or threatening or as lacking in some important aspect (Kanner, Kafry, & Pines, 1978) and one's resources for managing it are deemed inadequate or of doubtful efficacy. In contrast, positively toned emotions, such as happiness or joy, arise whenever a transaction is appraised as benign or favorable, or one's resources have been successfully used to control or master harm. Without debating the specifics, this kind of analysis of the cognitive constructions or appraisals underlying each emotion quality is very much in line with Beck's (1971) writings.

Since most social transactions are quite complex, several cognitive themes, each connected with different emotions, can occur at once or in succession, based on subtle differences or changes in meaning or on shifts in attention from one aspect of an encounter to another. A difficult question then arises about how we shall classify the fundamental themes and the emotions they generate, and where we draw the boundaries among them. To divide emotions into discontinuous cognitive categories (which are, in reality, categories of meaning), such as anxiety, fear, anger, jealousy, sadness, guilt, shame, joy, love, hopefulness, or whatever, creates the risk of reifying the categories that are said to describe basic relationships with the environment, thus losing the subtle variations (shadings of meaning) that occur within any category. Put differently, the response term "anger" leaves out the obvious fact that there are many forms of anger, as is probably true of each of the other broad, existing categories, despite the conviction that in all likelihood the between-category differences are greater and perhaps more important than the within-category differences.

This difficulty of classification is especially prominent for theorists such as ourselves who argue that each emotion probably has its own unique somatic response pattern, and for theorists such as Ekman and Friesen (1975) and Izard (1971), for whom each emotion is said to have its own unique set of facial muscle movement patterns. As we noted earlier, the problem is not pressing at the sociological level, where the focus is on the eliciting social relationships, but it is particularly urgent in psychophysiological analysis. The best solution, we think, is to take a tentative stand on broad categories and then to test their capacity to reflect useful social and psychological eliciting conditions, cognitive appraisals, and patterns of behavioral and physiological response.

Thus, at any given time, we may want to treat anxiety as a general category or distinguish it from fear (see Lazarus & Averill, 1972), while always being ready to recognize that important distinctions among anxieties may have to be drawn later on the basis of evidence about antecedents and consequences. This latter is precisely what happened in the case of agonistic behavior when ethologists became aware that the eliciting conditions, behavioral configuration, and physiological response differed between predatory aggression and defensive aggression (Moyer, 1976). Increasing sophistication in observation and research led to the abandonment of the overly general category of aggression and to the creation of various distinctions, such as between interspecific and intraspecific forms. This has also led to different theories about the evolutionary origins of aggression. The same prospect exists with respect to human emotion categories such as anger, anxiety, envy, joy, love, etc. We must be prepared to evolve new categories, some of which may fit within existing broad ones while others may emerge as independent categories based, for example, on careful social and psychological study (e.g., on cognitive appraisals).

Cognitive theory points also to another consideration related to the question about the number and kinds of basic emotions. Since humans share with all mammalian life a number of evolutionary-based neurochemical systems that make certain patterned reactions possible, it is reasonable to assume that a number of basic emotion-relevant cognitive themes stem from this common history. To be basic in this sense, however, does not mean to be simple or even the same. Anger may be a more basic emotion in the phylogenetic sense than the probably uniquely human emotions of nostalgia and smugness, but appraisals of the social situations eliciting anger may be every bit as complex as those that make us feel nostalgic. Furthermore, some forms of anger may arise from quite special and complex social and cognitive circumstances, such as those necessary to invoke righteous indignation.

Implied above is that many human emotions arise from the special, subtle, symbolic, cognitive distinctions of which only humans are capable, and it does not seem persuasive to us to argue that every human emotion has a counterpart in infra-human life. With evolutionary changes in our nervous systems have come new and complex patterns of emotional response that may or may not have counterparts in simpler species.

POSITIVELY TONED EMOTIONS

Traditionally, theories of emotion have concentrated on negatively toned emotions, ignoring or virtually ignoring the positively toned ones (see Leeper, 1948). One reason for this is that emotions have been viewed in the evolutionary context of biological adaptation, which emphasizes the capacity of an animal to rise to a survival-related emergency. From time to time, writers have noted the preoccupation of biology and psychology with stress and negatively toned emotional states to the exclusion of the positively toned. However, tension-reduction views of psychodynamics have predominated in psychological thought for a long time.

As in the case of general theory in psychology, psychoanalytic theory has followed the tradition of treating negatively toned emotions as prototypical and as sources of pathology. Illustrative is a recent collection of major psychoanalytic papers on emotion (Socarides, 1977), most of which are explicitly concerned with negatively toned emotions. Those that address positively toned emotions concentrate on their pathological aspects.

The tension-reduction orientation, and the emphasis on emotion as reflecting conflict and pathology, has resulted in a bleak view of human psychological experience, that is, as being oriented essentially toward defense against aversive conditions or impulse rather than toward positive experience and transcendence. It has also resulted in the theoretical and empirical neglect of positively toned emotions. Even cognitive approaches can make this error when the focus is on pathology. An illustration is Ellis's (1962) concept that irrational assumptions or beliefs are the basis of troubling or distressing emotional reactions. If one makes this assumption, then there is likely to be no place in one's thought for positively toned emotions, which could also arise from false assumptions and the cognitive appraisals they foster. If one's starting place is pathology, then even a cognitive approach to emotions is apt to ignore or minimize the importance of positively toned emotions and to overstate the importance of negatively toned emotions and their pathological implications. Our purpose in this section is to begin redressing the imbalance by discussing positively toned emotions, despite a number of difficult problems they present to traditional emotion theory.

The cognitive–phenomenological concept of appraisal gives us no trouble in dealing with positively toned emotions because the way a person evaluates the potential outcome of a transaction is said to determine the emotional response, both its intensity and its quality. Positively toned emotions arise when the transactional outcome is appraised as desirable. At first glance, the only remaining set of questions concerns how a person comes to evaluate cues about anticipated outcomes and to interpret transactions as good or bad.

There are, however, sticky issues about how to fit positively toned emotions into general emotion theory, issues that no approach has fully resolved and that few have even tackled. One of the most difficult issues concerns the place of physiological changes in positively toned emotions. This is an acute problem for any theory that defines emotion as necessarily including somatic arousal or mobilization or that assumes that such mobilization has had evolutionary-adaptive value. A second issue concerns the relationship between positively toned emotions and coping. As we shall see, theories that center attention on negatively toned emotions such as fear and anger ordinarily would not lend themselves to postulating any connection between positively toned emotions and coping.

THE FUNCTIONS OF PHYSIOLOGICAL CHANGES

From an evolutionary-adaptive perspective, it is easy to see why emotions such as fear and anger were and are important in survival. The physiological changes linked to these emotions as part of the mobilization for fight or flight (Cannon, 1935) are of enormous value despite the fact that, carried to the extreme, they would also exhaust the organism's reserves and do great tissue damage (Selye, 1976). Such somatic changes during emergencies were incorporated easily into psychological thought, which was heavily based on the organizing principle of tension reduction, and were expressed in the concept of arousal and drive theory (Duffy, 1951; Lindsley, 1951; Malmo, 1959). Drive (tension in psychological terms) and arousal (physiological mobilization) provided a unidimensional concept—varying from low to high—depending on the adaptational pressures. Emotion was subsumed under this doctrine as a unidimensional state of arousal and as a drive.

Arousal theorists such as Duffy, as well as neobehaviorists such as Brown and Farber (1951), were quite willing to reduce emotion to an intervening drive. Thus, emotion as we know it in experience was for several decades virtually written off as a viable psychological concept and, instead, was conceptualized as an intervening drive that has no substance beyond the defining antecedent and consequent conditions.

Nevertheless, as long as arousal or somatic disturbance is considered one of the defining attributes of emotion, as in our preceding treatment, a perplexing problem is posed by positively toned emotions such as joy, love, happiness, exhilaration, hopefulness, relief, peacefulness, etc. Stated differently, one might ask: Why *jump* for joy? Even more difficult is finding an answer to the question of why there should be any somatic activity associated with hope, curiosity, relief, and peacefulness.

The adaptational importance of positively experienced physiological activity can be found in occasions in which a person explores, plays, or displays curiosity. For example, Murphy (1974), White (1974), and Erikson (1963) have pointed to the role of play in the development of coping skills. Yet the essence of play is that it is highly stimulating; that is, it is accompanied not by stress and negatively toned emotions but by pleasurable emotions such as joy, a sense of thrill, and happiness, none of which is possible when one feels threatened and insecure. Moreover, as is well illustrated in research by Tolman (1941), Harlow (1953), and Harlow, Harlow, and Meyer (1950), exploratory activity occurs more readily in a biologically sated, comfortable, and secure animal than in one greatly aroused by a homeostatic crisis. The human infant will not venture far from a parent unless it is feeling secure, at which point it will play and explore, venturing farther and farther away but returning speedily if threatened or called by the mother (Bowlby, 1973). If positively toned emotions were generally characterized by quiescence, they would have less adaptive value in mobilizing play and exploration.

The issue of physiological change is especially troublesome considering that positively toned emotions have been understood as end-states of positive adaptational outcomes. If positively toned emotions are the result of successful adaptation, then mobilization would seem to have no function, although it obviously would when we are in jeopardy and must act in order to survive. Pleasurable emotions have even been treated as involving a decrease in arousal occurring after coping (Berlyne, 1960). If one argues that positively toned emotions occur only during a decrease in arousal, then there is a need to explain the function of increases in arousal that occur during pleasurable emotions such as passion, thrill, exhilaration, joy, and ecstasy. However, Tomkins (1963) has stated that, although both positively and negatively toned emotions can occur during rises in activation levels, only negatively toned emotions are associated with enduring high levels and positively toned emotions are exclusively linked to decreasing activation levels. Such a claim, we think, is unsubstantiated, and it does not seem to fit intuitively. People experience intense hope, curiosity and joy, strong exhilaration, glee, passion, and ecstasy, and some of these states seem capable of being sustained quite as long as episodes of anger and fear.

Another argument is that it is not generally accurate to regard positively toned emotions as end-states except in the most limited, transitory sense. The mistake has been to see the moment of joy as an outcome, as if it were the end to a commitment, rather than as one of a series of steps or stages. When one passes through one stage, the next one awaits. In effect, the experience of a positively toned emotion that is the result of successful striving may be not only an expression of positive appraisal for having passed an obstacle, but also a contribution to future coping and commitment efforts.

There are at least two ways that arousal in positively toned emotions enhances subsequent efforts required by long-range commitments and goals. Positive arousal can stimulate or even inspire the effort necessary to turn toward another task. For example, if an author's work is favorably reviewed, she or he is likely to begin the next writing task in a more enthusiastic state of mind. Positive arousal can also increase feelings of self-efficacy (Bandura, 1977), even to the extent that a task that would have been appraised as too difficult is instead seen as manageable. Consider the student who, upon receiving an ''A'' in a difficult course, decides after all to go to a job interview that previously was too threatening. Here the increased sense of self-efficacy that was generated from the first episode provides the impetus for tackling another problem that is essentially unrelated. Moreover, the effects of positive arousal on subsequent efforts are not limited to the onset of new endeavors, for the recollection of positive emotional experiences during particularly trying undertakings can reinspire efforts and restore belief in self-efficacy. These ideas are central to the role played by positive emotions in the coping process.

POSITIVELY TONED EMOTIONS AND COPING

Coping and positively toned emotions do not, at first, seem like suitable bedfellows. Coping naturally seems to go with stress and, hence, with negatively toned emotional states. Researchers sensibly reason that fear, anxiety, anger, guilt, etc., arise during stressful transactions or in anticipation of them and, once having occurred, are themselves sources of stress (Lazarus, 1966; Mechanic, 1962). Parallel to this, coping involves actual attempts either to change stressful transactions between person and environment or to regulate the negatively toned emotions that result from them. However, positively toned emotions are not sources of stress except on those occasions when they inspire guilt, shame, or anxiety, and, although it makes sense to ask, "How do people cope with threats, or how do they manage threat-based emotions?" the complementary question, "How do people cope with positive experiences, or how do they manage the joy they bring?" sounds odd indeed unless one presumes that reports of joy are merely instances of denial.

When positively toned emotions are viewed solely as end-states of successful adaptation, a position we have already challenged, we are led to two erroneous assumptions about the relations between emotions and coping. The first is that only negatively toned emotions *signal* the need for coping. For instance, Blatt and Feirstein (1977) have proposed that stressful emotions can be either a necessary instrumental component of adaptation or an undirected discharge of tension or anxiety. When they are a component of adaptational endeavors, negatively toned emotion involves information processing in which the emotion serves a signal function, "alerting the individual to the occurrence of important events and occasions" (Blatt & Feirstein, 1977, p. 122). The important events and occasions signaled by negatively toned emotions must be those that tax or exceed the person's resources and therefore require coping (Lazarus & Cohen, 1977; Lazarus & Launier, 1978). In the same tradition, Berlyne (1960) has stated that positively toned emotions during effective functioning may arise as a result of a decline in physiological arousal (as in relief) after successful completion of a task or as a function of "the equilibrium following discharge" (p. 115). Thus, positively toned emotions are seen as signals of positive transactions or outcomes, or that coping has been successful, but are not usually regarded as signals that coping might be necessary.

Our concept of challenge, which is one form of a stress-related cognitive appraisal, shows this view to be inadequate. As we stated earlier, in challenge, the person's thoughts center not on the possibility of harm–loss, but on the potential for mastery or gain. Although threat and challenge appraisals are similar in that they both require coping, and they generate substantial physiological and psychological mobilization when the stakes are high, they differ importantly in that challenge is accompanied by positively toned emotions such as excitement, hope, eagerness, and even joy, as in the "joy of battle." There is a certain parallel here with recent research on and assessment of what has been called "sensation seeking" (Zuckerman, 1979). In any case, excitement, hope, eagerness, and joy can help keep a person alert and vigilant to important inputs with which to cope and to the transactions requiring anticipation and planning for success.

Thus, it can be said that such positively toned emotions can signal the need for coping just as readily as do negatively toned emotions such as anxiety, guilt, anger, etc. If, indeed, the signal function of emotion is to be taken seriously—and there are some difficulties with it (Folkman *et al.*, 1979; Lazarus, 1966, 1968)—it must not be limited to negatively toned emotions or, as is commonly the case, to anxiety alone.[3] Rather, it is necessary to recognize that coping can be experienced positively and in positive transactions as well as negatively as in threat.

The second erroneous assumption is that only negatively toned emotions are linked to coping activities or can be held responsible for arousing and sustaining coping activity. Drive theory has traditionally emphasized the motivating role of anxiety (Dollard & Miller, 1950; Miller, 1960). Similar roles could be suggested for depression, as when it is said to motivate defensive hypomanic behavior, for anger, as when it is said to motivate reaction formation, and for guilt, as when it is said to motivate moral or restitutive behavior. We would argue, however, that coping activity can be aroused and sustained also by positively toned emotions. In fact, a number of related suggestions along these lines have already been made by others.

For example, Plutchik (1970) has suggested that pleasurable emotions evolved from the adaptationally critical but primitive *approach* response. Approach responses include "patterned bodily reaction(s) such as reproduction, incorporation, exploration, orientation, or some combination thereof" (Plutchik, 1970, p. 12). Extrapolating from this, one might say that curiosity, surprise, and wonder—emotions that are exploratory in nature—inherently contain a certain degree of anticipatory coping. Also considering emotions and survival in evolutionary terms, Hamburg (1963) has emphasized the bonding function of positive emotions: "The physiology of emotion insures fundamental acts of survival: the desire for sex, the extraordinary interest in the infant, the day-to-day reinforcement of interindividual bonds. . . . Social life is rooted in emotion and is basic to survival" (pp. 316–317).

Hamburg's comments also bring to mind recent thought and research on the importance of human social networks and social support systems in health, morale, and social functioning (Berkman, 1977; Cassel, 1976; Cobb, 1976; Kaplan, Cassel, & Gore, 1973). That such supports and, by implication, the positive emotions they engender can play at least an indirect role in coping

---

[3] The signal function of emotion is usually interpreted in one of two ways. In the first interpretation, the assumption is made that the presence of anxiety signals to the ego that there is danger. The dilemma is that the ego must already have assessed danger for anxiety to occur. There is, therefore, an inherent circularity in this notion. It makes more sense to argue that emotion (anxiety) amplifies the sense of danger (see Tomkins, 1963) or helps by creating the bodily mobilization required for alertness or vigilance in the face of danger. However, these are not signal functions.

In the second interpretation, a dissociated ego process is assumed wherein an unconscious ego process could sense danger while a conscious decision-making ego process would be unaware of it. In such an instance, the mobilization of action designed to cope with danger, which could require conscious processing, could benefit from a system in which the unconscious cognitive activity, by means of the anxiety it generates, informs (signals) the conscious cognitive system that there is danger. In short, for the signal function to make logical sense requires that there be dissociation of ego processes so that the mobilization of action would not readily proceed without some emotion-based cue (e.g., anxiety) that the person is in jeopardy.

has also been suggested by Moos (1977). Still other writers, such as Cousins (1976), Stotland (1969), and even Selye (1974) in his distinction between eustress and distress, have suggested or implied that positively toned emotions can facilitate coping. All told, the explanations thus far proposed to explain why positively toned emotions facilitate coping include primitive approach responses, social bonding, prior or concurrent emotional experience, and direct biochemical processes. However, we think there are still other ways in which positively toned emotions may facilitate coping, to which we turn now.

Positively toned emotions serve three basic psychological functions in coping, namely, as breathers from stress, as sustainers of coping effort and commitment, and as restorers. To our knowledge, these functions, though features of everyday living, have neither been noted nor studied in research on human adaptation.

Breathers. Positively toned emotions often provide or are part of a break from stress. The need for a *breather,* as we have chosen to call it (a chance to "get away"), is institutionally recognized almost universally in the form of a vacation, siesta, coffee break, or school recess. However, the purpose of a breather is not only to free oneself temporarily from a stressful experience, but also to engage in pleasurable diversionary activity. A boring coffee break or dull recess or vacation may not be particularly refreshing. The most effective breather should be one during which a positive emotional experience occurs. For this reason, we treat breathers as breaks from an ongoing stressful situation during which a positive emotion occurs.

The vacation, siesta, coffee break, and school recess are instances of institutionalized breathers. At the individual level, people differ in the frequency and quality of breathers that they allow themselves. Breznitz (1971), Horowitz (1976), Shapiro (1965), and Jenkins (1976), for example, describe the worried or obsessive person as one who persistently ruminates; the worried or obsessive person may also be unable to take breathers easily, and, when doing so, the problems promoting stress are brought right along. Obsessive worrying, ruminating, or working under pressure without a breather perpetuates distress and can reduce effectiveness in problem solving (Breznitz, 1971).

The significance of breathers has also been acknowledged in the creativity phenomenon often referred to as "incubation" (Poincaré, 1970; Sinnot, 1970; Wallas, 1970). Wallas, for example, has provided this relevant quotation from the great German physicist Helmholtz:

> He [Helmholtz] said that after previous investigations of the problem "in all directions . . . happy ideas come unexpectedly without effort, like an inspiration. So far as I am concerned, they have never come to me when my mind was fatigued, or when I was at my working table. . . . They came particularly readily during the slow ascent of wooded hills on a sunny day" [p. 91].

A slow ascent, one would guess, that is accompanied by pleasant emotions, that is, a breather.

In an attempt to explain the unconscious activity that he believed occurred during incubation, Poincaré (1970), the renowned mathematician, made the surprising comment that unconscious creative mathematical ideas "are those which, directly or indirectly, affect most profoundly our emotional sensibility." By this he meant that, since creative thoughts are aesthetically pleasing, the strong, positive emotional reaction to such ideas provides an opening through which they are ushered into consciousness. Chances are that much coping, problem solving, and creating occur during an effective breather. The speculations of Poincaré remind us that virtually nothing is known about the intervening mechanisms by which positive emotions as an aspect of breathers might facilitate coping.

Sustainers. Positive emotions can also *sustain* coping, so that even when situations become very taxing coping efforts are more likely to persist. Izard and Tomkins (1966) have stated it as follows: "Certainly positive affects, such as excitement and its accompanying autonomic activity, may sustain rather than interfere with performance" (p. 93). Examples of two different sustaining roles played by pleasurable emotions are the excitement of challenge and the optimism of hope.

Challenge carries with it the sense that the demands of a situation, although difficult, can eventually be met and the obstacles overcome. It holds the promise of the development of abilities, skills, and increased confidence, as well as the attainment of meaningful rewards. These possibilities can generate a positive excitement and mobilization that support effective and sustained coping. Not only are the possible benefits of challenge a source of support, but the utilization of one's resources while coping in a situation appraised as challenging is in itself a source of joy. This, in turn, reinforces and sustains coping efforts.

What has recently been referred to as "flow" (see Csikzenlmihalyi, 1976; Furlong, 1976) appears to be an extremely pleasurable, sustaining emotion that arises when one is totally immersed in an activity and is utilizing one's resources at peak efficiency. Examples of flow are the basketball player who is "hot" and the inspired performance of a musician, actor, or speaker. The person in flow "finds, among other things, his concentration vastly increased and his feedback from the activity greatly enhanced" (Furlong, 1976, p. 35). Although the experience of flow is characterized by a feeling of effortlessness, it occurs at times when great coping effort is usually required and during these times serves as a powerful sustainer of coping.

Norman Cousins' (1976) account of his fight against *ankylosing spondylitis* provides another example of the benefits of challenge-related emotions as sustainers. In his battle with the disease, Cousins researched it thoroughly, changed his medication with the approval of his doctor, and removed himself from the hospital setting to a hotel, which he considered more conducive to his major form of therapy, laughter. Above and beyond this, according to Cousins, his challenge-centered approach provided him with the energy and inclination to take such unusual steps: "Deep down I knew I had a good chance and *relished* the idea of bucking the odds" (p. 1462, emphasis ours). His discussion of the experience is peppered with phrases such as "I thought as hard as I could" (p. 1459), and, as the treatment began to work, he makes reference to the elation his success was bringing him. It could be hypothesized that Cousins was helped to sustain coping efforts through the positive emotional state that resulted from each successful step, and from the satisfaction of trying as hard as he could not to give in to the despair a life-threatening and debilitating disease usually brings. Joy and satisfaction, in turn, reinforced his effort to appraise the situation as a challenge, operating as a feedback loop from coping to modest success, to joy and satisfaction, to renewed and sustained coping effort, and so on.

Challenge depends on a sense of efficacy or control (Averill, 1973; Lefcourt, 1976) over the encounter. Hope, on the other hand, can occur even when an individual's efforts are known not to be sufficient. The belief, often ambivalently held, that there is even a slim chance that things will work out is enough to create and sustain hope, which, in turn, provides motivation to keep going, that is, to continue coping. Hope and challenge can operate simultaneously in the coping process and are mutually reinforcing.

Hope can occur in the face of very severe or even desperate threat. For example, the cancer patient who can do little to curb the progress of the disease can still feel hope through faith in the doctor, God, luck, denial (Weisman, 1972), or whatever. Yet the devastating effects of the absence of hope, or the state of hopelessness, have received far more attention (Engel, 1962; Lazarus, 1966; Schmale & Iker, 1966; Seligman, 1975). Despite theories to the contrary, hopelessness is probably not as common as is claimed, nor do we understand well the capacity of people to hope in the face of there being little or no basis for it. Ironically, although ambiguity or uncertainty has traditionally been regarded as a basis of anxiety, it is often an important basis of hope. When a member of the family, a friend, or a physician avoids presenting the bleakest of details about a patient's condition and outlook, the attempt is often being made to provide a basis for hope, since such a state of mind is easier to achieve when the person experiences some uncertainty about the facts than when everything is crystal clear. It would be profitable to give the same attention to the power of hopefulness to sustain coping and commitment as that given to hopelessness.

Although challenge and hope both sustain coping, their differences may provide clues to important individual differences in the situation and in personality. Challenge occurs when the potential for control of the situation appears to reside within the person, while hope often occurs when the situation seems beyond control (Lefcourt, 1976; Rotter, 1966). Optimists apparently come in many forms, including both the hopers and the challenged. However, being consistently a hoper or consistently one who is challenged could be maladaptive. A person who is always challenged may be unable to turn to hope in situations where nothing constructive can be done, while hopers may fail to act to change the situation when the opportunity does present itself. Approached from another vantage point, while gambling in Las Vegas the same situation may elicit fervent prayer (hope) from a vacationing church member while mobilizing the sleight-of-hand skills of the more challenged cheat. Challenge and hope both sustain coping, but do so differently depending on the person and/or the situation.

Restorers. The third function of positively toned emotions is that of *restorer.* While sustainers can enter the coping process at the outset and operate throughout a stressful transaction, and breathers occur primarily during the coping process, restorers come into play toward the latter stages of coping, when healing and recovery take place. Restorers are positively toned emotional experiences that facilitate the individual's recovery from harm or loss by replenishing damaged or depleted resources and/or developing new ones.

Lowered self-esteem, for instance, is a common reaction to the physical damage caused by polio (Visotsky, Hamburg, D. A, Goss, & Lebovits, 1961), mastectomy (Sutherland, Orbach, Dyk, & Bard, 1952), and severe burns (Hamburg, Hamburg, & DeGoza, 1953). In recovering from these traumas, restoration of self-esteem often occurs as a result of the rest, protection, acceptance, and care given by others. Along these lines, Hamburg *et al.* (1953) noted the facilitating role of hope in "the restoration of interpersonal relationships and restoration of self-esteem [in the] recovery and restoration of pre-illness function both physical and mental" (p. 20).

Restorers are also critical in recovery from depression. Klinger (1975, 1977) has suggested that depressed people have lost the incentive to engage in life; that is, that which used to involve them in one activity or another no longer does so. Little in life has any value. Klinger (1975) argues, however, that depressive withdrawal has an adaptive function since the negative experiences associated with it provide a mechanism whereby an organism may "annul . . . its commitment to an inaccessible incentive" (p. 14), such as attaining the love of a now deceased spouse. However, as Klinger points out, long periods of depression are maladaptive and a recovery phase is necessary.

The determinants of the onset and duration of the recovery phase following disengagement are unknown, although we do know that this phase is characterized by a gradually increasing appreciation of new incentives and, to quote Klinger (1977) again: "At some time during clinical depression patients become unusually responsive to small successes. For instance, depressed patients working on small laboratory tasks try harder after successfully completing a task than after failing one, which is a pattern opposite to that of nondepressed individuals, who try harder after failure (Loeb, Beck & Diggory, 1951)" (p. 169). During recovery, then, small successes are more likely to evoke positively toned emotions than at other times.

All this makes sense if we consider another adaptive component of depression. During early depression, attention is riveted on the object of actual or potential loss, so much so that any cue in the environment even vaguely associated with the loss is enough to trigger depressive ruminations. During this time, a person is evaluating the meaning of the loss, with all that it implies for reassessment of the past, present, and future and for changes in self-esteem. In time, though, such ruminations become utterly repetitive and of little adaptive value. Subsequently, the depressed person may become bored or simply tired of the whole depressive process. Attention becomes less focused and begins to drift or shift. If at this point opportunities exist for engagement or enjoyment that do not require too much risk (since self-esteem is typically low) and the ability to mobilize (which is also low), then attention may turn to small pleasurable activities.

The positively toned emotions that accompany these small endeavors are capable of at least temporarily breaking the depressive "set" and can remind the depressed person of other, more pleasant ways of experiencing and appraising the world. Through such repeated episodes involving greater risk and engagement, new incentives are discovered and/or interest in old ones is revived, and the depression lifts. In this example, which may be only one of several ways that recovery from depression occurs, positively toned emotions reinforce successful new activities and, by virtue of their intrinsic pleasurable nature, help put the person in a different, more optimistic "state of mind."

As just noted, the reevaluation that occurs during depression and the positively toned emotions that nurture recovery not only permit disengagement from old incentives but also are instrumental in the development of new values and incentives. This is likely to be one major way, for instance, that new levels or stages of ego development, which are characterized by new values, goals, and current concerns, are acquired and maintained (see Loevinger, 1976). That is, growth is one result of successful coping with crisis or recovery from depression. In this vein, Mages and Mendelsohn, (1979) have concluded from their study of cancer survivors that current conceptual approaches to coping are inadequate in that they fail to describe the opportunities experienced by many cancer survivors to "constructively reorganize [their] life, to understand [themselves] and others better, and to deepen close relationships."

CONCLUDING THOUGHTS

We have come to a new, yet in some ways very old, conceptualization of emotion by viewing it as a product of cognitive activity. However, unlike writers of the Middle Ages and classical times, we do not regard emotions as inferior or more animal-like compared with the higher mental processes of thought or reason. Emotions are a fusion of highly developed forms of cognitive appraisal with action impulse and bodily changes. It is only a matter of convenience of analysis that we separate cognitive, emotional, and motivational processes, and we think it unwise to be seduced into thinking of them as independent processes when each affects the other in a complex fashion.

Furthermore, in contrast to the tradition that treats coping only as a consequence of emotion (drive), we see coping as part of the transactional process from which emotions arise and change. The intensity and quality of the emotional response, and the inevitable emotional flux that occurs in any encounter, are products of how the person copes; such coping alters the person–environment relationship as perceived and construed by the person. Emotions are always appraised outcomes of actual, imagined, or anticipated transactions, the most important of which in human affairs are usually social. Each emotion quality involves a distinctive appraisal of the positive or negative significance of the encounter.

Positively toned emotions, which have been singularly underemphasized in psychological and biological thought, pose some especially sticky problems for a theory of emotion. First, it is difficult to conceive of why there should be physiological changes in positively toned emotions, especially hope, curiosity, relief, and peacefulness. Aside from simply excluding these as emotions, a sensible possibility is to reject the notion of positively toned emotions as end-states of striving and instead to regard them as inspirational way stations toward longer range commitments. Second, although coping processes seem like strange bedfellows for positively toned emotions, the latter do serve important coping functions as breathers, sustainers, and restorers. Such a position helps integrate emotion theory in general, especially that part of it which relates to positively toned emotions, to the theory of stress and coping from which our cognitive–phenomenological approach to emotions stems.

In thinking about emotions we must abandon the usual tendency to view things as discrete and either/or, and instead begin to see emotion, motivation, and cognition as highly interdependent, indeed fused, processes. These processes are tied to complex adaptational requirements in a species of animal that is able, more than any other, to transcend biologically wired-in boundaries in the search for meaning and value. In our view, we do not do well to overstate the ties and parallels between humans and lower animals, because ultimately this leads us toward a reductionism that distorts the actual nature of human adaptational activity and experience. It is appropriate and advantageous to be truly comparative, but this does not mean we can understand human emotions solely through reference to animal emotions, any more than we can understand animal emotions from the perspective of the human variety. Ultimately, this forces theories of emotion to emphasize cognitive processes, since it is this aspect of mind that has so strikingly changed and developed in the course of evolution.

ACKNOWLEDGMENTS

Writing this chapter was supported in part by a research grant from the National Institute on Aging (AG 00799*).

REFERENCES

Altman, I. Environmental psychology and social psychology. *Personality and Social Psychology Bulletin,* 1976, *2,* 96–113.

Arnold, M. B. (ed.) *Feelings and emotion.* New York: Academic Press, 1970.

Averill, J. R. Personal control over aversive stimuli and its relationship to stress. *Psychological Bulletin,* 1973, *80,* 286–303.

Bandura, A. Self-efficacy: Toward a unifying theory of behavioral change. *Psychological Review,* 1977, *84,* 191–215.

Beck, A. T. Cognition, affect and psychopathology. *Archives of General Psychiatry,* 1971, *24,* 495–500.

Berkman, L. *Social networks, host resistance, and mortality: A follow-up study of Alameda County residents.* Unpublished doctoral dissertation, University of California, Berkeley, 1977.

Berlyne, D. E. *Conflict, arousal and curiosity.* New York: McGraw-Hill, 1960.

Blatt, S., & Feirstein, A. Cardiac response and personality organization. *Journal of Consulting and Clinical Psychology,* 1977, *45,* 115–123.

Bolles, R. C. Cognition and motivation: Some historical trends. In B. Weiner (ed.), *Cognitive views of human motivation,* pp. 1–20. New York: Academic Press, 1974.

Bowlby, J. *Attachment and loss.* New York: Basic Books, 1973.

Breznitz, S. A study of worrying. *British Journal of Social and Clinical Psychology,* 1971, *10,* 271–279.

Brown, J., & Farber, I. E. Emotions conceptualized as intervening variables—with suggestions toward a theory of frustration. *Psychological Bulletin,* 1951, *48,* 465–495.

Cannon, W. B. Stresses and strains of homeostasis. *American Journal of Medical Science,* 1935, *189,* 1.

Cassel, J. The contribution of the social environment to host resistance. *American Journal of Epidemiology,* 1976, *104,* 107–123.

Cobb, S. Social support as a moderator of life stress. *Psychosomatic Medicine,* 1976, *38,* 300–314.

Cousins, N. Anatomy of an illness (as perceived by the patient). *New England Journal of Medicine,* 1976, *295,* 1458–1463.

Csikzenlmihalyi, M. *Beyond boredom and anxiety.* San Francisco: Jossey-Bass, 1976.

Dember, W. N. Motivation and the cognitive revolution. *American Psychologist,* 1974, *29,* 161–168.

Dollard, J., & Miller, N. E. *Personality and psychotherapy.* New York: McGraw-Hill, 1950.

Duffy, E. The concept of energy mobilization. *Psychological Review,* 1951, *58,* 30–40.

Easterbrook, J. A. The effect of emotion on cue utilization and the organization of behavior. *Psychological Review,* 1959, *66,* 183–201.

Ekman, P., & Friesen, W. *Unmasking the face.* Englewood Cliffs, N.J.: Prentice-Hall, 1975.

Ellis, A. *Reason and emotion in psychotherapy.* New York: Lyle Stuart, 1962.

Engel, G. L. *Psychological development in health and disease.* Philadelphia: W. B. Saunders, 1962.

Erikson, E. H. *Childhood and society.* New York: W. W. Norton, 1963.

Folkman, S., Schaefer, C., & Lazarus, R. S. Cognitive processes as mediators of stress and coping. In V. Hamilton & P. M. Warburton (eds.), *Human stress and cognition: An information-processing approach.* London: Wiley, 1979. Pp. 265–298.

Furlong, W. The fun in fun. *Psychology Today,* June 1976, 35–38 and 80.

Goldfried, M. R. Anxiety reduction through cognitive–behavioral intervention. In P. C. Kendall & S. D. Hollon (eds.), *Cognitive–behavioral interventions: Theory, research and procedures.* New York: Academic Press, 1979, in press.

Grastyán, E. Emotion. In H. H. Benton (ed.) *Encyclopedia Britannica,* Chicago: Encyclopedia Britannica, Inc., 1974, pp. 757–766.

Hamburg, D. A. Emotions in the perspective of human evolution. In P. Knapp (ed.), *Expressions of the emotions in man and animal,* pp. 300–317. New York: International Universities Press, 1963.

Hamburg, D. A., Hamburg, B., & DeGoza, S. Adaptive problems and mechanisms in severely burned patients. *Psychiatry,* 1953, *16,* 1–20.

Harlow, H. F. Mice, monkeys, men and motives. *Psychological Review,* 1953, *60,* 23–32.

Harlow, H. F., Harlow, M. K., & Meyer, D. R. Learning motivated by a manipulation drive. *Journal of Experimental Psychology,* 1950, *40,* 228–234.

Holmes, T. H., & Masuda, M. Life change and illness susceptibility. In B. S. Dohrenwend & B. P. Dohrenwend (eds.), *Stressful life events: Their nature and effects,* pp. 45–72. New York: Wiley, 1974.

Horowitz, M. *Stress response syndromes.* New York: Jason Aronson, 1976.

Izard, C. E. *The face of emotion.* New York: Appleton-Century-Crofts, 1971.

Izard, C. E., & Tomkins, S. S. Affect and behavior: Anxiety as a negative affect. In C. D. Spielberger (ed.), *Anxiety and behavior,* pp. 81–125. New York: Academic Press, 1966.

Jenkins, C. D. Recent evidence supporting the role of psychologic and social risk factors for coronary disease. *New England Journal of Medicine,* 1976, *294,* 987–994 and 1033–1038.

Kanner, A., Kafry, D., & Pines, A. Conspicuous in its absence: The lack of positive conditions as a source of stress. *Journal of Human Stress,* 1978, *4,* 33–39.

Kaplan, B., Cassel, J., & Gore, S. *Social support and health.* Paper presented at American Public Health Association meetings, San Francisco, California, November 9, 1973.

Kelly, G. A. *The psychology of personal constructs* (2 vols.). New York: W. W. Norton, 1955.

Kemper, T. Toward a sociology of emotions: Some problems and some solutions. *American Sociologist,* 1978,.

Ketal, R. Affect, mood, emotion, and feeling: Semantic considerations. *American Journal of Psychiatry,* 1975, *132,* 1215–1217.

Klein, G. S. *Perception, motives and personality,* pp. 162–231. New York: Knopf, 1970.

Klinger, E. Consequences of commitment to and disengagement from incentives. *Psychological Review,* 1975, *82,* 1–25.

Klinger, E. *Meaning and void.* Minneapolis: University of Minnesota Press, 1977.

Korchin, S. J. Anxiety and cognition. In C. Scheere (ed.), *Cognition: Theory, research, promise,* pp. 58–78. New York: Harper & Row, 1964.

Lacey, J. J. Somatic response patterning and stress: Some revisions of activation theory. In M. H. Appley & R. Trumbell (eds.), *Psychological stress,* pp. 14–37. New York: Appleton-Century-Crofts, 1967.

Lazarus, R. S. *Psychological stress and the coping process.* New York: McGraw-Hill, 1966.

Lazarus, R. S. Emotions and adaptation: Conceptual and empirical relations. In W. J. Arnold (ed.), *Nebraska Symposium on Motivation,* pp. 175–265. Lincoln: University of Nebraska Press, 1968.

LAZARUS, R. S. *The stress and coping paradigm.* Paper presented at the Proceedings of The Critical Evaluation of Behavioral Paradigms for Psychiatric Science, Nov. 3–6, 1978. Salishan Lodge, Gleneden Beach, Oregon.

Lazarus, R. S., & Averill, J. R. Emotion and cognition: With special reference to anxiety. In C. D. Spielberger (ed.), *Anxiety: Current trends in theory and research,* Vol. II, p. 242. New York: Academic Press, 1972.

Lazarus, R. S., Averill, J. R., & Opton, E. M., Jr. Toward a cognitive theory of emotion. In M. Arnold (ed.), *Feelings and emotions,* pp. 207–231. New York: Academic Press, 1970.

Lazarus, R. S., & Cohen, J. B. Environmental stress. In I. Altman & J. F. Wohlwill (eds.), *Human behavior and the environment: Current theory and research,* Vol. 1. New York: Plenum, 1977.

Lazarus, R. S., Cohen, J. B., Folkman, S., Kanner, A., & Schaefer, C. Psychological stress and adaptation: Some unresolved issues. In H. Selye (ed.), *Guide to stress research.* New York: Van Nostrand Reinhold, 1980, in press.

Lazarus, R. S., Deese, J., & Osler, S. F. The effects of psychological stress upon performance. *Psychological Bulletin,* 1952, *49,* 293–317.

Lazarus, R. S., & Launier, R. Stress-related transactions between person and environment. In L. A. Pervin & M. Lewis (eds.), *Perspectives in interactional psychology.* New York: Plenum, 1978,

Leeper, R. W. A motivational theory of emotion to replace "emotion as a disorganized response." *Psychological Review,* 1948, *55,* 5–21.

Lefcourt, H. M. *Locus of control, current trends in theory and research.* Hillsdale, N.J.: Lawrence Erlbaum, 1976.

Lindsley, D. B. Emotion. In S. S. Stevens (ed.), *Handbook of experimental psychology,* pp. 473–516. New York: Wiley, 1951.

Loeb, A., Beck, A. T., & Diggory, J. Differential effects of success and failure on depressed and nondepressed patients. *Journal of Nervous and Mental Disease,* 1971, *152,* 106–114.

Loevinger, J. *Ego development.* San Francisco: Jossey-Bass, 1976.

Mages, N. L. and Mendelsohn, G. A. Effects of cancer on patients' lives: A personological approach. In G. A. Stone, F. Cohen and N. E. Adler (eds.), *Health psychology.* San Francisco: Jossey-Bass, 1979.

Mahl, G. F. Relationship between acute and chronic fear and the gastric acidity and blood sugar levels in *Macaca mulatta* monkeys. *Psychosomatic Medicine,* 1952, *14,* 182–210.

Mahoney, N. J. Cognitive therapy and research: A question of questions. *Cognitive Therapy and Research,* 1977, *1,* 5–17.

Malmo, R. B. Activation: A neuropsychological dimension. *Psychological Review,* 1959, *66,* 367–386.

Mandler, G. *Mind and emotion.* New York: Wiley, 1975.

Mason, J. W. A historical view of the stress field, Part I. *Journal of Human Stress,* 1975, *1,* 6–12.

Mason, J. W., Maher, J. T., Hartley, L. H., Mougey, E., Perlow, M. J., & Jones, L. G. Selectivity of corticosteroid and catecholamine response to various natural stimuli. In G. Serbin (ed.), *Psychopathology of human adaptation,* pp. 147–171. New York: Plenum, 1976.

Mechanic, D. *Students under stress.* New York: The Free Press of Glencoe, 1962.

Meichenbaum, D. *Cognitive-behavior modification.* New York: Plenum, 1977.

Miller, G. A., Galanter, E. H., & Pribram, K. *Plans and the structure of behavior.* New York: Holt, 1960.

Moos, R. (ed.) *Coping with physical illness.* New York: Plenum, 1977.

Moyer, K. E. *The psychology of aggression.* New York: Harper & Row, 1976.

Murphy, L. B. Coping, vulnerability and resilience in childhood. In C. V. Coelho, D. A. Hamburg, & J. E. Adams (eds.), *Coping and adaptation,* pp. 69–100. New York: Basic Books, 1974.

Plutchik, R. *The emotions: Facts, theories and a new model.* New York: Random House, 1962.

Plutchik, R. Emotions, evolution and adaptive processes. In M. Arnold (ed.), *Feelings and emotions,* pp. 3–24. New York: Academic Press, 1970.

Poincaré, H. Mathematical creation. In P. E. Vernon (ed.), *Creativity,* pp. 77–88. Baltimore: Penguin, 1970.

Polanyi, M. *Personal knowledge.* Chicago: University of Chicago Press, 1958.

Roskies, E., & Lazarus, R. S. Coping theory and the teaching of coping skills. In P. Davidson (ed.), *Behavioral medicine: Changing health life styles.* New York: Brunner/Mazel, 1980, in press.

Rotter, J. B. Generalized expectancies for internal versus external control of reinforcement. *Psychological Monographs,* 1966, *80* (Whole No. 609).

Sarason, I. G. Experimental approaches to test anxiety: Attention and the uses of information. In C. D. Spielberger (ed.), *Anxiety: Current trends in theory and research,* Vol. II, pp. 383–403. New York: Academic press, 1972.

Schachter, S. The interaction of cognitive and physiological determinants of emotional state. In C. D. Spielberger (ed.), *Anxiety and behavior,* pp. 193–224. New York: Academic Press, 1966.

Schachter, S., & Singer, J. E. Cognitive, social and physiological determinants of emotional state. *Psychological Review,* 1962, *69,* 379–399.

Schmale, A., & Iker, H. P. The affect of hopelessness and the development of cancer. *Psychosomatic Medicine,* 1966, *28,* 714–721.

Seligman, M. E. *Helplessness.* San Francisco: W. H. Freeman, 1975.

Selye, H. *The stress of life.* New York: McGraw-Hill, 1956.

Selye, H. *Stress without distress.* Philadelphia: Lippincott, 1974.

Selye, H. *The stress of life* (rev. ed.). New York: McGraw-Hill, 1976.

Shapiro, D. *Neurotic styles.* New York: Basic Books, 1965.

Sinnot, E. W. The creativeness of life. In P. E. Vernon (ed.), *Creativity,* pp. 107–115. Baltimore: Penguin, 1970.

Socarides, C. (ed.) *The world of emotions: Clinical studies of affects and their expression.* New York: International Universities Press, 1977.

Stotland, E. *The psychology of hope.* San Francisco: Jossey-Bass, 1969.

Sutherland, A. M., Orbach, C. E., Dyk, R. B., & Bard, M. The psychological impact of cancer and cancer surgery. I. Adaptation to the dry colostomy: Preliminary report and summary of findings. *Cancer,* 1952, *5,* 857–872.

Tolman, E. C. Motivation, learning and adjustment. *Proceedings of the American Philosophical Society,* 1941, *84,* 543–563.

Tomkins, S. S. Simulation of personality: The interrelationships between affect, memory, thinking, perception and action. In S. S. Tomkins & S. Messick (eds.), *Computer simulation of personality,* pp. 3–57. New York: Wiley, 1963.

Visotsky, H. M., Hamburg, D. A., Gross, M. E., & Lebovits, B. Z. Coping behavior under extreme stress. *Archives of General Psychiatry,* 1961, *5,* 423–448.

Vogel, W., Raymond, S., & Lazarus, R. S. Intrinsic motivation and psychological stress. *Journal of Abnormal and Social Psychology,* 1959, *58,* 225–233.

Wallas, G. The art of thought. In P. E. Vernon (ed.), *Creativity,* pp. 91–97. Baltimore: Penguin, 1970.

Weiner, B. (ed.) *Cognitive views of human emotion.* New York: Academic Press, 1974.

Weisman, A. D. *On dying and denying.* New York: Behavioral Publications, 1972.

White, R. Strategies of adaptation: An attempt at systematic description. In G. V. Coelho, D. A. Hamburg, & J. E. Adams (eds.), *Coping and adaptation,* pp. 47–68. New York: Basic Books, 1974.

Yerkes, R. M., & Dodson, J. D. The relation of strength stimulus to rapidity of habit formation. *Journal of Comparative Neurological Psychology,* 1908, *18,* 459–482.

Young, P. T. The role of affective processes in learning and motivation. *Psychological Review,* 1959, *66,* 104–125.

Zimbardo, P. G. *The cognitive control of motivation: The consequences of choice and dissonance.* Glenview, Ill.: Scott, Foresman, 1969.

Zuckerman, M. Sensation seeking. In H. London & J. Exner (eds.), *Dimensions of personality.* New York: Wiley, in press.

Chapter 9

THE GENERATION OF EMOTION:
A PSYCHOLOGICAL THEORY[1]

GEORGE MANDLER

ABSTRACT

The intent is to develop a psychological theory defining the processes and mechanisms that produce emotional experiences and behavior. The background of the theory is found in modern developments toward a cognitive psychology, as well as in the analysis of private experience. The effects of interruption, the role of limited capacity conscious processes, the effect of cognitive evaluations, and the psychological function of peripheral autonomic reactions are discussed and their function in generating emotions is demonstrated. While the common language is rejected as a basis for psychological theory, its function in some common views and experiences of emotion is discussed. The generation of an integrated emotional experience out of autonomic and cognitive variables is extended to a discussion of related topics, including anxiety, facial expression, sexual emotion, and the adaptive role of the

---

[1] I have taken as my task in this chapter the presentation of a body of incomplete theory that I have advanced over the past 25 years. It aims at an understanding of human emotional experience and behavior, and a full exposition of its ancestry and ramifications would require much more space than I have available here. I have therefore talked only about the theory as such and about some of its assumptions and implications. I have kept the encumbrances of scholarly niceties such as specific references and footnotes to a minimum. More of these are available in the (incomplete) list of references to my own papers and books.

Emotion: Theory, Research, and Experience
Volume 1: Theories of Emotion

autonomic nervous system. Some current views on the biology of emotion are rejected, but further investigations of the evolutionary role of specific psychological mechanisms are suggested. The testability of the theory is discussed and further directions indicated.

THE INTENT OF A PSYCHOLOGY OF EMOTION

With the advent of new approaches to traditional problems of psychology, it is appropriate to base this discussion on some of these metatheoretical developments, specifically the liberation from orthodox behaviorism, rigid positivism, and inappropriate operationism. A new cognitive psychology has developed, which has borrowed its concepts from movements and disciplines as far ranging as Gestalt theory, neurophysiology, systems theory, and computer technology. It has combined concepts from these various endeavors, postulated useful and imaginative theoretical fictions, and—most important—insisted that empirical reality (be it experimental or phenomenal) must be constructed out of underlying psychological theory.

What distinguishes modern cognitive psychology from its somewhat unrelated namesakes earlier in the century (and behaviorists and others still mistake one for the other) is its insistence—to borrow a term from the linguists—on developing the deep structure of human mental events and actions. With that intent, the umbrella concept of emotion will also become superfluous as we investigate and discover the variables that generate the events that the common language and older psychologies have labeled "emotional." Just as the psychologies of memory, perception, or thought concentrate on processes rather than definitions, so a psychology of emotion should stress the underlying psychological processes and mechanisms that produce the sort of events that we call emotions. Such an approach not only avoids the question "What is an emotion?" (*pace* William James), but, in fact, denies its psychological relevance. It does not deny the historical utility of such question asking; rather, it assumes that we have achieved the kind of cumulative maturity that obviates its further pursuit. Parenthetically, I might note that the question "What is consciousness?" is still appropriate, but again the hope is that eventually that question too will become unnecessary.

A theory of emotion should attempt to identify those mechanisms and processes that do, in fact, generate most of the phenomena thought to be part of the family of concepts sheltered by the term "emotion." Specifically, such a theory must clearly state which "emotional" phenomena it will not, or cannot, address. Clearly such an attempt will be most successful if it is catholic in the phenomena with which it deals and at the same time parsimonious in the processes and mechanisms it invokes.

It is not my intent to address other theories critically in the pages to follow, but I do want to draw attention to the limited usefulness of some current theories, incurred by their restriction of intent to highly circumscribed definitions and phenomena. Thus, a theory that stresses the subjectivity of emotional experience must deal with that subjectivity directly and empirically: We must eventually be able to predict and control, not just describe and explain. Specifically, the conditions of the real world, as well as the personal cognitive world of the individual, must be addressed and accounted for. Or, a listing of "emotions" should, at least, be accompanied by a mechanism that accounts for the open-ended nature of emotional experience. It is an open-ended set of experiences because the number of different possible emotional experiences is at least very large, consisting of the concatenation of values on several continuous cognitive variables. As another example, the invocation of stress should address both the subjective interpretations and the external conditions that might be necessary, though not sufficient, for its occurrence. Similarly, effects of stress and threat should be derivable from a theory of emotion rather than providing its starting point as undefined primitives. Furthermore, the reverse of Morgan's canon should be taken seriously, and observations from a lower species should not be generalized to a higher one without equally good evidence from the latter group. Finally, speculations about the central nervous system should be given the same status as speculations about the conceptual nervous system (the mind).

HISTORY OF A THEORY: PARENTS AND COUSINS

My general view of emotional experience and behavior grew up, as I did intellectually, with the development of the new cognitive psychology. This psychology asserts, with James and the behaviorists, the importance of autonomic events, but at the same time assigns these events a contributory rather than a defining role. William James saw the experience of autonomic and skeletal events as *the* emotion, and the behaviorists looked at the visceral events themselves as the observables that constituted emotions. (I have retained the experience of autonomic events as a central argument, but have integrated it with the cognitive evaluative functions of the mind, the continuous and automatic meaning analysis performed by the mental apparatus. The impetus for this integration came from the work of Stanley Schachter and his collaborators [Schachter, 1971; Schachter & Singer, 1962].)

The emphasis on cognitive factors arose from an interest (often misplaced) in the measurement and prediction of anxiety. Though not labeled as such, that approach was cognitive because it concentrated much of its effort on the determination of people's perceptions and evaluations of their internal states and the conditions under which the "anxiety" was experienced. In particular, it was an approach that drew attention to the competition between emotional or task-irrelevant states and performance.

Seeing emotion as the confluence of experiences of autonomic activity, cognitive analyses of the current state of the world, and interactions with other cognitive processes focused special attention on a problem that became dominant in cognitive psychology—the analysis of the limited capacity of the human processing system—that is, the limited capacity of consciousness and attention placed firmly in the center of modern concerns by George Miller (1956). It became obvious that the interactions of autonomic perceptions, meaning analyses, and task-relevant processes had to be seen from the vantage point of a limited conscious system.

A PERSONAL RECAPITULATION

My original interests and attentions to "emotion" were fostered and guided in graduate school by Seymour Sarason. We developed the Test Anxiety Questionnaire and the theoretical interpretation of anxiety as an interfering, task-irrelevant state in a series of papers starting with that by Mandler and Sarason (1952). The next excursion was marked by a series of studies on autonomic feedback, the relation between the perception of autonomic activity and intellective performance (e.g., Mandler, Mandler, & Uviller, 1958), culminating in a monograph on the response to threat (Mandler, Mandler, Kremen, & Sholiton, 1961). These forerunners of the current interest in biofeedback established my commitment to the importance of autonomic perception in emotion. At the same time, William Kessen convinced me of the importance of seeing anxiety and distress both as nonreactive and as related to states of helplessness (Kessen & Mandler, 1961).

In a sense, these attempts toward an understanding of anxiety were prolegomena to looking at emotion writ large. Under the influence of Schachter's work, as well as John Lacey's guidance on physiological matters, I wrote my first, somewhat immature, and in retrospect still behavioristically accented, attempt at a statement on emotion (Mandler, 1962).

By now I was seriously concerned with more general statements about anxiety, threat, and emotion and, partly derivative from my work with Kessen, investigated and speculated about the effects of behavioral and cognitive interruption (Mandler, 1964). This was quickly applied to problems of anxiety (Mandler, 1972; Mandler & Watson, 1966) and set in the broader perspective of anxiety theories (Mandler, 1968).

With the radical shift to cognitive and information-processing theories, I pursued organizational analyses of memory and soon became concerned with the limited capacity system and with the role of consciousness in cognitive theory in general. By 1971 these interests had merged with my concern with emotion, and I wrote the first draft of my book, *Mind and emotion,* during a sabbatical at Oxford in 1971–1972. With its publication in 1975, I had essentially completed the outlines of the position presented here, though it still benefits from additional cogitation. A chapter on the history of the psychology of emotion gave me an opportunity to learn more about my historical forebears than I knew when I wrote the book (Mandler, 1979a). A recent chapter on stress and thought processes brought me full circle when I wrote at length about stress-induced emotional states and their interactions with performance, memory, and problem solving (Mandler, 1979b).

EXPERIENCE AND BEHAVIOR: TOWARD A THEORETICAL PHENOMENOLOGY

William James had insisted that his theory was a theory about emotional experience. During the behaviorist doldrums in the United States, such a direction for psychology was denied or ignored, but the emergence of the new cognitive psychology has made it possible once again to ask about the processes and mechanisms that produce emotional experience rather than about observationally rich but explanatory-poor skeletal and visceral "responses."

However, the behaviorist period has not gone without its lessons. It has taught us that private experience and public behavior are different categories of scientific events, and it has also imbued us with the conviction that psychologists can and should act as observers and theorists of other people's (or lower animals') minds and behaviors. This subject–scientist distinction avoids the circular pitfalls of philosophical phenomenology, but also presents us with formidable theoretical problems. These are problems that must be faced, particularly by a psychology of emotion that aspires to an explanation of human emotional experience.

An individual's private experience is exactly that: It is private, that is, not accessible to anyone else. Any attempt at a comprehensive cross-individual phenomenology must fail. I can—still within some limits—know my phenomenal life, but I cannot know yours. Phenomenal contents are a conglomeration of visual, auditory, linguistic, and relational (to mention a few) representations that cannot be expressed—except in the most crude fashion—in words. Phenomenology, at best, shows us how these experiences might bear some crude resemblances to their verbal translations. In fact, one of the formidable tasks we face is to show how the private life can be translated (though not in a one-to-one fashion) into language. Thus, while one asserts the importance of individual private experience, one can—for the other—*only* assert it and infer it. The fundamental problem for a theoretical phenomenology is the postulation of private experiences on the one hand and the construction of their content (as a *theoretical* endeavor) on the other. One of the conundrums of a modern psychology is how best to use the observations of one's own private experiences as a heuristic device without letting those observations mislead us about the inferred contents of other consciousnesses (see Mandler & Mandler, 1974).

A psychology of emotional experiences will therefore postulate the inferred private experience of its objects of study (other people) and it will postulate certain processes that have their primary effects on those experiences. At the same time, such a psychological system must build additional explanatory structures that will permit us to move from the theoretical experience of people to the final observable outcomes. These theoretical structures must not only construct a language for the representation of the private experience, but also incorporate specific statements as to how these representations are transferred into recordable language, gestures, facial expressions, and other indicators.

At the present time these additional explanatory structures are not available, except in rather crude forms. Since I do want to talk about emotional experience as a theoretical outcome, I do want to stress that—in practice—this is not an easy step for any psychology of emotion.

To what extent can a psychology that aims at explaining both the experience and the behavior of emotion claim to use or address emotional phenomena in lower animals? Again, the answer must—as in the case of human experience and behavior—be asymmetrical. First, it is dangerous to use the heuristics of our own minds to infer similar structures in lower animals; such inferences would be purely theoretical with the attendant difficulties of finding testable consequences. However, private experiences can be ascribed to animals if these are useful for purposes of explanation. One could support such an enterprise by the suggestion that it is unlikely that something as complex as human consciousness was sprung on us in full flower by evolutionary pressures; the usual slow processes of mammalian evolution are more likely candidates and would support some rudimentary conscious processes in other animals. Second, the use of animal *behavior* in support of theories of emotion that address the human experience seems to be much more easily supported. To the extent that the observed behavior (be it skeletal or visceral) shows similarities across the phylogenetic scale, one can with some caution use the animal observation (and experiment) to say something useful about human emotional behavior. The single best example is the observation of emotional behavior in the presence and absence of intact autonomic nervous systems.

Given these boundary conditions, a cognitive–autonomic theory should have much to say about animal behavior and experimentation, and such extensions should be encouraged. Excursions of this sort are much to be preferred to the converse position taken by biological behaviorists who insist that the limitations be imposed by animal observations and that experimentation must be translated *pari passu* to a psychology of human emotion. Surely, we know more about the human cognitive apparatus than about that of the apes or of rats. The fear of theory, which characterized much of radical behaviorism, led to the poverty of psychological explanation. We cannot be limited in theory by the limitations of some animals. Just as we have learned from the behaviorists (while rejecting their approach), so can we learn from the phenomenologists (while rejecting their assumptions) about the richness and importance of human experience.

INTERRUPTION AND CONFLICT THEORIES

Given the importance that I place on autonomic arousal, a central issue concerns the conditions under which such arousal will occur. The major source of my suggestions is encompassed in interruption theory, which asserts that the interruption (blocking, inhibition) of ongoing organized thought and behavior is followed by autonomic nervous system activity. I had originally ascribed the ancestry of this notion to Kurt Lewin's tension model and its extension to completed and uncompleted tasks. More recently I have become more familiar with an extensive, but discontinuous, line of reasoning, embodied in the conflict theories of emotion. These theories started at least with Herbart in the late eighteenth century, reached full flower with Paulhan and Dewey in the nineteenth century, and continued into the twentieth century in some behaviorist speculations. Their common insight is that many if not all emotional states arise out of the interruption of ongoing psychological events, out of the conflicts and the discrepancies among them, or from the frustrations of actions. Curiously, there has never been any sense of continuity among these proposals. They rise and fall without building on one another.

My own entry into the field is distinct in one sense. The earlier "conflict" theories ascribed the emergence of complete and specific emotions to specific conflicts—I do not. Rather, I claim only that the visceral component is due to interruption (or conflict or discrepancy), but that the quality of the emotional state that ensues is dependent on other cognitive evaluations. In that fashion, the "same" conflict or interruption may lead to different emotions, depending on the outcome of the individual's meaning analysis at the time.

With that caveat, however, there is still no doubt that at least part of what I present as a theory of emotion is in the line of the conflict theorists, individuals who do not usually receive proper credit for their contribution to psychological analyses of human emotion.

BUILDING BLOCKS AND CEMENT

This section reviews the psychological processes and mechanisms developed from a variety of sources, which must be ascribed to the human organism in order to construct an "emotional" system. Such a system will generate some subset of the class of events that the common, and sometimes the psychological, language calls emotion.

LIMITED CAPACITY CONSCIOUSNESS

The insight that human beings are limited in the amount of information they can process, or the number of events that they can apprehend at any one time, is quite old. It is only in the past 20 years, however, that any systematic attempt has been made to investigate the nature and function of that limited capacity. The endeavor started with the fact that only a limited set of events or values of variables are available to the individual in immediate memory tests or in psychophysical judgments. Further explorations then extended this limitation to the nature of focal attention, the number of alternatives that can be simultaneously considered for judgment and decision tasks, and the interaction between the central focus of attention and other peripheral attention-demanding events. These investigations have fed into a now generally accepted notion that consciousness, focal attention, or some aspects of short-term memory are indeed best characterized by a limited capacity process that—and the jury is still out on this issue—is limited either in the number of organized chunks of information it can process or in the amount of immediately available effort or capacity.

If we are concerned with emotional experience, then the generation of emotion must take place within that small conscious window to the mind; it is then "experienced." And if the class of psychological events that generate the "emotional" experience consists primarily of the perception of autonomic events and the product of the cognitive evaluation of the current internal and external situation, then the construction of the emotion out of these events and products must fit within the limited capacity that consciousness provides. Thus, consciousness of emotion implies the results of two sets of unconscious mental processes: autonomic activation (which is then perceived in a conscious process) and cognitive meaning analyses, the outcomes of which are, in turn, presented in a conscious process. The conscious experience of the emotion (inadequately labeled something like joy, or fear, or elation, or depression) arises as a single experience out of its components. Like other Gestalt-like experiences, it is different from the sum of its parts. This does not prevent us, however, from seeking the separate antecedent mechanisms that give rise to this unitary experience.

PSYCHOLOGICAL FUNCTIONS OF
PERIPHERAL AUTONOMIC REACTIONS

In dealing with autonomic nervous system (ANS) activity as a determinant (not an index or symptom) of emotion, it must clearly be viewed in the first instance as an event external to the mental system—an event to be registered and perceived. At the same time, we must consider those mental processes that, in turn, give rise to autonomic nervous system activity. I shall deal with the latter problem in the next section. As far as the perception of autonomic (visceral) response is concerned, we must consider the kinds of receptors available for its registration. These are essentially insensitive and few, thus resulting in a perceptual system that can register only gross changes in either variability or intensity. I follow here Walter Cannon's argument against James's belief that specific emotions could be assigned to specific autonomic and skeletal patterns. Despite repeated attempts to demonstrate the existence of discrete patterns, there is currently no evidence that different patterns of autonomic activity occurring *prior* to the experience of an emotion determine that experience. Let me emphasize that such a demonstration would easily be accommodated by my theoretical position: Such specific patterns would provide specific perceptions to be integrated with the cognitive components of the emotional experience. At present, however, the evidence suggests that ANS activity is primarily perceived in terms of intensity and provides the intensity dimension of emotional experience, while the cognitive components determine emotional qualities.

None of these arguments denies that different emotional experiences might be *accompanied* by different patterns of ANS activity. For the time being, though, we do not yet know whether these patterns have any specific psychological (in contrast to physiological) functions. However, there do exist some very few autonomic events (to be discussed) that are differentially perceived and that are possibly causal for some specific "emotional" experiences.

SOME CONSEQUENCES OF INTERRUPTION: EVENTS THAT PRODUCE AUTONOMIC REACTION

My interest in the effects of interruption was fathered, in part, by a pursuit of the origins of anxiety. However, in part, it arose out of a sense of frustration in trying to find some systematicity in physiological (as well as psychological) discussions of autonomic activity and its antecedents. In brief, physiologists can at best point to some central nervous system (CNS) structures that seem to be involved whenever ANS activity is observed, and psychologists typically either parrot their reductionist brethren or speak vaguely of threat and stress, which, in turn, are circularly defined. Typically one is presented with lists of events such as tissue injury, pain, threat, stress, etc., that are said to be responsible for the activation of the ANS.

I shall expand later on an analysis of the ANS from an adaptive, evolutionary point of view. For the time being, I shall simply assert that one can consider the ANS as a system that alerts the organism to important events in the environment. It is here that I want to connect with the concept of interruption. One of the most important sets of events to which the organism's behavioral attention has to be drawn consists of the occasions when well-developed, well-organized, habitual, and previously adaptive actions fail, cannot be completed, or in some way are inhibited. I refer to all of these as interruptions—The unintended noncompletion of organized actions or thoughts not only alerts the organism directly but also brings about ANS activity. That activity, in turn, singles out the occasions of interruption by marking them in memory as being accompanied by ANS activity. On subsequent occasions retrieval of the events or occasions will be distinguished by the accompanying ANS activity—This sequence singles out the interrupted event for special attention and for special memorial processing.

Once one has considered interruption as a likely candidate for the categorical definition of events that produce ANS activity, further reflection provides extensive support for that notion and it is in this context that my position makes contact with the tradition of conflict theories of emotion. Those theorists also noted that emotions followed interruptions, blocking, frustration, discrepancy, and conflict. However, to repeat, I only claim the occurrence of ANS activity following interruption, not necessarily any specific emotional reaction—That kind of event depends on the accompanying cognitive evaluation.

One of the consequences of this view is that interruption is stripped of its negative connotation; that is, the quality of an emotion following interruption depends on the evaluative cognitions, which may range from extreme joy to utter despair. I must add that some of the conflict theorists also included positive emotional states among the sequelae of conflict or discrepancy.

MEANING ANALYSIS—
AUTOMATIC AND PERVASIVE

In a sense, too much and too little is known of the cognitive mechanisms that provide the emotional experience with its evaluative quality. Too much because it is now generally accepted that the human organism constantly and automatically scans its external and internal environment and constructs interpretations in terms of existing mental structures and expectations. Too little is known because we do not, as yet, understand the precise mechanisms that generate specific cognitive evaluations, make decisions among competing ones, or generate the categories of thought that find their expression in the evaluative categories of the common language.

The active organism perceives and categorizes its environs, interprets the surrounding events, and produces (often, but not always, within the limited processes of consciousness) some categorical construction of the meaning of these events. In fact, the structural relationship among these perceptions and interpretations *is* the meaning of the world in which we live. These meanings are constructed, which implies, first, that no two individuals find exactly the same meaning in the identical external "objective" world and, second, that meanings are strong interactions between events in the world and the structures and expectations of the interpreting individual.

The source of these meaning analyses—and their products, the cognitive evaluations—resides in the complex networks of past experiences, perceptual expectations, and relational organizations that are ascribed to the mind of the individual. Current work in the field variously describes these mental structures as semantic networks, organizational structures, belief systems, cognitive organizations, etc. Given that no two meaning analyses will be alike, that no two constructions will be identical, it follows that the range of possible different emotional experiences is numerably infinite. In other words, the range of emotional experiences cannot be categorized into narrow classes in terms of its antecedents. The fact that such classes exist in the common language (and again in some psychological languages that mirror it) derives from another characteristic of human mental organization—the preference for categorization and classification. That preference has its sources in the need to reduce the contents of the mind to manageable proportions, to categories that permit easy memorial access as well as categorical action. Thus, to the extent that our semantic networks contain some fairly clean classifications of emotions (such as joy, fear, anxiety, and love), these classifications do not arise out of the mechanisms that generate the emotional experiences, but rather are categorizations that operate on the outcome of the emotion-generating mechanisms.

GENERATING EMOTIONS— GENERALITIES AND SPECIFICS

The intent of the previous sections has been to bring the reader to the point where the comprehension of the psychological mechanisms alone should lead to an understanding of how they generate emotional experiences. The experience arises out of a Gestalt-like concatenation of two major components: visceral arousal and cognitive evaluation. This experience is subjective and, as I have argued, necessarily theoretical and inferred. What we observe are symptoms of that inferred emotional state—symptoms that range from language to action, from visceral symptoms to facial ones, from tender words to violent actions. From these symptoms, together with an understanding of the prior state of the world and the individual's cognitions, we infer a private emotional state.

In addition, there are special states in which one or the other of the two major contributors to the emotional experience occurs in isolation and relatively independent of the other. These are unusual cases, because typically the conditions that generate visceral reactions are, with a high probability, also conditions that generate cognitive evaluations at the same time. However, autonomic reactions can and do occur in "nonemotional" situations in the world and in the laboratory (as in Schachter's experiments). I assume that classes of prior emotional concatenations are stored and remembered. At least in the adult the occurrence of visceral arousal may be compared with these stored past experiences, particularly with reference to their cognitive aspects—the quale of the emotion. When the ANS reaction occurs, a search for these past experiences may be initiated or some proper cognitive evaluation of the current state of affairs may be sought. If these evaluative cognitions are not found, then the individual will only experience the ANS perception. Thus, ANS arousal may result from exercise and be experienced as mere ANS arousal, or it may be assigned to the excitement associated with sports or referred to some drug or other artificial induction. ANS reactions do not automatically produce emotional experiences; they do so only in connection with the appropriate (usually previously acquired or assigned) cognitive evaluation. I shall return shortly to a discussion of those evaluations that are typically called emotional (e.g., judgments of good and bad).

The converse of "pure" ANS reaction is a much simpler case. A variety of cognitive evaluations and judgments can occur without any direct "emotional" import, that is, in the absence of ANS activity. One can talk about being sad and happy, angry and loving without "having" the emotional experiences referred to. In fact, in contrast to the ANS activity, which seems to seek some cognitive explanation, the cognitive experience does not "seek" emotional intensity, that is, ANS activity. This supports the notion of the primacy of the cognitive systems and the function of ANS activity in emphasizing, underlining, drawing attention to, and coding some subset of possible meaning analyses.

On the other hand, there are cases where "pure" cognitive activity can generate visceral actions and produce the full-blown emotional reaction. The retrieval of emotional experience is possible; we can reinstate the appropriate cognitive cues for the production of either imagined or real autonomic activity. The retrieval of the autonomic accompaniment is apparently dependent on the retrieval of the appropriate context. It seems that to retrieve "feeling happy" requires the retrieval of a cognitive representation of a condition under which we felt happy. Pure feelings, in the absence of some cognitive representations, are probably not stored and, from my theoretical point of view, should not be available. However, the possibility exists that some abstraction of a set of autonomic cognitive experiences can be stored and retrieved, but these are the rare, rather than the usual, cases. It is difficult to "remember" pain or joy in the abstract.

I have made reference to imaginary autonomic reactions, and the topic of autonomic imagery needs to be briefly examined. I proposed the concept in connection with our early work on autonomic feedback, and I suggest that, just as visual and auditory images can be experienced in the absence of physical stimulation, so can autonomic images occur in the absence of actual ANS reaction. The concept of autonomic imagery is useful for the exploration of some of the paler retrieved emotional states, for the occurrence of reported visceral reaction in situations that have frequently in the past produced emotional reactions, and for the persistence (but not the acquisition) of avoidance behavior in the absence of autonomic reactions.

THE EXPRESSION OF VALUE— LANGUAGES OF EMOTION

It should be obvious from all the above that I neither endorse nor accept a theoretical position on human emotional experience that postulates the existence of a specific set of innate, fundamental emotions or feelings or neural programs or affects. The appearance of such classes derives from the cognitive, linguistic characteristics of human beings and not from some pre-wired set of primary feelings. I have argued that the postulation of innate ideas or feelings belongs to another century and that contemporary psychology must deal with the processes and mechanisms (which well might be innate) that produce these ideas and feelings.

The classificatory, categorical tendency of the human cognitive system is unquestioned, and we do not need here to inquire into the basis for such a pervasive tendency. It is obvious, however, that it is particularly in the communicative skills (in the human languages) that these categories are most noticeable and useful. Given that languages communicate about states of the world, it is not surprising that much of the cognitive side of emotional states, which evaluates states of the world, is affected by language categories. I include among languages essentially all human communicative skills, but in particular for present purposes verbal language and the expressive languages of the face and body. These categorizations of the external world and of internal states are the main avenue of the cognitive evaluations that color the emotional experience. The label that something is good or the cognate facial expression of acceptance or approval influences the quality of the emotional experience. We know that the occurrence of some easily labeled social situations as well as the production of evaluative facial expressions influence the consequent emotional state (in the presence of visceral activity). In contrast to conventional wisdom, I do not consider facial expressions to be the necessary consequences of some innate primary affect or the mere expression of some prior fundamental or constructed emotional state. Rather, I read the evidence on facial expression as evidence for an ancient system of communication, probably pre-linguistic, that is used to code and communicate major categories of human experience—namely, cognitive evaluations.

SEX AND AGGRESSION

I indicated earlier that there do exist autonomic patterns that produce unique autonomic and emotional experiences. The most interesting of these are the autonomic consequences of sexual stimulation. These include not only parasympathetic and sympathetic events in general, but also specific, and sometimes pleasingly localized, bodily experiences arising from the genital areas, as well as sexual reactions such as lubrication and erection. The best category names we have for these concatenations of bodily and cognitive experiences are lust and sexuality. We know that in cognitively highly developed organisms, like human beings, the meaning analyses of the conditions under which these bodily events take place significantly affect the nature of the experience. In lower animals, the purely bodily experience seems to be dominant. In any case, I would consider these emotional experiences to be a separate but manageable subcategory of a more general theory of emotional experience. Furthermore, it is fairly obvious that the relationship between the separable categories of lust and love deserves special attention in the analysis of human emotional life, particularly because the cognitive accompaniments of love and lust are strongly influenced by different social conditions and are frequently discordant.

Sex is one topic that is frequently subsumed under the chapter heading of emotion; another one is aggression. If one puts primary emphasis on private emotional experience, it is difficult to include aggression because it is only tangentially the description of an internal state. People do not feel aggression; they feel anger. The analysis of the subjective experience of anger (and hostility) deserves more extensive treatment than is possible here. It might well start, however, with the observation that aggressive behavior (doing physical, social, or psychological harm to others) may be the expressive, communicative component of the feeling of anger. This would suggest (reminiscent of some of James's analyses) that people do not strike out because they are angry, but are angry because of actual or incipient aggressive behavior. I recognize the very tentative nature of such a suggestion, in particular because it is difficult at this point in time to talk about a simple category of either aggression or anger. Because aggressive behavior, and even the definition of aggressive behavior, is so strongly dependent on the social and cultural conditions under which a particular episode occurs, it is clear that such social analyses must precede the psychological task. The latter task will involve an analysis of the subjective experience of anger, the meaning analyses that are involved in these experiences, and the cognitive and external conditions that give rise to the ANS activity that accompanies the feeling of anger.

There are a variety of other so-called emotions that fall on the borderline of the intent of my theoretical considerations. Among these are disgust, one subset of which may well fall under the category of specific bodily patterns when it is accompanied by reverse peristalsis. Other categories that the common language sometimes insists as being emotional simply press for further analysis before they can be brought under the umbrella of these considerations. Among these are the "emotions" of pride, of patriotism, of boredom, of familiar ease, and many others. Are they categories that involve some combination of ANS arousal and cognitive evaluation? If not, they lie beyond the range of these speculations. Only intensive situational and psychological analyses can provide proper answers. For example, I have indicated elsewhere how certain aesthetic judgments and creative efforts are relevant to the framework of psychological mechanisms that I have proposed (Mandler, 1975).

PERSONALITY, PATHOLOGY, AND OTHER APPLICATIONS

In this section I shall address a set of topics that have frequently been considered to be central to the umbrella concept of emotion. They are, however, from my point of view, peripheral, and possibly premature, considerations. I refer to the broad area of individual differences and specifically to the subsets of personality factors and psychopathology. I consider individual differences peripheral not because they are either uninteresting or unimportant—quite the contrary. However, the demands of theory construction argue that the general theory must be established before one can deal constructively with the parameters of the theory represented by individual differences. In general, I argue that the role of the psychologist must be first to identify the important and determinative variables, to develop a measurement theory relevant to these variables, and to find out which theoretical variables are subject to individual differences. Only then will it be possible to develop meaningful measures of or to define theoretically interesting individual differences. I shall indicate some of the directions in which these endeavors might go.

I shall not present an exploration of problems of psychotherapy, a description of early emotional and cognitive development, or a general discussion of psychopathology. These issues, while clearly relevant to problems of emotion, are best dealt with in the context of general considerations of cognitive structures, their development and change. I have presented the beginnings of such an exploration in *Mind and emotion*. What I shall discuss here are, first of all, some special problems of anxiety and, second, some speculations about the individual difference parameters that might be specific to the visceral–cognitive model of emotion.

ANXIETY—ITS PRESENCE AND ABSENCE

I have argued that the concept of anxiety, with its variegated parentage, should disappear from a truly psychological language in the same fashion as the concept of emotion. A specific set of visceral–cognitive interactions accounts for a reasonably large subset of the phenomena that have been phenomenally and theoretically labeled as anxiety. In brief, that subset of anxious experiences arises out of the combination of the interruption of ongoing behavior and thought on the one hand and the unavailability of appropriate, situation-relevant task- or problem-solving actions on the other. The interruption is, of course, assumed to lead to the arousal of ANS activity and represents the visceral component of the anxiety reaction. The unavailability of situation-relevant actions or thought I have labeled helplessness; the individual is faced with a situation (either in the external or the internal world) that he or she cannot adequately address—The anxious individual does not know what to do in the problem-solving sense. Interruption accompanied by a lack of appropriate problem-solving actions or thoughts is represented in private experience as a subjective emotion that is frequently categorized as anxious (or nervous, or tense) in the common language. I have discussed the similarities of this anxiety concept to the explorations of Freud and Kierkegaard, as well as its affinity to behaviorist conceptions of anxiety, in *Mind and emotion*.

It might be noted that helplessness has sometimes been associated with the experience of depression, a concept that I prefer to refer to as hopelessness (i.e., generalized helplessness). The niceties of trying to distinguish between helpless and hopeless illustrate the danger—for me and for others—of relying on common language expressions.

If anxiety is the concatenation of visceral arousal with the cognition of helplessness, then we can explore conditions under which interruption (or disruption) is harmful or interfering, and when it is not. I stress this point again in order to remove once more the stigma of negativity from the concept of interruption. Under conditions of interruption and helplessness the cognitive content will be the predominant emotion ("anxiety"), which is by definition task irrelevant. But there are other cognitions that may compete for conscious capacity; among these are the explorations of alternative means of coping with the situation—which, if unsuccessful, further enhance the degree of helplessness—and ruminations about second-order effects of anxiety and helplessness—thoughts about inadequacy and low self-esteem. These preoccupations have the usual effect of preempting limited capacity consciousness and attention, and as a result the individual is less able to find new and effective means of coping with the world and becomes stereotyped in behavior and thought, which further limits his or her ability to find solutions to problems. In fact, one of the most popular sets of individual measures in the field of emotion—the anxiety scale—is predicated on the existence of a continuum of individual reactions based on perceptions of failure, low self-esteem, visceral reactions, inability to cope, etc.

Consider, on the other hand, an interruption that is swiftly followed by the cognition of the appropriate problem solution and adequate coping thoughts and action, for example, when a student is faced with an apparently difficult and not immediately obvious examination question. The ongoing thought processes are interrupted and some arousal occurs. But, if the appropriate solution becomes first vaguely and then specifically apparent, if the interruption is accompanied by self-appreciation, then the subjective emotional state is positive, often described as a sense of mastery or success, which can be quite as intense as the feeling of anxiety. It is interesting to note as an addendum that if the examination is very easy and the answers obvious from the beginning, the typical reaction is not "emotional" (no interruption or arousal has occurred) and the subjective experience is one of disinterest and low affect.

At the other extreme of the symptomatology of anxiety we find the individuals usually described as psychopaths or sociopaths. Evidence exists that psychopathic individuals tend to ignore their visceral reactions and are ANS insensitive, and are also less able to control their ANS reactions. This suggests that, whether by not expending attentional capacity on visceral sensations or because they are not able to differentiate their internal responses, psychopathic individuals lack the autonomic component for many of their "emotional" reactions. In the clinical literature they are often described as being unable to experience anxiety, guilt, or conscience. It is also possible that the psychopath cannot distinguish among the usual levels of autonomic variation and can only experience emotions when these automatic reactions are unusually high. If so, then this line of thought would make comprehensible the thrill-seeking behavior of some psychopathic individuals and groups.

INDIVIDUAL PARAMETERS
FOR AN AUTONOMIC–COGNITIVE THEORY

There are two directions in which the search for theoretically relevant individual parameters might lead. The first is found in the habitual interpretation of the world as threatening and failure inducing. Not just the anxiety scales, but a number of other personality instruments approach individual differences from the point of view of the differential cognitive interpretation of the world, on the one hand, and of the individual's potential, in terms of confidence, self-esteem, etc., on the other. Clearly, if such consistent, habitual, and pervasive modes of handling the world and the self can be established, they should interact strongly with the variables of a visceral–cognitive theory. Their failure to do so consistently, or at least at a level that is predictively useful, suggests that a good part of cognitive evaluation is significantly a function of the current state of the external world. Such a position underlies the currently popular view that personality reactions are situationally determined.

The other aspect of individual differences addresses perceptual and attentional variations in response to autonomic arousal. If it is the case with the psychopathic individual, then it is possible also within normal ranges that individuals differ in their perception of internal events. The theory states specifically that such variation should lead to changes in the intensity of emotional experiences. We have demonstrated such differences in the study of perceived autonomic feedback (e.g., Mandler, *et al.,* 1961), while others have shown them to occur as a result of physical (surgical or accidental) interruption of the feedback from peripheral autonomic events (e.g., Hohmann, 1966).

Finally, the theory makes weak predictions about the effect of variations in actual level of autonomic peripheral activity. These predictions about objective levels are weak because predictions about variations in the *perception* of autonomic activity are the more important ones. Clearly the perception of ANS activity may either vary with or stay constant across levels of arousal. Since I believe that the effective variable as far as emotional experience is concerned is the perception of visceral activity, I am not certain whether variations in ANS activity themselves will have large observable effects. What evidence exists is encouraging. Drugs that reduce ANS activity tend to reduce levels of experienced emotion, and training individuals to produce lower autonomic levels of response reduces the intensity of their perception of noxious events (e.g., Sirota, Schwartz, & Shapiro, 1976).

EXTENSIONS AND ELABORATIONS

In this section I shall address one specific and one general set of topics. The specific issue concerns the interface between psychological theories of emotion and psychobiological facts and speculations. I shall propose an approach to evolutionary biology that seems promising, and in the process I shall also elaborate on some aspects of ANS functioning discussed earlier. Under the heading "Some Further Extrapolations," I shall range more widely in the elaboration of some of the conjectures introduced earlier.

THE BIOLOGY OF EMOTION

The argument for a biology of emotion is not an argument about psychobiological versus physiological explanations of thought and action. The reason my approach has been seen at times as non- or anti-biological is not to be found in my preference for psychological over physiological mechanisms. These two approaches, the neurological versus the psychological, have reached a rather amiable stage of agreeing to disagree and, at times, even to cooperating in neuropsychological enterprises. No, the objection to a primarily psychological approach is its failure to ascribe to evolutionary and genetic factors large chunks of the thoughts and actions to be explained. I do not believe that appeals to innate primary or fundamental emotions, or to action patterns whose origins are sought in evolutionary history, or to primate observations are either advisable or necessary until possible explanations at the psychological level, in terms of the life history, society, and the culture of individuals, have been explored.

The main reason for my argument has an observational basis. Human behavior and thought in the areas of sex, aggression, and socialization (to name just the major objects of current concerns) are so variable and unpredictable across cultures, societies, and classes that a genetic, evolutionary explanation is simply unlikely. Such an explanation should, at least, predict low variability and high predictability across cultural and social groups. In fact, it makes few predictions, but rather emphasizes the low variability and predictability of the target behaviors among lower animals (a point not to be argued here) and then extends these observations by analogy and anecdote to the human experience.

Having observed at least one cycle in the recurring popularity of either environmentalism or nativism, having seen fashion change from the extreme environmentalism of Watson and the early Skinner to the nativism of Chomsky and Wilson, I am primarily concerned with what is scientifically feasible. Just as environmentalists have inhibited the investigation of the constraints on human thought and action, so have the nativists inhibited the exploration of the development of complex behaviors. We should learn from the genetic–environmental investigations of lower animals that assignments to genetics and environment are not just difficult but may at the present stage of knowledge be futile. The biologist Medawar, for example, has noted that as simple a problem as the eye color of water shrimp cannot be subjected to simple genetic calculations. This simple animal shows the inheritance of eye color according to strictly Mendelian laws only under specific ambient temperatures, and, conversely, it is possible to postulate a genetic makeup that will make eye color appear to be entirely under environmental (temperature) controls. Medawar (1977) concludes that it would make "no sense" to assign differential weights of heredity and environment to eye color. If that problem is so difficult, how much more so is an attempt to ascribe outbursts of anger, the induction of lust, or the occurrence of grief to specific genetic, adaptive, evolutionary mechanisms.

Rather than engage in speculations about naked apes and territorial imperatives, it might be useful to gather repeatable, useful and coherent data about human thought and action. Rather than engage in saltatory extrapolations from apes to humans or in the distribution of genetic recipes for intelligence, we might concentrate on observations and analyses of specifically human behavior and variation. Adequate psychological theories, bounded by observations, will then evolve to the point where their user will note invariances that cannot be accounted for by environmental constraints, or variabilities that speak for plasticity in response to the environment. Eventually the pendulum on the nativism–environmentalism argument will probably come to rest at a position that uses environmental and hereditary assignments as needed and not as prescribed.

I do believe that there exist a number of questions within the framework of my own approach that suggest a more concentrated attack in terms of evolutionary and genetic analyses. One of these concerns a reanalysis of the function of the autonomic nervous system. I have suggested two functions—one directly and the other indirectly relevant to a psychology of emotion. Both of them go beyond the current view of the ANS, which sees it as a passive preserver of the internal economy expressed in the concept of homeostasis.

The first suggestion asserts the role of the ANS as a mediating organizer of experience and memory. It starts with the fact that some experiences are accompanied by visceral arousal while others are not. This "tagging" in experience and memory of some events sets them apart, both in their retrieval from memory (i.e., they can be retrieved as part of a class of events so tagged) and in their cognitive significance. Specifically, the organism presumably knows that events and memories so tagged have played a special role in its past life—They are important events; they are "emotional" events. In this fashion, ANS activity plays a special role in singling out important events in the life history of the individual.

The second suggestion, derived largely from the work of John and Beatrice Lacey, assigns to ANS activity a special role in alerting the organism to important events in the environment and in facilitating attention to them (e.g., Lacey & Lacey, 1974). In brief, the possibility exists that, following the initiation of peripheral ANS activity, there occurs a reduction of sympathetic activity that may function to reduce internal noise and to make attention to the environment easier and more effective. I have suggested that these secondary results of ANS activity form part of an auxiliary signal system that directs the organism's attention to important environmental events.

Another related characteristic of human (and mammalian) adaptiveness follows from interruption theory. If it is the case that all interruptions (as defined previously) produce some degree of peripheral autonomic activity, a further analysis of the evolution of the response to interruption seems at least interesting. As I have noted above, it makes good sense that the interruption of well-organized and habitual thoughts and actions should provide a special signal to the cognitive system. In general, these suggestions contravene another popular view of emotions, which sees them as chaotic, nonadaptive, and obsolete. Somehow the emotional side of modern life is considered to be out of step with the requirements of the modern world, an evolutionary hangover that interferes with a rational approach to our problems. In contrast, I do not believe that evolution is out of step with humankind, and, given that we see such an infinitesimal slice of the process, such judgments are unlikely to be objective. Rather, I believe that emotional behavior can be seen as being just as adaptive and useful in this millennium as it probably was in prior ones.

SOME FURTHER EXTRAPOLATIONS

Closely connected with the biological view of emotion is the analysis of facial and bodily expressions as expressions of underlying and prior emotional states and feelings. The data on facial expressions are consistent with a position that sees them as an ancient, adaptive system of communication. They are the result of cognitive evaluations of the world and of internal states. The simple fact that human beings can display facial expressions in the absence of any emotional states suggests the parallel to language in general. I can make a face to signal disgust without being disgusted just as I can say "That is terrible" without referring to anything at all. I grimace the one and say the other, often in the absence of the appropriate reference. The primary function of these expressive facial and laryngeal movements is evaluative communication. In consequence, I would argue for an investigation of facial and bodily movements in terms of their role as remnants of a preverbal language. There is enough generality to facial expression, though not nearly as much invariance as some investigators, such as Izard (1971), claim, to consider the possibility that these expressions are old and adaptive enough to have been built into the behavioral genetic repertory of the species.

A closely related issue that needs further investigation and elaboration is the source of the most pervasive cognitive-evaluative judgments that people make—the assignments of the judgments of "good" and "bad." Given the commitment to the discovery of psychological mechanisms that generate conscious processes, I want to sketch two possible origins of these cognitions. One is that "good" and "bad" are commentaries on learned or unlearned approach and avoidance actions. Originally the organism has built-in tendencies to withdraw from or approach certain events (pain, sexual stimulation, some smells, etc.) and as, for example, the avoidance behavior occurs the cognitive system notes and perhaps comments on that behavior. Thus "bad" may originally be a commentary on appropriate avoidance behavior and may then be used in linguistic contexts to generalize to other situations; with respect to approach behavior, there is a similar procedure for the word "good." Another, and not alternative, source of the good–bad continuum may be found in cognitive activity itself. Thus, the ability to assimilate an event easily and effectively to existing cognitive structures may be equivalent to a "good" cognition, whereas the inability to assimilate the event or to accommodate it to a static and inflexible structure may define the cognition as "bad." The search for the familiar and the avoidance of the novel and unfamiliar illustrate one aspect of this suggestion.

PROSPECTS AND PROBLEMS

I am somewhat reluctant to describe the propositions and speculations discussed here as a theory. The term theory should be reserved for a body of general, hopefully quantitative, statements from which specific consequences can be deduced. Psychological concepts have not been specific enough, nor the relational statements unambiguous enough, nor the quantification developed enough to aspire to the kind of theoretical structure that the older sciences can invoke. However, in the early stages of theory development, more general verbal statements are permissible, and particularly in the fields of emotion and motivation we have had few specific and prescriptive theories. Thus, I am willing to let the foregoing stand as a "theory" if it is understood that it has a long way to go before it fully deserves the term. At the same time, there is no competitive theory that can make a stronger claim, nor can many theories make a claim that I think all theories (however vague) must make—and that is to testability, that is, verifiability and/or falsifiability in some sense.

There are two sets of observations that are strongly implied by my position: first, that the intensity of experienced emotion should increase with increases in ANS activity (or its perception) and, second, that the quality of experienced emotions should be a function of the cognitive evaluation of the self and the environment. The evidence that is available is very good for the first proposition and complex for the second, primarily because it is so difficult to obtain independent measures of cognitive evaluations.

As far as the interruption hypothesis is concerned, the visceral–cognitive theory does not stand or fall with it. However, some more abstract statement about the causes of ANS activity than a mere listing of antecedents would be desirable. I should add that the interruption hypothesis is not intended to be an exhaustive statement about the causes of ANS activity; interruption is sufficient but not necessary. There are a number of obvious conditions that produce peripheral ANS activity that do not easily fall into the rubric of interruption. Among these are tissue injury, pain (which is, however, related to interruption), extreme temperatures (but not their sudden onset), and others. All of these invite further exploration of the adaptive functions of the autonomic nervous system.

One of the reasonable criticisms of the model is that I am not quite clear whether it is a theory of emotional behavior or emotional experience. My own emphases have changed with the times as psychologists generally have moved from theories of behavior to theories of cognition. In fact, this chapter emphasizes private emotional experience even more so than previous explorations. I would like to think that the theory should (and does) address both thought and action, that its explanatory power should extend to both sets of phenomena, and that both thought and action should be seen as emerging from a complex model of the human mind. In order to be viable, modern cognitive theory must be a theory of action as well as thought, and developments in recent years have encouraged me to see such extensions. In contrast to earlier attempts at cognitive theories, current models do care about the organization of behavior and action and promise to be general models rather than parochial ones restricted to knowledge and thought.

In the same sense, my position has been seen as ambivalent between pure cognitive theories and theories that stress direct effects of environmental states on thought and action (with interruption theory as one example). Thought processes are molded by actions and by the consequences of actions. At the same time, some actions are invariant responses to important environmental events; they require no or few mediating choices or transformations. The autonomic response to interruption is one such example. On the other hand, the processes that determine what constitutes an interruption are, of course, cognitive ones.

The strongest objections to my position derive from my rejection of the essentially Darwinian model of emotion—the postulation of unanalyzable fundamental and primary emotions, feelings, and affects. That rejection is most directly obvious in my position on autonomic patterning and the function of facial expression. I have dealt with these issues in the preceding sections, and I hope that I have shown that even this position allows for the possibility of physically distinct emotions and indicates directions for further evolutionary analyses.

Finally, I have distanced myself from positions that rely heavily on the analysis of the common language of emotion. I reject theories that take as their starting point common language usage and the partitioning of emotions in terms of the categories used by common parlance to describe both the experience and the social context of emotions. It certainly is not surprising that the common language has developed fairly stable categories of emotions and that we speak about emotion in terms of these categories. However, a theory based on these categories is implicitly a theory of the development of language usage, not of emotion. I do not consider efforts in that direction useless or fruitless. On the contrary, much is to be learned from an analysis of the partitioning and structure of the common language of emotion. But it is not a theory that tells us what processes and mechanisms produce the thoughts, experiences, and actions that interest us.

The rejection of the vocabulary of the common language as a basis for a theory of emotion also entails the rejection of the explanations that are used in common parlance to explain emotional events. Psychologists concerned with emotion must accept what psychologists concerned with memory or social behavior have learned to accept, namely, that introspective accounts of causes and reasons are frequently useless in the determination of efficient causes and determinants of thought and action. People explain their thoughts and actions to themselves and construct theories in order to make the world at least appear consistent and explicable. When we have access to knowledge about actual causes and actions, these descriptions often bear little if any resemblance to them. Without a theory that informs us about the antecedent determinants of introspective accounts, we cannot sensibly use these accounts to construct a causal explanation of human behavior. In this sense, then, I consider the common language as nothing more than a heuristic starting point. What is needed is a theoretical account of phenomenology and of the transformations that lead to introspective accounts.

Where do we go from here? I believe the guideposts already exist within parts of cognitive psychology. A new paradigm seems to be emerging in psychology that combines approaches to the structure of thoughts with steps toward an understanding of the structure of action, of emotion, and of motivation. The information-processing approach and its partial successors in artificial intelligence have made increasingly heavy demands on psychological theory to become more precise, less ambiguous, and better testable. The computational paradigm has forced us to say what we mean exactly. If that trend continues, the present spate of vague verbal theories should be the last, and the next generation of psychologists might be able to devote themselves to specification, disambiguation, and experimental and conceptual tests of existing formulations. In the process they will discover, as we already have in the arena of knowledge representation, new problems and new challenges.

ACKNOWLEDGMENTS

The preparation of this chapter was supported in part by Grant MH–15828 from the National Institute of Mental Health to the Center for Human Information Processing, University of California, San Diego. I am also most grateful to the hospitality of the Department of Psychology, University College London, where this chapter was written.

REFERENCES

Hohmann, G. W. Some effects of spinal cord lesions on experienced emotional feelings. *Psychophysiology,* 1966, *3,* 143–156.

Izard, C. E. *The face of emotion.* New York: Appleton Century Crofts, 1971.

Kessen, W., & Mandler, G. Anxiety, pain, and the inhibition of distress. *Psychological Review,* 1961, *68,* 396–404.

Lacey, B. C., & Lacey, J. I. Studies of heart rate and other bodily processes in sensorimotor behavior. In P. A. Obrist, A. Black, J. Brener, & L. DiCara (eds.), *Cardiovascular psychophysiology: Current mechanisms, biofeedback and methodology.* Chicago: Aldine-Atherton, 1974.

Mandler, G. Emotion. In R. W. Brown, E. Galanter, E. Hess, & G. Mandler, *New directions in psychology.* New York: Holt, Rinehart, and Winston, 1962.

Mandler, G. The interruption of behavior. In D. Levine (ed.), *Nebraska symposium on motivation: 1964.* Lincoln, Nebraska: University of Nebraska Press, 1964.

Mandler, G. Anxiety. In D. L. Sills (ed.), *International encyclopedia of the social sciences*. New York: Crowell-Collier, 1968.
Crowell-Collier, 1968.
Mandler, G. Helplessness: Theory and research in anxiety. In C. D. Spielberger (ed.), *Anxiety: Current trends in theory and research,* Vol. 2. New York: Academic Press, 1972.
Mandler, G. *Mind and emotion.* New York: Wiley, 1975.
Mandler, G. Emotion. In E. Hearst (ed.), *The first century of experimental psychology*. Hillsdale, N. J.: Lawrence Erlbaum Associates, 1979. (a)
Mandler, G. Thought processes, consciousness, and stress. In V. Hamilton & D. M. Warburton (eds.), *Human stress and cognition: An information processing approach*. London: Wiley, 1979. (b)
Mandler, G., Mandler, J. M., Kremen, I., & Sholiton, R. D. The response to threat: Relations among verbal and physiological indices. *Psychological Monographs, 1961, 75,* No. 9 (Whole No. 513), 22 pp.
Mandler, G., Mandler, J. M., & Uviller, E. T. Autonomic feedback: The perception of autonomic activity. *Journal of Abnormal and Social Psychology, 1958, 56,* 367–373.
Mandler, G., & Sarason, S. B. A study of anxiety and learning. *Journal of Abnormal and Social Psychology, 1952, 47,* 166–173.
Mandler, G., & Watson, D. L. Anxiety and the interruption of behavior. In C. D. Spielberger (ed.), *Anxiety and behavior.* New York: Academic Press, 1966.
Mandler, J. M., & Mandler, G. Good guys vs. bad guys: The subject–object dichotomy. *Journal of Humanistic Psychology, 1974, 14,* 63–78.
Medawar, P. B. Unnatural science. *New York Review of Books, 1977, 24,* 13–18.
Miller, G. A. The magic number seven plus or minus two: Some limits on our capacity for processing information. *Psychological Review, 1956, 63,* 81–97.
Schachter, S. *Emotion, obesity, and crime.* New York: Academic Press, 1971.
Schachter, S., & Singer, J. E. Cognitive, social and physiological determinants of emotional state. *Psychological Review, 1962, 69,* 379–399.
Sirota, A., Schwartz, G. E., & Shapiro, D. Voluntary control of human heart rate: Effect on reaction to eversive stimulation: A replication and extension. *Journal of Abnormal Psychology, 1976, 85,* 473–477.

Chapter 10

THE BIOLOGY OF EMOTIONS
AND OTHER FEELINGS[1]

KARL H. PRIBRAM

ABSTRACT

There is a convergence between earlier biological theories of emotion and a current, far more comprehensive view. The medieval humoral theories find a berth in current endocrine research. Lange's visceral theory is confirmed as taking part in the arousal mechanism that provides feelings of interest, novelty, familiarity, and more painful disruptions of stable states. James' emphasis on a report to the brain of bodily responses is shown to be a manifestation of the brain's representation of familiar body responses so that departures from the familiar are arousing. Cannon's thalamic theory is supported by the documentation that the diencephalon is a prime locus for receptors sensitive to the humors that determine the body's chemical response systems and thus central to the (homeostatic) maintenance of the stable representations of body states. Papez' and MacLean's extension of Cannon's brain locus to the limbic forebrain is also amply supported—and one must now add (as foreshadowed by Nina Bull's attitude theory) the basal ganglia as well—in that limbic formations and basal ganglia are shown

---

[1] This chapter was written in response to a request to contribute an up-to-date "biological theory of emotion" to this volume because I have attempted to formulate such a theory in the past (see Pribram, 1967, 1969, 1970, 1971; Pribram & Melges, 1969). P. T. Young (1973) has characterized these attempts as "comprehensive," a tribute to the wealth of data on the topic that had been accumulated over the past few decades by neurobiological scientists. The flow of data has not slowed since the earlier reviews were written. The current revision of the theory is therefore extensive.

Emotion: Theory, Research, and Experience
Volume 1: Theories of Emotion

to be part of the neurochemical regulating mechanisms responsible for stable states and the sensing of departures from such stable states. Such departures were at an earlier time encompassed by Lindsley, by Duffy, and by Malmo under the banner of activation theory. Finally, as demanded by clinical evidence and social psychological experiment, the cerebral isocortex is not exempt from playing a critical role in the organization of emotional and motivational experience and expression. Laboratory evidence has shown that the intrinsic portions of the cerebral cortex, the "association" corteces of the posterior convexity and of the frontal pole, exert their influence via the basal ganglia, the forebrain focus of the arousal and readiness systems. This cortical control accounts for the specific epicritic "labeling" of feelings.

It was not so very long ago that I attended a symposium on "emotion" at an international congress in Montreal. The participants discussed factor analysis, limbic neuroanatomy, and operant conditioning. Somewhere in the agenda emotions were hidden from view, lurking in the dark alleys of our ignorance. No one even dared to use the term, and certainly no one discussed emotion as would the man in the street.

Let us therefore listen for a moment to ordinary discourse: "She's really emotional—so easily upset." "She's certainly an up and down person—so moody." "He's completely hung up on death; it would help him if he weren't so emotional about it." "Aren't they a warm emotional family?" "He makes me angry." "She is a loving person."

Common to these expressions is the theme of a cyclically recurring process—some steady state and its control. "Upsets" and "hang-ups" indicate malfunctions of control; "warmth" suggests that the regulatory mechanisms controlling emotional state are functioning flexibly and smoothly. It is these states and their regulation about which today's scientists have attained such a considerable body of evidence.

Current scientific knowledge regarding emotion has its roots in the Galenical medicine of the Middle Ages. Four "humors," sanguine, choleric, phlegmatic, and melancholic, were considered to determine temperamental differences in reactivity. The humors were thought to be bodily secretions, and modern biomedical research has supplanted these primitives with a host of endocrine hormones. The hormones must, of course, even today be seriously considered in any comprehensive treatment of the biological regulations that determine emotions.

In addition to the multiplication and specification of humors, two other major developments have occurred in the scientific study of the biology of emotions. One of these developments points to the role of nonhumoral mechanisms in the emotional process: Lange's (1887) "visceral" theory, made famous by William James (1890), and Nina Bull's (1951) "muscle"-based attitude theory are probably the most important of these.

The second major development shows brain mechanisms to be central and critical to understanding. The realization that the brain is involved in the experience and expression of emotions began with the work of Gall and Spurzheim (1809/1969) at the beginning of the nineteenth century and achieved considerable sophistication by its end. Thus, William James (1890) could write:

> If the neural process underlying emotional consciousness be what I have now sought to prove it, the physiology of the brain becomes a simpler matter than has been hitherto supposed.

> Supposing the cortex to contain parts, liable to be excited by changes in each special sense-organ, in each portion of the skin, in each muscle, each joint, and each viscus, and to contain absolutely nothing else, we still have a scheme capable of representing the process of the emotions. An object falls on a sense-organ, affects a cortical part, and is perceived; or else the latter, excited inwardly, gives rise to an idea of the same object. Quick as a flash, the reflex currents pass down through their preordained channels, alter the condition of muscle, skin, and viscus; and these alterations, perceived, like the original object, in as many portions of the cortex, combine with it in consciousness and transform it from an object-simply-apprehended into an object-emotionally-felt. No new principles have to be invoked, nothing postulated beyond the ordinary reflex circuits, and the local centres admitted in one shape or another by all to exist [Vol. II, pp. 472–474].

And Sigmund Freud (1895/1966) could develop a detailed neurological model of emotional development in his Project for a Scientific Psychology:

> The primary brain . . . would, to put it plainly, be a *sympathetic ganglion* [S. E., p. 303].

> There must [therefore] be "secretory" neurones which when they are excited, cause the generation in the interior of the body of something which operates as a stimulus upon the endogenous paths of conduction [S. E., pp. 320–321].

> The endogenous simuli consists of *chemical products,* of which there may be a considerable number [S. E., p. 321].

> At first, the human organism is incapable of bringing about the specific action. It takes place by *extraneous help,* when the attention of an experienced person is drawn to the child's state. In this way this path of discharge acquires a secondary function of the highest importance, that of *communication,* and the initial helplessness of human beings is the *primal source* of all *moral motives* [S. E., pp. 317–318].

These early formulations capture the essence of what needs to be covered in any comprehensive theory of emotions. Understanding in psychology comes when there is a sufficiently precise delineation of the variables—both environmental and organismic—that determine the behavior which reflects the psychological category under investigation. Thus, for example, we begin to understand color vision when we can specify the stimulus dimensions, the wavelengths of the electromagnetic spectrum that are involved, and something of their interactions. We achieve more understanding when we find in the retina three photochemicals that possess characteristics similar to those derived as "primary" from studies of the interactions among spectral components (as proposed in the Young–Helmholtz theory). And we begin to feel that we know a considerable amount when De Valois (1960) shows us that cells in the lateral geniculate nucleus reflect an opponent process which accounts for otherwise inexplicable perceptual phenomena (according to the Hering theory, 1964).

A comprehensive theory of emotion must begin by specifying the manner in which emotional behavior differs from other behavior, the stimulus dimension that elicits such behavior, and the brain mechanisms that process this dimension. We begin, therefore, by defining the limits of what we mean by "emotional behavior," just as psychophysics initially had to establish the limits of what is meant by color vision.

EMOTIONAL BEHAVIOR AS AN EXPRESSION OF THE EXPERIENCE OF INTERNAL STATES

Since Darwin's classical treatise on the expression of emotion (1965) it has been customary to separate emotional experience from emotional expression. Emotional experiences are classes of feelings, and I have elsewhere (Pribram, 1970, 1971) made the case for utilizing the category "feelings" to encompass a range of experiences that can be separated from those that allow us to perceive objects beyond our skin:

> I once had the opportunity to examine some patients in whom the medial part of the temporal lobe—including the amygdala—had been removed bilaterally. These patients, just as their monkey counterparts, typically ate considerably more than normal and gained up to a hundred pounds in weight. At last I could *ask* the subject how it felt to be so hungry. But much to my surprise, the expected answer was not forthcoming. One patient who had gained more than one hundred pounds in the year since surgery was examined at lunch time. Was she hungry? She answered, "No." Would she like a piece of rare, juicy steak? "No." Would she like a piece of chocolate candy? She answered, "Umhumm," but when no candy was offered she did not pursue the matter. A few minutes later, when the examination was completed, the doors to the common room were opened and she saw the other patients already seated at a long table eating lunch. She rushed to the table, pushed others aside, and began to stuff food into her mouth with both hands. She was immediately recalled to the examining room and the questions about food were repeated. The same negative answers were obtained again, even after they were pointedly contrasted with her recent behavior at the table. Somehow the lesion had impaired the patient's *feelings* of hunger and satiety and this impairment was accompanied by excessive eating!

As yet we understand little of how this impairment comes about. Nevertheless, this example points clearly to the folly of believing that a direct match exists between observations of any particular type of behavior and introspectively derived concepts. Are we to say that the patient *felt* hungry because she ate ravenously despite her verbal denial? Or are we to take her statements at face value and seek elsewhere for an explanation for her voracious eating? The paradox is resolved if, as in earlier chapters on perception, we consider the behavioral function to be composed of several processes, one of which is the feeling state reported verbally.

At the hypothalamic level a similar paradox has plagued investigators. As already noted, when lesions are made in the region of the ventromedial nucleus of the hypothalamus, rats will eat considerably more than their controls and will become obese. But this is not all. Although rats so lesioned ate a great deal when food was readily available, they worked less for food whenever some obstacle interfered (Miller, Bailey, and Stevenson, 1950).

It was also found that the more palatable the food, the more the lesioned subject would eat (Teitelbaum, 1955), giving rise to the notion that the lesioned animals did not show greater "drive" to eat but were actually more "finicky" than their controls. Recent experimental results obtained by Krasne (1962) and by Grossman (1966) added to the paradox: electrical stimulation of the ventromedial nucleus stops both food and water intake in deprived rats and chemical stimulation of the cholinergic mechanism produces foot stamping (in gerbils, Glickman, personal communication) and fighting if provoked (King and Hoebel, 1968).

Grossman summarizes these results with the succinct statement that medial hypothalamic manipulations change affect not appetite. But we are once again faced with our earlier dilemma. If the medial hypothalamic mechanism does not deal with motivation, how does eating, drinking, etc., come about? The data hold the answer. The ventromedial and lateral hypothalamic regions form a couplet, the lateral portion serving as a feeding, a "go" mechanism (which, when ablated, will produce rats which tend to starve), and the medial portion contains the "stop" mechanism.

The paradox is resolved by the hypothesis that processes ordinarily involved in taking the organism "out of motion" also generate affects or feelings of e-motion. Thus an important distinction between motivation and emotion becomes clarified: the term "motivation" can be restricted to the operations of appetitive "go" processes (such as those converging in the lateral hypothalamic region) that ordinarily result in behavior which carries forward an action, and the term "emotion" to the operations of affective "stop" or satiety processes of reequilibration [Pribram, 1971, pp. 192–194].

Thus, neurobehavioral data make imperative a reference to an encompassing category, feelings, with the subcategories emotion and motivation clearly distinguished. Emotion is found to be derived from processes that *stop* ongoing behavior: affective reactions accompanying the satiety mechanisms as in the quotation above, arousal as in the orienting reaction to distracting stimuli (see the following and Pribram & McGuinness, 1975), and more generally when behavior is interrupted (Mandler, 1964). By contrast, the organism is considered motivated when his readiness mechanisms are activated (see also following and Pribram & McGuinness, 1975), when he is ready to "go" and to continue "going." These responses are (as will be detailed below) critically organized by the basal ganglia (Pribram, 1977b) and have as their physiological indicators the contingent negative variation of DC brain potentials (Walter, 1967) and heart rate slowing (Lacey & Lacey, 1974).

The distinction between emotion and motivation is not a novel one. In his opening paragraph on emotions William James suggests that "emotional reaction usually terminates in the subject's own body" while motivation "is apt to go farther and enter into practical relations with the exciting object" (1890, Vol. II, p. 442). In a similar fashion, J. R. Kantor, whose interbehavioral analyses of psychological processes influenced B. F. Skinner so profoundly, distinguishes between affective and effective interactions: In affective interactions "the person is responding above all with internal body mechanisms" while effective interactions generate "implicit" (i. e., readiness) or overt responses toward the stimulus object (Kantor & Smith, 1975).

In short, for behavior, as well as for the neurophysiology of feelings, it becomes useful to distinguish emotional from motivational antecedents. Motivational antecedents imply that the organism is preparing to or actually acting on the environment, whereas emotional antecedents imply only that internal processing (internal control mechanisms) is in force. The distinction becomes manifest in the connotative differences between the meaning in English of the term "behavior" and its continental counterpart in German and French: "Verhaltung" and "comportment" both connote how one "holds oneself"—one's positive and negative attitudes—whereas the English "behavior" has the more pragmatic and active meaning of "entering into *practical* relations with the environment."

An important consideration arises at this point. If the expression of emotions is affective (rather than effective), that is, emotional expression terminates in the subject's own body, how then can we observe and work with such expressions in terms of their practical effect on the environment? Ordinarily, a behaviorally oriented experimentalist is concerned with the environmental consequences of behavior (e.g., the cumulative record in an operant situation). In these situations, according to our definition, behavior is motivated, not emotional. Thus, the behaviorist has had some difficulty in finding measures of emotional expression. Conditioned suppression of responses, bolles of rat feces, and the like have been used, but they fail to reflect the richness of (especially the pleasant and positive) emotional states that the observed organism can experience. Furthermore, ethologists working with social behavior have followed Darwin's lead and shown that organisms can "read" each other's emotional expressions and be influenced by them.

In these situations, emotional expression does have a practical influence beyond the emoting organism, *but only because of the communicative setting.* In such a setting the practical influence is completely dependent on the ability of other socially receptive organisms to sense the meaning of the expression. Effectiveness therefore does not depend on what the emoting organism does but on what the socially sensitive recipient is able to do. However, an intelligent self-aware organism such as *Homo sapiens* can use these emotional expressions motivationally, that is, to manipulate the social situation. Such manipulations, when deliberate and planned (see the following), characterize the "con" artist, actor, and administrator. But often, through imitation and conditioning, the emotional expressions become automatic, leading to stereotyped interactions. Much of the social display behavior of animals (e.g., birds) is apparently of this type: Internal and/or external stimuli set in motion an emotional reaction which, when expressed, triggers another emotional reaction in a socially receptive conspecific (e.g., Hinde, 1954a,b, 1960). In these animals, behavior sequences are thus concatenated of emotional expressions (and labeled "instinctive"). Such concatenations comprising instincts can also be elicited when an organism becomes completely adapted to an ecological niche in the nonsocial environment (see Miller, Galanter, & Pribram, 1960, Chapter 5). By contrast, organized motivations ("plans") are constructed within the organism's brain and *mean* to enter into practical relations with the exciting object. The adaptive consequence of emotional expression is a function of the social matrix in which this expression occurs.

In summary, emotional behavior is defined as an expression of positive and negative emotional feelings which are inferred as reflecting certain internal neurological states of the organism. The term "feelings" is therefore not synonymous with the term "emotion" since it is possible to identify additional internal neurological states and the behaviors they determine. One such additional category encompasses motivational feelings and behavior. Emotions are distinguished from motivations in that emotional reactions ordinarily "terminate within the organism's body," whereas motivations are "apt to go farther and enter into *practical* relations with the exciting object." An exception arises in social behavior, however. When a socially sensitive organism can be influenced by the expression of emotions or when an organism is totally adapted to his ecological niche, the sequential triggering of emotional expressions can lead to automatic (instinctive) behavior that is often, though not always, highly adaptive. Note, however, that the adaptation is due not to the expression of emotion but to the forces operating in the social and physical environment. We must next explore, therefore, what constitutes these "triggering" stimuli for emotional expression. What stimulus dimension addresses a physiological state experienced as an emotion? And what neural control mechanisms determine how an emotional feeling will be experienced?

THE PROTOCRITIC DIMENSION OF STIMULI

The importance of humoral factors in determining emotional states has already been noted. Hormones are chemicals that exert their influence on the brain via receptors located in its core. In addition to this sensitivity to hormones produced by glands such as the gonads, thyroid, adrenal medulla, and cortex, the core-brain receptors monitor a host of other chemical and physical constituents of the internal environment of the organism. A respiratory control mechanism is sensitive to the partial pressure of CO_2; a temperature sensor monitors the warmth of the blood stream; sex hormones are selectively absorbed at one location and adrenal steroids at another; the difference in the concentration of sugar in the venous and arterial circulation is monitored as is the concentration of salt and, therefore, reciprocally, the concentration of water. Chemicals secreted by the walls of the gut and by the kidney and a host of other chemicals are being investigated because some experiments indicate that they too are sensed by cells in the core of the brain (see Pribram, 1971, Chapters 9 and 10, for a review).

Furthermore, this part of the brain is a veritable cauldron of chemicals locally secreted by aggregates of cells in one or another location. Catecholamines such as norepinephrine (closely related to the hormone epinephrine–adrenalin, which is secreted by the adrenal medulla) and dopamine (which metabolizes into norepinephrine), indole amines such as serotonin, and peptides such as endorphin (an endogenous morphine-like substance) abound. As might be expected, sensitivities to these neurohumors are also built into the mechanism.

Walter Cannon (1927), in his classical studies, determined that the relationship between the sensor and its chemical was such that the concentration of the chemical, though fluctuating, was maintained constant around some set point. He enunciated this relationship as the principle of homeostasis. The sensor monitors the quantity of the variable and signals by way of neural pathways or chemical secretions when the variable rises above or falls below a certain level. Such signals compose a negative feedback because their sign is opposite to that which characterizes the deviation of the quantity of the variable from baseline. Often the mechanism that counteracts the decrease of the variable, the appetitive phase, is separate from that which counteracts the increase, the satiety phase.

Individual homeostatic mechanisms are multiply interlinked into complex organizations. Thus, the thermostat regulating temperature is linked to the glucostat regulating food intake and these are linked to the osmoreceptors (the salt–water sensors) to control thirst and the thyroid-sensitive mechanism controlling activity. Through various metabolic interrelations (such as breathing) that take place in the body, these homeostatic mechanisms in turn regulate the partial pressure of CO_2, etc. (see Brobeck, 1963, for a review).

In short, the core of the brain (mesencephalon, diencephalon, and the basal ganglia and limbic systems of the forebrain) utilizes chemical regulations to control body functions. The configuration of concentrations of these chemicals, though fluctuating around some set point, is sufficiently stable over periods of time to constitute steady "states." These states are apparently experienced—as hunger, thirst, sleepiness, elation, depression, effort, comfort, etc. (For a more complete discussion of how an experimenter infers what an observed organism might be experiencing see Douglas and Pribram [1966] and Pribram [1971, Chapter 6]. More direct evidence is obtained by psychopharmacological experiments where the effect of drugs of known neurochemical action on psychological state is assayed.) Although the chemical characteristics of each state are as yet incompletely specified, enough is known to allow one to say that the concentration of glucose is involved in the hunger mechanism, the concentration of salt in the thirst mechanism, the concentration of the indole amine serotonin and norepinephrine (a catecholamine) in the sleep mechanism (norepinephrine in dreaming), the concentration of dopamine (another catechol) in feelings of effectiveness (i.e., of elation and depression), the concentrations of endorphins (endogenous secretions of morphine-like substances) in those of temperature, novelty, and pain, and the concentrations of the enkephalins (adrenocorticotrophic hormones of the pituitary, see below) in those of effort and comfort (for reviews, see the following and Pribram, 1971, 1977a; Stein, 1978).

Note that the control of temperature and of pain falls into the homeostatic mold. But temperature and pain are also skin senses which share a common spinal pathway, and the question thus arises whether the skin components of these sensitivities are processed separately from those involved in internal regulations. The answer to this question is that parts of the skin components of temperature and pain are processed separately and parts are processed in conjunction with the chemical homeostats of the core brain.

The part of the skin components of temperature and pain sensitivity that is processed separately (in the parietal lobes of the cortex) from the homeostatic mechanism is characterized by what is called in neurology "local sign." This means that the sensation can be located on the skin and that the duration of the sensation is limited. Henry Head (1920) labeled such sensory experiences "epicritic" to distinguish them from more diffuse experiences that are obtained during early regrowth of severed nerves.

The remainder of the skin's temperature and pain sensitivities are processed in conjunction with the chemical core homeostatic mechanisms. The spinal temperature and pain tracts end in structures (such as the substantia gelatinosa of the dorsal spinal cord, the periaqueductal gray of the midbrain, and the amygdala of the forebrain) that are loaded with endorphins. Responses to hot and cold and pain are dramatically altered by electrical stimulations of these core portions of the spinal cord, brain stem (Liebeskind, Mayer, & Akil, 1974), and forebrain and are not affected by stimulations of the parietal cortex or the tracts leading to it (Chin, Pribram, Drake, & Greene, 1976; Richardson & Akil, 1974). The assumption is that the stimulations increase the local (and perhaps general) secretions of endorphins.

What is common to the homeostatic internal mechanisms and these aspects of pain and temperature processing is that they are sensitive simply to *amounts,* the quantities, of chemical and neural excitation. Processing does not lead to identification of location in time and space (or to other qualitative aspects of the stimulus such as color). Head (1920) termed the quantitative "diffuse" aspects of sensitivity "protopathic" because, in his experiments, they arose while the regenerating nerves were in a pathological condition. The term needs to be modified to *protocritic* in order to include current evidence that such sensitivities are part of the *normal* control of the temperature and pain (and probably other sensory) mechanisms. As noted, protocritic processes are homeostatic; that is, they control the quantitative aspects of stimuli and are thus determinants of neural *states* (for a more complete review see Chin *et al.,* 1976; Pribram, 1977a).

The protocritic dimension of experience, devoid of epicritic local sign, is therefore characteristically dependent on the quantity (the intensity) of the stimulus. Quantity (and therefore intensity) in a homeostatic system is in turn dependent on change and rate of change of the state of that system. Controlled changes of moderate amounts are apparently experienced positively, while more abrupt and overly intense changes of state lead to negative feelings (the Yerkes–Dodson law [see Hebb, 1955]). Here we are at the frontier of knowledge. As noted, the pain and temperature systems run together in the spinal cord and brain stem to terminate in and around the amygdala and frontal cortex. Do the elaborations of the temperature systems accrue to the experiencing of comfort as the elaborations of the pain systems accrue to suffering? Or is suffering experienced only when the limits of tolerable comfort are exceeded? Brain stimulations in man that protect against pain are accompanied by the feeling of cold (Richardson & Akil, 1974). In short, are there two neural systems, one for pain and one for temperature, or is there only one? And if there are two, how do they interact to produce a more or less unitary experience along a hedonic dimension?

An area of current investigation in our laboratory is aimed at establishing the individual (and situational) differences in band width (range) of tolerance of the intensive dimension of stimulation: What are the limits of comfort between changes sensed at all and those sensed to be uncomfortable? How much effort must be expended in control of the band width (i.e., how much attention must be *paid* in order to expand the range over which stimuli are sensed comfortable)? How do differences in attitudinal set and the situational setting influence the nature (positive [comfort] versus negative [effort]) of the emotional experience? These investigations are based on earlier work that discerned a distinction between a neural system that controls the comfort–effort dimension and two others upon which the comfort–effort system operates. The next section examines the evidence for this distinction.

PROTOCRITIC PROCESSING BY CORE-BRAIN CONTROL MECHANISMS

Historically, the humoral theory of emotions gave way to the visceral theory of Carl Lange, which was promulgated by William James. As already noted, however, James emphasized the visceral (and somatic) components of stimulation to the brain rather than the visceral phenomena per se (as is ordinarily suggested). Cannon (1929) performed a series of experiments designed to show that visceral stimulation per se did not account for emotional experience and expression. Cannon's experiments pointed to the diencephalon as the locus involved in organizing the states responsible for emotion. The evidence has already been reviewed that confirms the essence of Cannon's conclusions but extends the locus posteriorly to include the mid- and hindbrains, and even the spinal cord, and anteriorly to include the limbic formations and basal ganglia of the forebrain.

However, additional evidence, much of it from my laboratory, has shown that input from the body, including the viscera, through the autonomic nervous system is, after all, specifically involved in the organization of the neural states basic to emotional and motivational feeling. This work has shown that three classes of influence can be discerned and that this influence is necessary to stabilize the states rather than acting as a cue to emotional feeling. Some years ago Lindsley (1951) proposed an activation theory of emotions based on the fact that during emotional upset the electrical activity of the brain becomes desynchronized. Our evidence (reviewed in Pribram & McGuinness, 1975) showed that three separate systems could be discerned to influence electrocortical desynchronization. One system regulates phasic desynchronization i.e., brief, lasting at most several seconds), another regulates tonic desynchronization, and a third coordinates the other two (over a longer period of time—the duration of an attention span).

We called phasic desynchronization arousal. The system responsible for arousal centers in the forebrain on the amygdala, a basal ganglion of the limbic forebrain. Removal of the amygdala eliminates the visceral and autonomic responses that ordinarily accompany orienting and alerting to a change in stimulus conditions (Kimble, Bagshaw, & Pribram, 1965; Bagshaw, Kimble, & Pribram, 1965; Bagshaw & Benzies, 1968; Pribram, Reitz, McNeil, & Spevack, 1974; reviewed by Pribram & McGuinness, 1975). Furthermore, this elimination of the visceroautonomic responses apparently leads to a failure of behavioral habituation, which normally occurs rapidly when the novel stimulus is repeated: The visceroautonomic reaction speeds familiarization. *Thus, contrary to Lange and James, the visceral input appears not to be experienced directly as an emotion but leads to rapid habituation of the input. As shown by Sokolov (1960), habituation forms a stable neural representation. Such a stable state is necessary for appreciating subsequent change—the novelty which then arouses (emotional) interest and, when the novelty exceeds certain limits, the experiencing of (emotional) upset. James and Lange were correct in suggesting that visceral input is important to emotion but erroneous in the specific role they assigned it in the emotional process.*

The second system involved in the desynchronization of cortical electrical activity [in this instance a tonic (minute long) activation] is centered on the nonlimbic basal ganglia of the forebrain: the caudate nucleus and putamen (reviewed by Pribram, 1977b). These structures are concerned with maintaining the (motivational) readiness of the organism: postural readiness, motor readiness, and the readiness produced by the establishing of sensory (i.e., attentional) sets (Lassonde, Ptito, & Pribram, 1975; Reitz & Pribram, 1969; Spinelli & Pribram, 1966, 1967). It is this second system that forms the neural basis for "attitudes," much as suggested by Nina Bull (1969) except that, in the context of the proposals made here, her book would be entitled "The Attitudinal Theory of Feelings" rather than "of Emotion."

A third system centers on the hippocampus and coordinates arousal and readiness (see Pribram and McGuinness [1975] for a review of the evidence on which this statement is based). Arousal phasically interrupts ongoing tonic readiness. The balance between interruption and continuation must be coordinated, and neurobehavioral and neurophysiological evidence points to the hippocampal system as serving such a function. Coordination has been shown to involve neural work, that is, to take effort (see book edited by Ingvar & Lassen, 1975).

Neurochemically the three systems also differ (reviewed by Pribram, 1977a). As already noted, the amygdala is rich in endorphins and the caudate and putamen are characterized by dopamine. The hippocampal system is involved in the pituitary–adrenal hormonal controls, selectively absorbing adrenocortical hormone (see, e.g., Bohus, 1976; McEwen, Gerlach, & Micco, 1976) and being acted upon by ACTH (adrenocorticotrophic hormone) and related enkephalins (van Riezen, Rigter, & Greven, 1977).

The humoral, visceral, and activation theories of emotion (and motivation) are thus converging into a more comprehensive view that subsumes the earlier ones. The momentary arousal produced by novelty appears to be related to endorphin homeostasis, the activation of motivational readiness is based on a dopaminergic system, and coordinating effort (or its inverse, comfort) is experienced as a result of operations of the brain representation of the pituitary–adrenal hormonal stress mechanism.

The model of feelings (including emotional feelings) that emerges from these data centers on a set of core-brain neurochemical states that comprise the experience of a feeling of "familiarity." Such a feeling implies equilibration, a feeling of a reasonable amount of stability and a smooth transition from one state to another. This set of stable states can be altered by novel or pain-producing events, and what is perceived as novel, or painful, is dependent on the configuration of the states that determine what is familiar. The distinction between a feeling of novelty and pain is one of intensity *only* (e.g., electrical stimulations of the amygdala in animals and man produce orienting [interest], avoidance [fear], attack, and escape [pain] as a function of ascending stimulus intensity [Gastaut, 1954]. In contrast to the arousing disequilibrations produced by the novelty–pain mechanism, the maintenance of states is effected by tonic operations of the readiness system. This system may have evolved from, or in close coordination with, the temperature system.

There is considerable evidence that the maintenance of a stable basal temperature involves the food appetitive, water balance, and tonic muscular readiness systems, among others (see Brobeck, 1963, for a review). When the demands of arousal are pitted against those of continuing readiness, the feelings of stress and effort are experienced. These experiences are allayed by a coordinating mechanism that adjudicates the smooth transition from state to state within some comfortable band width of tolerance.

THE CORTICAL CONTRIBUTION
TO A LABELING OF FEELINGS

The biological contribution to an understanding of feelings in general and emotional feelings in particular cannot rest here. A basic problem set out at the beginning of this chapter in the quotations from William James and Freud has to be faced. Freud proposed that the critical neurological mechanisms involved in emotion are neurochemical and derive from body stimulation (the endogenous paths) that affects a certain portion of the brain. The work reviewed here has given substance to Freud's proposal and enlarged upon it: A protocritic dimension of stimulation was identified, a dimension describing much of the input through visceroautonomic (endogenous) paths but also receiving a contribution from exteroceptors (exogenous paths), especially those of the pain and temperature senses. Furthermore, the processing of this protocritic dimension was found to take place in limited portions of the brain: the core-brain systems of the brain stem and the limbic forebrain.

William James (1890), in the passage from which the earlier quotation was taken, faced the possibility that such separate neural processing of emotion occurs:

> And yet it is even now certain that of two things concerning the emotions, one must be true. Either separate and special centres, affected to them alone, are their brainseat, or else they correspond to processes occurring in the motor and sensory centres already assigned, or in others like them, not yet known. If the former be the case, we must deny the view that is current, and hold the cortex to be something more than the surface of "projection" for every sensitive spot and every muscle of the body. If the latter be the case, we must ask whether the emotional *process* in the sensory or motor centre be an altogether peculiar one, or whether it resembles the ordinary perceptive processes of which those centres are already recognized to be the seat. Now if the theory I have defended be true, the latter alternative is all that it demands [Vol. II, pp. 472–474].

James opted for the cortex, as we saw in the remainder of this quotation in the introduction to this chapter. Was he wrong?

I do not believe so. There is more to feeling than the protocritic dimension.

Schachter (e.g., Schachter & Singer, 1962), in a classical set of experiments, has delineated two aspects to feeling: one that devolves on its intensity (which has been discussed here as the protocritic dimension) and the other that "labels" the feeling. Labels are specific: They identify the feeling with respect to a spatial and temporal or other qualitative context. In short, labeling is epicritic, and we should turn, as James proposed, to the cerebral convexity in the search for the neural mechanisms that are involved.

According to James (1890), what needs to be demonstrated is that "the reflex currents pass down through their preordained channels, alter the condition of muscle, skin and viscus; and these alterations, perceived, like the original object, in as many portions of the cortex, combine with it in consciousness and transform it from an object-simply-apprehended into an object-emotionally-felt" (p. 253).

The work reviewed above has demonstrated that "the condition of muscle, skin and viscus" need not, in fact, be altered. A stable representation, a neural representation of bodily function including its quantitative hormonal composition, is interposed between "muscle, skin and viscus" and the cortex. All that needs to be established is that the representation (and its potential or actual perturbation) be addressed. The pathways whereby this can occur have now been thoroughly established both anatomically and physiologically (Goldman & Nauta, 1977; Kemp & Powell, 1970; Lassonde & Ptito, in preparation; Nauta, 1964; Reitz & Pribram, 1969).

The cortical contribution to the regulation of more primitive functions is, as might be expected, complex. Sense can be made of this complexity, however, by relating the myriad of observations on the effect of cortical lesions and excitations to the two simpler dimensions that have been delineated thus far. The cerebral isocortex is directly connected both to brain stem (core and shell portion) and to the remainder of the forebrain (basal ganglia and limbic formations). These connections can therefore modulate the epicritic–protocritic and the affective–effective dimensions of experience and behavior which are regulated by the more primitive structures.

The protocritic–epicritic dimension is reflected in the cortex by a front–back distinction in function. The anterior frontal cortex is so intimately related to the limbic systems that it can be conceived as the "association area" for these systems (Pribram, 1954, 1958a,b). Anatomically the anterior frontal (frontal intrinsic) cortex receives projections from the n. medialis dorsalis of the thalamus (an "intrinsic" nucleus because it is only indirectly connected with extracerebral inputs) which lies embedded within nuclei that project to limbic cortex. Behaviorally, resections of frontal intrinsic cortex result in deficits in delayed alternation performance, deficits also obtained when lesions are made of limbic structures but not when the posterior cortical convexity is damaged. By contrast, damage to the posterior cortical convexity (the posterior intrinsic cortex which receives its input from the pulvinar, another intrinsic thalamic nucleus) produces deficits in discrimination learning and performance which remain unaffected by frontal and limbic lesions. The difference between alternation and discrimination has been conceptualized to reflect the difference between context-sensitive, episode-specific reactions on the one hand and context-free, automatic information-processing on the other (Pribram, 1978). More on this follows.

Recent evidence from the human neurological and neuropsychological clinic and from the recording of electrical brain activity in man has suggested that the effective–affective dimension receives a cortical contribution which is to some extent lateralized, i.e., the left and right hemispheres of the cerebral cortex contribute unequally to the regulation of behavior and the monitoring of feelings (Galin, 1977; Gazzaniga, 1970; Schwartz, 1975; Sperry, 1974). The fact of right-hand dominance (dexterity) and that linguistic expression is regulated by the functioning of the left cerebral hemisphere in most right-handed persons has been well known for a long time. What is new is evidence that the right hemisphere may also be specialized in the direction of a more holistic, parallel processing, experiential mode of operation.

The front–back and right–left distinctions of cortical regulation converge to produce a new dimension which I have labeled esthetic–ethical (Pribram, 1968). This dimension is based on the distinction between the processing of "external space" and the processing of a "body image" or "self." Processing which results in the effective use of local sign (the epicritic dimension) is a function of a band of cortex surrounding the three major cerebral fissures: Sylvian, Rolandic (central), and Calcarine. (The continuity between peri Rolandic and pericalcarine cortex is established at the apex of the cortical convexity: In the monkey brain this is at the confluence of the intraparietal, superior temporal, and lunate sulci. The continuity between peri Sylvian and peri Rolandic cortex lies at the foot of the central fissure).

In primates including man, the growth of the cortex surrounding these major fissures has split the remaining cortex into two subdivisions: (1) a posterior focused on the inferior parietal lobule on the lateral surface and the precunens on the medial (connected via the medial extension of the confluence between intraparietal and lunate sulci); and (2) the cortex covering the poles of the frontal and temporal lobes (interconnected by the fibers of the uncinate faciculus and adjacent to the orbitofrontal—anterior insular—periamygdaloid cortex which is a part of the limbic systems). The functional connectivities of these divisions and subdivisions of the cortical mantle have been most clearly demonstrated by strychnine neuronography (Bonin and Bailey, 1947; Pribram and MacLean, 1953) and have been confirmed histologically by the use of silver staining techniques (Jones, 1973; Nauta, 1964).

The behavioral evidence showing that the perifissural cortex processes "external space" while the remaining cortex processes "self" is so extensive that only the highlights can be listed here: (1) Beginning with the precentral (preRolandic) cortex, Pribram, Kruger, Robinson, and Berman (1955) showed that the environmental consequences of movement, not movements or muscle contractions per se are encoded in this "motor" cortex (see review by Pribram, 1971). (2) The postcentral and superior parietal cortex deals with the somatosensory (haptic) discrimination of objects in external space (Brody and Pribram, 1978; Kruger and Michel, 1962; Mountcastle, Lynch, Georgopoulos, Sakata, and Acuna, 1975; Pribram and Barry, 1956). (3) The pericalcarine cortex deals with visual processing (see Weiskrantz, 1974, for review) and its extension into the inferior temporal gyrus, with making visual discriminations (see Pribram, 1974, for review). (4) The posterior perisylvian cortex is involved in auditory processing (see D. Neff, 1961, for review) and its extension into the superior temporal gyrus with auditory discriminations (Dewson, 1977; Dewson and Cowey, 1969; Dewson, Pribram, and Lynch, 1969). (5) The anterior perisylvian cortex in the depths of the fissure and extending forward to the temporal pole and orbital surface of the frontal lobe processes gustatory information (Bagshaw and Pribram, 1953; Pribram and Bagshaw, 1953), and is also involved in olfactory (Brown, 1963; Brown, Rosvold and Mishkin, 1963), and, as noted earlier, temperature discriminations (Chin, Pribram, Drake, and Green, 1976).

By contrast to these clearcut results of experiments relating the perifissural cortex to processing of "external space," the evidence for processing "self" by the remaining cortex is somewhat more difficult to interpret. Initially, data were believed to point to the anterior frontal cortex as the main source of an image of self. Recent experimental results show, however, that this conclusion was oversimplified and to a large extent erroneous (Brody and Pribram, 1978). Furthermore, clinical evidence has shown the inferior parietal lobule to be concerned with body-image: Lesions of this cortex lead to severe "neglect" of the opposite side of the body and this is especially severe when the lesion is in the right hemisphere. The lesions are often deep involving the precuneus and its connections (see Pribram and MacLean, 1953) with the cingulate and retrosplenical portions of the limbic cortex (Geschwind, 1965).

What seems to be a more accurate reading of current available evidence is that there is a balance between the parietal and frontal (including temporal pole) portions of this cortex which processes "self." While lesions of the parietal cortex lead to "neglect," lesions of the frontal and temporal poles lead to its opposite (Teuber, 1972; Geschwind, 1965). Patients with frontal and temporal lobe involvement tend to talk and write voluminously about themselves and, as noted, to lose control over behavior which is context-sensitive, i.e., depends on some stable mnemonically organized self. (See Fig. 10.1.)

To summarize: The cortical contribution to emotion relates the affective–effective dimension to the protocritic–epicritic in such a way that a new dimension, labeled ethical–esthetic, emerges. This new dimension is based on the construction of a self-concept which is organized and enhanced by parietal and selectively inhibited (made context sensitive) by frontal cortical functioning. The construction is achieved in man by combining a frontolimbic protocritic versus cortical convexity epicritic axis with a right hemisphere affec-

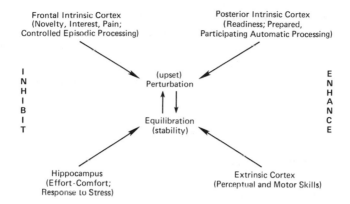

FIGURE 10.1 A highly schematic diagram that portrays cortical influences on the basic neuronal mechanisms that regulate stable states. The Perturbation $\rightleftarrows$ Equilibration couplet is composed of inhibitory interactions. Lateral inhibition pushes the couplet toward perturbation while recurrent inhibition acts as a negative feedback to stabilize and equilibrate. The data base for the arrows from the various cortical regions to the central couplet is derived from recovery cycle experiments. When a cortical stimulation increased the variance of an initial potential evoked by abrupt peripheral stimulation (in the visual, auditory, and somatosensory modes), the stimulus was considered to inhibit equilibration. This effect was obtained when the hippocampus was electrically stimulated. Conversely, a decrease in such variability signaled an enhanced equilibration, a result obtained when the primary sensory and motor cortical regions were stimulated. Furthermore, the second of a pair of such stimuli ordinarily evokes a diminished response (due to a lag in recovery of the channel) when administered over short interstimulus intervals (the recovery cycle). When the duration and level of diminution are increased, the input channel becomes desynchronized; that is, perturbation is enhanced. This effect is obtained when the posterior intrinsic cortex is electrically excited. The converse, inhibition of perturbation, is signaled by a more rapid recovery of the second potential evoked by the sensory stimulation. Such an effect is produced by electrical excitation of the frontal intrinsic cortex. Thus, the intrinsic cortical regions manifest their effect in the recovery cycle data; the extrinsic and hippocampal formations influence the variability of the initial evoked response directly. Both the intrinsic- and extrinsic-hippocampal effects are balanced: Frontolimbic formations exert their influence through inhibition (INHIBIT, a result that has been independently obtained in several series of experiments), whereas the cortical convexity operates via excitation (ENHANCE). This fourfold mechanism thus provides exquisite control over central neural stability and its potential and actual perturbations.

tive versus left hemisphere effective axis. The poles of each axis have been found to oppose each other (Lassonde and Ptito, in preparation; Pribram, Lassone, and Ptito, in preparation; Spinelli and Pribram, 1967) in such a way that a combinatorial balance of control is achieved (Jackson, 1873).

CONCLUSION

Clearly, considerable progress has been achieved in recent years in understanding the biology of emotion and other feelings. The intensive (protocritic) dimension of emotional experience is being correlated with neurochemical states and factors that control the changes in those states. Emotional expressions are related to these controls and are found to "stop at the skin" and, ordinarily, not to get into *"practical* relations with the environment," as William James so aptly stated. An exception to this occurs in social behavior, where emotional expressions are "read" by other persons and thus exert a practical influence through the exercise of the recipient rather than the emoting organism.

These experimentally based definitions of emotions distinguish them from motivational feelings and behavior. An affective–effective dimension is thus recognized as grounded in biological as well as in social fact.

The biological roots of the protocritic (intensive) dimension of emotional and motivational feelings concern two interrelated sets of systems:

1. Neurochemical (i.e., neurohumoral) control systems establish relatively enduring configurations, that is, stable states, by way of homeostatic regulations. To date, the catechol and indole amines and several peptides have been found to be especially important components of the neurohumoral configurations that determine such states.

2. Neuroelectric control systems ensure the stability and smooth changes of these states and involve arousal, activation, and effort. Arousal has been shown to be a phasic response to input experienced as interesting and novel or as disruptive. Arousal is regulated by a system whose forebrain locus is in the amygdala. Neurochemically this system is rich in sex hormones (among others) and in the neuropeptide endorphin, a regulator of pain. By contrast, activation is a tonic phenomenon whose forebrain locus centers on the basal ganglia, which are part of a dopaminergic neurohumoral system. Psychophysiological and neurobehavioral experiments have shown this system to provide continuing readiness to respond; it is therefore more directly involved in motivational than in emotional experience and expression.

3. A third control system whose forebrain locus centers on the hippocampus has been shown to regulate the coordination of arousal and activation. This system is intimately involved in the pituitary–adrenal cortical humoral response to stress by way of adrenocorticosteroid receptors and the pituitary secretion of adrenocorticotrophic hormones (ACTH) and peptides related to ACTH, the enkephalins. The system is thus responsible for the experiences (feelings) of effort and comfort and their expression.

Furthermore, current evidence attests to the involvement of body mechanisms in these brain regulations of state. Already noted is the role of the pituitary–adrenal axis in determining effort and comfort. Visceral involvement has been demonstrated as important in the registration of novelty (and familiarity). And the role of the motor system in attitudinal activation is clearcut. These muscular, skin, and visceral inputs are not directly responsible for emotional and motivational feeling as proposed by James and Lange, however. Rather, they are involved in the registration in memory of changes, so that the organism can habituate to them. They are thus the components of which stable neural (core-brain) representations of bodily states are put together. Changes in these core-brain states, not in the somatic inputs per se, appear to be related to the experiencing of the protocritic dimension of emotion and emotional feelings.

Thus, there is a convergence of earlier biological theories of emotion into a current, more comprehensive view. The medieval humoral theories find a berth in current endocrine research. Lange's (1887) visceral theory is confirmed as taking part in the arousal mechanism that provides feelings of interest, novelty, and familiarity and more painful disruptions of stable states. James's (1890) emphasis on a report to the brain of bodily responses is shown to be a manifestation of the brain's representation of familiar body responses so that departures from the familiar are arousing. Cannon's (1929) thalamic theory is supported by the documentation that the diencephalon is a prime locus for receptors sensitive to the hormones that determine the body's chemical response systems. The diencephalon is central to the (homeostatic) maintenance of the stable representations of body states. Papez's (1937) and MacLean's (1949) extension of Cannon's brain locus to the limbic forebrain is also amply supported—and one must now add (as foreshadowed by Nina Bull's [1951] attitude theory) the basal ganglia as well—in that limbic formations and basal ganglia are shown to be part of the neurochemical regulating mechanisms responsible for stable states and the sensing of departures from such stable states. Such departures were at an earlier time encompassed by Lindsley (1951), by Duffy (1934), and by Malmo (1963) under the banner of activation theory.

Finally, as demanded by clinical evidence (e.g., psychoanalysis and other verbal psychotherapies [see Pribram & Gill, 1976]) and social psychological experimentation (e.g., Schachter & Singer, 1962), the cerebral isocortex is not exempt from playing a critical role in the organization of emotional and motivational experience and expression. Laboratory evidence has shown that the intrinsic portions of the cerebral cortex, the "association" cortices of the posterior convexity and of the frontal pole, exert their influence via the basal ganglia, the forebrain focus of the arousal and readiness systems. This cortical control accounts for the specific epicritic "labeling" of feelings.

In short, as foreshadowed by William James, the entire brain is involved in the regulation of emotional experience and expression. But each part of the brain has a very specific role in the totality, and this role involves the sensing and control not only of other neural events but of body functions as well. The essence of an intensive protocritic dimension emotion—as experienced and expressed by the man in the street—is this regulation of changes in stable states, corebrain states, and body states. Brief episodic mild changes in stability are experienced as arousing and interesting (novel); more severe disruptions are painful and frightening. When control is exercised to contain such changes, it is experienced as effortful; when little control is needed, behavior is automatic and the experience is one of comfort. The intensive dimension of feeling is not the only dimension, however. Epicritic, specific labeling is also a prominent feature of emotional and motivational experience and expression. Evidence has been reviewed that shows a cortical contribution by way of input to core-brain structures to be responsible for the epicritic aspect, the labeling of feeling states.

But, in concluding, it should again be pointed out that a significant portion of the controls exercised are not through neural circuitry but by way of chemical regulations, that is, secretions or hormones in different concentrations that lay the foundation for differences in reactivity and thus differences in disposition and temperament. A single exposure to testosterone during a critical embryological period will change a female's reactivity to that of a male for the rest of its life (Young, 1961; Phoenix, Goy, & Young, 1967). Presumably that exposure programmed a brain mechanism that thereafter controlled behavior according to the testosterone program. Changes in adrenal cortical hormone level during disease (Cushing's syndrome), or by virtue of experimental excision, alter sensory thresholds and tolerances in several modalities (Henkin, 1970). Thyroid deficiency in infants produces cretins; in adults, activity levels are related to the amount of circulating thyroid hormone (Vernikos-Danellis, 1972a). Disturbed insulin and therefore sugar metabolism has been related to feelings of irritability and malaise (Vernikos-Danellis, 1972b). Could it be that Galen's theory was but a degenerate view of some more precise knowledge attained by the ancients, which we are only now regaining? Or is it that, like the concept of the atom, vague formulations which were held for centuries finally reached precision when subjected to scientific exploration? In either case, the search continues with just enough yield of novelty to maintain the interest of explorers of emotion—ensuring that profitable change in understanding continues.

REFERENCES

Bagshaw, M. H., & Benzies, S. Multiple measures of the orienting reaction and their dissociation after amygdalectomy in monkeys. *Experimental Neurology,* 1968, *20,* 175–187.

Bagshaw, M. H., Kimble, D. P., & Pribram, K. H. The GSR of monkeys during orienting and habituation and after ablation of the amygdala, hippocampus and inferotemporal cortex. *Neuropsychologia,* 1965, *3,* 111–119.

Basgshaw, M. H., & Pribram, K. H. Cortical organization in gustation (Macaca mulatta). *Journal of Neurophysiology,* 1953, *16,* 499–508.

Bohus, B. The hippocampus and the pituitary adrenal system hormones. In R. L. Isaacson & K. H. Pribram (eds.), *The hippocampus,* pp. 323–353. New York: Plenum, 1976.

Bonin, G. von, & Bailey, P. The neocortex of Macaca mulatta. *Illinois Monographs in the Medican Sciences,* Vol. 5, No. 4. Urbana: University of Illinois Press, 1947.

Brobeck, J. R. Review and synthesis. In M. A. Brazier (ed.), *Brain behavior,* Vol. II, pp. 389–409. Washington, D.C.: American Institute of Biological Sciences, 1963.

Brody, B. A., & Pribram, K. H. The role of frontal and parietal cortex in cognitive processing: Tests of spatial and sequence functions. *Brain,* 1978, *101,* 607–633.

Brown, T. S. Olfactory and visual discrimination in the monkey after selective lesions of the temporal lobe. *Journal of Comparative and Physiological Psychology,* 1963, *56,* 764–768.

Brown, T. S., Rosvold, H. E., & Mishkin, M. Olfactory discrimination after temporal lesions in monkeys. *Journal of Comparative Physiological Psychology,* 1963, *56,* 190–195.

Bull, N. *The attitude theory of emotion.* Nervous and Mental Disease Monograhs Series, New York: Johnson Reprint Corp., 1969.

Cannon, W. B. The James-Lange theory of emotions: A critical examination and an alternative theory. *American Journal of Psychology,* 1927, *34,* 106–124.

Cannon, W. B. *Bodily changes in pain, hunger, fear and rage.* New York: D. Appleton, 1929.

Chin, J. H., Pribram, K. H., Drake, K., & Greene, L. O., Jr. *Disruption* of temperature discrimination during limbic forebrain stimulation in monkeys. *Neuropsychologia,* 1976, *14,* 293–310.

Darwin, C. *The expression of the emotions in man and animals.* Chicago: University of Chicago Press, 1965.

De Valois, R. L. Color vision mechanisms in monkey. *Journal of General Physiology,* 1960, *43,* 115–128.

Dewson, J. H. III. Preliminary evidence of hemispheric asymmetry of auditory function in monkeys. In S. Harnard, R. W. Doty, J. Jaynes, L. Goldstein, G. Crauthamer (eds.), pp. 63–71. *Lateralization in the nervous system.* New York: Academic Press, 1977.

Dewson, J. H. III., & Cowey, A. Discrimination of auditory sequences by monkeys. *Nature,* 1969, *222,* 695–697.

Dewson, J. H. III., Pribram, K. H., & Lynch, J. Effects of ablations of temporal cortex on speech sound discrimination in monkeys. *Experimental Neurology,* 1969, *24,* 579–591.

Douglas, R. J., & Pribram, K. H. Learning and limbic lesions. *Neuropsychologia,* 1966, *4,* 197–220.

Duffy, E. Emotion: An example of the need for reorientation in psychology. *Psychology Review,* 1934, *41,* 184–198.

Freud, S. *Project for a scientific psychology* [orig. publ. 1895], Standard Edition, Vol. 1. London: The Hogarth Press, 1966.

Galin, D. Lateral specialization and psychiatric issues: Speculations on development and the evolution of consciousness. In S. J. Dimond & D. A. Blizard (eds.) *Evolution and lateralization of the brain.* Vol. 299, pp. 397–411. New York: Annals of the New York Academy of Sciences, 1977.

Gall, F. J., & Spurzheim, G. [*Research on the nervous system in general and on that of the brain in particular,* pp. 255–275. Paris: F. Schoell, 1809,] In K. H. Pribram (ed.) *Brain and behavior,* Vol. 1, pp. 20–26. Middlesex: Penguin Books, 1969.

Gastaut, H. Interpretation of the symptoms of "psychomotor" epilepsy in relation to physiologic data on rhinencephalic function. *Epilepsia,* Series III, 1954, *3,* 84–88.

Gazziniga, M. S. *The bisected brain.* New York: Appleton-Century-Crofts, 1970.

Geschwind, N. Disconnexion syndromes in animals and man: Part 1. *Brain,* 1965, *88,* 237–294.

Goldman, P. S., & Nauta, W. J. H. An intricately patterned prefrontocaudate projection in the rhesus monkey. *Journal of Comparative Neurology,* 1977, *171* (3), 369–384.

Grossman, S. P. The VMH: A center for affective reaction, satiety, or both? *Physiology and Behavior,* 1966, *1:* 10.

Head, H. *Studies in neurology.* Oxford: Oxford Medical Publications, 1920.

Hebb, D. O. Drives and the CNS (conceptual nervous system). *Psychology Review,* 1955, *62,* 243–254.

Henkin, R. I. The neuroendocrine control of perception. In D. A. Hamburg, K. H. Pribram, & A. J. Stunkard (eds.) *Perception and its disorders,* Research Publications, Association for

Research in Nervous and Mental Disease, Vol. XLVIII, pp. 54–107. Baltimore: Williams & Wilkins, 1970.

Hering, E. *Outlines of a theory of light sense.* Cambridge: Harvard University Press, 1964.

Hinde, R. A. Factors governing the changes in strength of a partially inborn response, as shown by the mobbing behavior of the chaffinch (*Fringilla coelebs*). I. The nature of the response, and an examination of its course. *Proceedings of the Royal Society of London, Series B,* 1954, *142,* 306–331. (a)

Hinde, R. A. Factors governing the changes in strength of a partially inborn response, as shown by the mobbing behavior of the chaffinch (*Fringilla coelebs*). II. The waning of the response. *Proceedings of the Royal Society of London, Series B,* 1954, *142,* 331–358. (b)

Hinde, R. A. Factors governing the changes in strength of a partially inborn response, as shown by the mobbing behavior of the chaffinch (*Fringilla coelebs*). III. The interaction of short-term and long-term incremental and decremental effects. *Proceedings of the Royal Society of London, Series B,* 1960, *153,* 398–420.

Ingvar, D. H., & Lassen, N. A. (eds.) *Brain work: Benzon Symposium VIII,* Copenhagen: Munksgaard, 1975.

Jackson, J. H. *Clinical and physiological researches on the nervous system.* London: J. & A. Churchill, 1873.

James, W. *Principles of psychology,* Vols. I and II (compl.). New York: Dover Publications, 1890.

Jones, E. G. The anatomy of extrageniculostriate visual mechanisms. In F. O. Schmitt & F. G. Worden (eds.) *The neurosciences third study program,* pp 215–227. Cambridge, Mass.: The MIT Press, 1973.

Kantor, J. R., & Smith, N. W. *The science of psychology: An interbehavioral survey.* Chicago: Principia Press, 1975.

Kemp, J. M., & Powell, T. P. S. The cortico-striate projection in the monkey. *Brain,* 1970, *93,* 525–546.

Kimble, D. P., Bagshaw, M. H., & Pribram, K. H. The GSR of monkeys during orienting and habituation after selective partial ablations of the cingulate and frontal cortex. *Neuropsychologia,* 1965, *3,* 121–128.

King, M. B., & Hoebel, B. G. Killing elicited by brain stimulation in rats. *Communications in Behavioral Biology,* Part A., 1968, *2,* 173–177.

Krasne, F. B. General disruption resulting from electical stimulation of ventro-medial hypothalamus. *Science,* 1962, *138,* 822–823.

Kruger, L., & Michel, F. A single neuron analysis of buccal cavity representation in the sensory trigeminal complex of the cat. *Archives of Oral Biology,* 1962, *7,* 491–503.

Lacey, B. C., & Lacey, J. I. Studies of heart rate and other bodily processes in sensorimotor behavior. In P. A. Obrist, A. Black, J. Bruner, & L. DiCara (eds.), *Cardiovascular psychophysiology: Current issues in response mechanisms, biofeedback and methodology,* pp. 538–564. Chicago: Aldine-Atherton, 1974.

Lange, C. *Ueber Gemuthsbewegungen.* Leipzig, Germany: Uebersetzt von H. Kurell, 1887.

Lassonde, M. C., & Ptito, M. Intracerebral influences on the microstructure of visual cortex. II. Striatal and cortical effects on response properties of visual cortex neurons. (Submitted to Journal of Neurophysiology, June, 1979).

Lassonde, M. C., Ptito, M., & Pribram, K. H. Are the basal ganglia only motor structures? In *Programs and Abstracts,* Washington, D.C.: American Physiological Society, 1975.

Liebeskind, J. C., Mayer, D. J., & Akil, H. Central mechanisms of pain inhibition: Studies of analgesia from focal brain stimulation. In J. J. Bonica (ed.), *Advances in neurology,* Vol. 4: *Pain.* New York: Raven Press, 1974.

Lindsley, D. B. Emotion. In S. S. Stevens (ed.), *Handbook of experimental psychology.* New York: Wiley, 1951.

MacLean, P. D. Psychosomatic disease and the "visceral pain": Recent developments bearing on the Papez theory of emotion. *Psychosomatic Medicine,* 1949, *44,* 338–353.

Malmo, R. B. On central and autonomic nervous system mechanisms in conditioning, learning and performance. *Canadian Journal of Psychology,* 1963, *17,* 1.

Mandler, G. The interruption of behavior. In D. Levine (ed.), *Nebraska Symposium on Motivation,* pp. 163–220. Lincoln: University of Nebraska Press, 1964.

McEwen, B. S., Gerlach, J. L., & Micco, D. J. Putative glucocorticoid receptors in hippocampus and other regions of the rat brain. In R. L. Isaacson & K. H. Pribram, (eds.), *The hippocampus,* pp. 285–322. New York: Plenum, 1976.

Miller, G. A., Galanter, E. H., & Pribram, K. H. *Plans and the structure of behavior.* New York: Henry Holt, 1960.

Miller, N. E., Bailey, C. J., & Stevenson, J. A. Decreased "hunger" but increased food intake resulting from hypothalamic lesions. *Science,* 1950, *112,* 256–259.

Mountcastle, V. B., Lynch, J. C., Georgopoulos, A., Sakata, H., & Acuna, C. Posterior parietal association cortex of the monkey: Command functions for operations within extrapersonal space. *Journal of Neurophysiology,* 1975, *38,* 871–908.

Nauta, W. J. H. Some efferent connections of the prefrontal cortex in the monkey. In J. M. Warren & K. Akert (eds.), *The frontal granular cortex and behavior,* p. 397. New York: McGraw-Hill, 1964.

Neff, D. Neural mechanisms of auditory discrimination. In W. A. Rosenbligh (ed.), *Sensory communication,* pp. 259–278. New York: Wiley, 1961.

Papez, J. W. A proposed mechanism of emotion. *Archives of Neurology and Psychiatry of Chicago,* 1937, *38,* 725–743.

Phoenix, C. H., Goy, R. W., & Young, W. C. Sexual behavior: General aspects. In L. Martini & W. F. Ganong (eds.), *Neuroendocrinology,* Vol. 2, pp. 163–196. New York: Academic Press, 1967.

Pribram, K. H. Toward a science of neuropsychology (method and data). In R. A. Patton (ed.) *Current trends in psychology and the behavioral sciences,* pp. 115–142. Pittsburgh: University of Pittsburgh Press, 1954.

Pribram, K. H. Neocortical function in behavior. In H. F. Harlow & C. H. Woolsey (eds.), *Biological and biochemical bases of behavior,* pp. 151–172. Madison: University of Wisconsin Press, 1958. (a)

Pribram, K. H. Comparative neurology and the evolution of behavior. In A. Roe & G. G. Simpson (eds.) *Behavior and evolution,* pp. 140–164. New Haven: Yale University Press, 1958. (b)

Pribram, K. H. The new neurology and the biology of emotion: A structural approach. *American Psychologist,* 1967, *22,* 830–838.

Pribram, K. H. Mind, brain, and behavior: Excursions into paradox. *Psychological Scene,* 1968, *2,* 30–33.

Pribram, K. H. Neural servosystems and the structure of personality. *Journal of Nervous and Mental Diseases* (Kubie issue), 1969, *140,* 30–39.

Pribram, K. H. Feelings as monitors. In M. B. Arnold (ed.), *Feelings and emotions,* pp. 41–53. New York: Academic Press, 1970.

Pribram, K. H. *Languages of the brain: Experimental paradoxes and principles in neuropsychology.* Englewood Cliffs, N.J.: Prentice-Hall, 1971. (2nd ed. Monterey, Calif.: Brooks/Cole, 1977).

Pribram, K. H. How is it that sensing so much we can do so little? In F. O. Schmitt (ed.) *The neurosciences third study program,* pp 249–261. Cambridge, Mass.: The MIT Press, 1974.

Pribram, K. H. Peptides and protocritic processes. In L. H. Miller, C. A. Sandman, & A. J. Kastin (eds.), *Neuropeptide influences on the brain and behavior.* New York: Raven Press, 1977. (a)

Pribram, K. H. New dimensions in the functions of the basal ganglia. In C. Shagass, S. Gershon, & A. J. Freidhoff (eds.), *Psychopathology and brain dysfunction,* pp. 77–95. New York: Raven Press, 1977 (b)

Pribram, K. H. Modes of central processing in human learning. In T. Teyler (ed.), *Brain and learning,* Stamford, Conn.: Greylock, 1978.

Pribram, K. H., & Bagshaw, M. Further analysis of the temporal lobe syndrome utilizing fronto-temporal ablations. *J. Comparative Neurology,* 1953, *99:* 347–375.

Pribram, K. H., & Barry, J. Further behavioral analysis of the parieto-temporo-preoccipital cortex. *Journal of Neurophysiology,* 1956, *99,* 99–106.

Pribram, K. H., & Gill, M. M. *Freud's "project" reassessed.* London: Hutchinson, 1976; New York: Basic Books, 1976.

Pribram, K. H., Kruger, L., Robinston, F., & Berman, A. J. The effects of precentral lesions on the behavior of monkeys. *Yale Journal of Biology and Medicine,* 1956, *28,* 428–443.

Pribram, K. H., Lassonde, M. C., & Ptito, M. Intracerebral influences on the microstructure of visual cortex: I. Classification of receptive field properties. (submitted to the Journal of Neurophysiology, June, 1979).

Pribram, K. H., & MacLean, P. D. Neuronographic analysis of medial and basal cerebral cortex. II. Monkey. *Journal of Neurophsyiology,* 1953, *16,* 324–340.

Pribram, K. H., & McGuinness, D. Arousal, activation and effort in the control of attention. *Psychology Review,* 1975, *82*(2), 116–149.

Pribram, K. H., & Melges, F. T. Psychophysiological basis of emotion. In P. J. Vinken & G. W. Bruyn (eds.), *Handbook of clinical neurology,* Vol. 3. Amsterdam: North Holland, 1969.

Pribram, K. H., Reitz, S., McNeil, M., & Spevack, A. A. The effect of amygdalectomy on orienting and classical conditioning. In *Mechanisms of formation and inhibition of conditional reflex* (Asratyan Festschrift). Moscow: Publishing office "Nauka" of the U.S.S.R. Academy of Sciences, 1974.

Reitz, S. L., & Pribram, K. H. Some subcortical connections of the inferotemporal gyrus of monkey. *Experimental Neurology,* 1969, *25,* 632–645.

Richardson, D. E., & Akil, H. Chronic self-administration of brain stimulation for pain relief in human patients. In *Proceedings of the American Association of Neurological Surgeons.* St. Louis, Mo.: AANS, 1974.

Riezen, van H., Rigter, H., & Greven, H. M. Critical appraisal of peptide pharmacology. In L. H. Miller, C. A. Sandman, & A. J. Kastin (eds.), *Neuropeptide influences on the brain and behavior,* pp. 11–27. New York: Raven Press, 1977.

Schachter, S., & Singer, T. E. Cognitive, social and physiological determinants of emotional state. *Psychology Review,* 1962, *69,* 379–397.

Schwartz, G. E. Biofeedback, self-regulation and the patterning of physiological processes. *American Scientist,* 1975, *63*(3), 314–324.

Sokolov, E. N. Neuronal models and the orienting reflex. In M. A. B. Brazier (ed.), *The central nervous system and behavior.* New York: Josiah Macy, Jr. Foundation, 1960.

Sperry, R. W. Lateral specialization in the surgically separated hemispheres. In F. O. Schmitt & F. G. Worden (eds.), *The neurosciences third study program,* pp. 5–19. Cambridge, Mass.: The MIT Press, 1974.

Spinelli, D. N., & Pribram, K. H. Changes in visual recovery functions produced by temporal lobe stimulation in monkeys. *Electroencephalography and Clinical Neurophysiology,* 1966, *20,* 44–49.

Spinelli, D. N., & Pribram, K. H. Changes in visual recovery function and unit activity produced by frontal and temporal cortex stimulation. *Electroencephalography and Clinical Neurophysiology,* 1967, *22,* 143–149.

Stein, L. Reward transmitters: Catecholamines and opioid peptides. In M. A. Lipton, A. DiMascio, & K. R. Killam (eds.), *Psychopharmacology: A generation of progress.* New York: Raven Press, 1978.

Teitelbaum, P. Sensory control of hypothalamic hyperphagia. *Journal of Comparative Physiological Psychology,* 1965, *59,* 275–279.

Teuber, H. L. Unity and diversity of frontal lobe functions. *Acta Neurobiologiae Experimentalis,* 1972, *32*(2), 615–656.

Vernikos-Danellis, J. Effects of hormones on the central nervous system. In S. Levine (ed.), *Hormones and behavior,* pp. 13–14. New York: Academic Press, 1972. (a)

Vernikos-Danellis, J. Effects of hormones on the central nervous system. In S. Levine (ed.), *Hormones and behavior,* pp. 29–39. New York: Academic Press, 1972. (b)

Walter, W. G. Electrical signs of association, expectancy, and decision in the human brain. *Electroencephalography and Clinical Neurophysiology,* 1967, *25,* 258–263.

Weiskrantz, L. The interaction between occipital and temporal cortex in vision: an overview. In F. O. Schmitt & F. G. Worden (eds.), *The neurosciences third study program.* pp. 189–204. Cambridge, Mass.: The MIT Press, 1974.

Wilson, M. Effects of circumscribed cortical lesions upon somesthetic and visual discrimination in the monkey. *J. Comparative Physiology and Psychology,* 1957, *50,* 630–635.

Young, P. T. *Emotion in man and animal, its nature and dynamic basis.* Huntington, New York: Robert E. Krieger, 1973.

Young, W. C. The hormones and mating behavior. In W. C. Young (ed.), *Sex and internal secretions,* pp. 1173–1239. Baltimore: Williams & Wilkins, 1961.

Chapter 11

THE COMMUNICATION OF EMOTION: THEORY OF SENTICS

MANFRED CLYNES

ABSTRACT

Theories and sentographic methods of measurement of the biologic basis of emotion communication are given. Specific biologic dynamic forms programmed into the CNS for the communication of specific emotions have been isolated and are called essentic forms. They may be produced through any motor output of sufficient dynamic flexibility, including the tone of voice and appear to be produced and recognized symbiotically. Essentic form and its corresponding emotion are seen to be a single entity with inherent feedback interaction between the expression and the emotional state. Essentic form and the corresponding emotional state exhibit the property of coherence so that only one essentic form can and does correspond to the experience of a particular emotion state. The theory predicts a new form of laughter, called motoric laughter, in which the voice is replaced by a suitable motoric pattern. Only when the motoric pattern replacing the voice corresponds in frequency to the "ha's" of laughter does the new laughter provide the same experience, confirming the coherence principle. Similar essentic forms have been isolated in various cultures for similar emotions. This, combined with the apparent impossibility to retrain individuals to express particular emotions with altered essentic forms, indicates a biologic rather than cultural origin of essentic form. It is proposed that emotion and its essentic form evolve simultaneously.

Emotion: Theory, Research, and Experience
Volume 1: Theories of Emotion

Nonverbal communication has been studied widely in terms of visual cues, such as body position and facial expressions (e.g., Birdwhistell, 1968; Ekman, 1972; Izard, 1971; Klages, 1950), and less widely in terms of auditory patterns (Bentley & Hoy, 1974). Subtleties of touch as a form of nonverbal communication are least of all studied. (Taste and smell have hardly been explored as possible media of voluntary nonverbal communication.) Painters and sculptors have to content themselves with momentary cross-sections in time to imply movement and expressive relationships. Yet the specific nature of live movement in time most powerfully influences communication. The time course of the expression defines its true character. But in the arts of music, dancing, and acting, the time course of the expression is allowed to reign. Communicating with subtlety and power depends on the almost infinite shades that can be produced in the course of expression. I have called the scientific study of dynamic emotional communication *sentics*.

Sentics aims to study the subtleties of temporal expression and has developed a new method for studying these experimentally. It has discovered some biological foundations of expressive forms through which individuals generate and communicate qualities and emotions. In this chapter, I shall briefly outline some of these findings (see Clynes [1977a, 1979] for a fuller exposition).

An expressive movement is an entity in time; it has a beginning, middle, and end. The first step in studying such entities is to note that it takes a certain amount of time to execute an expression of joy, of anger, of sadness, of love, and so on, and these times differ for different emotions. One may have a succession of such expressions, but each will partake of the character and duration of that particular emotion. The second thing is to recognize that the character of each expressive act is determined before it begins, that is, the time course of an expressive movement is preprogramed by the brain before it begins. This is very similar, for example, to the way a person might throw a ball to hit a particular target. The way he moves his arm to throw is preprogramed before he begins to throw: It is determined by his idea of hitting a particular spot. The more precise his idea and the more precise his execution, the more likely he will hit the target. Similarly, the time form of an expressive movement represents the state that seeks expression and is more powerful the more closely it corresponds to the expressive form of its quality.

It appears that there is a class of qualities of experience that are inherently linked with the motor system. Their expression and state may be considered as a single existential entity. Such a category inlcudes most emotions.

If expressive intercommunication consists of discrete spatiotemporal forms with clear beginnings and ends, we may ask the following question: Can these forms for specific emotions be isolated? Such elemental units of expression were, in fact, found to exist and could be precisely delineated by experimental methods to be described. We have called these elemental chunks or entities of expression *essentic forms*.

Essentic forms turn out to underlie expression regardless of the sensory modality in which they are expressed; thus, an expressive musical phrase, the tone of voice, a dance step, and an expressive touch partake of similar essentic forms when seeking to express a particular quality.

Once these entities characteristic of each quality have been identified, we can observe the way in which they act and interact. The nervous system appears to be programed in such a way as to be able to both produce and recognize these forms precisely (see Bentley & Hoy, 1974). They thus represent windows across the separation between individuals and allow contagion of emotion to take place, and they provide emotional understanding of one another.

Essentic forms have the power to generate emotion in the person who produces them, as well as in the one who receives them. Having isolated these elemental forms, it becomes possible to study the way in which they dynamically generate these emotional qualities. The studies summarized here represent a general systematic approach to this question. In the past, psychology and physiology have largely focused separate attention on either the study of the emotional state or the study of expression, rather than on their specific interaction. The generation of emotion affects bodily functions: The electrical activity of the brain, neurohormones, the hormonal system, and the cardiovascular system all respond to the generation of emotion through essentic form. This, in turn, affects the sense of well-being and modulates experience.

One approach to the question of what kind of entity constitutes an emotion is to consider those qualities of experience that can be communicated by means of direct temporal expression. If the contagion of experience through communication is selected as a common property, we obtain a class of qualities of experience nearly all of which are commonly called emotion. Love, grief, joy, anger, hate, laughter, sexual excitement, reverence, hope, and fear may be propagated through dynamic communication by using the tone of voice, expressive gesture, and facial expressive movement, for example. (Yawning is a quality of experience that is also contagious in this sense but is not usually classified as an emotion.)

In man-made information-processing systems, the transmitting units themselves (consisting of zeros and ones) have no meaning in terms of the message. They are like the dots and dashes in a Morse code message. In nature's system of communication of emotions, however, the message units themselves have analog (spatiotemporal form) features that act like keys in locks of our nervous system; the language, sender, and receiver are co-designed with vocabulary and meaning evolved by nature.

Some emotions, such as jealousy, are not communicable through a contagious process of expression. Jealousy, surprise, and to a large extent guilt, for example, are not capable of being embodied in temporal forms of expression that evoke similar feelings. Emotions like jealousy may be regarded as compounded of a number of existential factors of emotional meaning and significance. They have a special focus essential to their nature. Thus, emotions belonging to this second group, which includes jealousy, surprise, and guilt, require a special ideational content to become communicable. Music, for example, cannot portray the latter group in the same direct manner with expressive form as it can the emotions belonging to the first group.

EMOTION AND ITS EXPRESSION: SOME HISTORICAL ASPECTS

In the past, the emotional state and its expression have generally been studied separately, and very little systematic attempt has been made to study the consequences of regarding the state and its expression as one existential entity, incorporating inherent feedback (Laird, 1974). Studies of the psychophysiology of emotions generally have not concerned themselves with expression. Studies of human expression, on the other hand, have generally not investigated the psychophysiological ways in which successful or less successful expressions interact with the emotional state.

The most closely related systematic studies that we find are the studies by ethologists of the function of innate releasing mechanisms (IRMs) in animals. The action of IRMs resembles the function of dynamic expression in a number of ways. However, knowledge of IRMs in animals (predominately birds and fish) does not provide a sufficient framework for understanding the function of human expression in relationships between people and the function of expression in art and music.

Ethologic theories point out the genetic basis of communicative patterns in animals. These theories are in accord with the findings of genetic bases of the dynamic forms of emotion communication, called essentic forms which have been observed and identified through sentographic studies over the last decade.

Darwin (1872), in his study of the expression of emotions, regarded the mind–body interaction as a superstructure resulting from repeated association with earlier physiological processes. Thus, crying was related by him to earlier phylogenetic experience of the presence of foreign bodies in the eye, such as sand. Or, quite strangely, the "vulgar" scratching of one's head as an expression of puzzlement (an irritation according to Darwin) was supposedly a consequence of an abundance of lice among the uneducated, lice-irritated masses. It did not seem possible for Darwin to assume that an expressive phenomenon involving both mind and body should have evolved *in toto*. The sequence had to be, first, a bodily component and then mental associations that would go with it.

Freud, forced to make a choice between mind and body, chose Eros and Thanatos as origins of drives from which other emotional experiential characterizations and satisfactions were supposedly derived.

The view described in this chapter, which is derived from extensive sentographic observation of dynamic emotion communication, is that a particular dynamic form of emotion communication, such as laughter, anger, or even yawning, evolved as a single mind–body entity; the same genetic change that produces the form of expression also produces its corresponding experiential quality. (We are led to this conclusion through the existence of the property of coherence, affirmed through prediction of new psychobehavioral experience that can be experimentally confirmed [e.g., the predicted new form of laughter].)

We may need to go back to the sixteenth century philosopher Spinoza to find an antecedent to this view of emotional entities. Spinoza regarded emotions as natural entities comprising both mind and body and anticipated a biocybernetic approach that partakes of both mental and bodily aspects. His theory of emotions, as part of his ethics, dealt with the specific dynamic interaction of various emotions.

For a review of studies of the nature of expression, the reader is referred to Klages (1950), who, in addition to his own extensive studies, published a comprehensive historical review of the study of expression from the fifteenth century until 1950. For contemporary work in the study of expression, the work of Ekman (1972) and Izard (1971) and the school of body language centered around Birdwhistell (1968) are cited. None of these attempt to study the power of expression to generate, or to discharge, the emotional state. For that aspect, the work of Marañon (1950) is cited. Marañon examined the power of evocative speech: the emotion contagion of demagoguery displayed by the totalitarian dictators.

Of the two classical types of theories of emotion represented by the James–Lange and Cannon points of view, respectively, neither one alone can account for the full nature of emotional experience. It can be readily shown that aspects of emotional experience take place before there has been time for the special bodily changes to occur. On the other hand, individuals with spinal injuries are unable to experience emotion in the same way as individuals with intact spinal cords (Hohmann, 1966).

The perspective on the nature of emotion given by Schachter and Singer (1962) is that if arousal is provided by administration of adrenalin, subjects will as readily label their state one emotion as another, depending on an environment in which an actor is made to portray these specific emotions. These experiments are taken to signify nonspecificity of the emotions. However, in my view, they show the following:

1. Arousal predisposes a person to experience emotion.
2. Communication by actors can contagiously affect the state of a subject. (These experiments include the communication of emotion, unwittingly, as it were, as part of their demonstration.)

My experiments show, by contrast, that the emotional process can begin with labeling and lead to various states of arousal, some measured parameters of which may appear to show similar changes. Thus, if oxygen consumption is found to increase in anger, joy, and sex and decrease in love, reverence, and grief, this does not mean that emotions are not specific, but that emotional experience can be different, even if certain parametric measures appear to indicate a similar "arousal" measure. The correlate to the specific experience simply lies elsewhere in the organism. Where this might be shall be discussed later in this chapter.

EXPERIMENTAL MEASUREMENT OF ESSENTIC FORM

To avoid confusion between the words "feeling" and "emotion," I have introduced the term *sentic state* (derived from the Latin root *sentire*) to denote the emotion or feeling state, a generic term applicable at various intensities (a weak emotion is often termed a feeling).

I have further named a simple, single, voluntary movement together with its command decision an *acton* (Clynes, 1969, 1977a). Voluntary raising of the finger is an example of an acton. Such a simple single movement is capable of being modulated by the emotion seeking expression, and one may call such a modulated movement expressing a particular emotional state an *E-acton*. In this chapter, all references to expressive acts refer to E-actons.

The expressive character of an emotion appears to lie in its dynamic form or modulation of the E-acton, rather than to be specific only to a particular part of the body. Thus, for example, angry gestures can be made with the arm or leg or can be expressed by the tone of voice using different motor outputs in each case. If one wishes to extract and isolate the dynamic character (if it exists) that expresses the quality of anger, one would want to have a method of production and of measurement that is reliable, repeatable, and quantifiable. To make such a measurement of essentic forms possible, one may choose to measure the dynamic character of an emotion through the transient pressure of a finger on a finger rest. This has the possibility of being readily repeatable, can be measured easily, and thus can become a standard means for measuring and comparing various expressive forms.

Figure 11.1 shows the finger rest used in the experiment. Details of the method and procedure for the use of the apparatus may be found in Clynes (1977a).

Pressure rather than movement is used to measure essentic form for several reasons. First, it is a convenient form of measurement. Second, in using pressure rather than movement, it is more readily possible to characterize passionate states: Certain essentic forms include the experience of muscular tension that is provided by pressing against a finger-rest. Pressing is more suitable than pulling. Even so, because of the resilience of the fingertip, a small amount of movement necessarily ensues. (Small movements of one-

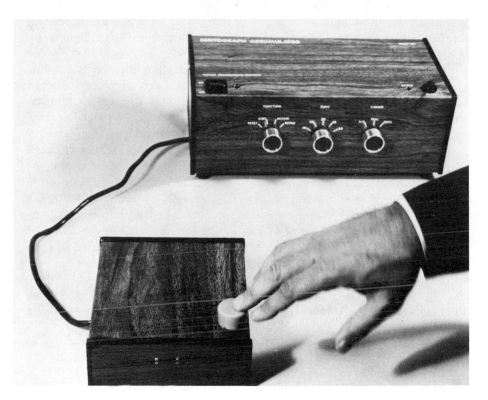

Figure 11.1. Sentograph for measuring vertical and horizontal components of transient pressure. Touch transducers and arm position for the measurement of essentic form. Two sets of strain gauges are mounted on a cantilever arm of square cross section, placed at right angles to the directions of measurement. Each is part of a bridge circuit, from which the pressure signal is obtained by amplification. Frequency response is 0–300 Hz. Deflection is .05 mm/100 g. In the background is the averaging computer which stores and sums individual expressions with a resolution of 200 ordinates and 12-bit AD conversion. Sampling rate is 10 msec. A special plastic touch surface is provided which is "gray" to the touch, i.e., does not itself cause tactile pleasure or irritability.

eighth of an inch or so on the finger-rest in a direction away from or toward the body are also acceptable.)

An important feature of these expressive pressure transients is that the direction of pressure is different for different sentic states. In expressing some states, the pressure tends to be away from the body; for other states, it has a neutral, close to vertical, direction. For still other states, it tends to be more toward the body. These distinctions have important significance.

It is necessary to measure not only the amount of the momentary pressure but also the angle of its direction. This is done with two pressure transducers, one measuring the vertical component of pressure and the other the horizontal component. By knowing each of the components at any one time, both the magnitude and the direction of pressure at that moment are known. In practice, the horizontal and vertical components of pressure are recorded as separate curves and the shapes of these curves constitute the visual representation of essentic form (Figure 11.2).

Since producing a single expression or E-acton may not adequately generate a clear sentic state in a subject, each subject is requested to produce a series of expressions for a particular sentic state. For instance, a subject is asked to express "anger." He then hears a sequence of soft, single clicks spaced at varying intervals a few seconds apart. He is requested to express anger as precisely as he can each time he hears a click with a single, expressive finger pressure action. The clicks are not spaced evenly in time but occur at quasi-random intervals; the subject cannot predict when the next click will occur. On hearing each click he expresses a quality of anger as precisely as he can with a single expressive pressure action and then waits for the next click, before he may express again. During the seconds of waiting for the next click the intensity of anger mounts. As he goes through this process, anger is generated in him. Thirty to fifty expressive acts are measured in this way and their forms in time are often averaged to obtain a more precise shape. The averaging may be done by a digital computer, such as the computer of average transients (CAT), or other similar instrument available in most physiology laboratories. Averaging

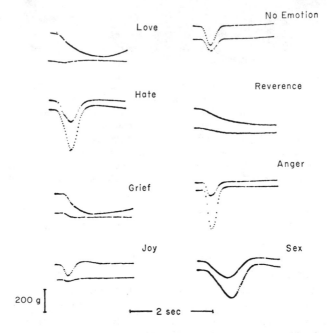

FIGURE 11.2. Sentograms of the essentic forms of emotions, as measured by the sentograph (subject, 42-year-old male). The upper trace for each emotion marks the vertical component of transient finger pressure; the lower trace marks the horizontal component (at twice the scale). No emotion is the form of expression recorded when a subject is asked to express mechanically, as if depressing a typewriter key. Each form is measured as the average of 50 actons. The subtle differences in forms (e.g., between love and grief) are as significant as the more obvious ones.

the space–time shapes of many expressive acts minimizes the effects of minor fluctuations of the sentic state and fluctuations in the precision of executing the expression. (Although averaging results in some loss of accuracy in regard to timing of each expressive form, it is helpful in establishing systematic differences.)

The essentic forms as expressed through transient finger pressure are recorded, as are (in some experiments) the specific actions of various muscles that are involved in the production of essentic form, including muscles of the forearm, upper arm, shoulder, and back (Figure 11.3). The action of these muscles is measured through the electrical activity produced at the neuromuscular junctions. In addition to such electromyograms, the electrical activity of the brain may be measured simultaneously.

The clearest measure of essentic form is provided by the recordings of transient finger pressure. The arm is in fact a biological filter through which activity of the brain not connected with expression of a particular essentic form is eliminated. The brain's electrical activity, in addition to aspects related to essentic form, contains all other activity related to the innumerable conscious,

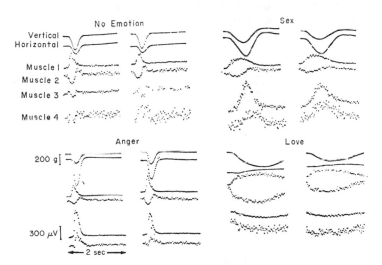

Figure 11.3. Sentograms of essentic form as vertical and horizontal components of finger pressure; also, four groups of muscle potentials integrated and rectified with a time constant of .01 sec. Each group is the average of 50 expressions. Muscle potentials are recorded from the forearm, upper arm, front shoulder, and back, respectively. Groups represent repeated recording from the same individual showing the stability of the patterns. "No emotion" consists of a mechanical movement, such as used for typewriting. In "anger" there is a marked accentuation of the horizontal component, indicating a tendency for the acton to be outward, away from the body. The characteristic shape for "love" (not sexual) shows a longer curved action, often with a slightly reversed horizontal component, indicating a pulling inward or embracing mode of behavior. The muscle actions reflect the differences of the essentic form. The preprogrammed time of the acton for love is considerably longer. The characteristic form for sex shows a strong secondary thrust with emphasized late muscle activity. This secondary thrust is characteristic of the purely sexual expression.

unconscious, and autonomic functions. Thus, the expression of essentic form can at present be noted only by averaging the brain's electrical activity as measured from the scalp.

Processes that reflect changes related to particular sentic states, rather than to each separate expression, such as changes in heart rate, cardiovascular function, respiration, oxygen consumption, and the electrical activity of the brain for the duration of each state, have also been measured in various experiments.

It is noted that the essentic forms as observed in this manner have vector properties. There is a specific angle as well as magnitude of the pressure as a function of time. The direction of the vector is rather constant for each dynamic expression and, for most states, changes only slightly during the expression. The tangent of the angle is given by the instantaneous ratio of the horizontal and vertical components of pressure. Anger and hate have outward components of pressure. Joy is vertical. Reverence is slightly outward.

Some expressions display a late, secondary muscular action. These late muscular actions occur approximately .7 sec after the beginning of the acton and are characteristic of certain "passionate" states in which there is a late developing tension in the acton (e.g., hate, sex). These actons contrast with the free character of other actons in which there is no late developing tension (e.g., joy, anger).

E-Actons of specific sentic states have characteristic durations. If we compare a "mechanical" impulse movement such as a single action on a typewriter with the duration of an E-acton, we see that the durations of some of these emotion expressions are considerably extended. The duration of a love acton is at least 2.2 sec and may be considerably longer. Typical values (in seconds) for minimum duration of E-actons are as follows: anger, .7; joy, .9; love, 2.2; hate, 1.2; grief, 2.5.

From these and related observations, carried out over a decade and involving several thousand subjects (Clynes, 1968, 1973, 1975a, 1977a), a number of properties of the communication process have emerged. These properties characterize the natural design of emotion communication systems permitting the generation and contagion of emotion through expression.

In the following I shall enumerate and discuss the function of basic biological design properties that appear to govern the dynamic communication of emotions. These properties may be regarded as constituting the dynamic anatomy of biology's solution for how to communicate emotions. They are not statistical in nature, but reflect organization.

1. THE PROPERTY OF EXCLUSIVITY

A sentic state is a single-channel system; only one state can be expressed at any one time.

Different parts of the body cannot be simultaneously used to express different emotions and have the individual experience them all. This does not mean that a "mixed" emotion cannot be expressed, but that two different states (mixed or unmixed) cannot be simultaneously expressed in different outputs.

Experiments with hypnosis carried out by Bull and Frank (1950) showed that even under hypnosis a subject could not be made to express more than one emotion at a time by suggestion. Nor are animals known to be able to express more than one expressive pattern at a time.

2. THE PROPERTY OF EQUIVALENCE

A sentic state may be expressed by any of a number of different output modalities.

This describes the system property that a particular emotion, seeking expression, may be expressed by any motor output mode of sufficient degrees of freedom to accommodate the dynamics of the expressive movement. The experienced links between the expressive movement and the emotion state are similar, whether a leg, an arm, or the muscles involved in producing the tone of voice or other motor outputs are used.

Three main functions in which the expression inherently affects the state are experienced: the satisfaction gained (S), the generating power (G), and the discharging ability (D) in regard to the intensity of the emotion. Each occurs for various motor output modes, though not necessarily to the same degree.

Postural patterns lend additional impetus to the expressive communication, but are not absolutely essential for the perceiver, since expressive sound, for example, may fully communicate emotional quality without any information concerning body posture. Some postures are antithetical to a particular emotion and its expression. We can speak of a positive, neutral, or negative posture with regard to the expression of a specific emotion. For example, lying back in an armchair is not conducive to expressing anger; it is a negative posture with respect to expressing anger. Sitting upright in a chair is a neutral posture for various emotions and is effective for expressing many emotions by the pressure of a finger.

3. THE PROPERTY OF COHERENCE

Regardless of the particular motor output chosen to express a sentic state, its dynamic expression is governed by a brain program or algorithm specific for that state which shall be called essentic form.

This property, perhaps the most centrally important one, signifies that there is an innate coherence between the essentic form of an expression and the emotion state seeking expression. That is, there is a one-to-one correspondence between essentic form and the quality of experience, if the expression is genuine. A bond exists between the physiological manifestation, the dynamic expressive form—the character of movement—and corresponding psychic experience. The nature of this bond is one of the most remarkable of natural phenomena.

As a genuine expression occurs, there is an experience of integrity, a reinforcement of the quality of experience.

Departure from the true expressive form may be of two kinds:

1. Improper execution, due to accidental causes or to improper focusing of intent, so that an expression is produced that does not have the full impact of a true expression.
2. There may be an inhibition of the true expression and substitution of some other form for it.

A faithful expression is recognized by the person expressing it: He or she can be aware of the power of the expression to generate, discharge, and satisfy with respect to the state it expresses. A departure from a true expression will significantly alter these functions (but not necessarily in equal degrees). Psychophysiological coherence is evident even in such a complex expressive form as laughter, and minor fluctuations of expression are of considerable significance and cause a different quality of experience.

Attempts to re-train a person to express anger with the expressive form of love and vice versa have invariably failed.

With a coherently expressed form, a specific satisfaction may be felt about 1–1.5 sec after its completion. An improper execution is accompanied by a corresponding degree of frustration, felt even before it is completed.

These phenomena also result in the process of expression being self-centering (self-steering) in art, music, and dance (that is, repeated expression teaches); one may be gradually attracted, as it were, to the true form. This inner attraction is a very characteristic phenomenon of the expressive process. It can result in a gradual refinement, when opportunity is given for repeated practice. One can, so to speak, fall in love with the true expression; it reveals itself gradually, as one becomes more and more aware of its subtleties. In turn, it provides a more and more powerful effect (until a temporary satiation occurs). Opportunities for this kind of practice occur mainly in the arts, but everyday life and personal interactions also offer opportunities for this to manifest itself.

Coherence means that expression *can* arise from the depth of the psyche. It is a paradox that when expression is most authentic and individual it is also most universal.

Experimental studies of essentic forms measured sentographically in Mexico, Japan, and Bali show forms largely similar to those found in the United States, supporting the view of the universal and genetic origin of essentic form (Clynes, 1973) (Figure 11.4).

A mathematical differential equation describing essentic forms is given in Clynes (1973), and the forms computed according to the equation are compared with experimental forms.

4. THE PROPERTY OF COMPLEMENTARITY

The production and recognition of essentic forms are governed by inherent data-processing programs of the central nervous system, biologically coordinated so that a precisely produced form is correspondingly recognized. The recognized form in turn generates a sentic state in the perceiver.

Because they can be recognized, essentic forms gain power to make emotion contagious. The recognition process generally occurs through a modality different from the one in which it was produced. A gesture or facial expression can be perceived through the visual sense; auditory expressions are not recognized by the same structures that produce them. However, in expressing with the sense of touch, there is kinesthetic feedback in which at least a part of the producing system may be involved. That the recognizing function should correspond so well to the producing function is by no means self-evident, although it has generally been taken for granted by human society.

We need to distinguish between recognizing essentic form as it is being produced by the person who is producing and its recognition by another individual. In any particular expressive transmission the effective communication power will depend on the following:

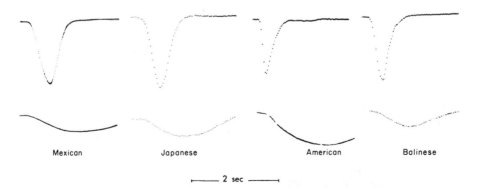

Mexican   Japanese   American   Balinese

|——— 2 sec ———|

FIGURE 11.4. A comparison of the essentic forms of love and anger in four cultures: Mexican, Japanese, American, and Balinese (vertical component shown). Similarities of the sentograms are apparent. Differences between individuals are typically of about the same order as variation between cultures.

1. Biological congruence between the innate capacity to produce and the innate capacity to recognize
2. Successful production
3. Attentive recognition

When there is no congruence between the production capacity and recognition capacity, as, for example, between a man and a beetle, no transmission of emotion occurs. Only when there is congruence between these is the possibility given of emotion communication in the present moment. We may call this the P–R (production–recognition) congruence. P–R congruence exists within a species but also across species to a lesser degree. Dogs, for example, recognize and respond to the expression of anger, fear, and joy from humans. When P–R congruence is largely absent, we experience a corresponding sense of isolation.

Biological P–R congruence has been beautifully demonstrated for crickets by the experiments of Bentley and Hoy (1974), which demonstrated that the production and recognition of crickets' mating songs were governed by the same genetic factor. In their experiments, a new hybrid species was bred, with a new mating song; the females of the new species were attracted exclusively to the new mating song without having previously heard any mating song. Lizards express aggressiveness and dominance by a characteristic up-and-down movement of the head and neck at a definite frequency. This pattern, too, is genetically controlled both in its production and in its recognition, as one of numerous examples that could be cited. In humans, laughter is a salient example of essentic form whose production and recognition are not learned in an arbitrary way, but are innately developed.

An example of a rudimentary essentic form that already has full power of contagion is yawning. Yawning does not necessarily have a primary communicating intent, yet it functions very much like essentic form. In man, the very word "yawning" may cause yawning. A highly specific contagious communicative mode, it shows the features of essentic form communication. (It displays all the seven dynamic properties of biological emotion communication systems listed.) Being little burdened with cultural superstructure, it makes an excellent example for study; this is even more so because of its interspecies application.

The principle of coherence also is well demonstrated in a yawn. The particular feeling of yawning belongs exclusively to a yawn; taking a deep breath by itself will not be accompanied by the feeling of yawning—the whole gestalt of the yawn dynamics needs to be present, including a specific tension in the jaw and back of the neck.

The faithfulness of the form of the yawn affects the recognition, so that we "receive" a yawn only when its form is appropriately "sent." Receiving is carried out without conceptualizing, or the need for symbols, through a direct program of the nervous system. No one is taught how to yawn or how to recognize a yawn. Indeed, it would be impossible because if the P–R congruence did not exist no amount of learning could provide the contagious feeling of yawning.

What seems clear for yawning applies also to the many essentic forms that allow contagious propagation of emotion. Sentographic experiments indicate that similar propagative processes occur. In its use of essentic form it seems nature has been distinctly parsimonious, providing a seeming unity in diversity, allowing the many to be linked together by finite strands. The patterns weaved do not end where our bodies do.

Through essentic form individuals can emotionally touch one another across time and distance. What we "touch," however, is not only the sense receptors but what appears to be a receiving "organ" at a level removed from these. Essentic form has primacy over the sensory modes in that its quality is perceived regardless of whether it is transmitted by sound, light, or touch and in the presence of other sensory input. The perceiving "organ" probably has differentiated internal neuroanatomical organization (this remains to be explored in the brain's organization). The production and recognition of essentic form both involve functions beyond the muscular production and sensory perception mechanisms. Yet without sensory and muscular input and output their communication is not possible.

5. THE PROPERTY OF SELF-GENERATION

The intensity of a sentic state is increased, within limits, by the repeated, arrhythmic generation of essentic form.

This describes the property that reiterated production of essentic form with appropriate timing can generate a state of emotion, without other causes. A single act of expression may increase intensity or discharge it. If circumstances allow more than one expression, and the iteration is appropriately timed, the intensity of the experience will generally tend to increase up to a certain level, remain there, with fluctuations, and thereafter gradually discharge.

Thus, for example, a person who laughs will find it easier to laugh as he continues to laugh. The threshold of laughter will drop, and at times the laughter will maintain itself without further stimulus. But eventually the person becomes satiated with laughter and has to have a period of recovery to be ready to laugh again. Expressions of anger or joy may take a similar course, building up and discharging intensity, though each on a different time scale.

Repetition has a clear role in many biological patterns of sensorimotor interaction. In scratching, for example, there is a gradual increase in sensation as one scratches, after which there is a gradual decrease in sensation and a feeling of satisfaction that lasts for a time. A similar process often occurs in sneezing, and sometimes in coughing and even in yawning. Another example of increasing intensity with repetition is the mounting intensity of feeling in sexual stimulation. Here, however, there is the additional special discharge of orgasm.

Inappropriate timing interferes with the way in which repetition of essentic form affects the intensity of the state. In everyday life, this often happens when a person is not free to produce such repetition as needed or when interaction with others forces him to change the timing.

The duration of essentic form is different for each emotion, and the mean rate of iteration generating intensity most effectively is also specific for each emotion. An even, or "mechanical," rate of repetition is inimical to the generation process. Such a mechanical rate of repetition entails predictability, effacing the newness of the expression. If an expression is not perceived as "new" it tends to be subsumed with the previous expression as one unit. It becomes part of an "anatural" unit: It is a double (or multiple) form of a single entity.

In generating emotion by repeated expressive finger pressure at repetition times given by external timing clicks, it was found (Clynes, 1973, 1975a,b, 1977a) that the quasi-random departure from regularity of the repetitions need to have a specific character (in addition to the mean rates being different for each emotion) for the most effective buildup and sustaining of emotion. Randomness of either a Gaussian or a Poisson distribution did not fulfill all requirements and included a certain number of irritating intervals during each sequence.

To provide effective generating power an interval is necessary between the end of one essentic form and the beginning of the next. During this time one experiences the following:

1. Satisfaction of having completed an essentic form
2. Preparation for the execution of the next essentic form
3. An increasing urge to express

The amount of time for these three aspects (which may be called renewal time) varies with the specific emotion and is in the range 1–8 sec. Thus, the mean repetition rate for generating a particular emotion is determined by the duration of the essentic form, plus the appropriate renewal time.

The mean rate is modulated by a randomness factor, which is different for different emotions.

6. THE PROPERTY OF GENERALIZED EMOTION

Sentic states may be experienced and expressed as pure qualities or identities, without reference to specific auxiliary relationships to generate or receive these qualities.

We tend to think of emotion as being generated mainly by relationships with others, by external events, or by specific fantasies and dreams. There is, however, a mode for generating and experiencing specific emotions and qualities that does not depend on particular interaction content, but is brought about by pure essentic form itself. The experience of essentic form itself generates a state that then may or may not draw specific fantasies to it. Thus, a person performing or listening to music can experience emotional qualities without reference to outside events or to recipients: Joy, love, and grief, for example, may be expressed in music.

Generalized experience of emotion is confined not only to the mode of music, although in the past it has been mostly experienced through music. Essentic form expressed through finger pressure is quite as effective in generating these qualities of experience (at the appropriate rates of repetition, as discussed under The Property of Self-Generation [p. 285], these rates are also similar to the sequence of musical phrases).

Such ability to feel emotions in a generalized way, without music, may seem surprising. The experience can be obtained, however, through other sensory modes capable of appropriate temporal relationships. They can be generated visually through modulated lines or simple forms (certain animated films, for example—the dance of simple lines alone can be highly and specifically emotionally meaningful).

The experience of the generalized state incorporates the following two aspects.

1. A virtual body image: This is a gestalt of specific body sensations characteristic of that emotional state, such as lightness in joy, heaviness in grief, etc. Such virtual body images have a fine structure; that is, in addition to general manifestations such as lightness and heaviness, there exist other more subtle special effects. Tensions also affect various parts of the body in different ways for each emotion.

In repressed emotion such body images may be experienced partially only, without the quality of the emotion itself being consciously experienced. Thus, for repressed grief, for example, sensations in the chest, or elsewhere (as part only of an emotional virtual body image complex), may be experienced for a long time, and one may become aware only later that these sensations are part of the virtual body image of grief. This is of considerable clinical importance.

2. A generalized emotion possesses a field of "knowledge." This knowledge is not of specific events or objects, but concerns relationships and attitudes. Each generalized emotion appears to incorporate a kind of world view. When feeling grief, for example, one will tend also to feel helpless and hopeless. Such knowledge will color all potential relationships in one's imagination, contributing to a particular point of view—that pertaining to grief.

A person in a generalized emotional state will tend to (a) remember specific past events related to that state; (b) create fantasies involving that state; and

(c) to a degree, act toward others as if they had caused the state or are recipients of it.

Generalized emotional states are as subject to organic influences as are other emotional states. For example, they are more easily induced at certain times of the day than others and are more difficult to experience after heavy meals. Fatigue also affects the intensity and/or repression of different generalized emotions differently. The experience of generalized emotion can in turn reduce fatigue. (Note that emotions in dreams, however, are experienced without the feeling of fatigue that may have been felt shortly prior to the onset of sleep.)

7. COMMUNICATIVE POWER AS A FORM FUNCTION

The power of essentic form in communicating and generating a sentic state is greater the more closely the form approaches pure or ideal essentic form for that state.

One of the most commonplace events that has defied analysis is that some expressions of a particular feeling have a far greater power of expression than others. We are familiar with this in daily life, in drama, in dance, in poetry, and in music. Among the ancients, Orpheus had a legendary power of expression. Particular gestures can have a major transforming power: witness the power of blessing and of cursing in various societies and at various times in history. The expressive power of Mozart, of Beethoven, or of Chopin on those who heard them play at their best was overwhelming.

One may study the relationship between communicative power and the particular form of an expression conveniently through expressive sound. It is possible to study single expressive sounds. Great differences in expressive quality are produced by small changes in certain of the parameters of the expression. A powerfully expressive form can be greatly reduced in expressive power by such changes. If one begins with a deliberately distorted essentic form, and has the means to remove the distortion, a subject will tend to adjust the parameters so as to restore the original form, without having heard it before. This applies to relatively small distortions, and it implies that there is an ideal essentic form for a particular quality of expression which may be approached asymptotically. To what extent the asymptotic form of one person for a given quality is identical to that of another is an experimental question that can be studied by successive approximation, narrowing the gap of uncertainty as more refined measurements are taken.

With an expression of exceptional purity, it is as if the essence of livingness has been revealed in that quality. The phenomenon of being able to feel such "essences of livingness" through some forms of sound in music phrased by Arthur Schnabel or Pablo Casals, for example, is a source of wonder; such wonder may at times be experienced in daily life also. An expression of this kind has the power to suffuse into a person not merely its own particular quality, but a sense of participation in what is felt to be a universal stratum of living, independent of time and place and person. It is accompanied by a special sense of security.

One needs to recognize that the power of pure essentic form exists. One needs equally to account for its rarity. Why should certain individuals have a far greater capacity to produce a pure essentic form? Certainly the capacity to recognize is far more prevalent than the capacity to produce such forms.

One needs to ask also why the sense of wonder that accompanies a pure form is absent in an imperfectly realized essentic form. Perhaps unconsciously a comparison may be taking place between the actual and the ideal form in the perceiver, and when they are identical then such wonder occurs. This could be likened to a control system whose setting directs toward the "livingest" quality of experience.

EXPERIMENTAL TESTS FOR DISTINGUISHING BASIC EMOTIONS

Sentic studies provide ways of approaching the question of "basic emotions" in an experimental way. A basic emotion, like a basic color, may be considered as one that cannot be thought of experientially as composed of others. This has been pointed out by Plutchik (1962) as well as by others. One may consider the spectrum of emotions to be composed of a number of distinct emotions, and their combinations and mixtures, in a manner similar to the spectrum of colors.

One experimental way, arising from sentographic methods, to determine which emotions are basic and which are mixed, or compound, makes use of the phenomenon of selective satiation. It is found that expressing a particular state for a number of minutes will generally produce satiation with respect to that state. After an initial period of rise in intensity, and a subsequently maintained level, with fluctuations, the intensity eventually decays to a low or extinguished level. The person then experiences satiety with respect to that particular emotion; however, at this point he or she is quite fresh for experiencing another, different emotion. The satiety is strongly selective.

To the extent that the two emotions are unrelated, the satiety with respect to the first will not affect the second. If, however, the second emotion contains an appreciable component of the first, as a mixture, we may expect satiety with respect to the first to carry over substantially to the second. We thus have a method for distinguishing between successive emotions that do not share a common emotional component and those that do.

A second approach that sentic studies offer toward the problem of basic emotions is by comparing essentic forms produced for specific emotions with those expressed as feelings toward specific individuals with whom the person who is expressing has a relationship. By studying a large number of people in this way, one can relate particular expressive forms of emotion to forms expressed for various types of relationships. The expressions of relationships contain a large spectrum of emotional meaning. In this spectrum one might expect to find sentograms corresponding to some of the basic emotions to be dominant to a certain extent so that, in large samples, correlations may be found between forms expressed according to the type of relationship and those expressed by emotion alone. In this way, one would expect basic emotions to factor out from their mixtures. (In studying this, however, one must bear in mind that the essentic form of a compound emotion is *not* the algebraic sum of the essentic forms of the components [see Clynes, 1977a].)

TIME FORM PRINTING BY THE NERVOUS SYSTEM

A function of the central nervous system that is especially relevant to the phenomena involved in the repeated expression of essentic form is the function I have named "time form printing," which concerns the way in which the nervous system generates repeated movement.

One of the special modes in which the voluntary motor system can function may be called the repetitive mode. Ordinarily, a separate command decision activates each voluntary movement; in the repetitive mode, however, one initial voluntary command decision sets the pattern, which either is repeated for a definite number of times as projected in the initial command or is repeated indefinitely until a new command to stop or to change the pattern is given. I have called the repetitive production of specific motor patterns with a single initial command *time form printing*.

It had been observed earlier (Clynes, 1970) that if a person started to tap with the hand, the initial rate of tapping would tend to maintain itself across minor beat-to-beat fluctuations that tended to average out. Errors deviating from this rate from beat to beat would tend to be self-correcting (some long-term drift was eliminated by thinking of a particular musical piece).

It was observed only later, however (Clynes, 1977b), that not only the rate but also the *shape* of a repetitive movement tended to be preserved. Whatever the form of the initial shape of a repetitive movement, say by the hand or arm, this form will maintain itself during the repetitions, *without further attention or command*. When a change of pattern is desired, a single new command must be given for the first modified pattern; thereafter, the modified pattern will preserve itself in the same manner as the original pattern.

Thus, the nervous system is capable of maintaining not only the rate of repetition, but also the specific form of a repetitive movement, with only a single initial command. This time form printing ability is of importance for understanding (*a*) the basis of the phenomena of rhythm in music and in dance; (*b*) the control of repetitive patterns such as walking or running; and (*c*) pathological behavior involving repetitive movement.

In relation to musical rhythm a further important property of time form printing is significant: the capacity of the process to be *modulated* by separate voluntary commands, enabling deviations from a "mechanical" repetition to occur, without stopping the nature of the repetitive process. This occurs in many types of music and is incorporated in expressiveness. In music, the specific form of the repetitive beat has an emotionally meaningful character (which may be experienced inwardly, or expressed outwardly by a motor pattern, such as the beat of a conductor).

Generating emotion by means of repeatedly expressed essentic forms, as in measuring essentic forms, we also encounter a process that is related (though not identical) to time form printing. There is a tendency to preserve a given form of expression once it is started. The process is different, however, from the musical pulse, since repetition is externally initiated by a tap or click, which, moreover, needs to come at unpredictable intervals.

A person who has begun a sequence of expressions expressing love, for example, according to a certain form, will tend to maintain a similar form for a few repetitions, even if the "mind is wandering." This ability to stay within a general region of expressive form acts in turn to stabilize the state itself. This relates to the concept of partial reciprocity as reported in Clynes (1973).

SOME PREDICTIONS OF SENTIC THEORY
CAPABLE OF VERIFICATION

The time relationships of essentic form and the principles of sentic communication permit us to make predictions about expressive behavior capable of experimental verification. The lawful behavior exhibited by the biological phenomena of communication and contagion of emotion enables one to treat the subject as a hard science, in that the properties, functions, and relationships observed are seen to be governed by specific design properties or principles and are not of a statistical nature.

In the following paragraphs, I shall describe two predictions of sentic theory that have been verified experimentally.

BLOCKING OF FEELING INTENSITY WITH
INCOMPLETE EXECUTION OF ESSENTIC FORM

An incomplete form causes frustration and a blocking, which prevents one from experiencing any other emotional state for a short period of time (as was initially noticed when switching from one emotion to another in sentic cycles: One always needs to complete the last expression of a state before switching to the next).

One could predict, however, that blocking would also occur within the *same* emotion if the essentic form of an expression was prevented from being completed, and it should not be possible to counteract the blocking incurred by one part of the body through another similar expression produced by a different part of the body out of phase with the first.

The prediction that blocking would occur within the same state, if essentic form cannot complete itself, is readily confirmed for interruptions occurring between 20 and 80% of the time course of the essentic form. Earlier interruption is not felt as blocking, but rather as a pause. Quite late interruption sometimes does not cause blocking; inner completion may still be possible, despite the interruption. The duration of blocking is variable, but is at least several essentic forms long.

That such blocking of feeling occurs within the same state, for example, for love and sex, may be quite surprising to many people; however, once understood, it becomes clear that precisely this kind of blocking often stands in the way of satisfactory intimate communication. A corollary is that one cannot *begin* another essentic form with a different part of the body while another part is producing one form, even within the same emotion, without causing blocking. (One can, however, initiate other parts of the body to participate in an ongoing essentic form, provided that the additional parts of the body enter at the same phase in which the essentic form is at the moment; then all of the parts of the body involved complete the remainder of the form together [Clynes, 1977a].)

PREDICTION OF A NEW FORM OF LAUGHTER

Laughter belongs to the category of essentic forms, albeit of higher hierarchical structure, and one may apply sentic communication principles to it. Laughter consists of an glottally chopped breathing pattern and a chopped voice pattern. Laughter also is a modulated carrier of other emotions (e.g., there is joyful, derisive, and sardonic laughter).

The voice pattern may be regarded as one of a number of possible motor output modes according to the principle of equivalence of sentic theory. Accordingly, we should be able to substitute a different motor output for the voice provided that we keep the same chopped breathing pattern. The substituted motor output needs to have adequate dynamic flexibility—that is a sufficient number of degrees of freedom, such as is provided by transient finger pressure.

It is readily confirmed that, if finger pressure is substituted at the same dynamic rate and manner as the chopped voice, all of the characteristic experiences of laughter are produced, including the sense of funniness, tearing of the eyes, twinkling of the eyes, and even paroxysms of laughing. The mean repetition frequency of the chopped voice (the "ha"s) and of the repeated finger pressure is 5.03 Hz ($\pm$.18 SD). The frequency chosen by a person laughing using repeated finger pressure is the same that he uses when laughing in the usual ways (Figures 11.5, 11.6, and 11.7). And, in every case, only when

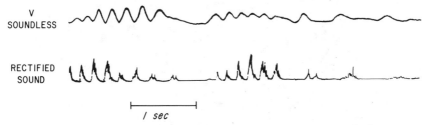

V
SOUNDLESS

RECTIFIED
SOUND

I sec

FIGURE 11.5. Shows the comparison of finger pressure (top) and sound when expressing voiced laughter also with finger pressure. The bursts of laughter have a somewhat different rise time and decay time for the motoric as compared with the voiced laughter, but the number of cycles is similar and the repetition frequency is the same.

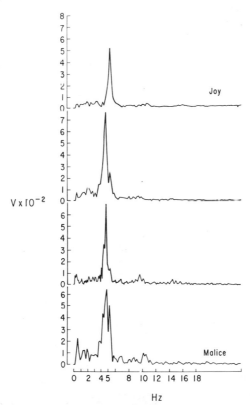

Hz

FIGURE 11.6. shows the low frequency amplitude spectrum of various types of voiceless motoric laughter expressed through finger pressure ranging from joyous to malicious laughter. The main harmonic component in all cases is near 5 Hz and corresponds to the repetition rate of the "ha"s. Side bands at 10 and 15 Hz appear progressively as the laughter becomes more malicious. The wave shape correspondingly becomes more pointed. The main frequency of 5 per second is the same as for voiced laughter.

293

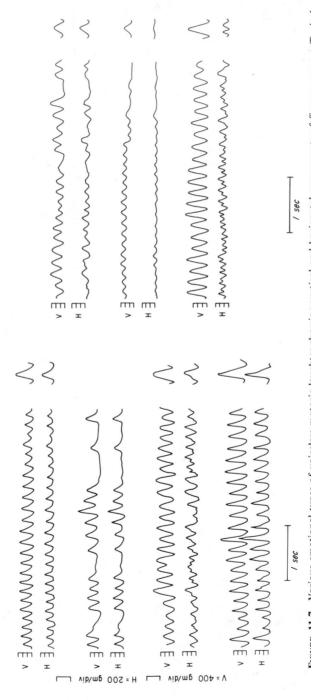

FIGURE 11.7 Various emotional types of voiceless motoric laughter showing vertical and horizontal components of finger pressure. Typical average wave forms are also shown on the right of each trace. The wave form and the angle of pressure are different for laughter with different emotional characteristics ranging from joyful to malicious. The main repetition frequency is closely similar.

the frequency is in that region does the sense of funniness "lock in." The significance of this form of laughter exceeds that of its own intrinsic interest. It constitutes an independent proof of the principle of coherence. It shows that only when the excessive behavior pattern is displayed according to the biologically programmed essentic form is its experiential quality realized.

Like other essentic forms, the essentic forms of laughter are universal, and the characteristic repetition frequency rate for laughter seems to center around 5 per second regardless of race, color, and culture.

YAWNING

Using reasoning similar to that used in the preceding section, it can be seen in yawning that the tension of the jaw and back of the neck that is an integral part of yawning might be substituted by other deliberately tensed parts of the body—for example, clasping the hands together and pressing them together, which would then result in a feeling of yawning without the usual tensions in the jaw and back of the neck. In fact, these tensions can be largely eliminated provided they are substituted by other dynamically similar tensions in the body. The experience of the quality of yawning does not occur without these tensions, such as taking a deep breath only, but does occur when these tensions are appropriately produced in another part of the body. This shows the nature of the coherence between the specific dynamic nature of the expression and the quality of feeling—that is, the specific mind–body link pertaining to the quality of "yawning."

INTENSITY

The intensity of an emotion experience presents a special theoretical problem that has not received adequate attention. A quality of experience of a unique character also has the attribute of intensity. What are the neuronal preconditions giving rise to emotional intensity?

Philosophers have concerned themselves with discrimination between various experiential qualities, but they have not given the phenomenon of intensity of emotion adequate specific attention, as a discriminated quantity of a quality. Preaching either moderation (as the Stoics did) or the synthesis of opposites (as did Goethe and Hegel) refers not to epistemologic but ethical considerations. Spinoza, however, is an exception: He states as an important principle that an emotion could be overcome only by another *more intense* emotion. Human language, however, has been more discerning and has at times provided different words for the same kind of emotion experienced at different intensities, for example, anger/rage, distaste/disgust, joy/ecstasy. While emotion may change in quality when driven through extremes of intensity, there remains a range of intensity within which its quality changes relatively little. That this is so forces us to consider that somewhere in the nervous system associated with its quality there must also be quantity.

The quantitative forms of perception known in brain function involve chemical concentration of numbers of molecules and rate of discharge of nerve firing, as well as associated synaptic and glial potentials. With every perceptual quality we associate an exterior receptor organ whose neuronal elements provide information concerning intensity, as patterns of neuronal discharge rates. These are processed by specific neuronal networks and brain structures, such as the visual cortex or the auditory cortex, and are eventually received and interpreted through the nonspecific parts of the brain. In general, the nervous system transmits intensity through the number of nerve discharges coming over specific channels or through the concentration of a neurotransmitter substance produced, by the message, at synapses. However, the nervous system does not exclusively limit itself to *external* receptor organs, although those have received the most scientific study.

We may consider that the experience of emotion may possibly involve the stimulation of *internal* receptors, in contrast to the *external* receptor organs of perception (Clynes, 1973). Such internal receptor organs for specific emotions might also be stimulated through transmitting substances released by a successful production of essentic form. We need to consider that there would be different processes involved for each emotion that would act as specific transmitters, that is, as endorphins, enkephalins, or neurohormones. For example, it may be that a specific chemical or electrochemical transmitter relates to laughter. As laughter is maintained, the accumulation of this chemical and its metabolites would be related to a transient decrease in the threshold for further laughter and eventually to satiation. Specific receptor sites and receptor processes may be involved and give rise to refractory periods. A similar dynamic interaction is likely for sexual stimulation and orgasm, followed again by a refractory period.

If specific chemicals and receptor sites are involved in specific emotions, it should be possible eventually to isolate these and identify them. Their action could also perhaps elucidate the function of essentic form as a specific focus of memories associated with the same feeling.

Although we have considered that the intensity of an emotion is increased, or discharged, through repeated essentic form production, we have not considered how single essentic forms might represent intensity as well as quality. It seems that, for this, other parameters and situational clues would need to be involved.

Consider, for example, an emotion portrayed by an essentic form produced in a soft sound. Would the same quality, but of greater intensity, be portrayed by a similar but louder sound? It may at times, but this simple analogy breaks down quite readily. A particular quality of expression may even be associated with a certain range of loudness. Thus, a loving expression in musical sound, for example, will lose its effectiveness when produced very loudly. (Postural and other visual cues give additional information on intensity, of course, but effects such as a flushed face, which may accompany an emotional state, are distinct from voluntary acts of expression involved in emotion communication.) It may be that intensity is not uniquely specified in essentic form; it would seem so at our present state of knowledge.

EMOTIONS AND KNOWLEDGE

How emotions are linked to aspects of knowledge is a subtle, though important, question and can be observed through generalized emotion, in which no situational cause is involved. The following represent some observations about this.

1. Generalized emotion tends to recall selectively past experiences associated with the same state. It acts as a memory search function for a class of experiences, which have in common a similar quality of emotion. This process occurs rather effortlessly. It should be emphasized that it is not an association of the present situational *content* of new experience with specific memories of the past, but that the generalized state acts as a focus or template that draws experiences in memory to awareness.

2. The generalized state also acts as a selective focus to create new fantasies with dynamic content and relationship engendered by the state or its expression. This function is one of the creative functions of the state of emotion.

3. The specific generalized state greatly affects our experience of the relationship of self to others. In anger, for example, we will tend to be angry with any person coming within our orbit, or even with a dog (with the implicit rejection that this implies), and use another person to satisfy the need to express. In the generalized state of love, we will tend to feel accepting and loving toward such others. Generalized emotion involves a world view, through which we experience ourselves as related, unrelated, or negatively related to our environment, or even the universe, in specific characteristic ways (e.g., love includes an experience of the fundamental rightness of the world; hate includes an inhibition of the life force, a feeling of separation).

4. Emotion can produce bias, injustice, and insensitivity to others, when experienced in a dionysian manner, as ego function. Because of this, attempts have been made to eliminate emotionality in creating an equitable social fabric. (Note, however, that most principles of social justice and morality are ultimately based on good will and love.) But when experienced in the Apollonian sense as pure existences, these qualities of emotion teach us to know the subtleties of human nature, to develop empathy; they enrich our knowledge and become the foundation for our understanding of human nature. We can improve our knowledge of the subtle forces of each emotion and see these subtleties in others as well as in ourselves. "Empathy" is a form of knowledge, and the knowledge of emotions is its prerequisite.

5. Emotion can govern action in ways similar to "instinctive" and "intuitive" behavior, as a necessary consequence of the relationship it implies.

A particularly interesting form of interaction between emotion and knowledge occurs with the special emotional condition of "empathy."

As a person functions with empathy, his actions are not constrained by specific emotions but by empathy, which includes understanding all of them.

PERSONAL–ACTIVE (DIONYSIAN) AND CONTEMPLATIVE (APOLLONIAN) MODES OF EMOTIONAL EXPERIENCE AND EXPRESSION

In addition to the properties already mentioned, an important distinction of the human capacity for experiencing and expressing qualities of emotion needs to be made, as shown by the methods of generating and expressing emotions described earlier. Human beings can experience emotions in two different modes of inner connectedness. In the first, most common mode, the energies associated with the emotion are experienced as linked directly with the self, or ego, of the individual and to his drives. The emotional experience is felt as an ego function and directly affects decisions and patterns of action of the individual. This mode may be called Dionysian (note that generalized emotion can be Dionysian, also).

In the other mode of experiencing the emotional qualities, which may be called Apollonian, the qualities are "considered" as existences. For example, a person can say the word "anger" and repeat it until he feels that the inflection expresses the quality of anger purely and precisely, and with such an inflection can feel and communicate the quality of anger without personal anger of the individual. In this mode, the emotions experienced are "considered" as existences in their own right, as natural existences belonging to the sphere of living. Joy and grief are experienced in this contemplative mode, not as *my* joy or *my* grief but as Joy, Grief—anybody's and everybody's joy and grief. It is quite remarkable, and of course important, that humans have the ability to experience and to savor emotional qualities in this mode. Music and art greatly depend on this capacity. (In mythology these dual modes of experience of emotion and their social function have found expression in the personae of the two Greek gods Apollo and Dionysius.)

The involvement of psychic energies in relation to the specific emotional qualities is very different in the two modes (for example, experiencing grief in the Apollonian mode does not drain energy, but escalates energies of compassion). The Apollonian mode of experience is directly linked to the development of empathy, as contrasted with sympathy. (See Clynes [1977] for a study of the different functions of empathy and sympathy.)

VIRTUAL BODY IMAGES IN RELATION
TO THE APOLLONIAN AND DIONYSIAN MODES

As one expresses emotion on the finger rest, and experiences a virtual body image of a particular emotion, say anger or love, the regions of the body involved in the virtual body image can be noted to have a geometric center, around which it is diffused. The feeling has a spatial extension, often an ellipsoid or lump-like shape, with vague boundaries. One can quite readily approximate a center for the space of the feeling as well as its approximate extension.

We may draw regional diagrams to denote the principal space of feeling for each emotional quality. Spatial differences of the virtual body images lie in

1. the place of the center of the space along the vertical axis of the body;
2. the extensiveness of the space;
3. the shape of the space.

Most virtual body images are related to the direction and magnitude of gravity. The heaviness of grief and lightness of joy are experienced in the direction given by gravity. Conflict between the virtual body image (which includes the influence of gravity) and the actual situation produces inhibition. This applies to both dynamic expression and the experience of the emotional state. (Thus, when one's body is floating in water, the virtual body image of anger or of grief, but not of joy, is in conflict with the actual situation.) Appollonian virtual body images center higher along the vertical axis than do their corresponding Dionysian forms.

In dreams, emotions are experienced as having virtual body images similar to those in the waking state. Just as we may dream of running, climbing, or falling, we also experience dream emotions with the same virtual body images, although our body is, so to speak, disconnected. The supine position of the body does not interfere in dreams with the experience of specific (dream) emotions as the same position would in the awake state.

CONCERNING THE EVOLUTION OF EMOTIONS
AND THEIR COMMUNICATION

Studies of the genetic basis of behavior in animals show that innate releasing mechanisms in the communication of animals are largely genetically preserved, as are mating dances and songs of various species.

It is proposed, as essentic forms appear to be also genetically preserved, that a mutation process would jointly evolve a new essentic form with a new emotional state. As an example of such a development in evolution, we may cite laughter. The universal character of laughter within the human species makes it highly likely that it derives from a common genetic mutation and that the specific experience of funniness with which it is linked evolved integrally with it. It seems absurd to suppose that the characteristic pattern of laughter evolved first and then by some further mutation the sense of funniness attached itself to it. Nor, vice versa, can laughter's quality be experienced without laughter's characteristic pattern. It is hardly likely that it could have been experienced earlier in evolution in the absence of the pattern of laughing.

What seems true of laughter appears to hold similarly from yawning to the more highly developed contagious patterns of emotional communication. Hunger and sex are very likely the first experiential entities evolved by nature that include specific knowledge. (Of these, sex already has communicative aspects and is probably the first contagious quality of experience evolved.) Hunger guides the individual in terms of what to eat, and how much, through the quality of its experience; sexual feelings guide individuals to choose mates for species survival. The specific nature of the feeling includes its own characteristic expression. If the coherence between the expression and the feeling were destroyed, survival could not take place.

The work outlined in this chapter represents a departure as a systematic theory of dynamic emotion communication, involving body and mind, and the study of the phenomena of emotional contagion. It is relevant to therapy, music, and art. Production and recognition of essentic forms are seen to constitute main elements of the biologic code of emotion communication.

ACKNOWLEDGMENT

The help of Lynn Kimber and Doris Sharpe in the preparation of this chapter is gratefully acknowledged.

REFERENCES

Bentley, D., & Hoy, R. R. The neurobiology of the cricket songs. *Scientific American,* August 1974, *213,* 34–44.

Birdwhistell, R. I. Communication as a multi-channel system. In *International encyclopedia of the social sciences.* New York: Macmillan, 1968.

Bull, N., & Frank. L. Emotions induced and studies in hypnotic subjects. *Journal of Nervous and Mental Disease,* 1950, *3,* 97–118.

Cannon, W. B. *Bodily Changes in Pain, Hunger, Fear, and Rage.* 2nd ed. New York: Appleton, 1929.

Clynes, M. Essentic form-aspects of control, function and measurement. *Proceedings of 21st ACEMB Conference,* 1968.

Clynes, M. Toward a theory of man: Precision of essentic form in living communication. In K. N. Leibovic & J. C. Eccles (eds.), *Information processing in the nervous system.* New York: Springer-Verlag, 1969.

Clynes, M. Toward a view of man. In M. Clynes & J. H. Milsum (eds.), *Biomedical engineering systems.* New York: McGraw-Hill, 1970.

Clynes, M. Sentics: Biocybernetics of emotion communication. *Annals of the New York Academy of Sciences,* 1973, *220,* 66–131.

Clynes, M. Communication and generation of emotion through essentic form. In L. Levi (ed.), *Emotions: Their parameters and measurement* (Proceedings of the Karolinska Institute Symposium of Parameters of Emotions), pp. 561–601. New York: Raven Press, 1975. (a)

Clynes, M. *Speaker recognition by the central nervous system* (abstract). New Orleans: Society for Neuroscience, 1975. (b)

Clynes, M. *Sentics, the touch of emotions.* New York: Doubleday, 1977. (a)

Clynes, M. *Space–time form printing by the human central nervous system* (abstract). Los Angeles: Society for Neuroscience, 1977. (b)

Clynes, M. Communication and generation of emotion through essentic form. In S. Weitz (ed.), *Non-verbal communication: Readings with commentary.* New York: Oxford University Press, 1979.

Darwin, C. *The expression of the emotions in man and animals.* London: Murray, 1872.

Ekman, P. (ed.) *Darwin and facial expression: A century of research in review.* New York: Academic Press, 1972.

Hohmann, G. W. Some effects of spinal cord lesions on experienced emotional feelings. *Psychophysiology,* 1966, *3,* 143–156.

Izard, C. *The face of emotion.* New York: Appleton-Century-Crofts, 1971.

Klages, L. *Grundlegung der Wissenschaft vom Ausdruck.* Bonn: Barth, 1950.

Laird, J. D. Self-attribution of emotion: The effects of expressive behavior on the quality of emotional experience. *Journal of Personality and Social Psychology,* 1974, *29,* 475–486.

Marañon, G. The psychology of gesture. *Journal of Nervous and Mental Disease,* 1950, *3,* 485–486.

Plutchik, R. *The emotions: Facts, theories, and a new model.* New York: Random House, 1962.

Schachter, S., & Singer, J. E. Cognition, social and physiological determinants of emotional state. *Psychological Review,* 1962, *69,* 379–399.

Part III

THE DYNAMIC CONTEXT

Chapter 12

A CONSTRUCTIVIST VIEW OF EMOTION

JAMES R. AVERILL

ABSTRACT

Traditionally, the emotions have been viewed from a biological perspective; that is, the emotions have been seen as genetically determined and relatively invariable responses. The present chapter, by contrast, views the emotions as social constructions. More precisely, the emotions are here defined as socially constituted syndromes or transitory social roles. A role-conception does not deny the contribution of biological systems to emotional syndromes; it does, however, imply that the functional significance of emotional responses is to be found largely within the sociocultural system. With regard to subjective experience, a person interprets his own behavior as emotional in much the same way that an actor interprets a role "with feeling." This involves not only the monitoring of behavior (including feedback from physiological arousal, facial expressions, etc.), but also an understanding of how the emotional role fits into a larger "drama" written by society. Some of the biological, personal, and situational factors that influence emotional behavior are also discussed.

The term "constructivist" in the title of this chapter has a double meaning. First, it means that the emotions are social *constructions,* not biological givens. Second, it means that the emotions are *improvisations,* based on an individual's interpretation of the situation. These two meanings are not independent. Very briefly, the emotions are viewed here as transitory social

305

roles, or socially constituted syndromes. The social norms that help constitute these syndromes are represented psychologically as cognitive structures or schemata. These structures—like the grammar of a language—provide the basis for the appraisal of stimuli, the organization of responses, and the monitoring of behavior, that is, for the improvisation of emotional roles.

The chapter is divided into five sections. In the first section, a definition of emotion is developed, a definition that takes into account both aspects of a constructivist view just described—namely, emotions as social constructions and as individual improvisations. In the second section, a role-analysis of emotion is presented in some detail. The third section deals with the problem of so-called "basic" emotions and, more generally, with the biological determinants of emotion. In the fourth section, three "paradigms" of emotion are introduced; these paradigms represent idealized models of the social–psychological mechanisms that help mediate emotional behavior. Finally, the fifth section concludes with a few observations on the idiosyncratic and nonnormative expression of emotion.

THE DEFINITION OF EMOTION

The concept of emotion encompasses a wide range of phenomena, and this fact accounts for much of the controversy in the area. Ostensibly competing theories are often not incompatible; they simply address different phenomena, or different aspects of the same phenomenon. It is therefore important to specify at the outset the scope of the analysis in this chapter. Basically, I am concerned with the concept of emotion as it is used in everyday discourse and with the kinds of emotions recognized in ordinary language, for example, anger, grief, fear, hope, love, etc. This means that the chapter deals primarily with *human* emotions. For reasons that will become evident during the course of the discussion, I believe that the application of emotional concepts to animals is primarily metaphorical or derivative. A focus on human emotions is not, however, a limitation. On the contrary, present formulation will have to be broad enough to encompass a wide range of emotions such as love, courage, hope, anxiety, and jealousy to mention but a few. These are as representative of human emotions as are fear and anger, the states most studied by psychologists.

At first, it might seem that, by taking commonly recognized human emotions as a starting point, the problem of analysis has been greatly compounded. Everyday behavior is, after all, highly variable, and the ordinary language of emotion often seems vague and confusing. However, any theory of emotion must eventually deal with the emotions as they are conceptualized and experienced in everyday affairs. By focusing on such phenomena from the outset, it may be hoped that our conclusions will be of direct relevance to our ultimate concerns. That is not the case with many current theories of emotion, which often represent little more than extrapolations to the area of emotion of constructs developed to account for other types of behavior. Most drive theories of emotion are, for example, offshoots of learning theory; and most physiological theories are based on animal studies and hence are only tangentially related to human emotions.

A focus on the emotions as ordinarily conceived does not, of course, obviate the need for precision. In this section, therefore, I will try to develop a definition of emotion that is precise and yet broad enough to cover the major categories of human emotions. In doing this, I will follow the classical method of *definition by genus and difference*. That is, I will first indicate the generic class of phenomena to which the emotions belong, and then I will indicate how the emotions can be differentiated from other members of that class.

THE GENERIC CLASS OF PHENOMENA TO WHICH EMOTIONS BELONG

Depending on the aspect of emotional behavior that one wishes to emphasize, the emotions can be classed with a variety of different phenomena. In what follows, I will consider, first, the commonalities between emotions and other *behavioral syndromes* and, second, the commonalities between emotions and *transitory social roles*.

Emotions as Syndromes

A syndrome may be defined as a *set* of responses that covary in a *systematic fashion*. The two key elements in this definition are "set" and "systematic." The notion of *set* implies that a syndrome consists of a variety of different elements; that is, a syndrome is not a unitary or invariant response. But not any set of elements can form a syndrome. The elements must also be related in such a manner that they form a coherent *system*. In this sense, syndromes could also be defined as systems of behavior, as opposed to specific reactions.

To illustrate the syndromic nature of emotional reactions, consider the case of anger. There are certain behaviors that are typical of anger (including the way the individual appraises the situation), but none of these is necessary for the attribution of anger. Thus, the person who is angry may lash out at his antagonist, or he may withdraw from the situation; he may experience a high degree of physiological arousal, or he may calmly retaliate; his subjective experience may vary from exhilaration to depression; in addition, under some conditions, he may not even realize that he is angry.

Of course, the individual must do or experience something, or else we would not classify his behavior as angry. This fact has led some theorists to postulate that the concept of anger must refer to events that lie "below the surface," so to speak. Depending on the theorist, the postulated event may be a neurological circuit, a subjective experience, or perhaps an intervening drive variable. But the basic idea is the same: There is some event that is common to all instances of anger, and to which the term "anger" ultimately refers.

A syndromic conception of emotion denies this last assumption. Emotional syndromes are "polythetic." This term was introduced by Sokal and Sneath (1963) to describe biological classes (e.g., species), but it has been extended by Jensen (1970) to behavioral classes as well. Polythetic classes or syndromes are not definable in terms of a limited number of common characteristics or "essences." It follows that what is true of one member of a polythetic class is not necessarily true of other members of the class. Moreover, the boundaries between polythetic classes are often indistinct, and members of different classes may share elements in common (e.g., a person may lash out in fear as well as anger).

The importance of the above considerations for an analysis of emotional behavior will become apparent in subsequent sections. For the moment, I only wish to emphasize the fact that an emotional syndrome may include many diverse elements, some of biological and some of social origin, but none of which is essential to the identification of the syndrome as a whole.

Emotions as Transitory Social Roles

The conception of emotions as syndromes can be misleading in several important respects. Diseases are also syndromes. And, although there are many close parallels between the notion of disease and the notion of emotion, I do not want to reinforce the hoary idea that emotions are diseases of the mind. But, even more important, because of its close association with medicine, the term "syndrome" has a strong biological or physiological connotation. By contrast, the view I am presenting here is that emotions are social constructions, not biological givens. Therefore, it will be useful to point out some commonalities between the emotions and another broad class of phenomena, namely, social roles.

A role may be defined as a socially prescribed set of responses to be followed by a person in a given situation. This definition is similar in certain respects to that of a syndrome described earlier. However, the notion of a syndrome, by itself, does not indicate the nature of the mechanisms or "rules" that govern the selection of, and covariation among, various response elements. In the case of social roles, the nature of the relevant rules are stipulated; they are, namely, social norms or shared expectancies regarding appropriate behavior.

In the second section of this chapter I will examine in detail the conception of emotions as transitory social roles. At this point, let me simply note that a role-conception is perfectly compatible with the definition of emotions as complex syndromes. To illustrate this point, let me digress briefly. The concept of a syndrome is commonly applied to disease states. But the symptomatology that a patient displays when ill is determined, in part, by the "sick role" he adopts (Parsons, 1951; Segall, 1976). This is true even in cases where the source of the illness can be traced rather directly to some physiological source, such as injury or infection. In the case of brain damage and other organically based mental disorders, the role-expectations of the subject may actually outweigh physiological factors in determining the nature of the syndrome. And when we consider "functional" or neurotic disorders, such as hysterical reactions, organic factors are by definition absent or minimal. Syndromes of the latter type are constituted by the role being played; stated somewhat differently, the syndrome is a manifestation of the sick role as interpreted by the patient.

Extending the above line of reasoning to the emotions, it may be said that any given emotional syndrome represents the enactment of a transitory social role. This assertion does not deny the importance of biological factors in many, if not most, emotional syndromes, as will be discussed in the third section of this chapter. It does mean, however, that emotions are not just remnants of our phylogenetic past, nor can they be explained in strictly physiological terms. Rather, they are social constructions, and they can be *fully* understood only on a social level of analysis.

DIFFERENTIAE

A definition of emotion in terms of syndromes and/or transitory social roles is incomplete, for other psychological phenomena could be similarly described. Some differentiae must therefore be added. The two most important of these have to do with the appraisal of emotional stimuli and the experience of passivity (being "overcome" by emotion).

The Appraisal of Emotional Stimuli

In saying that emotions belong to the class of transitory social roles, they already have been differentiated from syndromes that are primarily organic in origin. Social roles require an active interpretation by the individual for their enactment. However, there is another sense in which the emotions are dependent on cognitive activity, and this helps to distinguish emotions not only from other organic syndromes but also from certain other social roles. I am referring to the fact that emotions have objects. A person cannot simply be angry, fearful, or proud. He must be angry *at* something, fearful *of* something, proud *of* something, and so forth.

The object of an emotion is dependent on an individual's appraisal of the situation. The notion of appraisal was introduced systematically into the study of emotion by Arnold (1960) and Lazarus (1966). Emotional appraisals differ from "cold" perceptual judgments in that the former are *evaluative;* that is, they represent judgments about what is desirable and undesirable as opposed to judgments about what is true or false. Thus, if a certain picture disgusts me, it is because I consider it to be either aesthetically or morally in bad taste, regardless of whether or not I consider it to be an accurate portrayal of events. Of course, not all evaluative judgments are emotional. An art critic or a trial judge may strive to be impersonal and objective in making an evaluative judgment. Emotional appraisals, by contrast, are highly *personal.* For example, if I perceive another person to be in danger, I do not ordinarily become afraid (unless perhaps I have some personal interest in that other person). It is this feature that makes emotional appraisals so revealing of an individual's personality. If you know what makes an individual proud, angry, sad, joyful, fearful, etc., then you know what that person considers important about himself, even those aspects of his personality that he may not recognize or admit.

There has been much speculation about the mechanisms that help mediate emotional appraisals (see Leventhal, 1979; Mandler, 1975). This is not the place to review such speculations, for they are not particularly relevant to a definition of emotion. Our concern here is with the logical status of emotional appraisals, and not with explanatory mechanisms (which are, in any case, only poorly understood).

From a logical point of view, the process of appraisal is an aspect of an emotional syndrome, not something antecedent to it. That is, the appraised object is not something that exists out there, independent of the observer. Rather, it is a meaning imposed on the environment—a cognitive construction, so to speak. For example, I may be angry at John for insulting me, when in actuality John was only trying to be helpful by correctly pointing out a mistake I had made. John's insult is based on my appraisal of the situation; it is as much a part of my anger as is my feeling of hurt.

The fact that appraisals are part of emotional syndromes was pointed out quite forcefully by John Dewey (1894, 1895) in an attempt to resolve some inconsistencies in the James–Lange theory. More recently, a similar point has been made by Leeper (1970) and Solomon (1976), both of whom define emotions in terms of perceptual or evaluative judgments.

If appraisal is part of an emotional syndrome, then the appraised object becomes an important criterion for distinguishing one emotion from another and, ipso facto, emotional from nonemotional states. This can be illustrated easily by the following thought experiment. Try to distinguish between three closely related emotions, such as anger, envy, and jealousy. Exactly the same response (e.g., striking another person, rise in blood pressure, loathing, etc.) might be involved in each case. However, if the responding individual believes that another person has done him an injustice, then the response might be attributed to anger; if the individual believes that the other person has something (perhaps legitimately) that otherwise would be his, then the response might be classified as jealousy; and if the individual simply believes that the other person is in a more favorable position, though without any detriment to himself, then the response might be identified as envy.

At the risk of repetition, it must be emphasized that the relationship between an emotion and its object is logical as well as psychological. Revenge for wrongdoing is part of what we mean by anger; resentment over the good fortune of another is part of what we mean by envy, and so forth. In order to "discover" the object of an emotion, we therefore need to examine the meaning of the emotional concept. And the meaning of an emotional concept, like that of any concept, is primarily a matter of social convention.

The Experience of Passivity

Although an important differentia, the appraised object is not by itself sufficient to distinguish emotional from nonemotional phenomena. Thus, I may appraise a situation as involving wrongdoing and seek to punish the wrongdoer, but without ever becoming angry. An additional criterion must therefore be added to our definition of emotion. This criterion is readily identifiable if we consider the older and now somewhat archaic term for emotion, namely, passion. The term "passion" derives from the Latin, *pati*, which in turn is related to the Greek, *pathos*. Also derived from these same roots are such terms as "passivity," "patient," and "pathology." The root meaning of these concepts is that the individual is undergoing or suffering some change. An emotion, in other words, is not something we do (an action), but something that happens to us (a passion).

Colloquially, the passivity of emotion is expressed in many ways. We "fall" in love, are "consumed" by envy, "haunted" by guilt, "paralyzed" by fear, and so forth. Traditional theories have attempted to account for expressions such as these, and the experiences they ostensibly represent, in one or more of the following ways: (*a*) by relating the emotions to biologically primitive ("instinctive") reactions; (*b*) by emphasizing the role of the autonomic ("involuntary") nervous system in the mediation of emotion; and/or (*c*) by assuming that the emotions are basically noncognitive ("irrational") responses. The present analysis, by contrast, assumes that the emotions are social constructions and that they require the same level of cognitive capacity as do other complex forms of social behavior. How is the passivity of emotion to be explained on the basis of such an assumption?

Much of the remainder of this chapter will be devoted to answering the above question. To adumbrate briefly, the classification of a response as either an action or a passion involves an *interpretation:* Actions are responses that are interpreted as self-initiated; passions are responses that are interpreted as beyond self-control. No one would probably object to this statement as it applies to the behavior of others. But what I shall be arguing below is that the feeling or subjective experience of emotion also involves an interpretation of one's own behavior. This is, of course, a somewhat unusual way of speaking, for it is common to distinguish interpretations from direct experiences. Nevertheless, most psychologists recognize that even simple sensory experiences involve some interpretive elements, and the same is certainly true of more complex emotional experiences.

The idea that the experience of emotion involves an interpretation of one's own behavior has recently received considerable impetus from attribution theory (e.g., Schachter, 1971; Nisbett & Valins, 1971). It is not, however, limited to any one theoretical framework. For example, Alfred Schutz (1968), a phenomenologist, has argued that the experience of behavior as deliberate or emotional is not inherent to the response, but is a meaning bestowed on spontaneous activity. Similarly, Bem (1972), a behaviorist, has suggested that emotional reactions, like other responses, are emitted spontaneously or unselfconsciously, only to be interpreted in the light of antecedent and consequent events. And Schafer (1976), a psychoanalyst, has suggested that emotions be viewed as "disclaimed actions," that is, as responses that an individual performs but for which he does not, or cannot, accept responsibility.

In short, the experience of passivity (of being "overcome" by emotion) is not intrinsic to the response, as most biologically oriented theories imply. Rather, it is an interpretation of behavior. A major problem for a constructivist view of emotions is to elucidate the source and functional significance of such an interpretation.

A DEFINITION

To summarize the discussion thus far, the following definition of emotion may be offered: *An emotion is a transitory social role (a socially constituted syndrome) that includes an individual's appraisal of the situation and that is interpreted as a passion rather than as an action.* This definition does not cover all of the phenomena that in ordinary language are sometimes labeled "emotional." But no definition can be stretched to cover all borderline phenomena and still retain any precision. With certain qualifications that will be discussed more fully below, the present definition does cover most commonly recognized human emotions.

EMOTIONAL SYNDROMES
AS TRANSITORY SOCIAL ROLES

The part of the above definition that is most likely to cause misunderstanding is the contention that emotions are transitory social roles. This section, therefore, will be devoted to an elaboration of that contention.

In an earlier publication (Averill, 1976), I described a dialectical approach to the social construction of emotional syndromes. Basically, this approach extends to the problem of emotion the type of inquiry traditionally known as the sociology of knowledge (see Berger & Luckmann, 1966). A role-conception of emotion is a rather straightforward extension of that previous analysis. The present discussion also draws on the application of role-theory to other kinds of "passions," such as illness behavior (Parsons, 1951; Segall, 1976), temporary insanity (Szasz, 1968), and hypnotic states (Sarbin & Coe, 1972).

Not all aspects of a role-conception of emotion can be examined here. I will therefore limit discussion to four major issues: (*a*) understanding the meaning of emotional roles; (*b*) monitoring the performance; (*c*) involvement in emotional roles; and (*d*) factors that influence involvement in and/or performance of emotional roles. I will then consider briefly some of the limitations of an analysis of emotion in terms of social roles.

UNDERSTANDING THE MEANING
OF EMOTIONAL ROLES

Before a role can be enacted, its meaning must be understood, and its requirements must be perceived. This observation might seem so blatantly obvious that it hardly needs mention. Yet, what is obvious can also be overlooked. I will illustrate this by considering briefly Stanley Schachter's (1971) influential theory of emotion. According to this theory, emotions are a joint product of two factors: physiological arousal and cognitive appraisals regarding the source of that arousal. More specifically, Schachter postulates that feedback from the physiological arousal provides a nondescript affective tone to experience, while the cognitive appraisal of situational cues determines which, if any, emotion will be experienced. This means that precisely the same state of arousal might be "labeled" as anger, love, joy, fear, guilt, etc., depending on the cues present in the situation.

I do not wish to review here the many ingenious experiments stimulated by Schachter's theory (see Schachter, 1971; Nisbett & Valins, 1971; Dienstbier, 1978; Zillmann, 1978). Basically, I agree with much of what Schachter has to say. Like most good theories, however, his raises more questions than it answers. Consider for a moment Schachter's use of the term "labeling" to refer to the way people describe their emotional experiences. This terminology implies that there is a highly contingent relationship between emotional concepts and underlying states—as though a person could pick an emotional label out of a box and pin it onto bodily reactions, following instructions provided by situational cues. But the person who says "that makes me angry" or "I love you" is not simply labeling an internal state; he is entering into a complex relationship with another person. Any comprehensive theory of emotion must include within its scope an analysis of the meaning of such relationships, and the latter kind of analysis goes far beyond a specification of the cues, physiological or situational, that help determine the use of emotional "labels."

The relationship between emotional concepts and emotional behavior has been examined in some detail elsewhere (Averill, 1980). Suffice it here to note that, from a constructivist point of view, when a person makes a self-attribution of emotion he enters into a transitory social role, the meaning of which is only symbolized by the emotional "label" he applies to his behavior. Stated somewhat differently, a person's emotional behavior and experiences are determined by the meaning of the emotional role as he interprets it. The "labeling" of behavior is often an important part of this process, but only a part (and not even a necessary part, at that).

What is involved in understanding the meaning of an emotional role, aside from knowing how to apply emotional concepts in a manner appropriate to the situation? Perhaps most important, the person must be able to view his own behavior from the perspective of others. Within the symbolic–interactionist tradition (see Hewett, 1976), this is called "role-taking" as opposed to "role-making." That is, by taking the role of others, a person learns how to respond (role-making) so that his behavior conforms to social expectations.

Taking the role of another can proceed on two levels. In any concrete interaction, the person must take into account specific others when improvising his own responses. (I will have more to say about this level of interaction in a subsequent section on the importance of social feedback for role-enactment.) On a broader level, the person must also take into account the expectations of the cultural group to which he belongs, or what Mead (1934) called the "generalized other." When a person responds in a manner that conforms to the expectations of the generalized other, that is, when he construes his own behavior as others might construe it, then he understands the meaning of the role he is making.

The above account is incomplete in an important respect, as an analogy with a drama may illustrate. A drama is not simply a set of individual roles intertwined in a certain fashion. The drama also has a plot, and a plot is different (but not more) than the sum of individual roles. In order to perform a role adequately, an actor must not only know his own part, and the parts of others, but he must also understand how the various roles relate to the plot (and subplots) of the play.

In the case of social roles, the plot is the cultural system. This means that the emotions can only be fully understood as part of the culture as a whole. Of course, such understanding is seldom conscious on the part of individuals. A person understands most social roles in much the same way that he understands linguistic rules—on an intuitive rather than an intellectual level. One task for theories of emotion is to make such intuitive understandings explicit.

MONITORING THE PERFORMANCE

Earlier I suggested that the experience of emotion is basically an interpretation of one's own behavior. Such an interpretation has two aspects: (a) understanding the meaning of the emotional role and (b) monitoring behavior in light of that understanding. The first aspect was discussed above, and we may now turn to the second.

Two orders or kinds of monitoring may be distinguished (see Harré & Secord, 1972). All behavior is controlled and corrected by innumerable feedback loops, or what may be called "first-order" monitoring. In lower animals, first-order monitoring provides the stuff of consciousness; among humans, the conscious aspects of first-order monitoring correspond roughly to what phenomenological psychologists have called "prereflective" or "lived" experience. However, as a result of the same cognitive capacities that are reflected in language, human beings also are able to reflect upon and conceptualize their lived experiences. Such "reflective experience" (in phenomenological terminology) is the product of "second-order" monitoring.

The distinction between first-order monitoring (prereflective experience) and second-order monitoring (reflective experience) can be illustrated by the following example. Consider a music critic at a symphony. He may become completely absorbed in the experience. But subsequently, when writing about the experience, he must analyze the performance, relate it to other performances of the same work that he has heard before, etc. In the latter case, the critic is reflecting upon his original experience. The reflection in this example is retrospective, but that is not a necessary feature of reflective experience. Typically, a music critic analyzes a performance while listening to it; that is, he reflects upon his experience as it occurs.

Having drawn the distinction between prereflective and reflective experience for analytic purposes, an important qualification must immediately be added. Completely prereflective experience is a myth, at least on the human level. All experience is filtered, organized, and given meaning by the categories of reflective thought. Thus, continuing with the above illustration, a music critic listening to a new performance can never completely disregard his past learning and ways of thought, no matter how hard he tries to discard the role of critic and how engrossing he finds the experience to be. In fact, were it not for well-established categories of thought, he probably would not find the experience engrossing at all.

The emotions are often considered to be the epitome of prereflective or lived experience, as though they were the product of first-order monitoring only. But that is not the case. Emotional experiences are reflective, the product of second-order monitoring. Moreover, the categories of reflective thought that give an emotional experience its meaning are based on a person's understanding of the emotional role as discussed above.

INVOLVEMENT IN EMOTIONAL ROLES

The emotions do not occur in an all-or-none fashion. Rather, emotional episodes can range along a continuum from relatively mild to highly intense. From a role–theoretical point of view, this continuum can be analyzed in terms of involvement (see Sarbin & Coe, 1972). As points of reference, I will describe briefly three levels of involvement in emotional roles. I will then examine some of the personal and situational factors that help determine such involvement.

Low Involvement

At the lowest level of involvement, enactment of an emotional role is largely a formality. An example is the philanderer who falls in love with nearly every woman he meets or the teacher who scolds a child for being naughty while inwardly laughing at the child's antics. The most common expression of emotion at this level is a simple verbal statement: "It's all right, I love you"; "Don't do it again, it makes me angry"; "I am sorry to hear of your misfortune"; and so forth. Such statements are not necessarily insincere just because they lack a great deal of personal involvement. They are generally appropriate to the situation and sufficient to achieve the desired end. In fact, if a person becomes too involved in an emotional role when the situation does not call for it, he is liable to be considered insincere or "affected."

Medium Involvement

As involvement in an emotional role increases, physiological arousal, expressive reactions, etc., are called into play. Feedback from such organic responses adds greatly to the feeling tone of the experience. Indeed, following

William James's (1890) famous formulation, many theorists have considered organic feedback as a necessary condition for the experience of emotion. It is therefore worth emphasizing that such feedback is subject to second-order monitoring as described above, and it is the monitoring that determines the quality of experience, not the feedback per se. In fact, the mere belief that one is physiologically aroused may greatly facilitate involvement in an emotional role (see Nisbett & Valins, 1971). The importance of organic involvement is thus due as much to its symbolic significance as to direct physiological feedback.[1] This perhaps explains why people often try to work themselves into a state of physiological arousal when emotional. For example, a lover may engage in a variety of behaviors in order to stoke the fires of his passion; an injured person may brood about the provocation until his anger is at just the right pitch for revenge; and the bereaved may seek attention by wallowing in his grief. It is as though, without organic involvement, the emotional response will not be experienced as convincing—either by oneself or by others.

High Involvement

At the highest level of involvement, the person may become so engrossed in the emotional role that he no longer seems in control of his own behavior. The dictates of the role are paramount. After the episode the person may claim that he did not know what he was doing, or that he was not himself. When evaluating responses at this level of involvement, it must be remembered that it is part of the meaning of emotion to be "overcome," "gripped," "seized," etc. This meaning helps determine not only the kind of behavior that will be exhibited, but also how the response will be experienced.

Low Involvement and the Passivity of Emotion

The definition of emotion offered earlier stipulated that emotional roles be interpreted as passions rather than as actions. It is easy to see how this definition applies to high levels of emotional involvement. But how can a response at a low level of involvement be interpreted as a passion? At this level the individual does not experience any loss of control, and hence the response would seem to belong to the category of actions, not passions.

There are two reasons why a response at a low level of involvement might be interpreted as a passion rather than as an action. First, the more extreme occurrences of a response often determine how more mild occurrences are in-

[1]The symbolism associated with physiological arousal—especially visceral reactions—not only influences the personal experience (interpretation) of emotional responses, but it also has had a profound influence on scientific theories of emotion. For a historical review of this issue, see Averill (1974).

terpreted. For example, a violent attack on one occasion helps determine how a mild threat will be interpreted on other occasions. In other words, the meaning of emotional responses at a low level of involvement is determined, in part, by the knowledge that, under different circumstances, involvement in the role might be much greater.

To illustrate a second reason why a response at a low level of involvement might be interpreted as a passion rather than as an action, consider the following examples. If I tell my sweetheart that I love her, I may feel quite insulted if she interprets the remark as premeditated or deliberate, no matter how unpassionate I happen to be at the moment. The remark is meant to be interpreted as part of an emotional syndrome, which implies a degree of commitment and sincerity that is often lacking in more deliberate ("calculated") responses. Another example of the same principle: If I reprimand a friend for behavior I disapprove of, and if the reprimand turns out to be hurtful, I may attribute my remark to anger, thus abnegating responsibility; on the other hand, if the reprimand turns out to be helpful, I may interpret the response as an action, thus assuming credit for being so honest and forthright.

As these examples illustrate, the actual behavior exhibited (thoughts, remarks, etc.) represents only one factor contributing to the interpretation of a response as a passion. The other factor, as explained earlier, involves an understanding of the relevant emotional role. When a person interprets a perfunctory remark, say, as the manifestation of an emotion, he is asking that the remark be understood and judged by standards that apply to emotional reactions and not by standards that apply to deliberate, rational acts. These standards have to do with such matters as the degree of commitment and the assignment of responsibility, among other things.

FACTORS THAT INFLUENCE INVOLVEMENT IN, AND/OR THE PERFORMANCE OF, EMOTIONAL ROLES

There are a number of factors that influence how an emotional role will be enacted. Among these are such personal variables as the motivation, prior experience, and capacity of the actor, and such situational variables as the physical and social settings in which the response occurs.

Motivation

Typically, emotions have been treated as motives for other behavior (cf. the fear–avoidance paradigm). But, from a constructivist point of view, the emotions are themselves motivated. To illustrate this, we must first develop a concept of motivation that is applicable to both the motivating and motivated properties of emotional syndromes. The seeds of such a concept can be found in Aristotle's notion of a hierarchy of behavior and in his distinction between matter and form. Aristotle defined behavior by reference to some goal or object (i.e., as instrumental acts). Thus, the simple contraction of the muscles of my legs does not constitute a response, but walking to the door does. Moreover, responses in this sense form a hierarchy, with lower-order responses providing the "matter" for higher-order responses (which provide the "form"). Thus, looking upward in the hierarchy, walking to the door might provide the matter for a more inclusive response, namely, going to the store. But looking downward in the hierarchy, walking to the door provides the form for a number of subsidiary responses, for example, standing up, putting on my shoes, etc.

Recently, Chein (1972) has applied this type of hierarchical analysis to the problem of motivation. According to Chein, a superordinate act can be considered the motive for an act lower in the behavioral hierarchy if the latter is necessary for the completion of the former. At first, this concept of motivation might seem unusual, but it is actually quite close to common usage. Thus, in the preceding example, going to the store might be considered the motive for my walking to the door, and the latter might, in turn, be considered the motive for standing up, putting on my shoes, etc.[2]

In the preceding sense, all behaviors are both motivating (when treated as superordinate acts) and motivated (when treated as subsidiary responses). This is true of emotional as well as non-emotional behaviors. For example, an episode of anger may be considered the motive for a variety of subsidiary responses (e.g., yelling, striking, etc.). But looking upward rather than downward in the behavioral hierarchy, one might also ask: What is the motive (superordinate act) of which the episode of anger is a subsidiary part? This question is not always easy to answer, for a person need not be aware of the interconnectedness of behavior. We may then speak of unconscious motives. "Unconscious" in this sense does not refer, however, to deeply buried forces or drives; it refers, rather, to the lack of awareness of how one response relates to another.

To say that a person is motivated to perform an emotional role means that the behavior demanded by the role is subsidiary to some superordinate act or broader concern of the individual. We often do not speak of the emotion as motivated in this sense for two reasons. First, it is part of the meaning of emo-

[2]A related, though more cognitively oriented, approach to motivation is contained in George Kelly's (1955) theory of personal constructs. A construct is a way of interpreting events, and, according to Kelly, a higher-order construct determines subordinate elements in much the same way that a motive (as defined here) determines subsidiary responses. Klinger's (1977) notion of "current concerns" is also relevant to these considerations. Klinger defines the boundaries of a current concern "by the range of alternative outcomes that the individual would find acceptable substitutes for one another" (p. 351). Similarly, the boundaries of a motive can be defined by the range of subsidiary responses that would suffice for the completion of the superordinate act.

tion that the response be interpreted as a passion, that is, as beyond personal control. But by now I hope it is obvious that a response is not divorced from the remainder of a person's concerns simply because it is interpreted as a passion rather than as an action. Second, in everyday affairs, we typically ask about motives only when the reason for a response is not evident. In the case of emotional responses, however, the precipitating events are typically obvious. Thus, we are not tempted to ask about the motive for grieving at the death of a loved one, becoming angry at an insult, being frightened that a tumor will be cancerous, etc. In such instances, the individual is responding as *expected*.

The role-aspect of emotional behavior is especially evident when the motive for a response does not follow socially approved rules or expectations. For example, if the intensity of the emotional response is far out of proportion to the instigation, as when a person becomes enraged at an innocuous remark, we may wonder what the person is trying to achieve. Is he attempting to intimidate the other, break off a relationship, gain revenge for some past wrong?

When an emotional reaction is overly intense, it is liable to be regarded as somewhat "theatrical" or histrionic. This does not mean, of course, that the experience of the emotion is unreal or a sham. On the contrary, like the hysterical patient who cannot see what he does not wish to see, the highly motivated person may experience the emotion as entirely genuine.

A person may also lack the motivation to respond emotionally; that is, the emotion may be irrelevant to his broader concerns, and yet, social pressure may dictate that the role be performed anyway. Thus, a person might just as soon ignore an insult as petty and irrelevant, but he may feel that a display of anger is necessary for the sake of appearances. Or a person may believe it necessary to mourn the loss of a relative, even though the loss does not affect him personally. In cases such as these, the person himself typically recognizes that he is "playing a role," even if others do not.

In most instances, of course, the broader concerns of the individual are congruent with the demands of the role. A person normally *wants* to attack his provocateur, mourn the loss of a loved one, flee from danger, dance for joy, etc. In such cases the role-aspects of the emotion are no less important—only less apparent—than they are in cases where personal motives do not conform to social expectations.

Prior Experience

Like any complex form of social behavior, the emotions must be acquired through experience. This involves two factors: (a) coming to understand the meaning of the role and (b) learning the specific behavior appropriate to the role. Most of the research on the development of emotion has focused on the latter factor, generally within a conditioning or social-learning paradigm. Nevertheless, there are good reasons to believe that the first factor—understanding the meaning of the emotion—is much more important than the acquisition of specific responses. Appropriate responses can generally be improvised, provided the individual understands the requirements of the role.

The mechanisms by which children (and adults) internalize the social norms related to emotional behavior are not well understood. This is true for nonemotional behaviors as well; nevertheless, a few observations can be made. The emotions are related to the self in a particular way, that is, as passions rather than as actions. This means that emotional development must proceed simultaneously with ego development. The 1-year-old infant does not experience anger, jealousy, etc., except in a metaphorical sense. The infant is, of course, able to show a variety of different kinds of distress and pleasure reactions, but these have the same analogous relation to emotional development as does the babbling of an infant to language development. Also, emotional syndromes generally presuppose the prior development of nonemotional cognitive capacities. For example, the typical provocation to anger (as opposed to simple frustration-induced aggression) is an intentional wrong perpetrated by another (see Averill, 1979a). This means that, before a child understands the meaning of anger, he must also understand the meaning of intentionality and wrongdoing.

Children play at being angry, fearful, in love, etc., just as they play at being doctors, parents, garbage collectors, and the like. Such play, as well as the observation of the emotional reactions of others (both directly and vicariously in songs and stories), helps the child to understand the meaning of emotional roles. Much of this learning, it might be noted, proceeds simultaneously with the acquisition of language. As discussed earlier, emotional concepts do not simply name or label a response; rather, they help to explain behavior by relating it to systems of judgment (e.g., of a moral or aesthetic nature) and to patterns of social relationships. Thus, as the child learns to use emotional concepts correctly, he also learns a good deal about the meaning of emotional roles.

As adults, emotional reactions are likely to proceed automatically and in the absence of any verbal mediation. It is therefore easy to overlook the amount and kind of prior experience that is required for the proper enactment of an emotional role. We may be reminded of this fact, however, when confronted with a new role, such as falling in love for the first time, or grieving at the loss of a parent. In such instances, a person may rightfully wonder, "What should I do?" or "Are my feelings true?" With repeated practice, such doubts tend to disappear, and it becomes easier to show the appropriate emotion. In some cases, such as falling in love, it is part of the meaning of the emotion that it should happen only once, or at least not too often. But even here, as the words of a popular song indicate, the second time around is often better. And when it comes to such common emotional syndromes as anger, the facilitating effect of prior experience is often only too apparent.

Capacity

There are large individual differences in emotional reactivity. Such differences have traditionally been discussed under the rubric of personality traits. From a constructivist point of view, individual differences in emotional reactivity can better be conceptualized in terms of capacities or abilities. Stated somewhat differently, a personality trait might be defined as the capacity to enact an emotional role. It might be objected that personality traits represent tendencies to become emotional, not capacities. However, if a person has the capacity to respond, then, given the motivation (and the opportunity), he will respond. There is thus no need to introduce a concept of "tendency" in addition to the concepts of capacity and motivation.[3]

An interpretation of personality traits as capacities also has the advantage of placing emotional behavior on an analogous footing with intellectual behavior. The person who engages in some intellectual endeavor must have the capacity to perform the appropriate response. The motivation for actually engaging in the behavior is to be found in the broader concerns of the individual (e.g., to pass a course, to go to college, to become an engineer). Similarly, when a person becomes angry, falls in love, etc., he must have the capacity to perform the appropriate responses—and the motivation to do so.

Factor analytic studies of personality traits have typically yielded a broad dimension that has variously been called "emotionality," "neuroticism," or "anxiety." This suggests that there may be a general ability to become emotional, analogous to general intelligence in the intellectual domain. But before we accept the notion of a general emotional capacity, two facts should be noted. First, most situations do not require a great deal of involvement in emotional roles. Nearly everyone has the capacity to enter into emotional roles with at least some degree of involvement. Second, a general emotional capacity, even if it exists, is not sufficient for the enactment of specific emotional roles, since each emotion places unique demands on the individual. Anger, for example, requires the ability to retaliate; romantic love requires certain interpersonal skills; and so forth. The person who lacks these specific capacities is not going to be very effective, no matter how emotional he may become in a more general sense.

The capacity to perform any given emotional role is undoubtedly the joint product of prior experience and genetic endowment. The contribution of prior

---

[3]Wallace (1966) has also suggested that personality traits might be interpreted as the ability to perform emotional roles, and Willerman, Turner, and Peterson (1976) have provided some empirical support for such a suggestion.

experience has already been discussed and the contribution of genetic factors will be discussed in some detail when we consider the question of so-called "basic" emotions.

The Physical and Social Setting

Motivation, prior experience, and capacity are personal factors that help determine involvement in, and/or performance of, emotional roles. Equally important in this regard are the physical and social settings in which the response occurs. I am not referring simply to the focal stimulus that evokes the response. That is of such obvious importance as not to require discussion. I am referring, rather, to the ambient cues within the situation. To use a stage analogy, such cues correspond to the props (the physical setting) and the audience (the social setting).

With regard to the physical setting, it is easier to become angry in a barroom than in a church, to fall in love on a summer cruise than on a work project, to become frightened at night than during the day, to become jovial at a party than in the classroom, and so forth. Of course, the effects of the physical setting are not always so obvious as these anecdotal examples might suggest. As Berkowitz (1974) has demonstrated, rather subtle cues—such as the name of the provocateur or a weapon placed innocuously nearby—may potentiate anger, presumably because such cues have been previously associated with anger and/or aggressive responses. Similar observations could undoubtedly be made with regard to other emotions, although firm experimental evidence in this area is scarce. The environmental psychology of the emotions is largely an untilled field of research.[4]

As important as the physical setting may be for emotional behavior, the social environment is generally even more important. Some emotions, such as anger and love, typically demand some kind of response on the part of another person. However, the importance of social cues is not limited to emotions that involve mutual interaction between two or more persons. Many emotional roles are like soliloquies; only one actor is directly involved, but the response is played for and to an audience. Laughter, for example, is much heartier in the presence of others; embarrassment and shame do not occur in solitude; and any parent can testify how young children often await the arrival of a sympathetic audience before bursting into tears.

To illustrate not only the potency but also the subtlety of social feedback on emotional reactivity, consider the case of hysterical contagion. This refers to the appearance of emotion-like symptoms (or conversion reactions) among a group of individuals. The symptoms may include a wide variety of

---

[4]Even the stimulus value of weapons has proven to be ambiguous. Depending on the circumstances, the presence of a weapon may inhibit as well as facilitate the expression of aggression (see Buss, Booker, & Buss, 1972; Frodi, 1975).

physiological reactions, such as uncontrollable trembling or twitching, fainting, paralysis, and nausea, as well as bizarre behavioral responses (e.g., dancing manias).

Gehlen (1977) has analyzed hysterical contagions in terms of Parson's model of the sick role. Very briefly, one or two people may experience some reaction (perhaps due to stress, or even a physical illness). If the response is met with sympathy and social recognition, others in the group may be motivated to present similar symptoms. The reaction then spreads like a contagious disease. This is especially true if some credible agent is identified as the cause, thus providing social validation for the syndrome.

But we do not have to rely on hysterical or conversion reactions to illustrate the facilitating (or sometimes inhibiting) effects of social cues. Fear is notoriously "contagious"; so, too, are the calming effects of unafraid companions (Schachter, 1959). Anger also may be potentiated or mitigated as a function of the values conveyed by onlookers (Borden, 1975). Even falling in love can be facilitated by peer pressures, or short-circuited by the attitudes of parents and other reference-group figures (Rubin, 1973).

LIMITATIONS OF A ROLE–THEORETICAL APPROACH

In this section, I have tried to illustrate how the emotions might be analyzed in terms of social roles. Much more could be said along these lines, of course, but space does not allow a more detailed analysis. I will therefore conclude the section with a few observations on the limits of such an approach.

To begin with, the assertion that emotions are transitory social roles is a metaphorical way of speaking. The concept of a role has its primary application in stage productions. Shakespeare observed that "all the world is a stage," and role-theory is basically a working out of the implications of that metaphor. The role-metaphor is least strained when applied to professional occupations and other formalized behavior patterns. When applied to highly personal experiences, such as emotional reactions, it might seem that the role-metaphor is being stretched beyond meaningful limits. If the emotions can be conceptualized as social roles, is there any kind of behavior that cannot be so regarded? Probably not! As Goffman (1959) has equipped, "All the world is not, of course, a stage, but the crucial ways in which it isn't are not easy to specify" (p. 72).

If one cannot specify the ways in which some behavior does *not* conform to a role, then the entire analysis becomes a mere play on words; it allows neither proof nor disproof. The issue, however, is not whether the emotions are *really* social roles; the issue is, rather, whether the emotions can be fruitfully viewed from this perspective. I believe they can be. At the very minimum, a role-analysis forces us to consider the meaning (or functional significance) of the emotions within a social context.

Another limitation of a role-analysis is that it does not deal directly with some of the major problems that must be addressed by a theory of emotion. This is particularly true with regard to mechanisms (cognitive and physiological) that help mediate emotional reactions. Social roles represent functional units within a social system; they do not refer to psychological states as such. To be of psychological interest, the social role must be enacted. How are norms represented cognitively? And by what mechanism does the interpretation of a social role as a passion lead to the experience of being "overcome" by emotion? Some of these problems have been addressed in this section (especially in connection with the monitoring of behavior), and more will be said in the fourth section. The point that I now wish to emphasize is that a role-analysis can never be sufficient *by itself* to account for emotional behavior. But this is true of any approach that is limited to a single level of analysis, whether biological, psychological, or social.

Finally, it must also be recognized that a role-analysis is more appropriate to some emotions than to others. Startle, for example, does not lend itself to an analysis as a social role. And, on a more complex level, it would be fatuous to claim that a person who becomes frightened upon meeting the proverbial bear in the woods is enacting a role. However, this limitation may not be as serious as it at first appears. Startle might better be considered a reflex than an emotion, and most "natural" fears (e.g., of falling, and even of bears in the woods) are not very representative of emotions in general. Costello (1976) has posed the issue as follows: "Clear-cut events in the environment may produce what look like emotional behaviors such as fear and rage. But are these emotions in the same sense that we usually use the term?" (p. 14). He answers in the negative, and I largely agree.[5] To repeat what was stated earlier, emotions as we know them are the product of reflective experience. The person who meets a bear while alone in the woods must improvise and interpret his reactions according to categories of thought (cognitive systems) acquired during socialization; and it is such improvisation and interpretation that allows the response properly to be called fear.

In summary, a role-analysis capitalizes on metaphor and hence is difficult to prove or disprove; it is largely silent with regard to intervening psychological mechanisms; and it is more appropriate to some emotions than to others. Because of these limitations, I have defined emotions as syndromes as well as transitory social roles. Of course, the conception of emotions as syndromes is also somewhat metaphorical, since the notion of a syndrome has its primary application elsewhere (e.g., in medicine). The syndrome metaphor has the advantage of being somewhat more neutral and hence is less likely to lead to polemical argument than the role-metaphor. Nevertheless, I want to

[5]Dewey (1895) has made a similar point.

emphasize that these two metaphors are in no way incompatible. Emotional roles are socially constituted syndromes. Moreover, in spite of its limitations, the role-metaphor has a major advantage; namely, it serves as a constant reminder that emotions are social constructions and not just biological givens.

THE PROBLEM OF BASIC EMOTIONS

From a constructivist point of view, there are an indefinite number of emotions. That is, societies can shape, mold, or construct as many different emotions as are functional within the social system. In the English language, for example, there are over 550 concepts that refer more or less directly to emotional states (Averill, 1975). For purposes of analysis, this plethora of emotions must be reduced or simplified in some manner. One traditional approach to simplification has been to identify a small number of "basic" or "primary" emotions, out of which others might be compounded. In the present section, I will examine briefly the merits of this strategy; in the process, I also will consider the biological contribution to emotional syndromes.

Although it is logically possible to identify emotions as "primary" or "fundamental" on the basis of a number of different criteria, the criterion most commonly employed is biological; for example, Scott (1969) has associated emotional reactions with nine behavior systems, the latter being defined in terms of their "adaptive function" in an evolutionary sense. In Scott's view, there is not necessarily a one-to-one relationship between basic emotions and behavioral systems. Plutchik (1962), however, has postulated the existence of eight primary emotions, each of which is related to a "basic adaptive pattern" observable in all species from amoeba to man. Similarly, Tomkins (1970) has described nine primary emotions that he relates to "innately endowed" patterns of neural firings. And, building in part on the work of Tomkins, Izard (1977) has postulated the existence of "genetically determined universal behavior patterns that represent several fundamental emotions" (p. 70).[6]

SYSTEMS OF BEHAVIOR

The works of Plutchik, Tomkins, Izard, and Scott highlight the contribution of biological systems to emotional syndromes. However, systems of behavior can be defined at various levels of analysis, depending on the principles of organization that are being emphasized. In the case of biological

---

[6]For an example of a classification scheme that is not based on biological criteria, see Arnold (1960). She classifies basic emotions according to the appraisals involved, for example, whether the object of the emotion is appraised as good or bad, easy or difficult to obtain, and so forth.

systems, the principles of organization are genetic and evolutionary. More specifically, a biological system consists of genetically programmed but semi-autonomous elements—responses and the neurological structures necessary for their coordination—that have (or at one time did have) an adaptive value for the species. In addition to the biological level, systems of behavior can also be defined at the psychological and sociocultural levels of analysis. In the case of psychological systems, responses are organized with respect to other actions on the part of the individual. In the case of sociocultural systems, responses are organized around roles and the norms and symbols that help legitimize those roles.[7]

The definition of emotions as transitory social roles offered earlier places primary emphasis on the contribution of sociocultural systems. It must be emphasized, however, that any emotional syndrome represents an organic whole. The distinction among systems of behavior—biological, psychological, and sociocultural—is primarily analytical. That is, such systems are abstractions or ways of analyzing behavior. Any specific response, such as weeping at a funeral, may be analyzed as part of a biological system (e.g., when considered in relation to other genetically determined reactions), as part of a psychological system (e.g., when considered in relation to other responses within a person's motivational hierarchy), and as part of a sociocultural system (e.g., when considered in relation to other mourning practices). On the other hand, some responses have meaning primarily within one kind of system and not another. For example, the practice of wearing certain types of clothing during bereavement must be analyzed as part of the sociocultural system, while the fatigue and loss of appetite that often accompany bereavement may best be analyzed within a biological framework.[8]

THE CONTRIBUTION OF BIOLOGICAL SYSTEMS

With the above considerations in mind, let us now examine briefly some of the ways that biological systems contribute to emotional syndromes. The first thing to note in this regard is that any system will undergo progressive *segregation* in the absence of maintenance inputs (Hall & Fagen, 1968); that is, the elements of the system gradually become more loosely connected and independent. The opposite of segregation is *systematization*—the strengthening of preexisting relations and/or the incorporation of new elements into the

---

[7]This threefold division of systems is based rather loosely on the work of Parsons (1959). Actually, Parsons distinguishes among four "systems of action," each representing a mode of organization on the cultural, social, psychological, or biological level of analysis. Of course, at each level of analysis, a variety of different subsystems might also be recognized.

[8]For a detailed analysis of the biological, psychological, and sociocultural determinants of grief and mourning, see Averill (1968, 1979b).

system. In biological systems, segregation may result from such genetic processes as mutation, independent assortment, recombination, and the like, while natural selection acts as the major systematizing influence. However, as we ascend the phylogenetic scale, biological systems become increasingly segregated on a genetic level, while individual experience and social custom assume greater importance as systematizing factors.

In humans, most biological systems are highly segregated. This means that elements from a biological system can be incorporated into a variety of different behavioral syndromes—including emotional roles—as a function of learning and enculturation.

BIOLOGICAL SYSTEMS AND "BASIC EMOTIONS"

The above considerations have several important implications for theories of emotion. First, any given emotion may be related to more than one biological system; conversely, any given biological system may be related to more than one emotion. Second, emotional syndromes include culturally as well as biologically based elements. In some cases, such as a startle reaction or certain fears, the overlap between an emotional syndrome and a biological system may be almost total; in other cases, however, the overlap may be minimal. (It is, for example, difficult to relate an emotion such as hope directly to a biological system, or to a combination of systems.)

These two facts, it will be noted, preclude any meaningful attempt to identify biological systems with a limited number of primary or fundamental emotions. Consider, for example, romantic love (which includes elements of attachment as well as reproductive behavior on the biological level) and hope (which has little relationship to any biological system). In what sense are these emotions any less fundamental than, say, startle or fear? Of course, one may *define* a fundamental emotion in terms of a biological system. But then, with few exceptions, the defined emotion would not correspond to any actually existing emotional syndrome. Moreover, if such a definition were accepted, the assertion that fundamental emotions are related to biological systems would be little more than a tautology.

If emotions are complex syndromes that incorporate both biological and sociocultural elements, a major problem for any theory of emotion is the specification of the "rules" that determine the selection and organization of those elements. This problem has already been addressed. Biological and sociocultural systems interact to form emotional syndromes when people respond to one another in terms of transitory social roles. But an addendum may now be added to the role-analysis presented earlier. As previously explained, emotional roles are interpreted as passions rather than actions. The reasons for such an interpretation are primarily social (having to do with such issues as degree of commitment, the assignment of responsibility, etc.). However, to the extent that an emotional syndrome incorporates elements from one or more biological systems, the interpretation of the response as a passion may be facilitated. There is thus a grain of truth in the contention that the experience of emotion accompanies the activation of "instinctive" (biological) patterns of behavior. A grain of truth is not, however, sufficient to make a theoretical loaf.

PARADIGMS OF EMOTION

If we reject the idea that the emotions can be reduced to a fundamental few on the basis of biological criteria, we are still left with the problem of how to impose some order on the diversity of emotional phenomena. In the present section, I will approach this problem through the use of idealized models or paradigms. These paradigms describe the mechanisms that help distinguish certain classes of emotion; that is, they do not purport to represent particular emotions, nor do they imply that some emotions are more fundamental than others (although some may approximate the ideal of a paradigm more than do others).

Figure 12.1 presents, in block diagram, a model of emotion. I will use this diagram to explicate several different paradigms of emotion. But first, let me explain some of the general features of the model.

It will be noted that Figure 12.1 is symmetrical above and below the horizontal axis. That is, if the diagram were folded at the midline, the top and bottom halves would coincide. This is to illustrate the formal congruence between the sociological (top half) and psychological (bottom half) determinants of emotion. Another thing to note about Figure 12.1 is that the arrows do not necessarily represent causal sequences in the traditional sense. For example, social norms do not "cause" specific appraisals or response tendencies, as one event might be said to cause another event. Rather, social norms serve as standards against which responses can be compared and, if a discrepancy is detected, appropriate adjustments made.

The cognitive and physiological processes that help mediate emotional behavior are represented by a single "black box" along the horizontal axis. Included within this black box are the appraisal and monitoring functions discussed earlier.

Let us now examine the upper half of Figure 12.1 in more detail. Two types of social variables are of major importance for the understanding of emotional syndromes: social norms and defenses. As used here, the term "social norms" refers to demands or expectancies placed on the individual by society. Social norms may influence behavior in either of two ways: (a) The immediate prospect of positive and/or negative sanctions may induce compliance; (b)

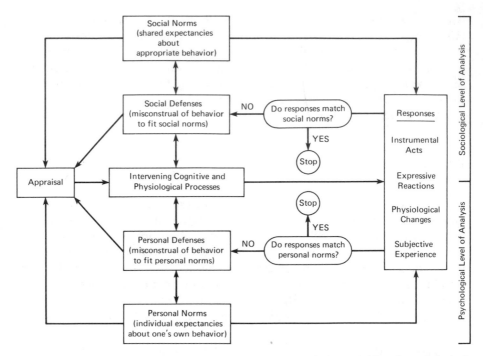

FIGURE 12.1. A model of emotion, depicting the sociological (top half) and psychological (bottom half) levels of analysis.

during the process of socialization, the individual may adopt as his own the relevant attitudes and beliefs of society, so that the expected behavior becomes "second nature," so to speak.

Sometimes, the practices fostered by society are detrimental to the interests of the individual (e.g., the person is encouraged to face the dangers of combat, to abstain from pleasurable activities, etc.), or, what amounts to much the same thing, equally compelling norms may call for incompatible responses. In such cases, the conflict may be resolved by another set of normative structures, which I have labeled "social defenses." These social defenses are analogous to psychological defense mechanisms, as described below.

The bottom half of Figure 12.1 represents the psychological level of analysis. Through a past history of conditioning and learning, a person develops a set of expectancies ("personal norms") about his or her own behavior. Some of these expectancies may be so strong that the individual cannot help but respond under given circumstances, in which case the response may be interpreted as a passion. But this is not the only source of passion on the individual level. When two or more expectancies are incompatible, intrapsychic conflict results. Psychological defense mechanisms allow a resolution of the conflict, for example, by symbolically transforming the conflicted response and divorcing it from the self-as-agent.

For the well-socialized individual, personal norms reflect social norms, and personal defenses are congruent with social defenses. In cases where the personal and social levels do not match, the resulting behavior is liable to be labeled "hysterical," which means simply that it is idiosyncratic to the individual and not standard within the social group.

Implicit in the above discussion is a distinction between two paradigms of emotion, which I shall call *impulsive* and *conflictive*. After describing each of these paradigms in further detail, I will then present a third paradigm to characterize what I have called *transcendental* emotional syndromes (Averill, 1976).

IMPULSIVE EMOTIONS

This paradigm of emotion represents straightforward desires and aversions that have become so "second nature" that they are not regarded as self-initiated. Examples are grief, joy, hope, sexual desire, and many common fears.

The paradigm of impulsive emotions bears some resemblance to older instinct theories of emotion. For example, according to McDougall (1948), "The operation of each instinct, no matter how brought into play, is accompanied by its own peculiar quality of experience which may be called a primary emotion. . . . The human emotions [are] then regarded as *clues to the instinctive impulses,* or indicators of the motives at work within us" (p. 128, italics mine). The linking of primary or basic emotions directly to biological systems (instincts) has already been criticized in the previous section. Otherwise, this statement by McDougall would apply well to the impulsive emotions. These are like states of strong motivation that (for any of a variety of reasons) are not completely identified with the self-as-agent.

The activation of biological systems may be one reason why a response is experienced as impulsive, but individual learning and socialization are also important in this respect. Thus, through a past history of reinforcement, an individual may acquire response tendencies that are as compelling as any biological "instinct." And the internalization of social norms, by whatever process, may result in behaviors that the individual experiences as beyond control. This last point has been made particularly well by Fox (1971). To paraphrase him, if a species (namely, mankind) were to lose its dependency on instincts, then a certain class of cultural behavior would have to become like instinctive behavior: unconscious, so that it did not require thought for its operation; reflexive, so that certain stimuli would automatically produce it; and common to all members of a society. Such a culturally produced "instinct" would be, in the words of McDougall, "accompanied by its own peculiar quality of experience," and it would constitute what I am calling an impulsive emotion.

The paradigm of impulsive emotions has a long history quite independent of its relationship to instinct theories. Arnold (1960), for example, has also described a class of "impulse emotions," which she defines as unhindered tendencies toward or away from some object appraised as good or bad. Arnold further postulates that, when simple tending becomes difficult (for example, due to some obstacle that prevents direct approach or avoidance) a "contending emotion," such as anger or despair, may result. Going back much further historically, Arnold's distinction between impulse and contending emotions is very similar to the medieval distinction between concupiscible and irascible emotions (cf. Aquinas); and the latter, in turn, has its roots in Plato's distinction between the appetitive and spirited elements of the soul.

CONFLICTIVE EMOTIONS

Arnold's (1960) conception of contending emotions may serve to introduce—by way of contrast—the paradigm of conflictive emotions. Within Arnold's system, the conditions that produce a contending emotion might best be described as frustration. But frustration is a much broader concept than is "conflict," and hence what Arnold calls contending emotions are different from what I am calling conflictive emotions.

If an impulse toward or away from some goal is simply blocked, a person may try to overcome the obstacle by aggression, or he may withdraw in despair. But in neither case need there be any real conflict. If, however, the person believes that aggression is wrong, or that despair is contemptible, then two opposing response tendencies will be present, and conflict will result.

Stated differently, simple frustration may give rise to new impulses (e.g., toward aggression or withdrawal); conflict, however, involves a transformation of behavior due to incompatible impulses. Sometimes, the response to conflict may resemble one of the original impulses; that is, it may appear that no transformation has occurred. But the resolution of a conflict always involves some compromise, or at least some justification as to why one impulse is acceded to while the other is not.

Conflictive emotions are more like conversion reactions in the Freudian sense than they are like contending emotions in Arnold's sense. In the case of a conversion reaction, the individual wishes to engage in some behavior that conflicts with personal norms or standards. The result is a compromise or symbolically transformed response, the meaning of which is dissociated from the self. For example, a person suffering from hysterical paralysis may be greatly troubled by his affliction and go to great lengths to seek help. However, the paralysis is not something that just "happens" to the person; it is, rather, a way of coping that the person cannot recognize or condone as such and yet that fulfills a definite function in helping to resolve intrapsychic conflict. By analogy, standard conflictive emotions can be viewed as conversion-like phenomena on a sociocultural as opposed to an individual level of analysis. That is, the source of the conflict and the "script" for the expression of the response are to be found within the sociocultural system, and are not due to intrapsychic conflicts peculiar to the individual.

Elsewhere, I have analyzed anger (Averill, 1979a) and romantic love (Averill & Boothroyd, 1977) as conflictive emotions within our culture. In the case of anger, the underlying conflict stems from two sets of norms, one of which condemns violence and the other of which calls for the retribution of perceived injustice. The conflict is resolved by a third set of norms ("social defenses" in Figure 12.1) that allow aggression to be expressed in the form of anger, thus preserving the strictures against *deliberately* harming another. In the case of romantic love, the conflict is between norms that encourage independence, self-reliance, and economic self-interest, on the one hand, and unselfish commitment to a spouse and children, on the other. The conflict is resolved by falling in love, which—if the script follows its traditional course—typically results in marriage and family.

TRANSCENDENTAL EMOTIONS

Impulsive and conflictive emotions presuppose well-defined cognitive structures and organized patterns of behavior. The third paradigm of emotion that I shall describe involves a breakdown in customary modes of thought, including the cognitive structures that help define the self as an active initiator of events. Cognitive structures may break down or become disorganized for many different reasons, for example, stimulus overload, sensory deprivation, drugs, meditation, brain damage, intrapsychic conflict, and the like. When such breakdown occurs, there can be no action, only passion. I have labeled such states "transcendental" because they involve a transcendence of the self, and because they tend to be diffuse, ineffable, and difficult to describe in ordinary language (Averill, 1976).

A few remarks about mystical experiences and anxiety reactions will serve to illustrate the nature of transcendental emotional states. Among the most common characteristics of mystical experiences are a disappearance of self-identity and a sense of unity with some underlying reality (see Deikman, 1966; Greeley, 1974). This underlying reality has been variously called "God," "The One," "Cosmic Consciousness," and "The Divine Ground," to give but a few examples. Whether or not such terms signify an actually existing reality, as the mystic often claims, they do symbolize the unifying and transcendental nature of the experience. And, like other unifying experiences (such as being in love, or even obtaining closure on some intellectual task), the mystical state is accompanied by contentment, peace, and a quiet joy. Perhaps the meaning of this emotional syndrome is best captured by the Buddhist concept of *nirvana,* which implies both unity and enlightenment.

The above considerations can be stated somewhat differently, more in line with the role-analysis developed earlier. During a mystical state, the customary distinctions between self and other, and between internal and external reality, are no longer recognized; and experience is guided by more encompassing categories of thought. These latter categories are often based on some philosophical or religious system within which the role of the mystic is defined, so to speak. In some instances, as in the case of the saint or shaman, the mystical role is quite explicit and formally recognized. But in other instances (such as the neophyte marihuana user who has to learn when he is "high"), the role may require a considerable amount of improvisation on the part of the individual.

In the absence of a supportive framework or belief system that lends meaning to experience, a breakdown in cognitive organization is more likely to result in anxiety than in nirvana. This accounts for the fact that anxiety is often occasioned by the same events that have also been found to trigger mystical experiences (see Bourque & Back, 1971; Noyes, 1972; Lazarus, 1976). Of course, a collapse of cognitive structures is seldom complete, and hence anxiety may occur in varying degrees, from vague feelings of unease and uncertainty to the catastrophic reactions described by Goldstein (1939). The latter occur when the individual is no longer able to impose meaning on reality, and, faced with an impending collapse of his own sense of selfhood, he becomes terrified. Yet, the individual is powerless to act, for the source of threat comes from within (a breakdown of cognitive structures) and not from any well-defined external danger.

Full-blown anxiety attacks are as rare as full-blown mystical experiences, and they are just as difficult to describe in ordinary language. However, the mere threat of anxiety can be a powerful motivating force, encouraging a wide variety of defensive maneuvers. This is why anxiety is so often invoked as an explanation for psychoneurotic symptoms. It is as though the individual were continually trying to shore up the walls of a crumbling edifice (cognitive structures) without ever repairing the edifice itself. The result is a rigid and unyielding personality, encrusted by defense mechanisms, and yet in constant peril of collapse.

Of the emotional syndromes considered thus far, anxiety would seem to be the one least suited to an analysis in terms of social roles. When anxiety is severe, the individual is in a state of psychological disarray. Such a state does not represent the enactment of a social role. Nevertheless, a role-analysis is not completely irrelevant to the problem of anxiety. For one thing, cognitive structures are, in large part, a product of socialization, and, when cognitive breakdown occurs, the residual structures that remain help determine the nature and quality of the experience. In this respect, it is meaningful to speak of culturally specific forms of anxiety. For another thing, when an individual is threatened with a collapse of cognitive structures, he may be assisted by a variety of formal and informal social roles. Many religious (and political) rituals can be viewed in this way (see, for example, Homans, 1941; Spiro, 1965).[9]

RELATIONSHIPS AMONG THE PARADIGMS

It must be emphasized that the threefold distinction among impulsive, conflictive, and transcendental emotions is primarily analytical. Any actual emotional syndrome may include aspects of all three paradigms, albeit to a greater or lesser extent. Moreover, the common name for an emotion is often a poor guide as to which paradigm best characterizes the syndrome. Consider the case of "fear." Many fears can be analyzed as impulsive emotions; for example, they involve straightforward responses to natural or socially defined dangers. But what begins as an impulsive fear may be transformed into a conflictive emotion. This may occur, for example, when a person comes to fear an object, not because of any realistic danger or past history of traumatic conditioning, but as a means of resolving some social or intrapsychic conflict. Fear can also be closely associated with anxiety, a transcendental emotional state. This association stems not only from the fact that both fear and anxiety have certain elements in common (e.g., physiological arousal, a feeling of dread); even more important, it stems from the fact that fear is often used as a defense against anxiety. That is, when an individual is faced with uncertainty, and normal cognitive processes prove to be inadequate, the "cause" of the problem may be projected on some external source. The latter then becomes the object of fear, which helps relieve anxiety by providing structure to the experience.

CONCLUDING OBSERVATIONS

I have defined emotions as "transitory social roles." I am not entirely satisfied with this definition, for it is based on metaphor. However, many psychologists may feel uncomfortable with the role-concept for another

[9]Before leaving the topic of anxiety, one final issue might be considered briefly. In the sociological literature, the concepts of anomie and alienation are used about as frequently as the concept of anxiety is used in psychology. And in casual discourse, the three terms are often used interchangeably. Yet, there are important distinctions among these concepts. Anomie involves a breakdown in social structures; such "normlessness" is, so to speak, the equivalent of anxiety on the social level of analysis. Anomie is often accompanied by anxiety, since social norms provide much of the support for cognitive structures; however, there is no necessary connection between these two conditions. Alienation, in contrast to anomie and anxiety, does not presume a breakdown of either social or psychological structures; rather, it represents a disjunction or mismatch between social and personal norms. Of course, if the disjunction results in a breakdown of cognitive structures, then alienation may lead to anxiety.

reason; namely, it implies that the emotions cannot be explained in strictly psychological or physiological terms. (Ironically, psychologists do not feel uncomfortable about the use of physiological metaphors—"conceptual nervous systems"—in the explanation of emotional behavior.) Concepts at the social level of analysis seem to carry a kind of "excess meaning" that is especially troublesome to psychologists. But is meaning "excessive" simply because it is not reducible to psychological or physiological terms? My answer to this question is, obviously, no. I would maintain that the meaning and significance of emotional syndromes can be fully understood only on the social level of analysis.

By this last statement, I am not suggesting that a social level of analysis is *sufficient* for an understanding of the emotions, only that it is *necessary*. But even this modest suggestion often meets with objection. Two of the reasons for objection deserve brief comment. First, the role-concept may make emotional reactions appear *too* meaningful or functionally significant. The parent who becomes angry at a child for spilling milk and the couple who fall romantically in love are not responding *in order to* fulfill some social obligation. Second, a role-concept, with its emphasis on the normative aspects of behavior, seems to ignore the abnormal and often harmful aspects of emotional behavior. The person who commits a crime of passion, the phobic who cannot leave the house, or the jealous husband who destroys his marriage—the behavior of such people is not explicable simply by reference to social norms.

With regard to the first objection, it is true that most persons do not become emotional in order to fulfill some social obligation. But a role-analysis is no more objectionable in this respect than is an analysis in terms of biologically based adaptive patterns. For example, two animals—or people—do not usually mate in order to produce offspring, and any particular act of mating may have no such effect. Nevertheless, the net result of mating by enough couples, a sufficient number of times, is reproduction of the species. Analogously, any specific episode of anger, love, fear, hope, pride, etc., may meet no social need. But if on the average, or over the long run, such emotional syndromes conform to social norms, then their net result will be functional within the social system.

With regard to the second objection, abnormal emotional reactions represent deviations from social norms. In general, three types of deviations may occur: (a) The emotion may be "flat," or fall short of social expectations; (b) the emotion may be exaggerated, or exceed social expectations; and (c) the emotion may be unsuited, as when a person laughs at a funeral, becomes angry at a favor, etc. The reasons for such deviation in emotional behavior are to be found in the motives, prior experience, and capacities of the individual, as well as in the immediate situation (e.g., conflicting demands and/or secondary gains). In this sense, the explanation of deviant emotional behavior is not fundamentally different from the explanation of normal emotional syndromes. The focus of attention is, however, different in each case. In the explanation of normal emotional syndromes, the focus is on commonalities (e.g., social norms), and the factors that contribute to individual differences are treated as background. In the explanation of emotional deviations, this figure-ground relationship must be reversed, and the factors that contribute to individual differences must become the focus of attention.

To summarize, then, emotional syndromes are among the roles societies create, and individuals enact, albeit with varying degrees of proficiency and fidelity. Often, an emotional role is built upon, or incorporates elements from, one or more biological systems of behavior. But the meaning of the emotion—its functional significance—is to be found primarily within the sociocultural system. The emotions are not remnants of previously serviceable habits, as Darwin maintained. Rather, they are presently serviceable, and one of the tasks of theory is to shed light on the functions that emotional syndromes now serve. This chapter is a prolegomenon to that task.

ACKNOWLEDGMENT

Preparation of this chapter was supported, in part, by a grant (MH 22299) from the National Institute of Mental Health.

REFERENCES

Arnold, M. B. *Emotion and personality* (2 vols.). New York: Columbia University Press, 1960.

Averill, J. R. Grief: Its nature and significance. *Psychological Bulletin,* 1968, *70,* 721–748.

Averill, J. R. An analysis of psychophysiological symbolism and its influence on theories of emotion. *Journal for the Theory of Social Behavior,* 1974, *4,* 147–190.

Averill, J. R. A semantic atlas of emotional concepts. *JSAS Catalogue of Selected Documents in Psychology,* 1975, *5,* 330 (Ms. No. 421).

Averill, J. R. Emotion and anxiety: Sociocultural, biological, and psychological determinants. In M. Zuckerman & C. D. Spielburger (eds.), *Emotion and anxiety; New concepts, methods and applications.* New York: LEA—Wiley, 1976.

Averill, J. R. Anger. In H. Howe & R. Dienstbier (eds.), *Nebraska Symposium on Motivation, 1978.* Lincoln: University of Nebraska Press, 1979. (a)

Averill, J. R. The functions of grief. In C. Izard (ed.), *Emotions in Personality and Psychopathology.* New York: Plenum, 1979. (b)

Averill, J. R. On the paucity of positive emotions. In K. Blankstein, P. Pliner, & J. Polivy (eds.), *Advances in the study of communication and affect,* Vol. 6: *Assessment and modification of emotional behavior.* New York: Plenum, 1980, in press.

Averill, J. R., & Boothroyd, R. On falling in love in conformance with the romantic ideal. *Motivation and Emotion,* 1977, *1,* 235–247.

Bem, D. J. Self-perception theory. In L. Berkowitz (ed.), *Advances in experimental social psychology,* Vol. 6. New York: Academic Press, 1972.

Berger, P. L., & Luckmann, T. *The social construction of reality.* New York: Doubleday, 1966.

Berkowitz, L. Some determinants of impulsive aggression: Role of mediated associations with reinforcements for aggression. *Psychological Bulletin,* 1974, *81,* 165–176.

Borden, R. J. Witnessed aggression: Influence of an observer's sex and values on aggressive responding. *Journal of Personality and Social Psychology,* 1975, *31,* 567–573.

Bourque, L. B., & Back, K. W. Language, society, and subjective experience. *Sociometry,* 1971, *34,* 1–21.

Buss, A. H., Booker, A., & Buss, E. Firing a weapon and aggression. *Journal of Personality and Social Psychology,* 1972, *22,* 196–302.

Chein, I. *The science of behavior and the image of man.* New York: Basic Books, 1972.

Costello, C. G. *Anxiety and depression: The adaptive emotions.* Montreal: McGill-Queen's University Press, 1976.

Deikman, A. J. Deautomatization and the mystic experience. *Psychiatry,* 1966, *29,* 324–338.

Dewey, J. The theory of emotion. I. Emotional attitudes. *Psychological Review,* 1894, *1,* 553–569.

Dewey, J. The theory of emotion. II. The significance of emotions. *Psychological Review,* 1895, *2,* 13–32.

Dienstbier, R. Attribution, socialization, and moral decision making. In J. H. Harvey, W. Ickes, & R. F. Kidd (eds.), *New Directions in Attribution Research,* Vol. 2. Hillsdale, N.J.: Lawrence Erlbaum Associates, 1978.

Fox, R. The cultural animal. In J. F. Eisenberg & W. S. Dillon (eds.), *Man and beast: Comparative social behavior.* Washington, D.C.: Smithsonian Institution Press, 1971.

Frodi, A. The effect of exposure to weapons on aggressive behavior from a cross-cultural perspective. *International Journal of Psychology,* 1975, *10,* 283–292.

Gehlen, F. L. Toward a revised theory of hysterical contagion. *Journal of Health and Social Behavior,* 1977, *18,* 27–35.

Goffman, E. *The presentation of self in everyday life.* New York: Doubleday Anchor, 1959.

Goldstein, K. *The organism.* New York: American Book, 1939.

Greeley, A.M. *Ecstasy: A way of knowing.* Englewood Cliffs, N. J.: Prentice Hall, 1974.

Hall, A. D., & Fagen, R. E. Definition of system. In W. B. Buckley (ed.), *Modern systems research for the behavioral scientist.* Chicago: Aldine, 1968.

Harré, R., & Secord, P. F. *The explanation of social behavior.* Totowa, N. J.: Rowman and Littlefield, 1972.

Hewett, J. P. *Self and society: A symbolic interactionist social psychology.* Boston: Allyn and Bacon, 1976.

Homans, G. C. Anxiety and ritual: The theories of Malinowski and Radcliffe-Brown. *American Anthropologist,* 1941, *43,* 164–173.

Izard, C. E. *Human emotions.* New York: Plenum, 1977.

James, W. *Principles of psychology,* Vol. 2. New York: Henry Holt, 1890.

Jensen, D. D. Polythetic biopsychology: An alternative to behaviorism. In J. H. Reynierse (ed.), *Current issues in animal learning: A colloquium.* Lincoln: University of Nebraska Press, 1970.

Kelly, G. A. *The psychology of personal constructs* (2 vols.). New York: Norton and Company, 1955.

Klinger, E. *Meaning and void: Inner experience and the incentives in people's lives.* Minneapolis: University of Minnesota Press, 1977.

Lazarus, A. A. Psychiatric problems precipitated by transcendental meditation. *Psychological Reports,* 1976, *39,* 601–602.

Lazarus, R. S. *Psychological stress and the coping process.* New York: McGraw-Hill, 1966.

Leeper, R. W. The motivational and perceptual properties of emotions as indicating their fundamental character and role. In M. B. Arnold (ed.), *Feelings and emotions: The Loyola Symposium.* New York: Academic Press, 1970.

Leventhal, H. A perceptual-motor theory of emotion. In K. Blankstein, P. Pliner, & J. Polivi (eds.), *Advances in the study of communication and affect,* Vol. 5: *Perception of emotion in self and others.* New York: Plenum, 1979.

Mandler, G. *Mind and emotion*. New York: Wiley, 1975.

McDougall, W. *An outline of psychology* (12th ed.). London: Methuen, 1948.

Mead, G. H. *Mind, self, and society*. Chicago: University of Chicago Press, 1934.

Nisbett, R. E., & Valins, S. Perceiving the causes of one's own behavior. In E. E. Jones, D. E. Kanouse, H. H. Kelley, R. E. Nisbett, S. Valins, & B. Weiner. *Attribution: Perceiving the causes of behavior*. Morristown, N.J.: General Learning Press, 1971.

Noyes, R. The experience of dying. *Psychiatry*, 1972, *35*, 174–184.

Parsons, T. *The social system*. New York: Free Press, 1951.

Parsons, T. An approach to psychological theory in terms of the theory of action. In S. Koch (ed.), *Psychology: A study of a science*, Vol. 3: *Formulations of the person and the social context*. New York: McGraw-Hill, 1959.

Plutchik, R. *The emotions: Facts, theories and a new model*. New York: Random House, 1962.

Rubin, Z. *Liking and loving: An invitation to social psychology*. New York: Holt, Rinehart, and Winston, 1973.

Sarbin, T. R., & Coe, W. C. *Hypnosis: A social psychological analysis of influence communication*. New York: Holt, Rinehart, and Winston, 1972.

Schachter, S. *The psychology of affiliation*. Stanford, Calif.: Stanford University Press, 1959.

Schachter, S. *Emotion, obesity, and crime*. New York: Academic Press, 1971.

Schafer, R. *A new language for psychoanalysis*. New Haven: Yale University Press, 1976.

Schutz, A. *On multiple realities*. In C. Gordon & K. J. Gergen (eds.), *The self in social interaction*, Vol. 1. New York: Wiley, 1968.

Scott, J. P. The emotional basis of social behavior. *Annals of the New York Academy of Science*, 1969, *159*, 777–790.

Segall, A. The sick role concept: Understanding illness behavior. *Journal of Health and Social Behavior*, 1976, *17*, 162–169.

Sokal, R. R., & Sneath, P. H. A. *Principles of numerical taxonomy*. San Francisco: W. H. Freeman, 1963.

Solomon, R. C. *The passions*. Garden City, N. Y.: Doubleday Anchor, 1976.

Spiro, M. E. Religious systems as culturally conditioned defense mechanisms. In M. E. Spiro (ed.), *Context and meaning in cultural anthropology*. New York: Free Press, 1965.

Szasz, T. S. *Law, liberty and psychiatry*. New York: Collier Books, 1968.

Tomkins, S. S. Affect as the primary motivational system. In M. B. Arnold (ed.), *Feelings and emotions: The Loyola Symposium*. New York: Academic Press, 1970.

Wallace, J. An abilities conception of personality: Some implications for personality measurement. *American Psychologist*, 1966, *21*, 132–138.

Willerman, L., Turner, R. G., & Peterson, M. A comparison of the predictive validity of typical and maximal personality measures. *Journal of Research in Personality*, 1976, *10*, 482–492.

Zillmann, D. Attribution and misattribution of Excitatory reactions. In J. H. Harvey, W. Ickes, & R. F. Kedd (eds.), *New directions in attribution research*, Vol. 2. Hillsdale, N. J.: Lawrence Erlbaum Associates, 1978.

Chapter 13

A PSYCHOANALYTIC THEORY OF AFFECTS

CHARLES BRENNER

ABSTRACT

Affects are complex mental phenomena. They include ideas as well as sensations of pleasure and unpleasure. Ideas plus pleasure-unpleasure sensations together constitute an affect as a mental (psychological) phenomenon.

Affects begin at the dawn of mental life, when ideas first become associated with sensations of pleasure-unpleasure. The latter are primarily connected with gratification and/or lack of gratification of instinctual drive derivatives (instinctual wishes). The development of affects and their differentiation from one another constitute an aspect of ego and superego development.

Some of the advantages of the psychoanalytic theory of affects proposed in this chapter are presented and discussed.

The data on which a theory of affects or emotions—I use the words synonymously—can be based fall into three categories. The first is subjective. It includes experiences we believe are common to mankind. The second is behavioral. Under this heading are included both actions mediated by skeletal musculature under voluntary control and such phenomena as changes in pulse rate, blood pressure, respiration, bladder or bowel function, lachrymal secretion, and hormonal release or production. The third includes observations of

Emotion: Theory, Research, and Experience
Volume 1: Theories of Emotion

the behavior of animals other than man—behavior that is believed to be relevant to what we identify as emotions in man. More briefly, then, the data are psychological, neurophysiological, and ethological.

Clearly, emotions are psychological phenomena. They are part of conscious mental life. The reason for our interest in them in the first place derives from subjective experience. Historically, therefore, the first classifications of emotions and the first attempts to study them systematically were based on introspection, since introspection was for a very long time the only method of study available.

The unreliability of introspection as a method of studying any psychological phenomena, emotions included, has long been evident on an empirical basis. More recently, psychoanalytic investigations have furnished a rational explanation for what had previously been only an empirical fact. These investigations have shown that the fundamentally decisive reason why adult human beings do not know all that they think and feel is that, throughout their lives, they go to considerable lengths to deceive themselves with respect to many of their most important thoughts and feelings. To depend on an adult subject's introspection for one's data, therefore, is to depend on data that are incomplete and that have been deliberately and systematically falsified and concealed.

The development of the psychoanalytic method, largely by Freud, has made it possible not only to understand the reasons for the unreliability of subjective data, as noted above, but also to overcome those reasons to a satisfactory degree in many cases. By applying the method under suitable circumstances, one gains access to subjective psychological data that are complete and reliable enough to serve as a satisfactory basis for theories of many previously obscure aspects of mental life, including that aspect we call emotions. To put it very briefly, the psychoanalytic method makes available psychoanalytic data to the investigator, that is, data from unconscious as well as from conscious mental life (Brenner, 1968, 1970). In what follows, I shall present what seems to me to be the most satisfactory theory of affect that can be derived from psychoanalytic data at the present time. In doing so, I shall draw heavily from a previous paper on the subject (Brenner, 1974). It will also be apparent that I assume that the reader has considerable familiarity with psychoanalytic theory in general and with the nature and extent of psychoanalytic data.

When one surveys the relevant psychoanalytic literature, one gains the impression that two major assumptions are operative in most discussions of affect theory. Both derive from Freud (1915a, 1919). One assumption is that each of the many affects listed in any dictionary can be descriptively differentiated from the others and studied as they are observed in each individual; for example, fear, terror, anxiety, and horror are separate though related affects and each is essentially the same, whoever the person may be who experiences it. In other words, it is assumed that basically everyone "knows" what each of these affects is, just as he knows what is sweet and what is sour, and that everyone may be expected to differentiate each affect in the same way.

The second assumption is that affects correspond to processes of instinctual discharge or gratification (Freud, 1915b, p. 178) and are to be understood primarily in economic, that is, in quantitative, terms. It is probably for this reason that psychoanalytic affect theory has usually been presented with relatively little reference to clinical data, though there have been many references to the importance of affects in clinical practice, and not a few articles devoted to the topic (e.g., Schafer, 1964).

THE PRESENT THEORY

The present theory departs from both of these assumptions. With respect to the first assumption, I suggest that it is not possible to differentiate affects from one another as sharply and as confidently as many have tended to do or to assume that they are uniform from one person to another. The theory I propose draws attention instead to the extremely individual nature of affects and to the degree to which they both vary from and overlap one another. With respect to the second assumption, the present theory adds to the purely economic considerations having to do with instinctual discharge (gratification) by stressing the importance of the role of psychic development with regard to both the nature and the development of affects. Moreover, the basis for both departures comes from the clinical data of psychoanalysis, that is, from data made available by the application of the psychoanalytic method. It is, in essence, a psychoanalytic theory and may be stated as follows.

Affects are complex mental phenomena that include (a) sensations of pleasure and unpleasure, or a mixture of the two, and (b) thoughts, memories, and wishes—in a word, ideas. Ideas and sensation together constitute an affect.

To avoid misunderstanding, it must be emphasized that either the idea(s), or the pleasure/unpleasure sensation(s), or both may be wholly or partly unconscious, that is, accessible only through the application of the psychoanalytic method. Only psychoanalytic data justify the statement that every affect includes both ideas and sensations of pleasure/unpleasure because either the ideas or the sensations of pleasure/unpleasure may be unconscious, that is, may be *apparently* absent from a given affective experience.

ONTOGENY OF AFFECT

Another important aspect of the present theory concerns the origins and development of affects—their ontogeny, as one may say. What analysts have learned of what they call ego development in general suggests that each affect has its beginning early in life when ideas first become associated with sensations of pleasure and unpleasure. Such sensations are most frequently and most importantly associated with the instinctual drives. They arise in connection with drive tension and drive discharge, that is, in connection with the satisfaction and the lack of satisfaction of instinctual wishes (i.e., derivatives of the instinctual drives). It is reasonable to assume that, for the most part, sensations of pleasure and unpleasure are not too different in adult life from what they are in childhood, that they undergo no special process of development. This assumption is, however, open to qualification, as, for example, most individuals do not experience orgasm before puberty. While the physical sensations that are part of the experience of orgasm are certainly special to that experience, it is very difficult to say whether the pleasure in orgasm differs from other and earlier sensations of pleasure except in its extraordinary intensity.

In any event, it seems fair to say that at present we have no certain knowledge concerning developmental changes in sensations of pleasure and unpleasure during the course of physical and mental maturation. On the other hand, it is obvious that the *ideas* that are part of an affect are wholly dependent on the level of psychic maturation and functioning (in psychoanalytic terms: ego development and ego functioning) with respect to their content and their complexity. It follows from this that the evolution of affects and their differentiation from one another depend on ego (and superego) development. It may be said, in fact, that the development of affective life is an aspect of psychic development, an aspect that can serve as one very important measure of the level of functioning that has been attained.

To repeat, one feeling of pleasure, or of unpleasure, can be differentiated from another only by its intensity and by the ideas and physical sensations associated with it. Pleasure and unpleasure are, as it were, biological givens in an infant's psychological development. Whenever it is during the first weeks or months after birth that mental life as such may be said to begin, the sensations of pleasure and of unpleasure of that early time are the undifferentiated matrix from which the entire gamut of the affects of later life develop as the mind matures.

As the theory of affects I have just advanced differs substantially from earlier formulations in the psychoanalytic literature, no detailed review of that literature will be offered here. It would be largely irrelevant. The interested reader is referred to Brenner (1974) for a list of the important references and a review of those most pertinent to the present theory.

The remainder of this chapter will deal with some of the implications contained in the theory just advanced. I shall emphasize implications of general psychological significance rather than those of primarily clinical importance for psychoanalytic or psychotherapeutic work. For a discussion of some clinical implications, the reader is referred to Brenner (1975, 1976).

THE LABELING OF AFFECTS

For one thing, the theory I have advanced offers a rational basis for defining various affects and for distinguishing among them, a statement that can best be justified by some illustrations. For instance, anxiety is unpleasure accompanied by an expectation that something unpleasurable is going to happen: in other words, unpleasure accompanied by ideas that in one way or another have to do with danger. Any affect, if it is to be called anxiety, must conform to this definition, according to the present theory. Under the broad heading of anxiety, however, different terms are often used to indicate variations both in the intensity of the unpleasure that an anxious person evidences and in the nature of the conscious and unconscious ideas associated with it. If the danger is perceived to be acute or imminent, we are likely to label the affect "fear." If the unpleasure is intense, we use the word "panic." If the unpleasure is mild and if the danger is slight, uncertain, or distant, we may well speak of worry or uneasiness.

The same considerations apply to other affects. When an affect is called "sadness," what is meant is unpleasure that is connected with ideas of something (bad) that has already happened—for instance, loss of a person important in one's life or physical injury (see Abraham, 1911/1927/1953). If, in the case of a person who is sad, the emphasis is on ideas of longing for a lost person, of wishing him back, we call the affect "loneliness." If, as Darwin (1872/1955) said, "We have no hope of relief," one speaks of despair. If the unpleasure is intense in such a case, it is called "misery" or "depression"; if the unpleasure is mild, it is called "discontent" or "unhappiness."

To turn to affects that are pleasurable, what we call happiness is a feeling of pleasure in connection with an experience or fantasy of instinctual gratification, no matter whether the gratification is wholly or in part unconscious. If the pleasure is intense, the affect is called "ecstasy" or "bliss." If the ideas have to do with having defeated a rival or rivals, the affect is called "triumph." Variants of triumph are called "omnipotence," "self-satisfaction," "mild superiority," or "smugness," depending on the intensity of the pleasure and the nature of the associated ideas. As one can see, in general, any attempt to define affects in psychological terms and to distinguish them from one another can only be done by (a) specifying the experience of pleasure or unpleasure and its intensity and by (b) making some reference to the content and origins of the associated ideas. Since the most significant ideas are often unconscious, it is also important to remember that an individual's own label is by no means always reliable. It may be or it may not be. Only a successful application of the psychoanalytic method can decide.

MIXED AFFECTS

It should be added that there are also affects characterized by a mixture of feelings of pleasure and unpleasure as well as by ideas that include various combinations of "good" and "bad" experiences and expectations. Such affects are rather the rule than the exception, at least in adult life, and are often to be understood as one aspect of what is called by analysts "ambivalence."

As an example of such a mixed affect, in some experiences of anxiety there is a conscious mixture of pleasure with unpleasure. In fact, in most clinical, psychotherapeutic experiences of anxiety one sees patients express unconscious pleasure (gratification of a repudiated childhood wish) as part of the experience called anxiety. Another clinical example is ideas of overcoming a rival, which often involve pity or compassion for the rival and an expectation of punishment for having defeated him. Such ideas and expectations are evidenced among persons who are not patients in psychotherapy—they are much more the rule than the exception to it. At any rate, in such cases, the winner experiences a mixture of pleasure and unpleasure along with the associated ideas of wanting and fearing to win, of being the loser's rival, and of being his ally, of dominating and of being dominated.

One is led by what has just been said to still another conclusion, namely, that the general categories of affect or emotion, such as anxiety, joy, rage, fear, and so on through all of the several hundred words that are listed under the headings of "affect" and "emotion," cannot be defined except in approximate terms. They are never precisely the same in any two individuals and may often be radically different from person to person. The same name may be used for very different constellations of pleasure, unpleasure, and ideas in different individuals. Moreover, even if those constellations are very similar, they are never quite the same in any two persons, and the differences are often of considerable importance. And the reverse is equally true. Different names may turn out to refer to very similar affective states. To take an example from clinical work, we customarily call some affective states "euphoria" instead of simple joy, precisely in order to emphasize their close kinship with sadness or depression. In such cases, what a euphoric person experiences *consciously* looks very much like joy. What his euphoria denies and conceals, however, is unconscious sadness, misery, or despair. In the same way, conscious courage, particularly recklessness, is often intimately related to unconscious anxiety, guilt, or even self-destructive tendencies.

Another implication of the present theory is that each affect is unique for each individual. Each person's affective life is his or her own and is never identical with that of another, since each person's wishes, memories, perceptions, fears, and expectations are never identical to those of another. More than this, an understanding of the connection between affects and mental development and functioning illuminates, at least in part, the vexing and otherwise unanswerable question of variations in the manifestations of affects, that is, the variations from one person to another of the ways of expressing affects. Why should it be that one person screams when frightened, another faints, and a third becomes nauseated? At least part of the answer to this question must derive from the fact that developmental influences in childhood are capable of such wide variations. Each person's childhood memories, wishes, and fears must greatly influence his or her particular forms of emotional expression in later life. They are at least in part determined by events of the past, which unconsciously shape behavior in the present—by events of childhood whose effects persist unconsciously throughout adult life.

In addition to individual variations in the manifestations of affect, there are also variations from culture to culture and from one social group to another. Here also, one can reach at least a partial understanding of the reasons for such variations by applying a developmental or ontogenetic approach. One of the important factors that must be involved has to do with identification. Children can be expected first to imitate and later to identify with and become like the significant adults in their environment with respect to manifestations of affect no less than with respect to various other aspects of behavior such as gait, speech, posture, recreational and vocational interests, etc. (Brenner, 1973, p. 216). The manifestations and expressions of affect must be unconsciously directed and influenced in their development in this and other similar ways that differ in different societies or cultures, leading to striking differences in the end results. Whatever other factors, both constitutional and experiential, may contribute to the manner in which affects influence behavior (in the broadest sense of the word) in adult life, an understanding of the connection between affective life and the whole complex sequence of psychic development in every individual must offer at least a significant part of the answer to the question of societal variations in affective manifestations as well as to the question of individual variations.

UNPLEASURE AND DEVELOPMENT

Another question of interest is the relation between physical pain and the evolution or development of affects in childhood. After all, unsatisfied instinctual wishes are not the only sources of unpleasure. Physical pain that results from injury or illness can cause intense unpleasure and, in many cases, intense unpleasure that is long continued, recurrent, or both. One might expect, a priori, that, in some cases at least, physical pain would play as important a role in the development of affects as unpleasure from instinctual sources. In fact, childhood illnesses and injuries, whether painful or not, are regularly woven into the fabric of instinctual life, as far as thoughts about them are concerned. They are experienced as evidence of mother's malice or of her faithlessness; they are thought to be consequences of incestuous fantasies, or punishments for the wishes giving rise to those fantasies; they symbolize castration, childbirth, or intercourse; they are seen as retribution for murderous and castrative wishes, and so on. Clinical experience demonstrates what one would not have expected, namely, that in childhood, especially in very early childhood, even pain and illness are secondary in their effect on mental development to the instinctual wishes and conflicts that so dominate the whole of mental life during those years.

This fact has interesting corollaries or consequences. Both in childhood and in adult life, physical pain is greatly influenced by unconscious psychological factors. Depending on those factors, pain may be greatly magnified or wholly extinguished. Thus, for example, a child who experiences as unbearably painful the sensations produced by having a tooth drilled or by being given a hypodermic injection in a pediatrician's office finds this experience painful because of what the drilling or the injection unconsciously symbolizes to him and the guilt and anxiety aroused as a result. His instinctual conflicts magnify the physical pain to an intolerable degree. On the other hand, every athlete and every soldier know that in the excitement of competition, as in the heat of battle, injuries that would otherwise be quite painful go wholly unnoticed. They begin to hurt only after the fray, not during it, and they do so, as in the example of the child, for reasons having to do with the individual's (often) unconscious instinctual life.

REFERENCES

Abraham, K. Notes on the psycho-analytical investigation and treatment of manic-depressive insanity and allied conditions. In *Selected papers of Karl Abraham*. London: The Hogarth Press and The Institute of Psycho-Analysis, 1927; New York: Basic Books, 1953, pp. 137–156. [Originally published 1911.]

Brenner, C. Psychoanalysis and science. *Journal of the American Psychoanalytic Association,* 1968, *16*, 675–696.

Brenner, C. Psychoanalysis: Philosophy or science? In C. Hanly, M. Lazerowitz, (eds.), *Psychoanalysis and philosophy,* pp. 35–45. New York: International Universities Press, 1970.

Brenner, C. *An elementary textbook of psychoanalysis* (2nd ed.). New York: International Universities Press, 1973.

Brenner, C. On the nature and development of affects: A unified theory. *Psychoanalytic Quarterly,* 1974, *43*, 532–556.

Brenner, C. Affects and psychic conflict. *Psychoanalytic Quarterly,* 1975, *44*, 5–28.

Brenner, C. *Psychoanalytic technique and psychic conflict*. New York: International Universities Press, 1976.

Darwin, C. *The expression of the emotions in man and animals.* New York: Philosophical Library, 1955. [Originally published 1872.]

Freud, S. Repression. In J. Strachey (ed.), *Standard Edition,* Vol. XIV, pp. 146–148. London: Hogarth Press, 1957. [Originally published 1915.] (a)

Freud, S. The unconscious. In J. Strachey (ed.), *Standard Edition,* Vol. XIV, pp. 177–179. London: Hogarth Press, 1957 (and the Institute of Psycho-Analysis). [Originally published 1915.] (b)

Freud, S. The 'uncanny', In J. Strachey (ed.), *Standard Edition,* Vol. XVII, pp. 219–252. London: Hogarth Press, 1957 (and the Institute of Psycho-Analysis). [Originally published 1919.]

Schafer, R. The clinical analysis of affects. *Journal of the American Psychoanalytic Association,* 1964, *12*, 275–299.

Chapter 14

A STRUCTURAL MODEL OF EMOTION
AND PERSONALITY: PSYCHOANALYTIC
AND SOCIOBIOLOGICAL IMPLICATIONS

HENRY KELLERMAN

ABSTRACT

A structural theory of personality is described that is based on a model of emotion. The theory proposes a specific network of relationships between various levels of personality. These include the levels of emotion, defense, diagnosis, and intrapsychic forces, as well as dreams and nightmares. The structural connections between these levels are understood in the context of psychoanalytic principles but the entire personality is presumed to be rooted in a biological program that provides predispositions for the development of personality. The theory suggests ways in which psychoanalytic and sociobiological forces interact. A series of postulates are presented to formalize some of these relationships.

The network of personality relationships that I have tried to develop here and in my book *Group psychotherapy and personality: Intersecting structures* (Kellerman, 1979) has its roots in the theoretical work done by Plutchik (1962, in press) on emotion. It will be proposed in this chapter that the theory of emotion may be utilized to show the connective links between various aspects of personality. Part of the conceptualization is supported by research and part still remains speculative and subject to the results of further empirical testing.

Emotion: Theory, Research, and Experience
Volume 1: Theories of Emotion

There are two important outcomes of the theory. First, it helps make sense out of the sea of facts and phenomena regarding the various levels and dimensions of personality, such as emotions, defenses, dreams, and so forth. Second, it makes possible the integration of personality theory with psychoanalytic precepts and offers a new way of understanding the connection between developmental conflicts and the intrapsychic apparatus.

The personality construction to be elaborated contains principles relevant to sociobiologists as well as to psychoanalysts. Genetic and biological dispositions are hypothesized to exist at birth and are defined as personality propensities. (Some of these include emotion and defensive inclinations.) It is presumed that the psychodynamic environmental interaction with these biological dispositions determines the extent to which conflict is generated in the personality. These genetically coded dispositions may be understood as epigenetic or biological given phenomena, whereas development viewed in a psychoanalytic context is considered to be adaptational.

EPIGENETIC AND EVOLUTIONARY ELEMENTS OF PERSONALITY

Freud obliquely referred to the interaction of epigenetic and evolutionary phenomena when he proposed that the content of the unconscious is phylogenetically determined. It might be more specifically proposed that emotions contain a deep structure that includes id or superego regulatory features. Kaywin (1960) focused precisely on this point by stating,

> The mental system is an epigenetic expression of . . . a hierarchic developmental outgrowth from a biological organization. . . . The mental system obviously has certain potentials, which are inherited givens. To what degree these potentials will be realized will depend on the dynamic interplay between the potentials and the conditions (organismic-environmental) to which they will be subjected.

Thus, the study of emotion and personality is presumed to contain psychological as well as sociobiological aspects.

Schafer (1964) begins to connect, however tentatively, the system of emotions, traits, defenses, psychosexuality and adaptation, and intrapsychic superego structure. Schafer states that an analysis of an affect may be compared to the analysis of a complex symptom; that is, the affect is determined by two distinct influences. First, there are tendencies that reflect instinctual gratifications; second, there are defenses and superego influences correlated to the emotion. Thus, as Novey (1959) also suggests, affect must be seen in terms of intrapsychic as well as interpersonal communication. The emotion or affect system is apparently far more complex than simply the study of anxiety. Needles (1964) states, "Metapsychological considerations alone are insufficient to account for the pleasure–unpleasure experience and the biological and evolutionary factors—in other words, our biological heritage—must be included in any such attempt.''

The structure of personality presented here is conceived as both epigenetic and evolutionary, and in this chapter, emotions will be related to defenses, diagnostic dispositions, and intrapsychic and psychosexual formulations.

PSYCHOANALYTIC BACKGROUND

There has been a great deal of psychoanalytic theory elaborating many of Freud's original formulations with respect to emotion, defense, diagnostic disposition, intrapsychic forces, and developmental stages. Most notably in emotion theory, Bowlby (1969, 1973), Brenner (1974, 1975), Kaywin (1960), Novey (1961), Rado (1956), and Schafer (1964) have attempted to provide new ways of explicating the psychology of emotion so that it is more than simply a theory of anxiety. On the level of mechanisms of defense and coping adaptations, work by such authors as Blum (1953), Anna Freud (1937), Hartmann (1950, 1959), Ostow (1959), Rado (1956), and Vaillant (1971) have shown that the study of ego-defense development is a much broader one than is implied only by the psychology of repression. On the level of symptoms, syndromes, and diagnostic and psychosomatic problems, Arieti (1974), Knapp (1958), Rapaport (1954), Waelder (1951), and White (1948) imply that such states are directly related to emotion and defense levels. With reference to intrapsychic structures and the appearance of psychosexual conflict stages, a wide variety of theoretical papers have suggested that both structural and psychosexual formulations are by no means well understood (Blum, 1953; Brenner, 1975; Kaywin, 1960; Klein, 1948; Novey, 1959).

Although Freud refers to the subject of affect throughout his publications (the terms affect and emotion are used interchangeably), it is never treated in a systematic way (Freud, 1915a, b, 1917, 1919, 1926). Rapaport (1953) and Kaywin (1960) describe three phases in the early history of psychoanalysis through which Freud's ideas with respect to emotion evolved. In each phase the nature of affect seemed to be implicitly tied to discharge of drive and to the management of impulse. In the first phase, affect was equated with mental energy or with a quantity of mental energy. This energy facilitated drive discharge. It ''fueled'' behavior. In the second phase, affects were instinct representations and served as ''safety valves'' to manage undue amounts of drive discharge. Here the affects were thought to require expression, and if blocked would overflow. The overflow occurred through the safety valve and implied that energy could be transformed into symptoms and diagnostic syndromes such as phobias and obsessions. This transformational quality became the basis for Freud's energy displacement hypothesis. In the third stage, affects were not considered to be safety valves but became signals of anxiety. As signals of anxiety, affects were psychic reasons for repression to occur.

Within the confines of this psychoanalytic view of affect, Freud apparently could not conceive of emotion without some corresponding statement of its relation to defensive function and to impulse. For example, in his earlier work, Freud conceived of anxiety as a result of repression. However, in his later formulations, anxiety became the reason for the repression. In this later formulation (Freud, 1926), the affects were now ego related and were used to perceive and to distinguish internal events from environmental ones. Freud's references to the relationships among emotion, anxiety, and repression were among the first theoretical statements that implied a connection between emotion, defense, and symptoms. He indicated that repression was always involved in the appearance of hysterical symptoms and that repression as a defensive operation was necessary in order to manage intense emotion (Freud, 1895, 1926). This led to the proposition that all defenses are reactions to emotion or to anxiety about emotion. For example, the idea referring to "anxiety about emotion" implied that repressed emotions may generate, in conscious form, tension or anxiety. Anxiety, therefore, was understood to be a reaction to the inability to cope with overwhelming stress and implied the presence of some underlying emotion.

Freud also postulated two kinds of instincts or drives, the sexual and the ego. In the analysis of these instincts, he implied that the intrapsychic forces of id, superego, and ego are related to aspects of personality such as emotion, defense and diagnostic disposition, or diagnostic type. He proposed a source, an aim, and an object for each drive. The object of the drive was presumably to satisfy interpersonal or intrapersonal needs. The source and the aim of each drive referred to whether the needs involved were id or superego ones, and it was this id–superego intrapsychic nature of the drive that implied its connection to emotion, defense, and diagnosis. These theoretical connections were rather speculative. They were not fashioned into a parsimonious system that could clearly show the specific relations between structural concepts, such as id or superego, and the concepts of emotion, defense, and diagnostic disposition. More specifically, although the introduction of the concept of repression as well as energy-displacement theory paved the way to the study of ego-defense development, it did not show how the structure of ego-defense mechanisms systematically related to the structure of emotions. In addition, although anxiety and symptoms were related to diagnosis as well as to psychosomatic disturbances, Freud left the task of discovering a basic diagnostic structure of personality to future writers; that is, he never formulated a basic system of diagnostic constructs that was related to the structure of intrapsychic forces or embedded within a system of emotion. Furthermore, although Freud attempted to show the formation of intrapsychic structures to be, in part, dependent on the vicissitudes of psychosexual development, he never completely designed a master plan that would, in fact, fully show these relationships.

In this chapter, an integration of various aspects of personality on the basis of a theory of emotion will be suggested. Some of the more recent literature on the levels of emotion, defense, and diagnostic states or dispositions will be introduced in support of this integration. Aspects of the work are new and speculative and are based on the theoretical and experimental work described in Kellerman (1979). Thus, some of the theoretical integrations of emotion and personality structure described in this chapter await further examination and evaluation by researchers who, it is hoped, may become interested in this work. The following sections of this chapter will include theoretical discussions and an attempt to create a structural model of emotion, defense, diagnostic dispositional states, and intrapsychic elements. I will begin by raising the problem of determining a basic system of emotion.

THE PROBLEM OF DETERMINING
A BASIC EMOTION SYSTEM

A key idea in the elaboration of affect theory was proposed by Bowlby (1969, 1973). In a general sense, Bowlby suggested that emotion terms refer to dispositions and as such are etched in the substrate of instinctive behavior. This proposition is a far-reaching one. It suggests an epigenetic view of personality that assumes that dispositional or diagnostic forces are infused within the emotion.

The idea of connecting emotion to basic instinctive or behavioral patterns has been suggested by several authors. McDougall (1921) formulated a basic list of instincts that were related to emotion. A similar formulation of behavioral categories is later stated in the research by Scott (1958) on comparative behavior and in the work of Plutchik (1962, in press) with respect to emotion theory. One of the fundamental questions asked by these writers is, How many basic emotions are there?

It was not until the 1950s that a formal attempt to determine a basic emotion system was undertaken by Plutchik, who, in a series of papers (1955, 1957, 1958, 1962, 1970), attempted to derive the complement of basic emotions as they are reflected in prototype basic behavioral patterns seen throughout the evolutionary scale. For example, anger may be considered a basic emotion and is reflected in a basic prototype variably called aggressive, agonistic, attack, or destructive behavior. The determination of all other basic emotions is similarly generated from an evolutionary–adaptational context. In this context, basic emotions are derived from a system of basic behavioral categories. Rado (1956) states in this respect that the "emotion is a component in a behavior pattern" and implies that the structure of emotions may be viewed with greater meaning in the presence of their corresponding prototype patterns. Rado (1956) lists at least seven affect patterns and McDougall (1921) also lists seven instincts and relates these to corresponding affect patterns. Scott (1958) lists nine patterns of behavior and Plutchik (1962) lists eight basic prototype behavior patterns and eight basic corresponding emotions.

Plutchik's concept of basic emotions has been described elsewhere (1962, 1970, in press) and is further elaborated by Plutchik in Chapter 1 of this book. There are many aspects to the theory other than the concept of basic emotions. However, it is that aspect of the theory—the formulation of basic emotions and their corresponding behavioral patterns—that is most immediately relevant to the theoretical construction of a personality system to be described here.

EMOTIONS AND DEFENSES

Both Brenner (1974, 1975) and Rado (1956) suggest that emotion is linked with defense mechanisms. Rado indicates through his theory of "emotion as emergency reactions" that the emotions are connected to coping behaviors and contain a regulatory feature. Brenner suggests that defenses are used to decrease feelings of displeasure, again implying the regulatory role of defenses in relation to emotion. Brenner further suggests that, when defenses become impaired or do not regulate well, symptoms may develop.

There are several questions that need to be raised when relating emotion to defense. First, is: can defenses specifically be derived from each basic emotion? Another important question relates to the qualitative differences between defenses; that is, it may be that certain defenses such as "identification" and "introjection" become utilized in the development of personality or character traits. Other defenses, the so-called traditional ego defenses such as displacement, projection, regression, and denial, may be utilized to manage emotions as transitory reactions in the personality, reactions not immediately concerned with, or involved in, the development of enduring trait formations. Therefore, in formulating a defense system, it would seem useful to ascertain a basic number of defense mechanisms that can be related to the basic emotions and, perhaps, to distinguish between those defenses that function to manage transitory emotions and those designed to aid in the construction of more enduring trait patterns.

HOW MANY DEFENSES ARE THERE?

The literature on ego defenses, starting with Freud, proposes lists of defenses that do not always overlap. For example, Freud (1926), in his paper "Inhibitions, Symptoms and Anxiety," listed regression, repression, projection, isolation, introjection, undoing, and reaction formation. In the work by Healy, Bronner, and Bowers (1930), 17 dynamisms (a euphemistic reference to defenses) are listed. These include displacement, transformation, symbolization, idealization, unconscious fantasy, repression, reaction formation, projection, isolation, undoing, conversion, introjection, identification, sublimation, rationalization, idealization, and dream work. Brenner (1975) lists the defenses of undoing, denial, reaction formation, displacement, repression, identification with the aggressor, isolation, projection, compensation, identification, and introjection.

Of all defenses listed, there are some that seem best to reflect defense processes in the service of character trait formation. These are introjection, idealization, and identification. These defenses are perhaps utilized in the service of trait formation or in the development of personality styles. This is what is meant by the development of more enduring traits. Other defenses that are listed, such as transformation, symbolization, unconscious fantasy, conversion, and dream work, seem more to be definitions of defensive processes or, for example, in the case of transformation, to be a synonym for the term defense itself. The remaining defenses of displacement, repression, reaction formation, projection, isolation, undoing, sublimation, rationalization, denial, and compensation may be utilized in the personality most often to manage transitory emotional reactions.

Anna Freud, in her well-known book *The ego and the mechanisms of defense* (1937), refers to those defenses listed by Sigmund Freud in his paper "Inhibitions, Symptoms and Anxiety" and adds sublimation and displacement to the list. Yet, she too does not distinguish between those defenses designed to manage intense transitory emotion and those involved more in character formation. She does, however, propose a hierarchical system of defense mechanisms, beginning with those considered most primitive, and implies that others may be considered higher-order defenses. The notion of hierarchies of defense seems to be an important one and is further considered by English and Finch (1964), Ewalt and Farnsworth (1963), and Semrad (1967). There are other authors with varying lists of ego defenses. Coleman (1956) lists 17 ego-defense mechanisms Frazier (1975) lists 23 ego defenses, and Vaillant (1976) lists 18 ego defenses. The lists overlap to varying degrees.

In terms of a hierarchical arrangement, Blum (1953) proposes that the defenses appearing earliest, more or less in the first year of life, include introjection, projection, denial, fixation, and regression. All other defenses are more sophisticated and appear as a function of further development. In a reference to work by Fenichel, Blum indicates that Fenichel considered successful defenses to create a "cessation of blocked impulses (sublimation)" while unsuccessful defenses produced repetition behavior utilizing defenses of denial, projection, introjection, regression, repression, reaction formation, undoing, isolation, and displacement.

Therefore, in the study of defense as related to emotion, it may be useful to establish a hierarchy of defense, a basic defense system—one that clarifies how many basic defenses there are—and a way of distinguishing defenses that deal with character development from those that manage momentary and transitory emotion. Vaillant (1971), after defining defense mechanisms as unconscious processes used to resolve conflict between instinctual needs, internalized prohibitions, and external reality, also suggests such a distinction. He notes that defenses can be used to manage affects in problematic situations, to resolve homeostasis, to buy time, and to manage loss and that, in addition, they can be seen as characteristic life styles.

This review of some of the psychoanalytic literature on affect and on defenses indicates that no single system has been developed that is accepted by the mainstream of psychoanalytic writers with respect to the organization of defenses and emotions. In the following section a model that shows the relationship between emotions and defenses shall be proposed. In this model, a system of eight basic defenses is derived from the theory of emotion set forth by Plutchik (1962; and in press).

A PROPOSED MODEL OF
EMOTION AND DEFENSE MECHANISMS

There are six postulates that are proposed with respect to the nature of the similarity structure of defenses and the relation of defense mechanisms to emotions. These are elaborated in Kellerman (1979).

POSTULATE 1:   *Specific defenses are designed to manage specific emotions.*

POSTULATE 2:   *There are eight basic defense mechanisms that have evolved to deal with the eight basic emotions.*

POSTULATE 3:   *The eight basic defense mechanisms show the properties of both polarity and similarity.*

POSTULATE 4:   *There are other defense mechanisms chiefly used in the service of character trait formation. These are the defenses that are usually labeled as identification defenses.*

POSTULATE 5:   *Major diagnostic personality types are derived from particular defensive styles.*

POSTULATE 6:   *An individual may utilize any combination of the defense mechanisms.*

The relation of some specific emotions to specific defenses has been occasionally cited in the psychological literature, but not in any systematic way.

However, when such connections are made they are usually discussed in a way that implies their close functional relations; for example, in social psychological studies of scapegoating and of the authoritarian personality, the expression of the emotions of anger and hate is frequently better understood when examined in connection with the defense of displacement. This sort of connection is also made with other emotions and defenses. In the following presentation, an attempt will be made to show some connections between the eight basic emotions and what are considered to be their corresponding defense mechanisms. These relationships are the basis for the postulates given above.

THE EMOTION OF ANGER AND
THE DEFENSE OF DISPLACEMENT

There is a wide cross-disciplinary literature suggesting the intrinsic relation between the emotion of anger and the defense of displacement; for example, in social psychological studies of scapegoating and hate, referred to above, when anger cannot be expressed directly it becomes indirectly expressed toward substitute target figures (Bychowski, 1968; Lasswell, 1952). In ethological studies (Kaufman, 1960; Lorenz, 1966), it was shown that this phenomenon of indirect displaced attack even occurs in animals. An example of this sort of connection is given in a study of a baboon troop, which has implications for the human group process (Kellerman, Buirski, & Plutchik, 1974). This relationship between anger and displacement is also traced in a theoretical study of personality (Kellerman, 1977).

THE EMOTION OF FEAR AND
THE DEFENSE OF REPRESSION

It is proposed that the emotion of fear is managed most generally by the defense mechanism of repression. Insofar as fear generates escape as well as withdrawal feelings, repression acts to eliminate threatening material from consciousness. Clinicians frequently find that it is generally fearful patients who show the most intense repression. The nature of the fear may concern unconscious feelings of anger, or it may simply be the desire to avoid painful memories. When fearfulness subsides, such patients generally begin to remember dreams, and clinicians then refer to "the lifting of repression." It is further proposed that, although repression is the central quality that defines all defenses, it is most prominent in the management of the emotion of fear.

In studies of hypnosis, for example, "fears" are frequently reported to become freed from their "repressions."

THE EMOTION OF JOY AND
THE DEFENSE OF REACTION FORMATION

In the psychoanalytic literature, the defense of reaction formation is considered to permit the translation of one emotion into its opposite. More specifically, reaction formation is designed to deflect one's attention from pleasurable attractions. As Jones (1929) stated, one affect can be the defense for another; for example, the appearance of a disgust emotion in a dream is usually interpreted to reflect the final point of the emotional experience. Presumably, what originally started with sexual attraction was converted by the defense of reaction formation to its opposite, disgust feeling. Ostow (1959) also indicates that reaction formation may deflect instinctual energy from a forbidden activity to its opposite, for example, from soiling to cleaning. It should be added that reaction formation is utilized because soiling is experienced as pleasurable. It is proposed here that reaction formation is utilized in the personality to translate any emotion into its opposite, provided that the conversion was originally based on pleasure and attraction. Therefore, the defense of reaction formation may be best understood as fundamentally related to the management of pleasure or the emotion of joy.

THE EMOTION OF SORROW AND
THE DEFENSE OF COMPENSATION

The emotion of sorrow or sadness may be generated from object-loss experiences or from a loss of self-esteem (Ostow, 1959). The relation between sorrowful feelings and self-esteem problems is frequently experienced during adolescence. The central defense utilized to manage such self-esteem- or object-loss-related problems is the compensation defense. Adolescent fantasies are almost entirely compensatory in character. During object-loss experiences, identification with the object as an internalized symbol produces a sense that something "inside" was lost. This identity loss experience needs to be replaced, or in some way regained. The compensatory mechanism manages, through aggrandizing fantasy or expansive behavior, to accomplish this aim. It is an attempt to overcome the effects of a real or perceived loss. Mahler's theoretical work (1968, 1971) on separation–individuation in infants in relation to the appearance of depressive feelings provides a partial basis for the connection of sorrow, self-esteem, and the defense of compensation.

THE EMOTION OF ACCEPTANCE
AND THE DEFENSE OF DENIAL

The emotion of acceptance is implied in traits of suggestibility, gullibility, the absence of a critical attitude, and the tendency to idealize. The defense of denial is tied to idealization needs (Lachman & Stolorow, 1977) and to the trait of suggestibility. Denial is a defense that becomes necessary in all ideal-izations, especially because the idealized object is accepted entirely and not only in part. Thus, it is proposed that the defense of denial is designed to manage the emotion of acceptance. A partial or part-object acceptance could not adequately constitute a full expression of the emotion of acceptance. The denial is designed to permit the full experience of acceptance. It acts as a selec-tive inattention device screening out all but a possible whole perception of the object; that is, it acts to screen out any possible criticism of even a small part of the object.

THE EMOTION OF DISGUST AND
THE DEFENSE OF PROJECTION

In several of Freud's papers (e.g., 1911, 1922) and in the general psychiatric literature, the emotion of rejection, disgust, loathing, or severe criticality is related to paranoia and the central defense mechanism of projection. The pro-jection mechanism creates a vehicle for nothing to be accepted and for everything to be criticized or disliked. The emotion of disgust is managed by the defense of projection so that the object of the disgust remains external and alien to the personality. Thus, it is not what is "inside" that is disgusting and needs criticism; rather, the "outside" objects are the ones that are disgusting and need criticizing. This relation of self-devaluation and projection is a key element in the dynamics of the paranoid personality.

THE EMOTION OF EXPECTATION AND
THE DEFENSE OF INTELLECTUALIZATION

The emotion of expectation is related to the expression of needs to control. Anticipation and "set" are synonyms of expectation at different intensity levels. The central defense mechanism of intellectualization is designed to help with control needs implicit in expectation. "The intellectualization implies control or non-motoric transformation of an impulse" (Plutchik et al., 1979). In clinical practice, psychoanalysts also understand the intellectual defense mechanism to be a regulator of needs to control or to anticipate. It is apparent in clinical practice that patients with severe intellectualized defenses need to anticipate events in the environment. These are persons who need to control impulse and to prevent motoric or impulsive acting-out. This is what is meant by a non-motoric transformation or control of an impulse.

THE EMOTION OF SURPRISE AND
THE DEFENSE OF REGRESSION

The emotion of surprise reflects a dyscontrolled, uncontrolled, or unexpected experience. Just as intellectualization is used to control impulse for the person needing such controls, so too is the defense of regression used to minimize controls for the person needing to maintain a "motoric," action-oriented way of functioning. Therefore, it is proposed here that the emotion of surprise or "needing adventure" or "action" contains an impulsive inclination seeking to be expressed. Regression is a defense mechanism that is frequently observed by clinicians to be utilized in the service of acting-out or in impulsive behavior. It is the regression that permits an ongoing motoric condition to exist so that the individual who needs to "move" may do so without restriction. There are diagnostic correlates to this formulation and they will be discussed in a later section.

Figure 14.1 shows the proposed similarity structure of emotions, defenses, and diagnostic dispositions. At a glance it is possible to see the specific emotion–defense relationships and the system of emotion–defense polarities. Inspection of Figure 14.1 shows the proposed opposition of the following pairs: denial and projection, reaction formation and compensation, repression and displacement, and intellectualization and regression. These are considered to be the main defense mechanisms designed to manage the basic emotions. Of all other defenses it may be said that they are of a different nature; that is, they are designed to manage other developmental and identification–introjection events. These other defenses include, for the most part, identification, and introjection. These second types of defenses are used to entrench character traits. The two types of defense mechanisms address the issue of distinguishing between primary and secondary defenses suggested by English and Finch (1964).

In Figure 14.2, a schema or mnemonic "it" device is used to show the proposed similarity structure of the defense system. It is an attempt to create a statement for each defense that implies a corresponding emotion. For example, the statement that reflects displacement is "attack something that represents it." The "it" represents an event, a person, or an impulse that evokes the emotion relating to that particular defense. Tracing the "it"

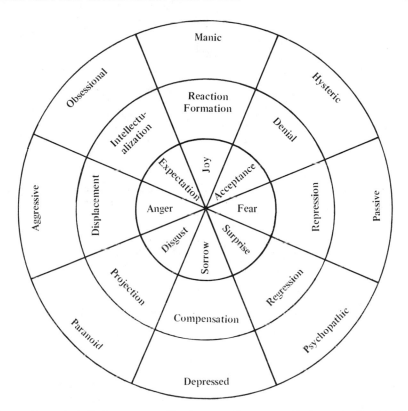

FIGURE 14.1.   A similarity structure of basic personality systems. Each emotion listed in the in-
nermost circle has a mechanism of defense associated with it that is listed in the middle circle. Personality dispositions are associated with each emotion–defense dimension listed in the outermost
circle. The system is constructed on the basis of the law of neighboring and of the law of polarity;
that is, those dimensions that are adjacent on the circle are most similar (e.g., manic and hysteric),
whereas opposite dimensions are most dissimilar (e.g., manic versus depressed). The associated
emotions, defenses, and personality dispositions are considered to be basic states of the personality from which all other emotions, defenses, and personality dispositions are derived [From
Kellerman H. & Plutchik, R. The meaning of tension in group therapy. In L. R. Wolberg, M. L.
Aronson, A. R. Wolberg (eds.), *Group Therapy 1977: An overview*. New York: Stratton Intercontinental Medical Book Corp., 1977.]

around the circle in Figure 14.2 creates a tentative logic in terms of how one
defense may be similar to another. In the discussion of emotion and defense,
it becomes apparent that diagnostic considerations are also intricately tied to
both emotion and defense. This idea is presented in Postulate 5 which states,
"Major diagnostic personality types are derived from particular defensive
styles." In view of this postulate, the relation between emotion, defense, and
diagnosis will be suggested in the following section.

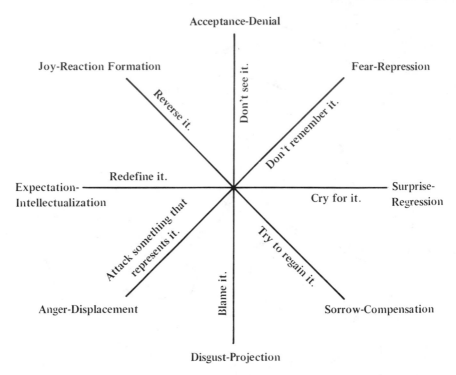

FIGURE 14.2. The "it." A mnemonic device to create an image of each defense mechanism. A similarity structure of defenses is revealed by the continuous images around the circle.

THE RELATION OF EMOTIONS, DEFENSE MECHANISMS, AND CLINICAL DIAGNOSIS

Engel (1962), Menninger (1963), Symonds (1945), and Vaillant (1976) suggest that a theory of ego mechanisms implies a theory of diagnosis. Figure 14.1 shows one way to understand these relationships. The idea that diagnostic types correspond quite closely to emotional types or to persons with specific defensive styles has been proposed by many other writers. Freud (1926) proposed the connection between particular disorders and special defenses in his paper "Inhibitions, Symptoms and Anxiety." He offered two main examples that show the relationship between diagnosis and defense. These were the hysterical diagnostic type associated with the defense of repression and the paranoid diagnostic type associated with the defensive syndrome of introjection, identification, and projection. The idea of a defensive syndrome that is utilized in the service of a particular diagnostic state is suggested in Postulate 6 which states, "An individual may utilize any combination of the defense mechanisms." Thus, the defense structure is a flexible one; that is, even though it is suggested that specific defenses may have been designed in the personality to manage specific emotions, the defense system nevertheless is a highly "selected" one because any number of defenses may be employed in a syndromal fashion or as an aggregate. For example, in clinical psycho-analytic usage, the diagnosis of paranoia is generally considered a dispositional state in which defenses of denial, rationalization, projection, reaction formation, introjection, and identification are used. Some of these defenses, as described previously, may be basically designed to manage diagnostic and emotional states other than paranoia. Nevertheless, the flexibility of the defense system allows for a diagnostic "borrowing-of-defenses."

The connection between emotion and diagnostic disposition was studied by Kellerman and Plutchik (1978). In this study, a group of drug addicts was tested with the Emotions Profile Index (EPI). This test is a paper-and-pencil forced-choice index in which a group of personality trait terms are paired in all possible combinations. Each trait term is coded for its underlying constituent emotions. Thus, subjects select trait terms as best self-descriptions but are scored in terms of underlying basic emotions. Subjects are required to choose one adjective in every pair that seems the best self-description. When all choices are accumulated, each of the eight emotions may be assigned a frequency rank; that is, based on one's choices, each of the basic emotions will have been chosen a different number of times. It is possible then to derive a rank ordering of each of the eight basic emotions from "chosen most" to "chosen least" (Plutchik & Kellerman, 1974).

In this study, each subject was rated on the EPI by every other subject. The EPI profile of each subject was matched against the EPI profile of every other subject. "Profile similarity" was then ascertained, and this technique allowed the creation of a sociogram-like diagram in which members of the group were located on the diagram in terms of their emotion profile similarity. The presence of certain emotions in particular areas of the diagram correlated with the location of particular subjects and with the location of diagnostic descriptions. For example, one sector of the diagram was described "as an area locating subjects who are diagnostically passive and withdrawn. Emotions such as fear, caution and remoteness" characterized subjects located there. The results of the study showed a close correspondence between emotions and diagnostic dispositions in a way that supports the relation between specific emotions and specific diagnoses to be outlined in the following section on the diagnostic system.

THE DIAGNOSTIC SYSTEM

In this section, the diagnostic system will be related to emotions and to defenses. Each basic diagnosis will be called a "disposition" to indicate that inherent in its essential derived nature is an inclination or propensity that has its roots in the genetic and biological organization of the system.

THE HYSTERICAL DISPOSITION

The dispositional state of the hysteric is characterized by high suggestibility. The hysteric needs to accept everything and criticize nothing. The high degree of suggestibility requires the use of a defense mechanism that can enable an individual to screen out any critical attitude regarding the perceived object. It is akin to utilizing selective inattention or perceptual defense. The emotion of acceptance and the defense of denial are the structural components of hysterical functioning that permit this dispositional type to engage in the idealization of the perceived object; for example, hysterical types fall in love frequently. The idealization of the perceived object and the warding off of any critical feelings permit this repetitive "swoon" to occur.

THE PARANOID DISPOSITION

The paranoid disposition is characterized by the absence of significant suggestibility and by the presence of a severely critical attitude. On the emotion level, disgust or rejection underlies this dispositional type. On the defense level, projection is used to fend off any possibility of self-criticism. All imperfections must be perceived as located in the external world. The dispositionally paranoid person is one who experiences profound personal incapacity and needs to defend against seeing it. The perceived object must be criticized. This type of person in everyday life experiences a "buyer's regret" in decisions to affiliate. This means that the paranoid person finds it very difficult to accept or to "buy" anything. The act of buying or the decision to affiliate means that something has been accepted. Whenever this occurs, this type of person experiences a regret. The regret is an attempt to reject the item or object that has been accepted.

THE PASSIVE DISPOSITION

The passive dispositional type is characterized by an inert, non-action attitude. Withdrawal, remoteness, and avoidance behavior also describe this kind of person. The emotion underlying the passive disposition is apprehension, fear, or terror, or any other degree of intensity of these emotions. To maintain the passive stance, massive repression is brought to bear on day-today experiences so that the repressive defense constitutes the central defensive core of the passive personality type. The repression permits the main withdrawal and avoidance reactions to exist. The utilization of repression as the chief defensive function of the passive type implies the need for a seventh postulate to be added to the six postulates regarding defenses that have been stated:

POSTULATE 7: *Although all defenses contain a repressive element, repression was originally developed to manage the emotion of fear, which is the chief underlying component of the passive dispositional diagnosis.*

THE AGGRESSIVE DISPOSITION

The aggressive person shows behavior quite opposite to that of the passive type. Typical behavior of the aggressive person reflects underlying anger as the chief emotion. The defense of displacement has been developed in the personality to manage the expression of anger and aggression. This means that, were it not for the operation of the mechanism of displacement, ongoing dissatisfactions in the personality would be continuously and directly expressed to on-target figures. Such behavior could cause untold upheavals, inappropriate reactions, and retaliations in many situations. Displacement permits the channeling of aggression toward substitute, safer figures, those who may absorb the anger without it causing immediate repercussions.

THE OBSESSIVE DISPOSITION

The obsessive type is one who needs to control or to map the environment. Anticipation and expectation are emotions that underlie the controlling attitude. The defensive condition designed to manage the need to control includes a syndrome of mechanisms. These are intellectualization, rationalization, sublimation, and undoing. The defense that best represents this aggregate is the intellectualization mechanism. This mechanism permits all impulses to be screened and sorted.

THE PSYCHOPATHIC DISPOSITION

The psychopathic dispositional type is opposite to that of the obsessive type. While the obsessive type needs to employ defenses in order to maintain control, the psychopathic type is inclined to do quite the opposite: This kind of person needs to maintain a control-free state amounting to an impulsive condition that permits the motoric expression of needs. As previously described, the defense of regression manages the need for the constant expression of impulse. The defense of regression permits a continual retreat "to earlier or more immature patterns of behavior and gratification" (Plutchik *et al.*, 1979). Apparently at deeper levels the psychopathic type feels extremely overcontrolled and is compelled to generate a counterforce in order to undermine these feelings of overcontrol that threaten to surface. The psychopathic type needs to create an abundance of stimulation or surprises in the external environment to counteract what is perceived to be a basic internal paralysis and "deadened" feeling. The basic emotion underlying this type is that of surprise.

THE MANIC DISPOSITION

The manic dispositional type is an energized type who needs to be involved in projects. Good feelings toward people and a gregarious and intense sociality characterize manic behavior. The emotion of joy or sexuality is inherent in this diagnostic type. The manic type contains in its basic nature the potential for needing an overabundance of pleasurable stimuli. It is suggested that the defense of reaction formation has developed, therefore, to manage undue amounts of pleasure-need in the personality. In psychoanalytic terms, the reaction formation results from superego prohibitions against the attraction to pleasurable stimuli, especially toward those objects that will become repressed based upon socialization requirements. One such example is the attraction to Oedipal figures. These attractions to pleasurable objects or stimuli contain sexual implications, which was discussed in the section on emotion and defenses (p. 354). The reaction formation acts to maintain a moderate degree of positive response to pleasurable perceptions by converting non-socialized attractions of a sexual nature to opposite avoidance experiences.

THE DEPRESSED DISPOSITION

The depressed personality type is one who suffers from real or imagined object loss, from a loss of self-esteem, or from a perceived low self-esteem. In any case, the depressed type presumably perceives loss. The underlying emotion of this diagnostic disposition is that of sorrow or sadness. The chief defense used to avoid feelings of depression or to manage potentially sorrowful feelings is proposed to be compensation. The compensatory defense is especially effective in helping to maintain higher self-esteem. It is the defense mechanism also through which restitutive processes are maintained; that is, in the period of reconstituting oneself from depressive or otherwise debilitating emotional states, the defense of compensation is chiefly used.

Inspection of Figure 14.1 shows the proposed network of relationships between the various emotions, defenses, and diagnoses. It may be seen, for example, that in this system depressive and paranoid dispositions are more similar, based on the proximity of their location to one another, than are depressive and manic diagnoses. On the emotion level, sorrow and disgust are more similar, based on the proximity of their respective locations, than are sorrow and joy. On the level of defense, the system suggests that compensation and projection may be more similar, based on their neighboring location to one another, than are defenses of compensation and reaction formation. An elaboration of these relationships appears in Kellerman (1979).

One of the questions that might be asked at this point is whether some subdivision may be made of the eight basic categories. For example, are there some types that are inherently "healthier" than others? In the following section an attempt will be made to show that the eight basic dimensions are divided into two kinds of categories. These two kinds of categories may contain implications for the relation between diagnosis and maladjustment.

ACCESSIBLE VERSUS IMPEDANCE STATES

In a study of maladjustment (Kellerman, 1965; Kellerman & Plutchik, 1968), hospitalized patients were divided into three groups. The first group consisted of "normal" female patients on an obstetrics ward in a general hospital. The other two groups consisted of female patients hospitalized for emotional or mental disorders in a state hospital, and these two groups were divided on the basis of degree of maladjustment: One group of patients was judged to be moderately disturbed while the other was judged to be severely disturbed. The Emotions Profile Index was administered to patients in each group. Results for patients in the "normal" group indicated that four of the eight basic emotions were activated to significantly higher levels than the levels to which their opposite emotions were activated. The emotions activated to higher levels in the normal group were acceptance, joy, fear, and expectation. Those activated to lower levels were disgust, sorrow, anger, and surprise. As maladjustment increased, that is, as an analysis of the moderately and severely disturbed groups was made, the emotions profile tended to change. The emotions that were highly activated in the normal group were activated to a lesser extent in the maladjusted groups. Those emotions hardly activated in the normal group became highly activated in the disturbed groups.

In Figure 14.3(A), the normal relative activation pattern of each of the eight emotion dimensions is seen. Categories of acceptance, joy, fear, and expectation are greatly activated, whereas the categories of disgust, sorrow, anger,

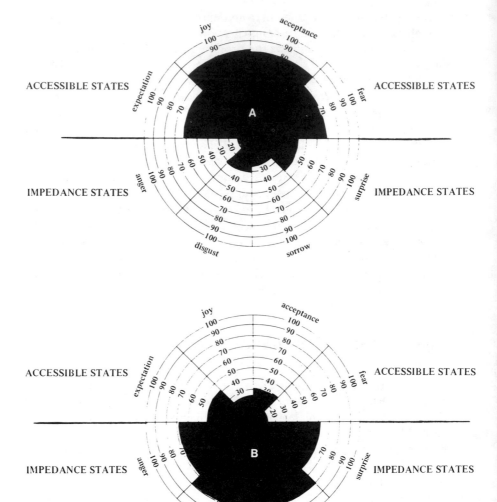

Figure 14.3 (A) A "normal" emotions profile showing the activation of the accessible categories. (B) A mirror-image "disturbed" emotions profile showing the activation of the impedance categories. The midpoint of the circle represents 0%. The outer rim of the circle represents 100%. [From Kellerman, H. *Group psychotherapy and personality: Intersecting structures.* New York: Grune and Stratton, 1979. Reprinted by permission. Copyright © 1979 by Grune and Stratton.]

and surprise are activated only to a minimal extent. In Figure 14.3(B), a hypothetical mirror-image profile is presented to contrast a disturbed profile with the normal one presented in Figure 14.3(A). This contrast suggests that the disgust, sorrow, anger, and surprise categories, if highly activated, may reflect more pathological states in the personality; that is, the higher activation of these emotions reflects greater maladjustment. Because of this implication, the emotions of disgust, sorrow, anger, and surprise are termed "impedance" states to suggest, as the concept does in engineering principles, a resistance or disturbance. The concept of the impedance state, therefore, is used here to reflect those emotion–diagnostic categories that are more problematic or that may potentially create greater difficulty for people in day-to-day living. In contrast to the impedance states, the emotions of acceptance, joy, fear, and expectation imply "accessibility." This means that as the normal profile is approximated, the emotions of acceptance, joy, fear, and expection will be highly activated, reflecting greater ease and less interpersonal difficulty for people in day-to-day living (Kellerman, 1979).

A SPECIAL FOCUS ON FEAR AND ANGER

It may seem difficult to understand why the emotion of fear is included among the accessible emotions. Yet, when all trait terms on the EPI were evaluated and rated in terms of their social desirability, results showed that all traits containing a component of fear were considered to be socially desirable. Traits such as "obedience" and "caution" are examples of fear-related traits considered to be desirable traits to have. Those traits that were least desirable contained anger components. Traits such as "quarrelsome" and "resentful" arc two examples. In the normal group, fear-related traits were among those frequently chosen as best self-descriptions, whereas anger-related traits were among those traits least chosen. As maladjustment increased, this pattern tended to become reversed; that is, in the maladjustment groups, anger-related traits were chosen as best self-descriptions while fear-related traits were chosen less as best self-descriptions. A normal accessible profile generally portrays high pleasure scores, low depression scores, high caution scores, and low anger scores. A maladjusted profile generally displays the opposite pattern: high depression scores, low pleasure scores, higher anger scores, and lower caution or fear scores.

It can be hypothesized that, were the "impedance" states to be highly activated and their opposite "accessible" states only minimally activated, the resulting profile would reflect a relatively disturbed individual. This was vividly portrayed in a study by Platman et al (1971) in which pre- and post-suicidal profiles were presented. Figure 14.4 shows both pre- and post-suicidal patterns. The pre-suicidal pattern showed a distinct impedance pattern while the post-suicidal pattern was more or less normal and showed the higher activation of accessible emotions. The differences between accessible and impedance categories as they relate to the entire personality system are described by Kellerman (1979).

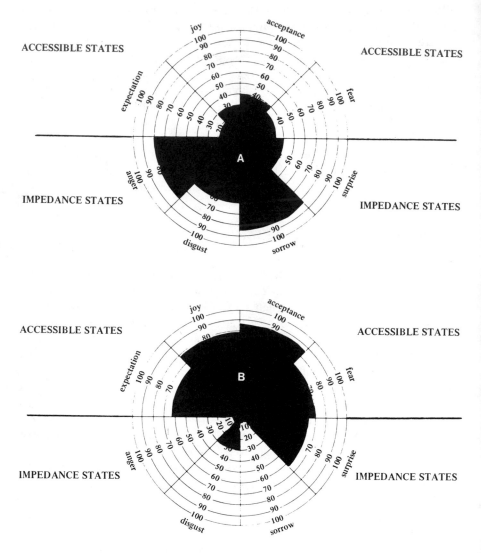

Figure 14.4 Comparison of emotion profiles of a hospitalized patient. (A) Immediately preceding a suicidal attempt. (B) Immediately following the suicidal attempt. The activation of impedance categories correlates to the pre-suicidal period. The activation of accessible categories correlates to the post-suicidal period. The midpoint of the circle represents 0%. The outer rim of the circle represents 100%. [From Platman, S. R., Plutchik, R., & Weinstein, B. Psychiatric, physiological, behavioral and self-report measures in relation to a suicide attempt. Reprinted with permission from *Journal of Psychiatric Research,* 1971, *8,* 127–137. Copyright © 1971, Pergamon Press, Ltd.]

DEFENSE MECHANISMS ASSOCIATED
WITH ACCESSIBLE AND IMPEDANCE DIAGNOSES

One question raised by the differences between accessible and impedance states is whether the defense mechanisms corresponding to these emotions serve different functions for those that are accessible as compared to those that are impeded. Analysis of defenses designed to manage emotions reflecting accessible diagnoses indicates that most of these serve to block impulse expression. For example, reaction formation is designed to *block* an over-response to pleasure, joy, or sexuality. Intellectualization is designed to *block* any impulse that could undermine the need to expect or to anticipate or the need for control. Denial is designed to *block* the perception of unpleasant realities.

In contrast, most defenses designed to manage emotions that reflect impedance diagnoses serve to release impulses. Compensation is designed to *release* impulses that increase self-esteem in order to manage feelings of loss, sorrow, or depression. Regression functions to *release* impulse in order to maintain an action-oriented attitude and to avoid any possibility of a non-motoric condition. Projection is designed to *release* criticism toward the environment in order to avoid self-criticism.

What emerges from this finding is that defense mechanisms have two distinct functions: Some have developed to permit impulse expression and some have developed to block it (Kellerman, 1979). This idea of defenses as either blocking or releasing mechanisms suggests that defenses are performing an intrapsychic function relating to each basic diagnostic state; that is, defenses designed to block impulse may be performing an id-management function while those designed to release impulse may be performing a superego-management function. The superego is understood in theory to serve withholding, punitive, and controlling functions, while the id is thought to aim continually for release and expression. The job of the defenses, therefore, is to regulate these intrapsychic forces: to moderate both id and superego aims.

Some interesting insights emerge from this formulation; for example, intellectualization serves to block impulse expression. This suggests that the obsessive clinical diagnosis of which intellectualization is the central defense is at its deepest layer guarding against a presumed basic id nature. The obsessive person may need to control an impulsive nature. The defense of intellectualization, therefore, may be considered to be a superego defense counteracting and managing the id nature of the obsessive. This is an illuminating finding since the obsessive is one who develops inordinate control mechanisms such as compulsions, ruminations, and rituals. The question that has been asked about the need for such inordinate controls may now be provided with one possible answer: The obsessional person needs to control an underlying desire to release impulse. For various psychodynamic reasons, this need is not considered to be safe, and so this kind of person develops control defense mechanisms such as intellectualization, rationalization, and undoing. As the underlying needs for release of impulse increase, control features of the obsessive also increase, and these include additional compulsions and the appearance of more and more ritualistic behavior. This kind of dynamic, the connection between the intrapsychic defensive purpose within emotion and diagnostic states, may be illustrated for each of the other accessible and impedance categories. Thus, this finding suggests that it may be possible to talk about the intrapsychic nature of emotions as well as of defenses and diagnoses.

The task remains of identifying each of the eight dispositional states in terms of their respective intrapsychic designations. One way of approaching this problem is through the analysis of dreams and nightmares. The appearance of a nightmare suggests that the defensive function in the dream was not performing properly. When defenses do function properly a person presumably remains sleeping. When the dreamer's defense is not operating effectively the dreamer will awaken with a nightmare in which emotion is experienced in its intense, undefended form. It is this nondefended, intense emotion that may reveal the underlying intrapsychic nature of each diagnostic state. Since nightmares are states in which emotions are expressed at their highest intensities, the following section will present a conceptualization of nightmares that helps reveal the basic underlying intrapsychic designations—id, ego, or superego—of each diagnostic state.

A BASIC SYSTEM OF NIGHTMARES
AND THEIR INTRAPSYCHIC DESIGNATIONS

A nightmare may be defined as a content of a dream that awakens the dreamer. This proposition broadens considerably the notion that nightmares are only dreams of terror since a multitude of dream emotion-contents may awaken the dreamer. It is proposed that, compared to the infinite number of dreams that people may dream, only a few basic nightmare emotion themes may exist (Kellerman, 1979). The nightmare is always experienced with some intense emotion. It is further proposed that there are only eight basic nightmares. These nightmares correspond to each of the eight basic structures of personality that contain emotion, defense, and diagnostic elements. All other non-nightmare dreams cannot be readily categorized with respect to any of the basic eight categories. When the nightmare occurs, the central underlying intrapsychic position of the dream is revealed. Thus, the infinite number of dreams that may occur becomes reduced to a few basic emotional themes when the dream develops into a nightmare.

In the following discussion I will attempt to outline each of these basic nightmare themes and try to show how they reveal the underlying intrapsychic nature of each basic diagnostic state. The system of nightmares and the resulting correlation with the entire personality system of emotion, defense, diagnostic disposition, and intrapsychic forces suggest a series of postulates. The theory and postulates are fully elaborated in Kellerman (1979).

POSTULATE 1:   *There are eight basic nightmare themes that correspond to the eight basic categories of the entire emotion–personality system.*

POSTULATE 2:   *Any basic nightmare is a reflection of the dreamer's current diagnostic disposition.*

POSTULATE 3:   *Any of the basic nightmare themes may be experienced; for example, a manic person may experience nightmares of grief that are characteristic of persons feeling depressed. This is possible because the manic person's feelings at the time of the dream may include depressive elements.*

POSTULATE 4:   *Each nightmare theme reveals the basic intrapsychic nature of each diagnostic state.*

POSTULATE 5:   *Although there are an infinite number of dream contents, when they become nightmares, they reveal only eight basic emotion themes.*

The following provides an analysis of each basic nightmare theme.

NIGHTMARES OF TERROR

The terror nightmare is one that reflects extreme fear. It occurs when the mechanism of repression is inadequate to release the basic impulse of the passive personality, which is to act out an urge to escape. Contents of such nightmares include running in terror from an attacker, being physically harmed, and being unable to escape from an attacker fast enough. The nightmare of terror in which fear, punishment, and the general feeling of dread prevail corresponds to a superego reference in which a sense that the dreamer is weak or bad exists. This reflects the existence of superego impulses in the personality called the passive type. Repression is the defense used to regulate these superego impulses. When the repressive defense does not fulfill its function, a nightmare will occur that reveals the superego nature of this personality type. The sense of dread and terror that the dreamer experiences is a result of superego pressure in the personality, which leads the dreamer to accept the role of the bad object or of the one who deserves punishment—an implicit superego demand. In this sense, it is proposed that the passive personality containing the central emotion of fear and managed by the repression defense produces a nightmare of terror and is revealed to be a superego dispositional type. In other words, the passive personality is revealed to be a diagnostic type in which an inherent superego nature is managed by the *impulse releasing defense* of repression.

NIGHTMARES OF RAGE

The rage nightmare reflects extreme anger and occurs when the mechanism of displacement is inadequate to block direct expression of anger or create safe overflow channels for the expression of anger. The appearance of the rage nightmare reveals the basically destructive nature of the aggressive personality type. Contents of such nightmares include harming someone else, shooting or stabbing someone, and screaming at someone instead of being screamed at. The nightmare of rage in which there appear anger, execution of punishment, and a general feeling of permission to assault is assumed to be based on an id formation in which there is a sense that the dreamer has been somehow vindicated. This means that, in the absence of the blocking defense of displacement, anger is expressed in its fullest most direct manner. The aggressive type is an id dispositional type insofar as anger and rage are expressed in an unbridled way. Instead of expecting punishment in the superego sense, as in the case of the nightmare of the passive type, the aggressive type becomes the attacker and is free of superego prohibitions. Because of an id nature, this type feels a sense of permission and feels vindicated to express anger in its fullest form. It is proposed that the aggressive personality containing the central emotion of anger and managed by the displacement defense produces a nightmare of rage and is an id dispositional type. In other words, the aggressive personality is a diagnostic type in which an inherent id nature is managed by the *impulse blocking defense* of displacement.

NIGHTMARES OF SEXUALITY

The sexual dream is one that can also develop into a nightmare when the dreamer is awakened by intense, undefended emotion. In this case, the dreamer is awakened by sexual orgasm or near orgasm. This can only be possible when the defense of reaction formation, which acts to block an overflow of pleasurable–sexual impulses, becomes momentarily impaired or for some other reason becomes inadequate to its task. In the absence of reaction formation, the manic person may be directing substantial energy toward sexual release. The reaction formation was originally designed to manage the joy–pleasure emotions. Contents of such nightmares include any playing out of sexual fantasies in the dream to a desired conclusion. This can include anything from the mere touching of various body parts to actual sexual intercourse or may involve any other erotic gratification whatsoever. The nightmare of orgasm or sexual arousal in which the general feeling of release is experienced is based on an id formation. This means that, in the absence of the defense of reaction formation, sexuality or pleasure is experienced in its fullest id expression. Therefore, it is proposed that the manic personality containing the primary emotion of joy and managed by the reaction formation defense produces a nightmare of sexuality and is an id dispositional type. In other words, the manic personality is a diagnostic type in which an inherent id nature is managed by the *impulse-blocking defense* of reaction formation.

NIGHTMARES OF GRIEF OR CRYING

The nightmare of grief or crying is one that reflects intensely sorrowful feelings. It occurs when the defense of compensation is not functioning effectively. Contents of such nightmares include variations of dreaming of the death of a loved one and awakening to find oneself sobbing or crying in grief.

The nightmare of crying in which sorrow and the general feeling of loss are experienced corresponds to a superego formation in which a sense that the dreamer has lost a last chance exists. Thus, in the absence of the compensation defense, the loss seems irretrievable. What this suggests is that in the personality of the depressive dispositional type there exist superego urges that generate feelings of inadequacy and a sense of extreme dependence on external figures for support and nurturance. The compensation defense is designed, therefore, as a releasing impulse mechanism in order to increase self-esteem. It is proposed that the depressed personality containing the primary emotion of sorrow and managed by the defense of compensation generates a nightmare of grief and is a superego dispositional type. The depressed type is a diagnostic type in which an inherent superego nature is managed by the *impulse-releasing defense* of compensation.

NIGHTMARES OF FALLING OR LOSS OF CONTROL

The nightmare of falling either off a building or mountain or other high place and awakening in fright reflects the basic fear of the overcontrolled intellectualized obsessive type. It occurs when the obsessive defenses are incapacitated. These defenses are designed to control any impulses and to guard against loss of control over them. These are blocking defenses. When they become impaired, for example, nightmares of falling or dreams in which bedwetting occurs awaken the dreamer. The bedwetting dream, frequently experienced by children, occurs when the child utilizes rationalization and dreams of already being in the bathroom, thereby making it unnecessary to control bladder activity. Children are surprised when awakened by the bedwetting not to find themselves in the bathroom.

There is a common misconception regarding "falling" dreams in which people believe that falling from a building or other high place and hitting the ground will actually prove fatal to the dreamer. This conception has no empirical or theoretical basis. Should the dreamer dream of hitting the ground but not awaken, then the dream cannot be considered a nightmare. This implies that the controlling defenses are not impaired and that the "falling" has a meaning other than loss of control. The nightmare of loss of control in which the dreamer awakens corresponds to an id reference in which, however momentary, a sense of release takes place. This suggests that, in the absence of controlling defense mechanisms such as intellectualization, the underlying id impulses of this obsessional type that usually necessitate overcontrol finally become fully expressed. As previously suggested the id impulses associated with the obsessive type may be inherently quite intense. This provides a rationale for the appearance of so many control features in this type—rituals, obsessions, compulsions, ruminations, and the use of several defenses (e.g., intellectualization, rationalization, undoing, and sublimation). It is proposed, therefore, that the obsessive personality containing the central emotion of expectation and managed by the defense of intellectualization produces a loss of control dream and is an id dispositional type. Thus, the obsessive personality is a diagnostic type in which an inherent id nature is managed by the *impulse-blocking defense* of intellectualization.

NIGHTMARES OF PARALYSIS OR OVERCONTROL

The nightmare of overcontrol is one in which the dreamer experiences an inability to move. This occurs when the defense mechanism of regression becomes impaired. Instead of impulses being released which occurs when regression is operating, they become blocked when regression is impaired. The dreamer awakens startled and deeply troubled by an excruciatingly experienced dream "paralysis." This is the typical nightmare of a psychopathic dyscontrolled personality. Contents of such nightmares include being buried alive, drowning, and being "hotly" pursued by a dangerous figure but not being able to move. The nightmare of paralysis and its resulting panic correspond to a superego reference in which there exists a sense that the dreamer is about to suffer dire consequences. This means that in the nature of the psychopathic personality there may exist strong superego impulses. This kind of person feels exceedingly vulnerable and, therefore, may need to feel completely free of physical restrictions. It must be remembered that this psychopathic type tries to create external stimulation in order to counteract a "deadened" internalized sense. This "deadened" sense is reflected in the feeling of paralysis that emerges in the nightmare. The regression defense ensures a condition of movement or ensures a continual motoric condition. In the absence of such defense, the worst fear of the psychopathic type is realized: to be completely "stopped" and therefore, perhaps, to feel vulnerable to the full punitive measure of the superego. It is proposed that the psychopathic dyscontrolled personality containing the central emotion of surprise and managed by the regression defense produces a nightmare of panic–paralysis and is a superego dispositional type. This dyscontrolled type is, then, a diagnostic type in which an inherent superego nature is managed by the *impulse-releasing defense* of regression.

NIGHTMARES OF LAUGHTER

The nightmare of laughter is one in which the dreamer awakens because of something said or seen that is apparently humorous. The dreamer begins to laugh and awakens. Laughing occurs because, in the absence of the denial defense, critical feelings toward external figures are likely to be expressed in the form of sarcasm or wit. The dreamer awakens because of the surprise or ego-alien nature of the dream; that is, this kind of dream seems to be produced by the hysteric personality type who wishes to accept all and to avoid seeing or experiencing any critical feelings toward external figures. The defense of denial is used to regulate this wish. In the absence of denial, the release of critical feelings reflects id aims. When denial mechanisms are incapacitated the dreamer may then experience a distinct boundary between experiences that are internal and those that are external. The external world now may be criticized. The dreamer usually awakens feeling either surprised, amazed, or perplexed. It is proposed that the hysteric personality containing the central emotion of acceptance and managed by the defense of denial produces a nightmare of laughter and is an id dispositional type. This hysteric disposition is, then, a diagnostic type in which an inherent id nature is managed by the *impulse-blocking defense* of denial.

NIGHTMARES OF FRAGMENTATION

The body fragmentation nightmare is generally produced by the critical paranoid diagnostic type. The dreamer awakens feeling perplexed and sometimes frightened. Contents of such nightmares include watching while one's arm falls off, seeing one's penis split apart and viewing other similar fragmentation of body parts. These sorts of nightmares also generate feelings in the dreamer of disgust, revulsion or nausea. These nightmares occur when the projection defense becomes incapacitated so that the critical paranoid type can no longer limit criticism to objects exclusively external to the self. In the absence of the projection defense, then, intense self-criticism occurs in the form of body fragmentation themes. The paranoid type needs to project criticism and to notice all imperfections in the world instead of confronting a profound sense of personal imperfection. Thus, in the absence of the projection defense, a nightmare occurs that reflects this extreme sense of imperfection in the form of a body fragmentation dream. This sort of nightmare seems to indicate that the basic nature of the paranoid type reflects superego formation. The superego element of this type is represented by a sense that the dreamer lacks solidity, is unworthy, and is therefore subject to punitive superego effects. It is proposed that the paranoid personality represented by the primary emotion of disgust and managed by the projection defense produces a nightmare of fragmentation and revulsion and is a superego dispositional type. The paranoid personality disposition, then, represents a diagnostic type in which an inherent superego nature is managed by the *impulse-releasing defense* of projection.

DISCUSSION OF THE PERSONALITY SYSTEM

In Figure 14.5, the intrapsychic id–superego forces are related to the basic nightmares and dispositional types, and in Table 14.1 these id–superego forces are summarized in terms of their defensive purpose. Each superego category is placed opposite an id category. This is meant to imply that, within the basic system of emotion described here, the entire personality structure, as it is arranged in terms of its particular polarities, is consistently paralleled by polarities on the levels of diagnosis and intrapsychic structure. Furthermore, in view of the categorization of nightmares and the relation of emotion to intrapsychic forces of id and superego, it may now be suggested that the emotions of joy, acceptance, anger, and expectation may be considered id emotions based on their expression in nightmares when unencumbered by defenses. Similarly, the emotions of sorrow, disgust, fear, and surprise may be superego emotions, since, in the nightmare state, in the absence of defenses, they seem to reflect superego formations or to be revealed with superego effects. It may also be suggested on the same basis that the manic, hysteric, aggressive, and obsessive diagnoses may be corresponding id diagnoses, whereas the depressed, paranoid, passive, and psychopathic diagnoses may be superego ones.

This proposal, in part, explains why the accessible diagnoses are activated

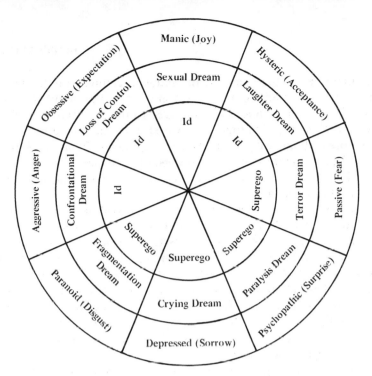

Figure 14.5 The intrapsychic structure of each of the eight basic emotion-dispositional categories. Typical nightmare themes are indicated. (From Kellerman, H. *Group Psychotherapy and Personality: Intersecting Structures*. New York: Grune & Stratton, Inc., 1979.)

TABLE 14.1

THE INTRAPSYCHIC NATURE OF DIAGNOSTIC STATES:
RELATION OF DEFENSES TO NIGHTMARES

Diagnostic disposition	Defense	Purpose of defense	Nightmare theme based on impaired defense	Intrapsychic force revealed by nightmare
Manic	Reaction formation	To block impulse	Sexual–Orgastic–pleasure	Id
Depressed	Compensation	To release impulse	Grief–sobbing	Superego
Obsessive	Intellectual-ization	To block impulse	Loss of control, falling–bedwetting	Id
Psychopathic	Regression	To release impulse	Paralysis, drowning, being buried alive	Superego
Aggressive	Displacement	To block impulse	Attacking–stab-bing–hitting	Id
Passive	Repression	To release impulse	Terror–running–escaping	Superego
Hysteric	Denial	To block impulse	Laughing–sarcastic wit	Id
Paranoid	Projection	To release impulse	Fragmentation–body parts falling off	Superego

(From Kellerman, H. *Group Psychotherapy and Personality: Intersecting Structures*. New York: Grune & Stratton, Inc., 1979.)

so much more on the Emotions Profile Index as compared to the impedance diagnoses in a "normal" profile. Apparently it is "normal" to experience higher levels of the id emotions as compared to the superego ones. When the superego emotions are abnormally activated, the emotions profile begins to reflect a more pathological pattern. This is suggested in Figure 14.4, where the pre-suicidal pathological pattern is superego-impedance dominated while in the postsuicidal pattern the id-accessible emotions are once again normally activated and thus dominant.

The system of nightmares presented here also reveals more about the nature of the dream work as described by Freud (1900). Freud proposed that the latent dream is converted to its manifest descriptive level through the process of dream work. This dream work includes the operation of translating mechanisms made up of condensation, symbolization, displacement, and secondary elaboration. The implication is that, if the constituent dream work mechanisms do not function properly, then the dreamer cannot remain sleeping. According to Freud, in the absence of the dream work an infusion of dream stimuli composed of primary process material would then surface, thereby producing a nightmare.

The new conceptualization of nightmares presented in this chapter may offer a refinement of a traditional Freudian understanding of the nightmare. Thus, it may be proposed that, when the dream work mechanisms do not function adequately, the dreamer will only experience what is commonly called an anxiety dream and, most important, will remain asleep. The nightmare will occur only when two conditions exist. First, there needs to be some impairment in dream work mechanisms, and, second, the central defense mechanism for that particular person's current diagnostic disposition must also be impaired; for example, if an individual is experiencing some loss, the defense mechanism of compensation must somehow be incapacitated simultaneously with the impairment of dream work mechanisms in order for that person to generate a nightmare characterized by sobbing, crying, or the experience of grief. When the dream work mechanisms do not operate, but the compensatory mechanism does, then it is suggested that this person will only experience an anxiety dream, will remain asleep, and will not produce a nightmare. The system of nightmares and personality structure presented here as it relates to the development of ego is described in Kellerman (1979).

A CONCLUDING NOTE

Traditional psychoanalytic understanding and object relations theory perceive identification as an ongoing unfolding process based on the conflict emerging during each psychosexual period. As the work with conflict confrontation produces character trait formations, superego and ego effects become increasingly visible in the personality. In the formulation proposed in this chapter, it is assumed that the entire program exists at birth as dispositions. Psychosexual conflict inherent in each bipolar pair of emotions then becomes expressed on the basis of whether the intrapsychic aim of each emotion is achieved—that is, whether the aims of id emotions and superego emotions are achieved. It is proposed here that the extent to which these aims are frustrated determines, in part, the psychosexual conflict that emerges during developmental stages.

The issue of refinement of structure or differentiation of it as a function of developmental considerations is an evolutionary–adaptational concept. The issue of an existing structure rooted in biology is an epigenetic one. Both phenomena, evolutionary adaptations and the effects of epigenetic programs, are integrally tied to the emergence of the complete structure of personality and reflect the sociobiological interaction with psychoanalytic principles.

In summary, it may be proposed that personality trait structure and the refinement of ego and superego structure are based on biological as well as developmental factors. Vicissitudes of psychosexual development become superimposed on existing basic personality structure, in part lending meaning to the psychosexual developmental experience. Therefore, the emotion–personality theory contains principles relevant to sociobiologists as well as to psychoanalysts. In this sense, the emotion–personality system is considered here to be both sociobiological and psychoanalytic, and future work with the theory should be able to develop this cross-disciplinary relationship further.

REFERENCES

Arieti, S. (ed.) *American handbook of psychiatry.* New York: Basic Books, 1974.

Blum, G. S. *Psychoanalytic theories of personality.* New York: McGraw-Hill, 1953.

Bowlby, J. *Attachment and loss.* New York: Basic Books, 1969.

Bowlby, J. *Separation.* New York: Basic Books, 1973.

Brenner, C. On the nature and development of affects: A unified theory. *The Psychoanalytic Quarterly,* Oct. 1974, *43* (4), 532–556.

Brenner, C. Affects and psychic conflict. *The Psychoanalytic Quarterly,* Jan. 1975, *44* (1), 5–28.

Bychowski, G. *Evil in man: The anatomy of hate and violence.* New York: Grune and Stratton, 1968.

Coleman, J. C. *Abnormal psychology and modern life.* New York: Scott Foresman, 1956.

Engel, G. L. *Psychological development in health and disease.* Philadelphia: Saunders, 1962.

English, O. S., & Finch, S. M. *Introduction to psychiatry.* New York: Norton, 1964.

Ewalt, J. R., & Farnsworth, D. C. *Textbook of psychiatry.* New York: McGraw-Hill, 1963.

Frazier, S. H. *A psychiatric glossary.* Washington, D. C.: American Psychiatric Association, 1975.

Freud, A. *The ego and the mechanisms of defense.* London: Hogarth, 1937.

Freud, S. Studies on hysteria. In Strachey, J. (ed.), *The complete psychological works of Sigmund Freud.* Standard Edition, Volume 2. London: Hogarth Press, 1955. [Originally published 1895.]

Freud, S. The interpretation of dreams. In Strachey, J. (ed.), *The complete psychological works of Sigmund Freud.* Standard Edition, Volumes 4 and 5. London: Hogarth Press, 1953. [Originally published 1900.]

Freud, S. Psychoanalytic notes on an autobiographical account of a case of paranoia. In Strachey, J. (ed.), *The complete psychological works of Sigmund Freud.* Standard Edition, Volume 12. London: Hogarth Press, 1958. [Originally published 1911.]

Freud, S. Repression. In Strachey, J. (ed.), *The complete psychological works of Sigmund Freud.* Standard Edition, Volume 14. London: Hogarth Press, 1957. [Originally published 1915a.]

Freud, S. The unconscious: III. In Strachery, J. (ed.), *The complete psychological works of Sigmund Freud.* Standard Edition, Volume 14. London: Hogarth Press, 1957. [Originally published 1915b.]

Freud, S. Introductory lectures on psychoanalysis. Part III. In Strachey, J. (ed.), *The complete psychological works of Sigmund Freud.* Standard Edition, Volume 16. London: Hogarth Press, 1956. [Originally published 1917.]

Freud, S. The uncanny. In Strachey, J. (ed.), *The complete psychological works of Sigmund Freud.* Standard Edition, Volume 17. London: Hogarth Press, 1955. [Originally published 1919.]

Freud, S. Neurotic mechanisms in jealousy, paranoia and homosexuality. In Strachey, J. (ed.), *The complete psychological works of Sigmund Freud.* Standard Edition, Volume 18. London: Hogarth Press, 1955. [Originally published 1922.]

Freud, S. Inhibitions, symptoms and anxiety. In Strachey, J. (ed.), *The complete psychological works of Sigmund Freud.* Standard Edition, Volume 20. London: Hogarth Press, 1959. [Originally published 1926.]

Hartmann, H. Comments on the psychoanalytic theory of the ego. In *The psychoanalytic study of the child,* Vol. 5, pp. 74–96. New York: International Universities Press, 1950.

Hartmann, H. *Ego psychology and the problem of adaptation.* New York: International Universities Press, 1959.

Healy, W., Bronner, A. F., & Bowers, A. M. *The structure and meaning of psychoanalysis.* New York: Knopf, 1930.

Jones, E. Fear, guilt and hate. *International Journal of Psychoanalysis,* 1929, *10,* 383–397.

Kaufman, C. Some ethological studies of social relationships and conflict situations. *Journal of the American Psychoanalytic Association,* Oct. 1960, *8* (4), 671–685.

Kaywin, L. An epigenetic approach to the psychoanalytic theory of instincts and affects. *Journal of the American Psychoanalytic Association,* Oct. 1960, *8* (4), 613–658.

Kellerman, H. Relating emotion and traits in the measurement of maladjustment. In *Proceedings of the 73rd Annual Convention of the American Psychological Association,* 1965, pp. 229–230.

Kellerman, H. Hate. In B. B. Wolman (ed.), *International encyclopedia of neurology, psychiatry, psychoanalysis and psychology.* New York: Van Nostrand Reinhold, 1977.

Kellerman, H. *Group psychotherapy and personality: Intersecting structures.* New York: Grune and Stratton, 1979.

Kellerman, H., Buirski, P., & Plutchik, R. Group behavior in a baboon troop: Implications for human group process. In L. R. Wolberg & M. L. Aronson (eds.), *Group therapy 1974.* New York: Stratton Intercontinental Medical Book Corp., 1974.

Kellerman, H., & Plutchik, R. Emotion–trait interrelations and the measurement of personality. *Psychological Reports,* 1968, *23,* 1107–1114.

Kellerman, H., & Plutchik, R. The meaning of tension in group therapy. In L. R. Wolberg, M. L. Aronson, & A. R. Wolberg (eds.), *Group therapy 1977: An overview.* New York: Stratton Intercontinental Medical Book Corp., 1977.

Kellerman, H., & Plutchik, R. Personality patterns of drug addicts in a therapy group: A similarity structure analysis. *Group,* 1978, *2* (1), 14–21.

Klein, M. *Contributions to psychoanalysis: 1921–1945.* London: Hogarth, 1948.

Knapp, P. H. Conscious and unconscious affects: A preliminary approach to concepts and methods of study. *Psychiatric Research Reports,* April 1957, *8,* 55–74.

Lachman, F. M., & Stolorow, R. Idealization and grandiosity: Developmental considerations and treatment implications. *The Psychoanalytic Quarterly,* 1976, *45, (4),* 565–587.

Lasswell, H. D. The psychology of Hitlerism as a response of the lower middle class to continuing insecurity. In G. Swanson, T. M. Newcomb, & E. L. Hartley (eds.), *Readings in social psychology.* New York: Holt, 1952.

Lorenz, K. *On aggression.* New York: Harcourt Brace, 1966.

Mahler, M. *On human symbiosis and the vicissitudes of individuation,* Vol. 1. New York: International Universities Press, 1968.

Mahler, M. A study of the separation–individuation process and its possible application to borderline phenomena. In *The psychoanalytic study of the child,* Vol. 26, pp. 403–425. New Haven: Yale University Press, 1971.

McDougall, W. *An introduction to social psychology.* Boston: Luce, 1921.

Menninger, K. *The vital balance.* New York: Viking Press, 1963.

Needles, W. Comments on the pleasure–unpleasure experience: The role of biological factors. *Journal of the American Psychoanalytic Association,* April 1964, *12* (2), 300–314.

Novey, S. A clinical view of affect theory in psychoanalysis. *International Journal of Psychoanalysis,* 1959, *40,* 1–11.

Novey, S. Further considerations on affect theory in psychoanalysis. *International Journal of Psychoanalysis,* 1961, *42,* (Pts. I, II), 21–31.

Ostow, M. The structural model: Ego, id and superego. *Annals of the New York Academy of Sciences,* 1959, *76,* 1098–1134.

Platman, S. R., Plutchik, R., & Weinstein, B. Psychiatric, physiological, behavioral and self-report measures in relation to a suicide attempt. *Journal of Psychiatric Research,* 1971, *8,* 127–137.

Plutchik, R. Some problems for a theory of emotion. *Psychosomatic Medicine,* 1955, *17,* 306–310.

Plutchik, R. Further comments on the definition of emotion. *Psychological Record,* 1957, *7,* 123–124.

Plutchik, R. Outlines of a new theory of emotion. *Transactions of the New York Academy of Science,* 1958, *20,* 394–403.

Plutchik, R. *The emotions: Facts, theories and a new model.* New York: Random House, 1962.

Plutchik R. Emotions, evolution and adaptive processes. In M. Arnold (ed.), *Feelings and emotions.* New York: Academic Press, 1970.

Plutchik, R. *The nature of emotion: A psychoevolutionary approach.* New York: Harper and Row, in press.

Plutchik, R., & Kellerman, H. *Emotions profile index.* San Francisco: Western Psychological Services, 1974.

Plutchik, R., Kellerman, H., & Conte, H. A structural theory of ego defenses and emotions. In C. E. Izard (ed.), *Emotions and psychopathology.* New York: Plenum, 1979.

Rado, S. *Psychoanalysis of behavior.* New York: Grune and Stratton, 1956.

Rapaport, D. On the psychoanalytic theory of affect. *International Journal of Psychoanalysis,* 1953, *34,* 177–198.

Rapaport, D. On the psychoanalytic theory of affects. In R. Knight (ed.), *Psychoanalysis, psychiatry and psychology.* New York: International Universities Press, 1954.

Schafer, R. The clinical analysis of affects. *Journal of the American Psychoanalytic Association,* April 1964, *12* (2), 275–299.

Scott, J. P. *Animal behavior.* Chicago: University of Chicago Press, 1958.

Semrad, E. The organization of ego-defenses and object-loss. In D. M. Moriarity (ed.), *The loss of loved ones.* Springfield, Ill.: Charles C Thomas, 1967.

Symonds, P. M. *Defenses: The dynamics of human adjustment.* New York: Appleton-Century-Crofts, 1945.

Vaillant, G. E. Theoretical hierarchy of adaptive ego mechanisms. *Archives of General Psychiatry,* Feb. 1971, *24,* 107–118.

Vaillant, G. E. Natural history of male psychological health. V. The relation of ego mechanisms of defense to adult adjustment. *Archives of General Psychiatry,* 1976, *33,* 535–545.

Waelder, R. The structure of paranoid ideas. *International Journal of Psychoanalysis,* 1951, *32,* 167.

White, R. W. *The abnormal personality: A textbook.* New York: Ronald, 1948.

EPILOGUE

ROBERT PLUTCHIK AND HENRY KELLERMAN

Emotion theory has reached a new stage of existence. No longer can students be told that the only theories of emotion worthy of the name are those attributed to William James and Walter Cannon. The chapters presented in this book create a sense of excitement because of the new ground they have broken and the new themes that are heard. What is especially exciting about the range of theories and ideas presented is that they come out of different intellectual traditions and different scientific disciplines.

One of the main ideas that emerges from a reading of these contributions is that emotion is a complex multidimensional concept. It has something to do with environmental events, cognitions, motivational states, brain mechanisms, autonomic changes, impulses to action, actions, and effects on the environment. Emotions are not only wide but deep. There are unconscious and nonverbal elements that are part of the determinants of this complex process called an emotion. Of equal importance is the fact that emotions have derivatives. These include such things as personality traits and coping styles.

We believe that these various connections reflect a deep structure and that this deep structure to emotion is tied in a fundamental way to the ongoing process of evolution. Some authors have emphasized the common evolutionary sources of emotion in humans and animals while others have emphasized the uniqueness of emotion in humans. Both are valid perceptions

Emotion: Theory, Research, and Experience
Volume 1: Theories of Emotion

and both also need to be connected. Although this issue is addressed in this volume, it is a problem that should and will be considered in further theoretical work.

The different theoretical schools did not develop in a historical vacuum. Each theoretical orientation has been responsive to a particular context and to a particular set of questions and problems. For example, Darwin attempted to show the relevance of his newly developed theory of evolution to emotional *behavior*. His primary concern was with expressions and not feelings, and his primary method was the observation of natural behavior in normal environmental settings. In contrast, William James was primarily concerned with feeling states and their relation to poorly understood and poorly specified physiological changes in the body. For each particular theoretical orientation there developed an appropriate method of investigation. For example, the problem of how bodily arousal contributes to emotional feelings in humans led to a tradition of laboratory research that deals with autonomic physiology. In a parallel way, Freud's concern with unconscious determinants of behavior led to the special methods used by psychoanalysts to identify implicit affective states. In other words, problems and methods of investigation developed in a kind of synchrony.

However, with the development of research and theory in recent years, as expressed by many of the contributors to this volume, there has been an increasing overlap of common problems and methods for the solution of these problems. We no longer see a sharp distinction between emotions in humans and in lower animals, and the examination of the variables that influence emotions relies both on naturalistic observations and on laboratory techniques. Fundamentally, whatever truths are found by any one investigator representing any one tradition must eventually be incorporated by all theories deriving from any context.

The fact that this volume has brought together the work of these major thinkers in this field has not automatically provided us with a synthesis, but it has provided us with the raw material from which a synthesis will evolve. The next decade will be a particularly exciting time as this process unfolds.

One of the important issues that will have to be considered in this future synthesis concerns the question of the complexity of the emotions. In the early writings on emotion in the nineteenth century, there was a tendency to assume that emotions had a linear, directed quality. In contrast, one of the most important contributions that has come out of the chapters presented in this book is the notion of emotion as part of a complex feedback system. Basically Darwin was right—emotions tend to have an impact on the environment, but the very process of expressing emotion leads to changes in the emotional state itself. This represents a new theme that needs to be explored in future work.

The theories of emotion presented in this book represent the beginnings of a search. They are guides to the future. They represent different ways of looking at a phenomenon. They suggest what is important to study and measure, and sometimes they have implications for the measurement technique itself. In future volumes a number of these implications will be explored. For example, the next volume in the series will examine developmental aspects of emotion. Other volumes will consider all major aspects of the study of emotion so that these works will constitute an archive of fundamental theory and fact.

SUBJECT INDEX